The History of Buddhist Thought

A BODHISATTVA: GANDHARA SCHOOL

The History of Buddhist Thought

By
EDWARD J. THOMAS
M.A., D.Litt. (St. Andrews)
Author of "The Life of Buddha as Legend and History".

LONDON
ROUTLEDGE & KEGAN PAUL LTD
BROADWAY HOUSE: 68-74 CARTER LANE, EC4V 5EL

First published 1933
by Routledge & Kegan Paul Ltd
Broadway House, 68–74 *Carter Lane*
London, *EC*4*V* 5*EL*
Second edition 1951
Reprinted 1953, 1959, 1963, 1967 and 1971

Printed in Great Britain by
Lowe & Brydone (*Printers*) *Ltd.*
London, *N.W.*10
ISBN 0 7100 4971 4

CONTENTS

ILLUSTRATIONS

PLATE.

Pl. I. Bodhisattva of the Gandhāra school. The figure, 5 ft. 9 in. high, probably from Yusufzai near Peshawar, is in the possession of Messrs. E. Goldston, 25 Museum Street, London, to whose kindness I am indebted for the reproduction. The sculptures of the Gandhāra school are found on the North-West Frontier, and belong to the Kushāna period from the first century B.C. to the fourth century A.D., but we have no means of exactly dating any of the figures. They were evidently produced by workmen with a knowledge of Greek sculpture, but the ideas that they reveal are purely Indian.

Pl. II. The Wheel of Becoming, from *Journ. As. Soc. Bengal*, 1893, vol. lxi, pt. 1, p. 133 ; described below, p. 69.

Pl. III. Gotama practising austerities before he found the true method of meditation. Gandhāra figure found at Sikri in the Peshawar District by Captain Deane in 1889, now in the Lahore Museum ; see *JA.*, 1890, i, p. 139.

The prominence on the head is one of a Buddha's thirty-two bodily marks, which appear also on bodhisattvas in their last birth (below, p. 142). One of these is that he is said to be *ushṇīsha-śīrsha* or *uṇhīsa-sīsa*, 'turban-headed,' a term which as applied to a bodily mark can only mean having the head in the shape of a turban. This is how it was interpreted by the later Indian artists, who represented a prominence of the skull covered with short curls, and it has been assumed that they were trying to copy the bunched-up hair of the Gandhāra figures. But this mark is mentioned in the list of marks as given by all known schools, and these lists must have been already in existence when the Gandhāra art arose. There is no reason to think that these artists were ignorant of the tradition, and the probability is that the bunched-up hair of the Gandhāra figures is their way of indicating the mark without making it appear as a deformity.

Pl. IV. The two scenes are from paintings in a MS. of the *Kāraṇḍa-vyūha* from Nepal in the possession of H. Wilkinson, Esq., C.S.I., C.I.E, who has kindly lent the MS. for reproduction. In the first the preaching of the First Sermon to the five disciples in the deer park at Benares (see p. 140) shows how Mahāyāna continued to preserve the old legend and recognize the Hīnayāna teaching. In the second the bodhisattva Sarvanīvaraṇavishkambhin is receiving the spell, *Oṃ maṇipadme hūṃ*, from a reciter of the Doctrine as described in the *Kāraṇḍa-vyūha* (below, p. 192), and Avalokiteśvara in the sky is giving his approval.

On Gandhāra art see A. Foucher, *The Beginnings of Buddhist Art* (1917). On the significance of art and religion M. Focillon's *L'art bouddhique*, Paris, 1921, is a work of deep penetration and sympathy.

PREFACE

A HISTORY of Buddhism in the sense of a connected account of the chief events of all the Buddhist communities throughout the centuries is an ideal not yet attainable. The monumental *Cambridge History of India* is blazing a path, but it has so far completed only the first volume of the Hindu portion. Merely to record the known facts of some two thousand years of Buddhism would require more than one volume.

During the last few years several important works dealing with the less explored regions of Buddhism have appeared. Dr. N. Dutt's *Aspects of Mahāyāna Buddhism* is more fundamental than appears from the title, and in *The Bodhisattva Doctrine in Buddhist Sanskrit Literature* Dr. H. Dayal has devoted much intensive research to one special development. A general treatment has been begun by Dr. McGovern in his *Manual of Buddhist Philosophy*, vol. 1, and in *An Introduction to Mahāyāna Buddhism*. From Dr. B. M. Barua we have *Prolegomena to a History of Buddhistic Philosophy*.

The earliest period has also received new attention. This period, according to Mrs. Rhys Davids, was so different from the picture that we find in our earliest records that she prefers to call it not Buddhism but Sakya. "Put away, for your origins, the word 'Buddhism' and think of your subject as 'Sakya'."[1] This is really a religious question, and the interest that Buddhism still rouses from this point of view can be seen from Bishop Gore's Gifford Lectures, *The Philosophy of the Good Life*, and the Bampton Lectures of Canon Streeter, *The Buddha and the Christ*. It is Buddhism as we find it actually recorded, not a hypothetical primitive system, which still forms a challenge to other religions.

Through the labours of Rhys Davids and his colleagues it has become possible to form a clear idea of one of the earliest schools of Buddhism, that of the Pāli tradition still flourishing in Ceylon, Burma, Siam, and Further India. It was no

[1] *Sakya or Buddhist Origins*, 1931. However, in her *Manual of Buddhism*, 1932, *Sakya* does not occur in the index.

fault of these investigators if they were satisfied that here we have the earliest known form, or even the primitive form, of Buddhism and that all that followed was degeneration. For Mrs. Rhys Davids even the earliest known form was degeneration. But other scholars have been at work, and we now know of other schools with an equal right to claim that they were holding the primitive teaching. The problem about the primitive teaching now becomes actual.

The problem of the later history of Buddhism has also become actual. Philosophically it was no degeneration, but a great advance. This has been brought out by Professor A. B. Keith in his *Buddhist Philosophy in India and Ceylon*. The existence of the documents of the later schools termed Mahāyāna was early made known through the labours of the Hungarian scholar Alexander Csoma de Kőrös, and it was in fact a misfortune that some of these documents were among the earliest to reach investigators in the West. There was then no possibility of placing in their historical order documents separated by half a millennium. But the actual texts are at last being edited and studied, and their relations to the earlier Pāli and Sanskrit works are being established.

We have now a long series of important texts in the *Bibliotheca Buddhica* edited by Professor S. Oldenburg, of Leningrad. It is to the work of the scholars who are contributing to this task, both in their editions and their independent investigations, that I owe the greatest debt, and first of all to those of T. Stcherbatsky and Professor L. de la Vallée Poussin. I am also much indebted to other scholars working on the same lines, especially Professor S. Schayer, of Warsaw, and Professor M. Walleser, of Heidelberg. In France we have the splendid achievements of É. Senart and S. Lévi, as well as others who are now contributing to the valuable researches in the series *Buddhica* edited by J. Przyluski.

Important texts are also being brought out by Indian scholars, especially in the *Gaekwad's Oriental Series* and the *Trivandrum Sanskrit Series*, and in these are appearing some of the epoch-making works and editions by the Italian scholar G. Tucci, chiefly on Buddhist logic and Yogāchāra. For a long time Japanese scholars have been making solid contributions. The works of the late Rev. Bunyiu Nanjio, J. Takakusu, A. Anesaki, U. Wogihara, J. Masuda, and others are well known, and the extensive and important studies of Professor D. T. Suzuki are given in the bibliography.

The legendary and earliest historical aspect was dealt with by the author in *The Life of Buddha as Legend and History* in the same series as the present volume. Although much work remains to be done regarding the chronology of Indian history, the sequence of thought in the development of Buddhist doctrine is becoming clear. The aim of the present work is to trace the growth of the Buddhist community, to indicate its relation to the world of Hindu and non-Hindu society in which it arose, and to follow the rise and development of the doctrines from their legendary origin into the system which has spread over a great part of Asia.

My special thanks are due to Miss C. M. Ridding, M.A., of Girton College, who has given me invaluable help in the collection of material, and to Miss G. Hjort, Ph.D., Research Fellow of Girton College, who has read, criticized, and discussed the whole manuscript.

EDWARD J. THOMAS.

PREFACE TO THE SECOND EDITION

The baneful results of the events of recent years may be seen from the losses that Oriental scholarship has sustained in the decease of some of its most eminent investigators, losses in some cases directly due to the hardships of that time. In Stanislaw Schayer we miss one of the ablest interpreters of the doctrine of the Void as developed by Nāgārjuna and his commentators. T. I. Stcherbatsky expounded the logical and epistemological theories both of the Sarvastivadins and the later Indian thinkers, and L. de La Vallée Poussin did invaluable work in making accessible the Abhidharma of the Indian schools and the intricacies of Vijñānavāda.

In two directions there has been progress. More and more of the Sanskrit originals of the Scriptures of the Buddhist schools in India are coming to light. Professor E. Waldschmidt's analysis of the *Mahāparinirvāṇa-sūtra* and its elaborations shows how it is becoming possible to trace out a relative chronology of the canonical matter and to determine more of the actual relations between the Pāli Scriptures and the recensions of the Indian schools.

It has been the fashion to speak of certain portions of the Canon as " early " or as belonging to a " sehr alter Zeit." Such phrases are either meaningless or they disguise an implied theory, which is of no value unless brought to the light and shown to be more than subjective guess-work. But there is a striking distinction in the texts themselves, which allows us to speak of earlier and later portions. Some of the suttas are discourses recorded as the direct words of the Master or his disciples. These claim not to be early but primitive. At the time of Buddha's death there must have been many discourses which the disciples knew by heart, and we need not doubt that they were collected and recited in a "chanting-together" or *sangīti*. How far this portion can now be distinguished is still a problem. But besides this there is a large class of poems, legends, short incidents, dialogues, and narrative ballads, which are clearly marked off by their style from the plain sermons. Evidently they belong to a period when literary composition was practised as an art. They show elaborate metres which never occur in the four Nikāyas, and use poetic phraseology, such as is found also in Jain poems and even the *Mahābhārata*. Dr. N. A. Jayawicknama is at present studying one of the most important works of this class,[1] the *Sutta-nipāta*, and revealing the complicated questions that still face us in this class of works.

E. J. THOMAS.

[1] See his articles in the University of Ceylon Review, 1947 ff.

ABBREVIATIONS

Dīgha : Dīgha-nikāya. (This and the next three are quoted by vol. and page of text. This reference serves also for the translations mentioned in the bibliography, as they repeat the page numbers of the text.)

Majjh. : Majjhima-nikāya.

Saṃy. : Saṃyutta-nikāya.

Ang. : Anguttara-nikāya.

Jāt. : Jātaka.

Dhp. : Dhammapada.

Sn. : Sutta-nipāta.

Vin. : Vinaya.

Dpvs. : Dīpavaṃsa.

Mhvs. : Mahāvaṃsa.

Mahābh. : Mahābhārata.

Mvyut. : Mahāvyutpatti.

Mbvs. : Mahābodhivaṃsa.

Dhs. : Dharmasangraha.

Lal. : Lalita-vistara.

Abhk. : Abhidharmakośa.

Mvst. : Mahāvastu.

Lotus : Saddharmapuṇḍarīka.

Divy. : Divyāvadāna.

Vism. : Visuddhimagga.

ERE. : Hastings' Encyclopaedia of Religion and Ethics.

JA. : Journal Asiatique.

JPTS. : Journal of the Pali Text Society.

JRAS. : Journal of the Royal Asiatic Society.

JAOS. : Journal of the American Oriental Society.

ZDMG. : Zeitschrift der deutschen Morgenländischen Gesellschaft.

IHQ. : Indian Historical Quarterly.

BEFEO. : Bulletin de l'École française d'extrême—Orient.

SBE. : Sacred Books of the East.

SBB. : Sacred Books of the Buddhists.

CHI. : Cambridge History of India.

As. Res. : Asiatic Researches.

PRONUNCIATION

IN Pāli and Sanskrit words the vowels are as in German or Italian, except that short *a* has the sound of *u* in *but*. The consonants are mostly as in English : *g* is always hard, *c* has the sound of *ch* in *church*. (In words more or less Anglicized *ch* has been used, as in *Chandragupta*.) The dentals, *t*, *d*, etc., are true dentals pronounced with the tongue against the teeth. The cerebrals, *ṭ*, *ḍ*, etc., are pronounced with the tongue against the hard palate, much as the English so-called dentals. In the case of the aspirated letters, *th*, *ph*, etc., the sound is a stop *plus* a simultaneous aspiration. The accent is on the long syllable as in Latin : *Suddhódana*, *udā́na*, *Lálita-vístara*.

CHRONOLOGY

B.C.

6TH CENT.

563. Birth of Gotama Buddha.
528. Enlightenment.

5TH CENT.

483. Death of Buddha: First Council at Rājagaha.

4TH CENT.

383. Second Council at Vesālī.

3RD CENT.

269–237. Reign of Asoka.
247. Third Council at Pāṭaliputta.
246. Mission of Mahinda to Ceylon.

2ND CENT.

Rise of Mahāyāna doctrines.

1ST CENT.

Kushāna kings established in N.W. India.
29–17. Reign of Vaṭṭagāmaṇi in Ceylon.

A.D.

1ST CENT.

78. Accession of Kanishka.
c. 100. Council of Sarvāstivādins under Kanishka.

2ND CENT.

Madhyamaka School of Nāgārjuna.

5TH CENT.

Yogāchāra School of Vasubandha and Asanga.

6TH CENT.

Logical School of Dignāga.

7TH CENT.

Śāntideva and Dharmakīrti.

7TH–10TH CENT.

Rise of Tantric Schools.

CHAPTER I

INTRODUCTION

AN account of a religion may be expected to begin with the biography of its founder. But in the case of Buddhism we are faced with the fact that all the biographies by ancient Buddhist authors are centuries later than the period of which they speak. They have all been composed after the time when the movement had broken up into separate schools, and they represent the traditions, often contradictory, preserved by these bodies, and modified in accordance with various dogmas concerning the nature of a Buddha and the means of winning release. The popular story of Buddha's life, as known to the West, is merely the modern version of one of these traditions, and it has been made plausible only by ignoring the other accounts and omitting all the marvels.

So far as these traditions preserve doctrinal teaching about the nature and career of a Buddha they are highly important, but it is not until the sacred literature and its doctrines have been examined that their historical elements can be considered. Fragments of biography are to be found in the Buddhist Canon. There we find the teacher represented as wandering from place to place as an ascetic, and claiming to have become enlightened and free from all worldly ties. His disciples, who all follow the same ascetic life, are instructed by him to follow the path which he has discovered and, unlike the priests of the prevailing religion, he also gives moral discourses to lay people. His high birth as a member of the kshatriya or warrior caste is often emphasized, especially in opposition to the brahmins. Several other rival schools are mentioned, the chief being the Nigaṇṭhas, the sect still surviving as the Jains. The sphere of his activity was almost entirely in the Magadha and Kosala country, corresponding to the modern Behar, the United Provinces, and Nepal.

There is no doubt that the central fact we have to deal

with is that the founder was a religious genius. However much a genius is influenced by his spiritual environment, his own contribution is something new and original. It may be that he claims to have acquired it by inspiration, or that he has been directly taught by a divine instructor.

Neither of these is the case with Buddhism, which represents its founder as having by his own unaided effort discovered "the doctrine unheard before", and as having shown a way of salvation which makes an end of pain. But this new teaching cannot be fully explained by itself. It was expressed in accordance with the conceptions of the Hindu world in the sixth century B.C., and as it continued to develop it took for granted all the current views on the nature of the world and man so far as they were not in conflict with its own principles. This is the Buddhism with which we have to deal, not merely the kernel of new doctrine, but the actual system with all that it assimilated from the thought and social conditions of its environment, or adopted as it attracted new followers. The history of Buddhism is the history of the developments, schisms, corruptions, and reforms which the system underwent as it spread in India and beyond, and as it became accepted and reinterpreted by the most diverse cultures of Asia.

The problem of the relation of Buddhism to Brahminism and of their interaction as religious and philosophical schools runs throughout the whole history. But Brahminism was not merely a rival; it was in the first place the system in the midst of which Buddhism originated. Brahminism had long grown out of the prehistoric nature religion of Aryan India, and, influenced doubtless by contact with non-Aryan peoples, had become by the sixth century B.C. an elaborate sacrificial and sacerdotal system. It had also originated the philosophical principles which have ever since dominated it. A consideration of this early form of Brahminism will be important in so far as it may have had an influence in determining the ideas of the thinker or thinkers who struck out a new path. We need to ascertain, if possible, the world of thought in which Buddha lived, what there was in it that he found inadequate or erroneous, and in opposition to which his teaching made such a powerful appeal.

Geography

Two preliminary questions which must first be considered are the geographical and the chronological. The geographical facts are of the first importance, for they show that the early Brahminism as known from its literature belonged to a region far distant from the cradle of the new religion. The brahmin region was in the north-west of India, where its chief centre during the compilation of these documents was between the Ganges and the Jumna. Buddhism originated in a region much further to the east, a district which is treated by the brahminical works as unfit for the residence of brahmins. We cannot, therefore, assume that this Brahminism was identical with that known to the early Buddhists. It moreover claimed to possess a secret doctrine confined to exclusive schools, and some of its teachings do not seem even to have been known to the reformers of eastern India.

The home of Buddhism lies in what is now South Behar, west of Bengal and south of the Ganges. This was the kingdom of the Magadhas, extending from the confluence of the Son with the Ganges towards the east some 150 miles as far as Bhagalpur, the ancient Champā. Forty miles to the south was the chief city Rājagaha (now Rajgir) and some 30 miles further south-west Buddha Gayā, the scene of Buddha's enlightenment, and still further south the Southern Hills (Dakkhiṇāgiri). The actual region of Bengal further east was then probably quite outside brahmin influence. Even to-day a linguistic map shows the Magadha region bounded on the south and east by tribes speaking non-Aryan (Muṇḍā) languages.[1]

In Buddha's time the aryanization of the country had begun but, as the anthropological evidence shows, it was the spread of an Aryan civilization over a more primitive population, and its introduction into this region was not by conquest but by gradual infiltration. In the eastern portion of Magadha dwelt the Angas, in Buddha's time no longer an independent people. North of the Ganges were a number of peoples still in the tribal stage. The chief of these were the Vajjis with the chief city Vesālī (now Besar), and further north the Kolas and Mallas. To the west of these, between

[1] *Linguistic Survey of India*, vol. i, pt. 1.

the Ganges and the Himalayas, were the Kosalas, a people who like the Magadhas were united into a kingdom, and had become paramount over other tribes. The capital was Sāvatthī (Śrāvastī), but another city is also mentioned, Sāketa or Ayodhyā,[1] and this appears to have been at a later time the capital. Among peoples subject to the Kosalas or under their suzerainty were the Kāsis in the south with capital Benares, and north of the Kosalas near the Himalayas a tribe destined to play an important part in later legend, the Sakyas (Śākyas), the tribe to which Buddha belonged. The Buddhist accounts speak of them as being ruled by a king, and say that if Buddha had not chosen to become a king of the Doctrine (*Dhamma*) he was destined to become a universal king (*cakravartin*) ruling from sea to sea. Nevertheless, there are indications that the rule of the Sakyas, like that of the adjoining tribes, was oligarchic. The district included part of what is now Nepal, and was probably never much more extensive.

It was within these districts that the first preaching of Buddhism took place, and we have good reason for holding that in Buddha's lifetime it did not extend beyond. This may be inferred, not from the statements of the legends (which are often quite unhistorical, and represent Buddha as going to the Himalayas, Kashmir, and even Ceylon), but from the undesigned evidence furnished by the discourses themselves. Each discourse is preceded by a statement saying where it was delivered. Doubtless many of these ascriptions are inferences or mere guesses, but they do belong to an early tradition, and we find that according to this tradition the places which are recognized by it are practically confined to the districts mentioned above—the Magadha and Kosala kingdoms and the various tribes to the north-east. This limitation is the more significant when it is compared with the anachronisms of the stories found in the commentaries and Sanskrit works. We there find the mention of peoples in the extreme north-west, the Gandhāras, the Kambojas, the City of Taxila, and in the east Bengal, as well as southern India and Ceylon. The spread of Buddhism by the great trade routes was along the Ganges and Jumna towards the

[1] Ayodhya is well known, being near the present Ajudhia in the Fyzabad District. The site of Sāvatthī is still disputed, but it is usually identified with Set Mahet, a large collection of ruins further north in the Babraich District of Oudh.

north-west and Kashmir and south of the Ganges along the Vindhyas, turning south to the west coast. Along these routes great Buddhist communities arose, and there is no doubt that legends connecting Buddha with these places were invented. But they are quite absent from the first four Nikāyas of the Pāli Scriptures, and these collections, even if they were revised in their present form as late as two centuries after Buddha's death, show us the only region which has a historical claim to be the cradle of Buddhism.

There is a single passage in the Pāli which appears to imply not a wider range of Buddha's activity than that described above, but a much wider geographical knowledge among the early Buddhists than that implied in most of the texts. It is in the *Anguttara Nikāya*, i, 213, repeated iv, 252, 256, 260, and consists of a list of countries which has been held to be a statement of the political divisions of India in or before Buddha's time.[1] But the collection of discourses in which it is found has less claim than some of the others to be considered early or as conveying contemporary information. It even contains a legend about king Muṇḍa, the fifth in descent from Buddha's contemporary Bimbisāra. The passage in question is not one that has any concern with giving geographical information, but merely introduces the names in an illustration. It occurs in a discourse on the merit of keeping the fast day (*uposatha*), and there it is said in verse :

> The moon's brilliance and all the host of stars
> Are not worth a sixteenth part
> Of the fast day kept with the eight precepts.

This is developed in the prose, where it is said :

> Just as if one should rule with supreme lordship over these sixteen great countries, namely the Angas, Magadhas, Kāsis, Kosalas, Vajjis, Mallas, Chetis, Vaṃsas, Kurus, Pañchālas, Macchas, Sūrasenas, Assakas, Avantis, Gandhāras, and Kambojas, they are not worth a sixteenth part of the fast day kept with the eight precepts.

The word for " part " is *kalā*, properly a digit, the sixteenth part by which the moon increases daily between new and full moon, and the phrase " not worth a sixteenth part " was proverbial.[2] The compiler wanted a list of sixteen countries, and he has evidently made it up from an earlier

[1] Rh. Davids, in *CHI.*, i, 172.
[2] Cf. *Dhp.*, 70 ; *Mahābh.*, xii, 174, 48 ; *Praśna Up.*, vi, 2.

list, for the first eight names down to the Sūrasenas occur in the *Janavasabha-sutta, Dīgha,* ii, 200). In that sutta Buddha is said to have explained the destinies of persons in these countries who had recently died, stating whether they had attained Nirvāṇa or in what stage of spiritual progress they were reborn. It is this list of twelve to which four others have here been added, the Assakas of south India, the Avantis of the west, and the Gandhāras and Kambojas of the extreme north-west. These names are frequent enough in later literature, but their almost complete absence from the four Nikāyas, and the fact that the list is preceded by a shorter one, makes it unlikely that it is due to someone who had a knowledge of the political divisions of India before Buddha's time.

Dr. Hemachandra Raychaudhuri [1] has pointed out a similar list of sixteen countries in the *Bhagavatī-sūtra* of the Jains, which he thinks is later than the Buddhist list. It certainly shows how such lists might come to be compiled. It has no mention of the northern Kambojas and Gandhāras, but it includes several south Indian peoples. All that this proves is that the Jain author wrote in south India, and compiled his list from countries that he knew.

This bare list of names (which are not local, but names of tribes or peoples) has little to do with explaining the geography of pre-Buddhistic India. The additional names suggest the directions in which Buddhism spread, but historically we start with the kingdoms of the Magadhas and the Kosalas. These continued to exist for more than a century after Buddha's death, until the usurper Chandragupta seized the Magadha kingdom, overran his neighbours, and extended his power over most of north India.

Chronology

Neither the Pāli nor the Sanskrit forms of the Canon give any help in determining anything about the dates of Buddha's career or even about the historical sequence of the whole story. This comes from the Chronicles composed in Ceylon and from Sarvāstivādin works known as Avadānas. There are two Pāli Chronicles giving the early history of Buddhism, its introduction into Ceylon, and its progress

[1] *Political History of Ancient India,* p. 46.

in the Island. The earlier of these is the *Dīpavaṃsa*, " history of the Island (of Ceylon)," a record in verse, assigned to the fourth century A.D. The *Mahāvaṃsa*, " the great Chronicle," also in verse, is a rewriting of the same subject matter with more completeness, and is about a century later. Both these works rest upon historical material which was contained in the old Sinhalese commentaries on the Canon, and most of the material with which we are concerned originated in India. It is unnecessary to consider the *Dīpavaṃsa* in detail here. Its relation to the *Mahāvaṃsa* has been discussed by W. Geiger in his editions of the text and translation of the *Mahāvaṃsa*.

The *Mahāvaṃsa* has been extended from time to time by continuations, but the original form was in thirty-seven chapters, ending like the *Dīpavaṃsa* with the reign of Mahāsena, king of Ceylon, early in the fourth century A.D. It begins with the resolve which " our Conqueror " made under the Buddha Dīpankara, and the prophecy by Dīpankara about his destiny, repeated by each succeeding Buddha, until in his last life as Gotama he attained complete enlightenment, and began to teach the Doctrine at Benares. The rest of the chapter gives the Sinhalese legend of his three visits to Ceylon, the first of them nine months after his enlightenment, the next five years later, and the third in the eighth year. So far we have purely imaginative legend. The actual history begins with the second chapter, and it is introduced, after the style of the Purāṇas, with the genealogy of Buddha from Mahāsammata, the first king of this age (*kalpa*) down to his father, king Suddhodana. It then continues :

Māyā and Pajāpatī were the queens of Suddhodana ; our Conqueror [1] was the son of Suddhodana and Māyā.

In the unbroken lineage of Mahāsammata, which thus became the head of the warrior caste, was born the Great Recluse.

The wife of prince Siddhattha, the Bodhisatta, was Bhaddakaccānā, and his son was Rāhula.

Bimbisāra and prince Siddhattha were friends ; and likewise friends were the fathers of both.

[1] *Jina* (conqueror), *muni* (recluse), *satthā* (teacher), *bodhisatta* (destined Buddha), *buddha* (enlightened), *tathāgata* (he who has gone thus or to such a state) are all titles of Siddhattha. His name Gotama (Skt. Gautama) was a kind of surname, as it was the common name of his clan or *gotra*, applied to all descended from the same supposed ancestor. This gotra, however, is a brahmin gotra, and was probably the gotra of the hotar priest who performed the sacrifices for this warrior tribe. See *Life of Buddha*, p. 22.

The Bodhisatta was five years older than Bimbisāra; and at the age of twenty-nine the Bodhisatta renounced the world.

He strove for six years, and in due course won enlightenment; and at the age of thirty-five he visited Bimbisāra.

Now the virtuous Bimbisāra at the age of fifteen was himself consecrated by his father; and after he had attained the kingdom (of Magadha),

In the sixteenth year, the Teacher taught the Doctrine; fifty-two years did Bimbisāra rule his kingdom.

Fifteen years was his reign before the Conqueror came, and thirty-seven more while the Tathāgata lived.

Ajātasattu, son of Bimbisāra, intent on murdering his father, ruled his kingdom for thirty-two years, a great injurer of friends.

In the eighth year of Ajātasattu the Recluse attained Nirvāṇa; thereafter Ajātasattu ruled his kingdom for twenty-four years.

When the Conqueror, living for forty-five years, had performed all duties in the world in every way,

At Kusinārā, between the excellent pair of sāla trees he, the light of the world, attained Nirvāṇa.

The third chapter continues with the funeral rites of Buddha and the holding of a Council by the monks of the Order six months later for the reciting and collecting of the Doctrine.

In the fourth chapter six successors of Ajātasattu are recorded, the last of whom was Kālāsoka. It was after ten years of his reign that the second Council was held, exactly a century after Buddha's death. This Council is said to have dealt only with disciplinary measures. It declared illegal ten practices in which relaxation of the rules had taken place among the monks of Vesālī.

The fifth chapter records the rise of "the doctrines of other teachers", resulting in seventeen new schools in the second century after Buddha's death, and later still six other schools in India and two in Ceylon. Authors belonging to Sanskrit schools also give lists of eighteen, and these lists contain the kernel of what we know of the history of the Order and the development of the doctrine in the earlier period. This chapter also continues the history of the kings of Magadha down to Asoka.

Kālāsoka was succeeded by his ten brothers, who reigned in all twenty-two years. Then followed the nine Nandas, who also reigned twenty-two years. The last of these, Dhanananda, was overthrown by Chandagutta (Chandragupta), who made himself master of northern India, and reigned twenty-four years. His son Bindusāra succeeded, and reigned twenty-eight.

Bindusāra's splendid sons were a hundred and one ; but of these Asoka excelled in merit, splendour, might, and wondrous power.
When he had slain ninety-nine of his brothers by different mothers, he attained the sole rule in all Jambudīpa.
It is to be known that from the Nirvāṇa of the Conqueror down to Asoka's consecration it is two hundred and eighteen years.
Four years after the famous one (Asoka) had attained sole rule he caused himself to be consecrated in the city of Pāṭaliputta (Patna).

The rest of the chapter tells of Asoka's conversion to Buddhism, and how his name became changed from Asoka the fierce (Chandāsoka) to Asoka the righteous (Dhammāsoka). He reformed the Order, expelling the heretical monks, and the third Council was held in the seventeenth year of his reign. The Chronicle then turns to the history of Ceylon, and tells no more of Buddhism in India beyond Asoka's sending of missionaries to various countries after the third Council and the official introduction of Buddhism into Ceylon by Asoka's son Mahinda.

This is the tradition as preserved by one school, the Theravāda, and the extent to which the details can be relied upon is much disputed.[1] It is unnecessary for our purpose to investigate the chronological problems beyond pointing out those which can be verified independently as historical facts. Chandagutta (Chandragupta), the grandfather of Asoka, has been identified with certainty as the Indian ruler known to the Greeks and Romans as Sandrocottus, who about 304–3 B.C. made a treaty with Seleucus Nicator. The historical character of Asoka's reign is proved by the decrees which he caused to be inscribed on rocks and pillars in various parts of India. All the earlier dates are problematical, though they agree to some extent with the chronology of the Jains and the Purāṇas. If we could be sure of the number 218 as the number of years between the death of Buddha and the Consecration of Asoka, all the rest would fall into a natural chronological sequence. The Sarvāstivādin tradition, however, puts Asoka one century

[1] An examination of the Pāli evidence compared with that of the Jains and the Purāṇas is given by W. Geiger in the introduction to his translation of the *Mahāvaṃsa*. Mr. Bhattasali, preferring the Jain dates, wishes to shift all the dates five years forward. How precarious the whole scheme is can be seen from the fact that Dr. Matsumoto, following Professor Ui, shifts the death of Buddha to 386 B.C., nearly a century later. See *Die Prajñāpāramitā-Literatur*, p. 25. Stuttgart, 1932. None of these dates agrees with the traditional dates accepted by the Buddhists themselves. In Ceylon, Siam, and Burma 544 B.C. is the date of Buddha's death ; in China 1067 B.C. and other dates are given. Mr. Bhattasali's calculation is given in *JRAS*. 1932, p. 273.

after the death of Buddha, and apparently confuses him with Kālāsoka. But, as it also omits Chandragupta from its list of kings, there is no reason to prefer it as the more correct. The relative dates as accepted by the Theravāda school thus become :

B.C.

563 Birth of Gotama Buddha.
559 Birth of Bimbisāra, king of Magadha.
543 Accession of Bimbisāra.
534 Great Renunciation of Gotama.
528 The Enlightenment.
491 Accession of Ajātasattu.
483 Death of Buddha and first Council at Rājagaha.
393 Accession of Kālāsoka.
383–2 Second Council at Vesālī and first schism.
365–343 The ten sons of Kālāsoka.
343–321 The nine Nandas.
321 Usurpation of Chandragupta and founding of the Maurya empire.
297 Accession of Bindusāra.
269 Accession of his son Asoka.
265 Consecration of Asoka.
247 Third Council at Pāṭaliputta.
246 Mission of Mahinda to Ceylon.

CHAPTER II

THE ASCETIC IDEAL

BUDDHISM appears first in history as an ascetic movement. It was one of a number of sects, bodies of mendicants who had " gone forth from a house to a houseless state " and who had cut themselves off from the hindrances of worldly ties and pleasures in the pursuit of their ideal.

Ascetic practices are found in very early stages of society. They appear in connection with ideas of tabu, or the sanctity of the priest and wonderworker, and the exercise of magic. These have no necessary connection with any particular type of religious belief, and in the earliest known form of religion in India little of an ascetic tendency appears. But the *tāpasin*, the performer of austerities (*tapas*), existed, and there was a strong belief in the results to be obtained by such practices. Probably pre-Aryan influences were at work. The adept might acquire marvellous powers and control the course of nature, and the belief that such powers were real certainly existed among the early Buddhists.

In the Vedic literature this aspect of religious expression is little in evidence. There we find the sacrifice as the centre and the religious instincts satisfied by the due performance of priestly rites.[1] But with the rise of the doctrine of rebirth human life and its value began to appear in a different aspect. Life with an unending chain of repeated existences became something to be escaped. Schools arose which broke away from the current view and taught a doctrine of release.

Even among the brahmins doubts as to the sufficiency of sacrifice arose. A way of permanent escape was sought, and in the Vedic schools themselves arose a secret doctrine expounding how by a method superseding the ritual of sacrifice emancipation might be won. The non-Vedic schools definitely rejected the brahminical method of sacrifice and the Vedic lore. Some teachers boldly denied the doctrine of the retribution of actions (*karma*), some declared that nothing could be done to escape it. Others, like the Jains and Buddhists,

[1] Cf. *CHI.*, i, 106.

held that escape from rebirth could be obtained by the knowledge of a special way of life. Both of these movements were ascetic in making renunciation of worldly life essential for final release. Buddhism in particular was a moral protest. There can be no doubt that it was due to the genius of its founder that it was able to moralize the doctrine of karma. It made a clear distinction between action in accordance with really ethical principles and action resting upon inherited beliefs in the mysterious efficacy of ritual and magical ceremonies.

There have been great movements in which the practice of the ascetic life has become an enthusiasm, but we always find that it is a new ideal which gives the inspiration.[1] Ascetic practices have seemed to be a wonderful means for attaining the positive end. For the Christian monks of Egypt in the third century the present life was a transitory period of no value in view of the glories soon to come. St. Antony, hearing in church how the apostles had left all, sold his goods, and in reply to the tempter said, " no one shall separate me from the love of Christ." St. Pachomius tried in the depths of the desert to " live the life of the heavenly ones through the love of virtue ". In those very words we may probably see the other side of the ideal, the attempt to live more than a human life, leading to results that have repeatedly shown themselves in the history of asceticism. What was wanted was a rule of life to guide the enthusiastic impulses. We need not now consider whether the ascetic life should be set up as a vocation at all. It is certain that there are natures to whom the thought of another world or a life beyond the mere pleasures of sense is so vivid that everything except the pursuit of that ideal is worthless and vain. Ascetic movements have succeeded when they have roused individuals to whom the ideal appealed, and when a guide has appeared who knew how to establish a wise rule of life through which such natures could find their realization.

This is one of the reasons for the great success and long continuance of Buddhism. Its founder had the genius to

[1] The term asceticism is ambiguous. It may mean self-mortification, the actual infliction of pain on himself by the devotee, or it may mean merely abstention from any or all of the pleasures of sense. Against the former practice Buddhism made a definite protest, though it did not entirely eradicate it from the discipline of its disciples, just as it did not destroy the belief in the acquisition of supernormal powers by such means.

establish a working system, not intended for all, but for those who realized that there was a life higher than "indulgence in the passions, low, vulgar, common, ignoble, and useless", and who felt that it could not be attained under the limitations of the social conditions of the time.[1] It was a system, ascetic indeed in its rules of strict celibacy and restrictions on eating, but one in which practices of self-mortification were discouraged. The goal was Nirvāṇa, a state of the individual described as bliss and freedom from rebirth; and the course of training required to attain it was hindered both by self-torture and by indulgence in the passions.

The positive doctrines of the teaching are called the four Noble Truths. (1) The truth that suffering exists; (2) the truth that suffering has a cause, which is "thirst" (*taṇhā*) or craving for existence; (3) the truth that this craving can be stopped; (4) the truth of the Noble Eightfold Path consisting of the eight practices of self-training by which the Truths may be realized and a permanent state of peace attained. This is the Doctrine,[2] which all schools have recognized as fundamental, and if it could have been kept free from the metaphysical problems lurking in the references to the self and the world, it might conceivably have remained essentially a religion, a doctrine teaching a way for the salvation of the individual, and discarding everything in human life and thought that appeared to hinder that goal.

But from the first it never was such a simple agnostic system of quietism. It inherited and took for granted many of the current Hindu dogmas, the belief in rebirth, karma, and cosmological theories. It had to defend itself against rival systems that taught their own methods of salvation, and it had to justify itself against the sacrificial system of the current Hinduism. There were other reformers, especially

[1] It should be noticed that it differs from Christian asceticism in teaching that the ascetic life is the only means of winning ultimate salvation. Even in medieval Christianity there is no necessary conflict between the two ends, temporal felicity and the beatitude of eternal life.

[2] Doctrine is here *dhamma* or *dharma*. In pre-Buddhistic use dharma is conceived as a prescribed course of action for anything in nature which may follow a natural or normal process. It may thus be translated "law". As applied to theories of human action it was much wider than morality, for it included all ritual, and was thus practically religion. The dharma of Buddha consisted in teaching the true doctrine (*saddharma*) of man's beliefs and actions, and this exists in the Buddha-word, the Doctrine. Another distinct use of the word is in the sense of thing or object, especially objects of the mind, thoughts, or ideas. See Ch. XII.

the Jains, following similar practices, but often with very different presuppositions underlying them. Later it had to meet the metaphysical arguments of the orthodox philosophical schools, and was compelled to find arguments in self-defence. It ended by becoming one—or rather more than one—of the most developed philosophical systems of Indian thought, and it has left its mark on the still existing philosophies of India.

Before we can inquire what the doctrine was, and especially what was its most primitive form, it has to be realized that Buddhism had split up into sects before it possessed any written records. This does not in itself imply divergent teaching in the Scriptures. It is clear that for a long period the different schools appealed to the same Scripture. Yet the fact that it was all preserved by memory inevitably led to divergences in the Canon. Owing to the deliberate inclusion of utterances of the great disciples or of discourses attributed to them, as well as any passages which might contain an utterance of Buddha, there was ready opportunity for accretions.[1] But the Buddha-word includes also the rules of the community which was founded for the purpose of practising the new life. To begin by analysing the Doctrine without first examining the community and the circumstances in which it originated would be likely to lead to quite arbitrary results. The movement began not with a body of doctrine but with the formation of a society bound by certain rules. These rules of discipline have developed into the first division of the Scriptures, the Vinaya, and they have not only remained practically identical in most of the early schools, but the Vinaya as a whole has been preserved in such a way that the older and later parts can be easily seen. We can, therefore, start, if not at the very beginning at least with what is one of the earliest documents for the history of the Buddhist community.

The *Vinaya* now forming the first part of the threefold division of the Scriptures consists essentially of the monastic rules together with a commentary. It is evident that from the first there must have been disciplinary regulations for the members of the Order, but it is also clear that among the existing rules, as now found in the Vinaya, there are

[1] Buddhaghosa says that of the 84,000 sections (*khandha*) of the Buddha-word 2,000 are by monks. *Vin. com.*, i, 29.

additions and modifications. Some rules, though still preserved, have been abrogated by new conditions, and others have been added owing to the necessity of considering special circumstances. But the nucleus, on account of its use as a formulary of confession, has been preserved separately in a very early form. This collection is known as the *Pātimokkha*.[1]

The Pātimokkha was used at the fortnightly fast-day (*uposatha*), when it was recited at the meeting of the monks held at new moon and at full moon.[2] Oldenberg held that in its present shape, or at least in its most essential parts, it might reach back to Buddha's own time or to that of his personal disciples.[3] This view is now strengthened by the fact that we are now able to compare the formulary as used by several schools, Pāli and Sanskrit, and there is essential agreement between them. The arrangement is exactly the same in all, and the rules for the most part agree in their actual wording and numbering.[4] This implies that we have it practically in the form it had assumed before any sects arose.

According to the regulations in the Vinaya, the Uposatha day (at new moon and full moon) must be formally proclaimed beforehand, and all the monks within one boundary-district must be present unless definite leave of absence has been

[1] In Sanskrit *prātimoksha*. In form it is an adjective formed from *patimokkha* " binding ", from *pati-muc-* " to fasten or bind on (as armour) ", and thus should mean " that which binds, obligatory ". This, however, is not recognized by the ancient Pāli authorities. Buddhaghosa derives it from *muc-* in the sense of freeing from the punishments of hell and other painful births, *Vism.*, 16. The oldest Buddhist explanation in *Vin.*, i, 103 (*Vin. Texts*, i, 263), is purely fanciful. The probability is that the term along with the Uposatha ceremony itself was borrowed from other sects, and like other obscure terms in this document was not clear to the Buddhists themselves. The spelling *pātimokkha* also suggests this; *pāṭimokkha* (with cerebral *ṭ*), says Childers, is unquestionably a Burmese error. Cf. S. Lévi, " Observations sur une langue précanonique du Bouddhisme," *JA.*, 1912, ii, p. 495. There is also a Pātimokkha for nuns modelled on the rules for monks. The Buddhist tradition is that an Order of nuns was formed during Buddha's lifetime, and though this is probable, the legends about its formation scarcely bear historical investigation.

[2] The word *uposatha* corresponds to the brahminical Sanskrit term *upavasatha*, which was the name for the day before the soma-sacrifice, from which the Buddhist term is no doubt derived. The Sarvāstivādins use the term *poshadha*, which was doubtless the form in their dialect before their Canon was turned into Sanskrit.

[3] *Vin. Texts*, vol. i, p. xi.

[4] The following analysis of the Pātimokkha rests upon the Pāli text (ed. by Minaev, St. Petersburg, 1869), the Sanskrit of the Sarvāstivādins, published by Finot, *JA.*, i, 1913, pp. 465 ff., and that of the Mūla-Sarvāstivādins in *Mvyut*, 256 ff.

obtained. The presiding monk begins the recitation of the Pātimokkha by declaring:

Let the Assembly, reverend ones, hear me. To-day is the Uposatha of the fifteenth day. If it appears the right time to the Assembly, let the Assembly perform the Uposatha and repeat the Pātimokkha. How is it with regard to the necessary preliminaries for the Assembly? Reverend ones, announce your purity (freedom from disability). I will repeat the Pātimokkha.—We are all listening well and reflecting on it.—He who has incurred a fault should declare it; if there is no fault he should keep silence. Now by your silence, reverend sirs, I shall know that you are pure. Now as there is a reply for each question, so in such a meeting as this it is proclaimed as many as three times. Now should a monk, when it is proclaimed three times, remember a fault that he has committed and not declare it, he is guilty of a conscious falsehood. Now a conscious falsehood, reverend sirs, has been declared by the Lord to be a hindrance (to advance). Therefore a monk who remembers that he had committed a fault, and wishes to be pure, should declare the fault committed, for when declared it will be easy for him (to advance).[1]

The introduction, reverend sirs, has been repeated. So, I ask the reverend ones, are you pure in this matter? A second time I ask, are you pure in this matter? A third time I ask, are you pure in this matter? The reverend ones are pure in this matter, therefore they are silent. Even so I understand it.

Then follows the recitation of the rules, which are arranged in seven classes according to the degree of gravity. An eighth section gives the rules to be followed at meetings where cases are decided.

1. *Four Pārājika rules*, violation of which involves permanent expulsion.[2]

1. Sexual intercourse of any kind is forbidden.
2. Taking what is not given is forbidden.
3. " A monk who shall knowingly deprive a human being of life, or seek out an armed person against him, or by uttering the praises of death shall incite to suicide, saying, 'ho, man! what is this evil, wretched life to thee?'—he is *pārājika*, and is not in association."
4. " A monk who, though not having the higher knowledge of possessing the superhuman qualities, shall give out with regard to himself that he knows and perceives that complete knowledge and insight has arisen, and then at another time, whether on being pressed or not, desiring to be purified, says, 'without knowing, friends, I said

[1] " In theory all sins must be confessed at the recital of the Prātimokṣa, but as this ceremony takes place only twice a month, and as an immediate confession is required, it is deemed sufficient that the sinner makes his confession to an elder brother. So at least is the practice nowadays in Ceylon and Burma." Kern, *Man*, 87.

[2] Buddhaghosa interprets *pārājika* as " suffering defeat ", and the Mūla-Sarvāstivādins appear to do the same (*Mvyut.*, 278, 9), but the earliest commentary in the Vinaya gives no suggestion of this meaning. The term was probably adopted from some already existing sect. S. Lévi (loc. cit.) has made it probable that it is the same word as the Jain *pāraṃciya*, in the sense of being (permanently) excluded.

I know, without perceiving, I said I perceive, speaking vainly and falsely', unless it was through undue assurance—he is *pārājika*, he is no longer in association."

The third and fourth rules illustrate two points of doctrine. Suicide is condemned without qualification. On Buddhistic and general Indian theory it could only result in another life still burdened with the consequences of the individual's previous karma. But the Buddhist scholastics appear to have raised the question as to what happens in the case of a person who, by winning the goal of arahatship, has escaped from the chain of birth and death, and for whom there is no rebirth. What if at the moment of escape he commits suicide? It appears never to have been more than an academic question, but the problem is illustrated by several stories of monks who are said to have taken this means to escape falling from arahatship. These are discussed below.

The fourth question speaks of superhuman (*uttarimanussa*) qualities.[1] They are superhuman only in the sense that they do not belong to the ordinary man, but have to be acquired by a long course of training, and they are the powers attained by means of the mystic practices of concentration (*samādhi*) known as yoga. These attainments are in the first place states of mind, in which the monk rises by stages so that he becomes gradually free from contact with the world of change. But they also bring with them supernormal physical powers (levitation, the power of projecting an image of oneself to a distance, clairvoyance, etc.), powers which were already claimed by pre-Buddhist adepts. Their mention here is important as early evidence for the view that yoga is an essential part of the primitive doctrine, as seen in the triple division of the disciple's practice into morality, concentration, and full knowledge.

2. *Thirteen Sanghādisesa rules.* Offences involving a period of penance and reinstatement by the Assembly.

Five of these deal with minor sexual offences, such as touching a woman or addressing her with wicked words. Two refer to the building of a monk's dwelling, two to the bringing of false accusations against monks, two to causing dissension in the Order and taking sides in disputes, and two to cases of insubordination, that of a monk who becomes abusive when admonished, and that of one who on account of his evil behaviour has been warned to leave the village where he begs and who refuses to do so.

[1] In *Vin.*, i, 97, they are specified as the trances, releases, concentration, attainments, the Way or the fruit of the Way. See Ch. IV.

These cases were dealt with at a formal meeting of the Order, and the sentence is thus described :

> If the monk becomes guilty of one or another of these offences, for as many days as he conceals it so many days must he, even though unwilling, be compelled to dwell apart. When the monk has passed this period of probation (*parivāsa*), he must still for another six nights undergo the *mānatta* practice [1] towards the (other) monks. When his period of *mānatta* is over, the monk is to be restored in a place where the Assembly of monks is as many as twenty. If the Assembly, being less than twenty even by one, should restore him, he is not restored, and those monks are blameworthy. This is the proper course in the matter.

Two of these rules (6 and 7) throw light on the earliest dwelling-places of the monks. Each monk lived in his own hut (*kuṭi*). If not having a donor he begged the materials and had it put up for him, he must have it made according to certain measurements, and it must be on a site not likely to cause injury (to living things) and with an open space round it. The other monks must come and approve. Similarly, if he had a large residence (*vihāra*) put up, given him by a donor [2] and intended for his own use, the monks must also give their approval.

3. Two *aniyata* rules, undetermined cases, in which the monk might be charged under one or other of the existing rules.

> These are (1) if a monk should sit together with a woman on a secluded seat, and (2) if he should sit with a woman on a seat not secluded, but convenient for addressing her with wicked words. In the first case a lay woman of trustworthy speech might charge him with a pārājika offence or a sanghādisesa or a pācittiya. In the second case she might charge him with a sanghādisesa or a pācittiya offence.

4. *Thirty nissaggiya pācittiya rules.* Offences requiring expiation [3] and involving forfeiture. Although the monk must have no possessions, there were four objects (requisites) that were considered indispensable, a set of three robes,

[1] Skt. *mānatva* and *mānāpya* ; on this passage in the *Vin.* Buddhaghosa (iii, 629) explains *bhikkhumānatta* as *bhikkhūnaṃ mānanabhāva*, the paying of some kind of respect to the other monks. This makes it probable that the culprit remained in a special state of subordination, but the origin of the term remains obscure.

[2] *Sassāmikam ;* " ayant un donateur " (Huber) ; not as in *Vin. Texts*, i, 9, " to belong (also) to others."

[3] This translation depends upon the derivation of *pācittiya* from Sanskrit *prāyaścittika*, but this is not the term used in the Sanskrit versions of the Pātimokkha, which have *pātayantika* and *pāyantika*. It is another example of the fact that the document is so old that the later Buddhists were not sure of the original terms. Cf. S. Lévi, loc. cit.

bowl, bed, and medicine,[1] but rules were made to prevent his obtaining absolute possession of them. They had in theory to belong to the Order, and as the monk might receive them as alms, rules were required to prevent his acquiring a store of property.

1. *Ten rules concerning robes.*

These refer to the length of time during which an extra robe might be kept, to repair and exchange of robes, and to receiving them as alms. He might not ask a lay person for a robe unless he had lost his own, nor might he suggest the kind he was to receive.

2. *Ten rules on material for rugs and the use of money.*

The material of which the rug was made was prescribed, and it had to be used for six years. The monk might accept the material for it under certain conditions. Gold and silver must not be accepted or used in transactions, and buying and selling were forbidden.

3. *Ten rules concerning bowl, medicine, and robes.*

A monk might not keep an extra bowl beyond ten days, nor exchange his bowl if it was broken in less than five places. Medicine (ghee, butter, oil, honey, raw sugar) must not be stored more than seven days. There are special rules for robes in the rainy season and for having them woven. Nothing intended to be given to the Order was to be applied by the monk to his own use.

5. *Ninety-Two Pācittiya rules.* Faults requiring expiation.

This miscellaneous set of rules chiefly contains regulations intended for the harmonious intercourse of the monks, and for the avoidance of abuses leading to luxury in dress or eating or to anything which might distract the monk in his striving to realize the Truths. Some of the most characteristic rules occur here. They are in no systematic order, but may be grouped as follows :

Moral rules, such as lying, abusive language, slander, prevarication which irritates, disrespectful behaviour, stirring up ill-will, reviving a decided matter, concealing a monk's serious offence, ordaining a person below the age of twenty, irregular behaviour at proceedings of the Order, suggesting difficulties of conscience to a fellow monk, eavesdropping during a quarrel, telling an unordained person of one's supernatural powers, or revealing a serious offence to him.

Rules for conduct towards women. Ten rules regulate the relations of the monks with the nuns, especially the official duty of giving them exhortation, restrictions on making gifts to a nun or doing services for her if she is not related.

[1] There was a later division of the requisites into eight : three robes, bowl, razor, needle, girdle, and water-strainer. The bed and medicine do not appear in it, probably because with the institution of large monasteries the monk would find them provided for him.

Behaviour in the vihāra, rules on sleeping, use of furniture, encroaching on a monk who has arrived before, turning another out of a common dwelling-place, or striking or threatening him.

Rules concerning food, eating at the wrong time, eating food that has been put by, going in numbers to receive a meal, beginning to eat again after having finished, asking for medicaments when not sick, drinking strong drink. A monk must not ask another to go with him for alms and then refuse to go, nor must he with his own hand give food to certain classes of heretics.

He must not travel by appointment with a caravan of robbers or with a woman, or cross the threshold of a king without being announced, or go and see an army on the march or in battle-array; if he enters a village late in the day he must inform a monk if one is there.

He must not cause an unordained person to recite the Doctrine word by word, or preach more than five or six words to a woman without a discreet man being present, or ordain a person under twenty years of age.

He must not deprive any living thing of life, or drink water with living things in it, or sprinkle such water on grass or clay, or dig or cause to dig the ground; he must not light a fire to warm himself or bathe oftener than every half month except at the proper seasons.

There are several rules for the use of the requisites, bedsteads, chairs, needlecases, etc. A new robe must be marked with blue or black (to distinguish it). The size of robes and rugs is prescribed.

Several rules in this section show a more developed communal life than that implied in the Sanghādisesa rules, and the whole section has probably been collected or put into shape at a later period than the previous rules. Besides the single huts as dwellings for the monks, we find vihāras belonging to the Order. There is also furniture common to the Order, beds, chairs, etc., and common sleeping places, and among the requisites a needle-case, which must not be of bone, ivory, or horn.

6. *Four Pāṭidesaniya rules.* Faults that must be confessed.

1. A monk must not accept and eat food from a nun who is on her begging rounds if she is not related to him.

2. If the monks are invited to a meal (by a layman) and a nun stands giving orders about serving the food, the monks must rebuke her and say " go away, sister, while the monks are eating ". If they do not, they must confess their fault.

3. If a monk (not being ill and not invited) accepts food from a believing family which is too poor to give alms, and which has been " put under discipline "[1] by the Order, he must confess his fault.

4. A monk who lives in the jungle must not have food brought to him without warning the givers (that the place is dangerous), unless he is sick.

[1] *Sekhasammata.* The term is interpreted as above in *Vin.*, iv, 178. The intention was to prevent the almsgiving becoming a burden to lay people who were willing but too poor to give.

7. *Seventy-five Sekhiya rules.* Rules of training.

These are chiefly rules of behaviour in the daily life of the monk. Six or seven refer to being properly dressed, others to behaving decently and modestly while on begging rounds and to special acts requiring modesty.

Twenty are rules of behaviour in eating. Ten rules prescribe the conditions for preaching the Doctrine to lay people. All the rules are given in the first person in a form convenient for being recited. " With downcast eye will I go among the houses. This is a training to be observed (8)." " Paying attention to my bowl will I eat my alms. This is a training to be observed (32)." " Not to a person wearing slippers, unless he is sick, will I preach the Doctrine. This is a training to be observed (61)." Similar rules follow forbidding preaching to a person with a sunshade, a stick, or a sword in his hand, wearing sandals, lying on a couch, having his head wrapped up, or walking in front, etc.

The differences in the Sanskrit rules are greatest in this section, but they are often more apparent than real. To the rule not to preach the Dhamma to anyone in a cart the Sanskrit adds rules that it is not to be preached to one on an elephant or a horse.

8. *Seven Adhikaraṇa-samatha rules.*

These are simply a classification of the different ways of proceeding in cases that arise under the above rules.

(1) When the accused or the disputants are present, in which case (2) the accused may claim that he is innocent, or (3) that he may have been out of his mind, or (4) he may confess his guilt. (5) Proceedings may be by a majority of the meeting. (6) The accused may be obstinate. (7) The proceeding called " covering with grass " may be followed when the disputants mutually agree to drop the charges and peace is made.

The Pātimokkha gives the rules of life for the monk, not for the man who may come into active association with any form of social life. For the monk some of these activities are entirely cut off, not on the ground that they are sinful in themselves, but that they are a hindrance to the attainment of the ideal at which he aims—the knowledge of the Truths. They become sins for anyone who has deliberately renounced them on the ground that they conflict with progress on the Noble Eightfold Way.

Besides these rules intended for the daily life of the individual monk, others were found necessary for the organization of the Order. These also in their essentials must have existed from the beginning. They are contained in the second part of the Vinaya known as the *Khandhakas*, and in the Pāli are divided into two series (*Mahāvagga*, *Cullavagga*). They give the rules for admission to the Order, the regulations for Uposatha (this part contains the introduction to the Pātimokkha, quoted above, p. 16), rules for spending Retreat (*vassa*), the ceremony at the end of Retreat (*pavāraṇā*), rules for foot-wear, medicines, food, and robes, the carrying out of legal proceedings and settling disputes, as specified in the last part of the Pātimokkha, and rules for the daily life of monks and novices.

Although it is clear that there must have been such rules from the first, we cannot separate the nucleus with the same certainty as in the case of the Pātimokkha. Nevertheless we find the classification of the Mūla-Sarvāstivādin rules [1] mostly in the same order and with similar titles, showing that the general arrangement goes back, like the Pātimokkha, to a time before the origin of distinct sects.

The different recensions of the Vinaya still extant all agree in keeping the nucleus of rules which form the Pātimokkha quite distinct. New rules had to be added to meet changed circumstances, and special interpretations were adopted to meet exceptional cases such as arise under any system of casuistics. But the added rules and new offences were not incorporated with the old. The old list with the special names of the offences remained, and rules for additional faults, though still attributed to Buddha, were described by new names. In the Theravāda and Sarvāstivāda schools this corpus of ecclesiastical law remained without violent change for centuries, and was even taken over by Mahāyāna, a movement which in doctrine produced such a revolution.

The Vinaya describes the monastic community as divided by boundaries (*sīmā*). Each boundary or parish had to be of convenient extent so that all the members who happened to be within it could attend the Uposatha meeting. Within this boundary each assembly (*sangha*) was self-governing.

[1] *Mvyut.*, 276. See below, page 268. L. Finot, "Fragments du Saptadharmaka," *JA.*, 1913, ii, p. 550. In Jan., 1874, J. F. Dickson was present at a recitation of the Pātimokkha in Ceylon. See his description of the ceremony with text and translation in *JRAS.*, 1876, pp. 62 ff. He has also given a description of the ordination service (*upasampadā*) with Pāli text and translation, as he witnessed it in May, 1872. (*The Upasampada-kammavācā*, Venice, 1875.) The Sarvāstivādin form has been translated from the Chinese by Huber in Finot's edition, and that of the Dharmaguptas by Beal in *A catena of Buddhist Scriptures* from the Chinese, London, 1871.

There was no hierarchy, but seniority was reckoned by the number of years from ordination, nor did a central authority exist to check any tendency to change or development in new directions. It is possible, says Oldenberg, that in the early period after Buddha's death the personal autnority of the disciples who had been nearest to the Master may have tended to repress any serious schism ; but a state of things resting on personal influence, not on the sure structure of legal institutions, bears in itself the germ of dissolution. Against this it is possible to maintain that a legal system seeking to enforce its authority over a wide area would have been the very thing to produce violent reaction and opposition. What we find, in fact, for a long period is not dissolution but gradual development. Schools arose, but of their origin we have little definite knowledge, and it is in those which have survived that we find the lines of the development of Buddhist thought.

There is a list of thirteen ascetic practices (*dhutangas*) which shows that there were differences of view about the extent to which austerities should be practised. These are (1) wearing clothes taken from a dustheap, (2) wearing only three robes, (3) getting food only by begging, (4) begging straight on from house to house, (5) eating food only at one place, (6) eating from one vessel only, (7) refusing food offered after the proper time, (8) living in the forest, (9) living at the foot of a tree, (10) living in the open air, (11) living in a cemetery, (12) taking any seat that is offered, (13) sleeping in a sitting posture. They do not appear to be primitive as a whole, as they are not mentioned in the Vinaya proper.[1] The vinaya, however, has a list of four " supports " (*nissaya*), which are to be taught to the disciple after his ordination as being the strict rule, though relaxations are permitted: (1) living only on broken meats (corresponding to the third dhutanga), (2) wearing clothes taken from a dustheap, (3) sleeping at the foot of a tree, (4) using only decomposed urine as medicine. These rules are still enjoined on the monk at the ordination service, and less severe practices are allowed

[1] They occur in the supplementary *Parivāra*, *Vin.*, v, 193. Buddhaghosa discusses them fully, *Vism.*, 59. In Sarvāstivādin works they are called *dhūtaguṇa*. *Mvyut.*, 49, and *Dhs.*, 63, have a list of twelve. They omit (4) and (6) and add *nāmatika*, wearing a certain kind of cloth. *Dhuta* means " one who has shaken off ", i.e. the bonds or depravities ; the separate practices are *angas* " items ", or *guṇas* " qualities ".

as "extras" (*atireka*).[1] Some of them also appear again in another connection.

In the rules of the Vinaya concerning schism the story of the schism of Devadatta, the cousin of Buddha, is told.[2] Towards the end of Buddha's life he aimed at becoming leader, and being repulsed he proposed that five rules should be made compulsory: (1) That monks should dwell all their lives in the forest, (2) that they should live only on alms begged, (3) wear only clothes taken fron a dustheap, (4) dwell at the foot of a tree, (5) not eat fish or flesh. The first four are among the dhutangas. Buddha is said to have refused to make them compulsory, but pointed out that all were permissible except sleeping at the foot of a tree during the rainy season. The schism is said to have been soon suppressed, and nothing more is heard of it. The Chinese traveller, Fa Hien, however, writing in the fifth century A.D., mentions the existence of a body that followed Devadatta. It has been assumed that this proves the continued existence of Devadatta's followers in complete obscurity for a thousand years. All it really tells us is that there was then a body that followed Devadatta's rules. Some schools certainly appear to have treated his memory more favourably than the Theravādins did, for the *Lotus* (ch. XI) says he is to become a Buddha, and that he helped Buddha in his former existence to attain the Perfections, apparently by putting hindrances in his way, which made the Perfections all the greater.

In the differences of the later schools there is little about discipline, but an interesting sidelight on the use of money is thrown in an Avadāna (*Damamūka*, No. 8). A child was born with two gold coins in his hand. Whenever he opened them gold coins appeared. In due time he entered the Order, and when asking permission of the monks he bowed down, placing his hands on the ground, and on getting up there were two coins. This was because in the time of Buddha Kanakamuni he had been a poor woodcutter, and seeing a great feast being given to the monks he had offered them two coins that he had earned. It was his reward to have been born wealthy ever after, for he of his want had given more than they all.

The question of meat-eating also led to differences in practice. There is a Vinaya rule (*Mahāv.*, vi, 23) which

[1] *Vin.*, i, 58. [2] *Vin.*, ii, 196.

forbids the eating of the flesh of elephants, horses, dogs, and certain other kinds. Evidently the usual kinds are not forbidden, and a little later (vi, 31) there is the story of Buddha accepting meat from a Jain general. He justified himself on the ground that the ox had been already killed, and not specially for him. This was the occasion for the promulgation of the rule that " no one shall knowingly eat meat intended (for the recipient). I prescribe that fish and meat are pure in three particulars : when it has not been seen, heard, or suspected (that it was intended for the recipient)". The word *macchamaṃsa* naturally means " fish and flesh ", though it has been translated merely " fish ", but the whole context shows that meat is permitted. A similar story is told in the *Majjhima* (i, 368), where the same three restrictions are mentioned referring only to meat.

This remained the rule, and Hiuen Tsiang tells how on his travels he met communities who " eat only the three pure aliments ", but he himself refused to accept them.[1] A custom had grown up in Mahāyāna of abstaining from all meat, probably due to rivalry with the stricter rules of other sects. This motive is quite clear in the *Lankāvatāra-sūtra*, which has a whole chapter on meat-eating. It points out that even the followers of heretical systems forbid it, and the followers of Buddha's teaching should avoid censure. But it also gives good reasons against the practice, one may be eating one's nearest relative, the practice is not good for health, and most of all it causes pain to living creatures. The three permissible conditions of the Vinaya are expressly condemned.

The rules for novices (sāmaṇeras) are contained in the ten rules of training[2]:

(1) Refraining from killing living things ;
(2) from taking what is not given ;
(3) from unchastity (or incontinence) ;
(4) from falsehood ;
(5) from intoxicants ;
(6) from eating at unseasonable times ;
(7) from seeing displays, dancing, singing, and music ;
(8) from the use of garlands, scents, and unguents ;

[1] *Life* (Beal), p. 38 ; cf. T. Watters, *On Yuan Chwang's Travels in India*, i, 53.
[2] *Khuddakapāṭha*, 2 ; *Vin.*, i, 83 ; cf. *Abhk.*, iv, 69.

(9) from the use of a high or a big bed ;
(10) from receiving gold and silver.

The first five form the rules for laymen, to which the next three are added during a period of fasting (*upavāsa*), i.e. on the Uposatha days.

It has been a matter of discussion whether a layman can win arahatship. The question is not properly put, for the real question is whether he can exercise the necessary training while living in a house. If he can and does, then he becomes an arahat, but he at the same time ceases to be a layman. The question seems to have arisen from the existence of certain legends which tell of laymen suddenly winning complete insight. If such a one does cast off all the fetters, he has freed himself from everything that binds him to a life of pleasure. But some schools held that arahatship could be reached even while he was enjoying such pleasures (*kāmabhogin*). This view is treated by the *Kathāvatthu* (iv, 1) as a heresy.[1]

[1] See the literature quoted by La Vallée Poussin in *Abhk.*, iv, 29 ; B. C. Law, " Nirvāṇa and Buddhist laymen," *Annals of the Bhandarkar Or. Research Inst.*, 1933, p. 80.

CHAPTER III

THE COUNCILS: EARLY SCHOOLS

THE FIRST COUNCIL

THE problems about the events of the first three centuries of Buddhism turn upon two chief points: the records of the first three Councils and the lists of seventeen schools or sects which began to arise in the second century after Buddha's death. The records have no claim to be considered historical accounts. They are legends full of astonishing miracles and impossible anachronisms. Even when the miracles are stripped off we find that the different schools disagree about the most important events.

All the schools hold that there was a Council (*sangīti*, lit. "chanting or reciting together") held at Rājagaha immediately after the death of Buddha. According to the oldest account (that of the Theravādins),[1] the elder Kassapa summoned a Council of 500 for the recital of the Dhamma and Vinaya, giving as a reason the conduct of Subhadda, a monk who had joined the Order in old age, and who, on hearing of Buddha's death, said they were well freed from the Great Ascetic and could now do or not do what they liked. The members decided to take the Vinaya first, on the ground, says Buddhaghosa, that the Vinaya is as old

[1] *Vin.*, ii, 284 ff.; *Vin. Texts*, iii, 370 ff. This is the eleventh chapter of the *Cullavagga*, which forms with the twelfth a supplement to the Vinaya containing the story of the first two Councils. On this the accounts in *Dpvs.*, ch. iv, and *Mhvs.*, ch. iii, are based. Franke says there is complete dependence. Certainly they give nothing in corroboration that adds to the credibility. Besides these there are the accounts of what used to be called the "Northern Schools", i.e. those accounts going back to the Vinaya of the Sarvāstivāda and related schools, which agree in essentials with the Pāli and show that there was a common tradition, but they make it probable that all the details are inferences as to what must have taken place, not actual memories preserved by the members of the Council. The account in the Vinaya of the Dharmaguptas, a Sarvāstivāda branch, is translated by Beal from the Chinese in the reports of the fifth Oriental Congress in 1881 (vol. ii, Ostasiat. Section, p. 13, Berlin, 1882; and *Abstract of four Lectures*, pp. 66 ff.). There is an account from the Tibetan in Rockhill's *Life of the Buddha*, ch. v. O. Franke gives an entirely destructive criticism in "The Buddhist Councils at Rājagaha and Vesālī", *JPTS.*, 1908. J. Przyluski has dealt in great detail with the Chinese sources in *Le Concile de Rājagṛha*, Paris, 1926–8.

as Buddha's teaching, and while the Vinaya stands the teaching stands. Kassapa, who presided, questioned Upāli, "the first of those who know the Vinaya by heart," about each rule, asking (1) the subject of it, (2) the occasion of its being given, (3) the person concerned, (4) the rule itself, (5) further rules resulting from it, (6) when it constitutes an offence, (7) when it does not. In the same way he questioned Ānanda about the Dhamma, beginning with the first sutta in the Dīgha Nikāya, and asking (1) where it was given, (2) about whom or to whom it was spoken. "In this way he asked the five Nikāyas, and question by question the elder Ānanda replied."

It will be seen that the account assumes that the Vinaya and Sutta were in the same state as we have them now. The Vinaya rules are treated as if they already had the commentary (which gives a fictitious account of the circumstances leading to the promulgation of each rule) as well as the additional rules and exceptions resulting from it. No Abhidhamma is mentioned. It is possible that when the account was composed there was an Abhidhamma not separated in a third Piṭaka, but we can be sure that whatever it was it did not consist of the works now known by that name. Buddhaghosa mentions a classification in which it is reckoned along with the fifth Nikāya. However, other schools hold that the Abhidhamma was recited, and that this was done by Kassapa himself.[1]

The account in the Vinaya goes on to say that Ānanda told the Council that Buddha before his death had told him that the Order if it wished might abrogate any of the minor rules. But Ānanda had forgotten to ask which these were, and as the Council could not decide, and further, as Kassapa pointed out that people would say that the rules were being given up because their Master was no longer with them, they accordingly decided neither to add to them nor to abrogate any. In the *Mahāvastu* (i, 69) this argument of Kassapa's is made the reason for summoning the Council. Oldenberg pointed out that the words of Subhadda, which in the Vinaya account are made the reason for the Council being held, occur in the *Mahāparinibbāna-sutta*, and in that sutta there is no mention of a Council. Therefore, he said, the sutta knew nothing of a Council, and, therefore, its existence is quite

[1] Rockhill, *Life*, p. 160. Schiefner, *Tib. Leb.* Hiuen Tsiang (Beal), ii, 164.

fictitious. Not only is this a mere argument *ex silentio*, but it is entirely fallacious. There is no reason why a Council should have been mentioned in that sutta. The statement of Subhadda was made in the midst of the funeral proceedings, and Kassapa could not immediately get up and propose a Council. It was afterwards that Kassapa is said to have addressed the monks and to have repeated to them what Subhadda had said.[1] Then it was that he proposed a Council, and not at the time when Subhadda spoke the words. It is true that we cannot say that the reason given for Kassapa summoning the Council was the actual one. It may have been wrongly attributed to him by the compiler of the Vinaya account, and the *Mahāvastu* in fact contradicts it, but as Kassapa did not and could not propose a Council during the funeral proceedings, the absence of any mention of a Council in the sutta proves nothing against the reality of the Council.[2]

When we come to ask what we may conclude about the historical circumstances of the Council, we do not get much further than the conclusion of Kern: "It is by no means incredible that the Disciples after the death of the founder of their sect came together to come to an agreement concerning the principal points of the creed and of the discipline." [3] All the accounts give us details which were written down centuries later, and from the point of view of those who assumed that the Buddhism and the Canon which they then knew existed as such from the beginning. We can infer that there was at Buddha's death a body of disciplinary rules in existence, and that many discourses of the Master had been remembered during his long years of teaching. To the extent to which we can infer what these were, we may be able to form some positive idea of the first Council, not from the recorded accounts.

The Second Council

The *Cullavagga* (ch. 12) also gives an account of the second Council. We are told that a hundred years after the death

[1] Yet Minaev did imagine that this proposal was made during the funeral proceedings. *Recherches*, p. 25.

[2] M. Finot has recently made it very plausible that the sutta and the Vinaya account were once a single work. As he says, there is not the shadow of a discrepancy. *Indian Hist. Quarterly*, 1932, p. 243.

[3] *Man*, 103.

of the Lord the Vajjian monks of Vesālī explained ten things to be permissible practices :

1. That salt might be kept in a horn.
2. That it was permissible to eat when the sun's shadow showed two fingers' breadth after noon.
3. And to go into the village for alms and eat again after having eaten.
4. That monks in one parish might hold separate Uposatha meetings.
5. That a party in the Order might perform an official act and decide to inform the rest.
6. That it was permissible to practise what was practised by one's tutor.
7. That milk which had begun to turn but had not become curd might be drunk by one who had had his meal.
8. That liquor which had not yet fermented might be drunk.
9. That a rug not of the prescribed length might be used if it had no fringe.
10. That gold and silver might be accepted.

The elder Yasa (one of the earliest converts of Buddha, and now over 165 years old) was going for alms in Vesālī, and found that the monks of the place had set up a bronze bowl filled with water and was asking the lay people for contributions in money. He warned the people that the sons of Buddha were not allowed to accept gold and silver. Nevertheless the monks collected the money and offered Yasa a share, which he refused. They therefore carried an act of expiation against him, requiring him to go and apologize to the laity for his action. He went, but he defended himself before the people with such effect that they concluded he was in the right. Then the monks decided to carry an act of suspension against him, but he rose in the air and flew to Kosambī, where he summoned a meeting of the monks of Pāvā, Avanti, and the south. They met on Ahoganga hill, and decided that as it was a difficult and delicate matter they had better get the elder Revata on their side. Revata was at Soreyya, but he heard them with his divine ear, and not wishing to be involved in a dispute decided to keep out of their way. He went from place to place, until they caught him up at Sahajāti, and there they succeeded in getting a satisfactory answer from him on the ten points.

The monks of Vesālī also thought it would be well to have Revata on their side. They approached him with a present of bowl, robes, and other requisites. He refused them, but they succeeded in bribing his attendant, so Revata dismissed him. Revata then decided that the matter should be decided where it arose, and the assembly met at Vesālī. But the speeches were aimless and their meaning obscure, so Revata proposed a motion that a committee of eight elders should be elected, four from the east and four from the west, and this was approved. Revata had already made sure of a majority by interviewing the elder Sabbakāmin, one of the eastern monks, the night before. The committee adjourned to the Vālika park, where Revata questioned Sabbakāmin on the ten points, and all were rejected.[1] Sabbakāmin then declared the questions settled, and asked Revata to question him again before the full assembly for the information of the monks. The account concludes: "So the elder Revata questioned the elder Sabbakāmin on the ten points also in the midst of the assembly, and question by question the elder Sabbakāmin replied. Now in this Vinaya-council there were seven hundred monks, no more and no less; therefore, this Vinaya-council is called that of the seven hundred."

In this account some links in the actual procedure appear to be missing, but the records in the Chronicles do not make it any clearer. The Mahāvaṃsa says that it was held in the tenth year of Kālāsoka, that 12,000 monks were present, and that "then the elder Revata selected seven hundred monks who were arahats, who knew the science of meaning and so forth and had the three Piṭakas by heart, from the whole number of monks to form a Dhamma-council". They then met in the Vālika park and made a collection of the Dhamma. It goes on to say that the wicked monks, 10,000 in number, who had been defeated by the holders of the second Council, formed a school (*ācariyavāda*)[2] named the Mahāsanghika. This term means "belonging to the Great

[1] The sixth point, that the practice of one's tutor might be followed, may be permissible according to circumstances, but could not form a rule.

[2] Lit. "teacher-school"; these teachers appear to have been the heads of sects, and the names of several—Dharmagupta, Kāśyapa, and Bhadrāyaṇa—probably appear in the names of heretical schools.

Order or Community of monks ", but there is nothing in the *Mahāvaṃsa* to imply that they held a council. The *Dīpavaṃsa*, however, states that the 10,000 wicked monks assembled and made a collection of the Dhamma, and therefore this Dhamma-council is called the Great Council. It seems that the author of the *Mahāvaṃsa*, who must have known this statement, deliberately rejects it. He also omits the next statement of the *Dīpavaṃsa*, which goes on to say :

> The monks of the great Council made a reversed teaching. They broke up the original collection (of the Scriptures) and made another collection.
>
> They put the Sutta collected in one place elsewhere. They broke up the sense and the doctrine in the five Nikāyas . . .
>
> The Parivāra, the summary of the sense (of the Vinaya), the six sections of the Abhidhamma, the Paṭisambhidā, the Niddesa, and part of the Jātaka—so much they set aside and made others.

Oldenberg declared that the account of the dispute at the second Council bears the stamp of being in the highest degree trustworthy. Yet it is part of the same document which tells us of the first Council, an event which he considered pure invention. We at least have to reject the details. The Council, we are told, was held 100 years (or 110 in Rockhill's account) after Buddha's death. Yet the eight elders had all seen Buddha,[1] so that they were all at least 120 years old if they had been ordained at the lowest possible age of twenty. The various accounts all speak of the ten practices, but they do not agree what these were. In Rockhill's account only the last four agree with the Pāli. Four in the Dharmagupta account also agree, but not the same four. The list was preserved by means of ten mnemonic words, *singiloṇakappa* " horn-salt-practice ", *dvangulakappa* " two-finger-practice ", etc., and it is clear that some of them have been misunderstood. For the Dharmaguptas the two-finger-practice refers not to the shadow of the sun being two fingers' breadth after noon, but to eating after meals by taking food with two fingers. Evidently the writers had to guess at the meaning. Nor can we infer that the Pāli is the only trustworthy version, for, in the case of the eighth practice, *jalogikappa* should mean the practice of sucking like a leech (*jaloga*), as the Dharmagupta account takes it.

[1] Geiger thinks this an embellishment intended to exalt the authority of the elders. In that case it must have been another Yasa, for Yasa is identified with the Yasa who was one of Buddha's first converts.

We thus cannot be certain what all the points of dispute were about, but the list does not appear to be an arbitrary invention. The probability is that it records a real set of practices which were once in dispute, but it is also probable that their condemnation at the Council is mere inference. This is all the more likely when we find that Vasumitra, in his account of the first schism,[1] gives an entirely different reason for the origin of the Mahāsanghikas. It was due, he says, to five points of doctrine about the nature and attainments of the arahat, which were brought forward by a certain Mahādeva. These five points need not be inventions any more than the ten points, as they appear again later, but they show that one party or other (or both) knew nothing of what took place at the second Council.

The same conclusion may be drawn about the story of the Great Council in the *Dīpavaṃsa.* What is there told about the different recension of the Scriptures is true in substance. There was such a recension, and the author inferred that it was part of the disputes at the second Council. But the story that it was deliberately drawn up at this time by the Mahāsanghikas is ignored by the author of the *Mahāvaṃsa.* As the *Mahāvaṃsa* is a deliberate rewriting and improving of the *Dīpavaṃsa,* "a conscious and intentional re-arrangement," as Geiger says, it must have definitely rejected that story.

The Third Council

The story of the third Council of Pāṭaliputta is given in the *Mahāvaṃsa* (ch. 5) at the end of the legendary account of the reign of Asoka. Much of the material of this comes from Indian sources, as we find most of the legend in Sarvāstivādin works,[2] but it is only in the Pāli that there is any mention of this Council. We are told in the *Mahāvaṃsa* that owing to the prosperity of the Order under Asoka, who was ruling in Pāṭaliputta, heretics had come to live with the monks. These heretics are expressly spoken of as non-Buddhists,

[1] "Origin and Doctrines of Early Buddhist Schools," from the Chinese by J. Masuda, *Asia Major*, ii, p. 14; from the Tibetan by Vasiliev, *Der Buddhismus*, p. 247.

[2] The chief difference is that the Theravādins connect Asoka with their great elder Tissa Moggaliputta, while the Sarvāstivādins connect him with their own hero Upagupta. *CHI.*, i, 498, boldly identifies the two.

not as members of any Buddhist party. No reference to Buddhist sects appears. Asoka sent for Tissa Moggaliputta, assembled all the monks on the earth, and turned out all those who wrongly answered his question, " What was the teaching of the Buddha ? " The king then asked the righteous monks, and they replied, " He was a Vibhajjavādin." Asoka was delighted, and ordered the Uposatha to be held, and they assembled.

The elder (Tissa) from the numerous assembly chose a thousand monks, learned, possessing the six higher knowledges, knowing the three Piṭakas, versed in analysis, to form the Council of the true Doctrine.[1]

With these in the park of Asoka he formed the Council of the true Doctrine. Just as the elder Mahākassapa and the elder Yasa had held a Dhamma-council, so did the elder Tissa hold it.

And in the meeting of the Council he spoke the work *Kathāvatthu* for the refutation of other sects.

So under the protection of King Asoka this Dhamma-council was completed by the thousand monks in nine months.

In the seventeenth year of the King the Sage, seventy-two years old, closed the Council with a great pavāraṇā ceremony.[2]

Thus all we are told of the Council is that it was held and that the *Kathāvatthu* was spoken. Later accounts tell us no more. Buddhaghosa merely paraphrases the *Mahāvaṃsa*, and the *Mahābodhivaṃsa* (110) repeats him.

The Sarvāstivādin accounts have much in common with the Pāli. They agree essentially in the reports of the first two Councils, although they put Asoka not two centuries but one after Buddha's death.[3] Both accounts tell much of Asoka and repeat some of the same legends. They have similar lists of the early schools, and their Scriptures are arranged in the same four chief divisions. But the Sarvāstivādins have no word about the third Council. They speak of a Council under Asoka, but this is the second Council, and they may have confused this Asoka with Kālāsoka. Kern supposes that the third Council was but a party meeting, so much so that no other party ever heard of it, but the fact that it is ignored by all other sects makes it necessary to

[1] *Saddhammasaṃgahaṃ*. Geiger says " to make a compilation of the true doctrine ". But in *Dpvs. saṃgaha* is used all through in the sense of " council ". Buddhaghosa (*Vin. com.*, 61), who paraphrases *Mhvs.*, speaks only of *saṃgīti*.

[2] *Mhvs.*, v, 275–280.

[3] The supposed 200 years mentioned in a Sarvāstivādin document (Burnouf, *Intro.*, 432) rests on a misreading. See Speyer, *Av. Śat.*, ii, 200. Other later sources give various dates. Bhavya gives 160 years, but still makes Dharmāśoka king at the second Council. Rockhill, *Life*, p. 182.

consider the other alternative, that there never was a third Council.

Even the Pāli data lend support to this view. There is fairly early evidence for the first and second Councils in the *Cullavagga*, but that account has no mention of a third. This has usually been taken to imply that the *Cullavagga* account was composed before Asoka's time. It may equally imply that the third Council had not then been invented. The earliest evidence for it is confined to the testimony of the much later Ceylon Chronicles. The Chronicles had already added the story of a Dhamma-council to the account in the *Cullavagga* of the second Council, and had garnished the story of the first Council with the patronage of Ajātasattu, and the second with more elaborate legends of Kālāsoka. There are cogent reasons why a third Council under Asoka should have been imagined, and Tissa is said to have held it " just as the elder Mahākassapa and the elder Yasa had held a Dhamma-council ". The Abhidhamma books were rejected by other schools, and in particular the *Kathāvatthu*, which Tissa had promulgated at it. This especially needed the support of a Council, or perhaps to the mind of disciples implied one.

The commentary on another Abhidhamma book, the *Dhammasangaṇi*, represents an objector as saying, " why is the *Kathāvatthu* accepted ? Was it not fixed by the elder Moggaliputta Tissa more than 218 years after the enlightened Buddha had attained Nirvāṇa ? Therefore reject it as being the utterance of a disciple." Even the authority of a Council was not enough for this objector. The commentator meets this by admitting that the discussion of the doctrines was composed by Tissa following the method given by the Master, but that the list of doctrines discussed was first given by Buddha when he visited the Heaven of the thirty-three gods and taught the doctrine to his mother.

V. A. Smith remarks that Asoka after he had been reigning for some thirty years issued a fresh series of documents, the seven Pillar Edicts, which reiterate his earlier teaching, and conclude with a formal retrospect of the measures adopted by him in furtherance of the ethical reforms which he had at heart. Yet he seems surprised that there is no mention of the Council of Buddhist elders.[1] Mrs. Rhys

[1] *The Early History of India*, 3rd ed., p. 161.

Davids accepts the Council, but subjects the evidence for it to the severest criticism, pointing out first that the evidence is six or seven centuries later than the Council. She also holds that it was a Congress rather than a Council, that the "collection of the Dhamma" was a "gigantic task of revision", that the actual revisers and judges were not a thousand but only eight,[1] that as the revision of the English Prayer-book took twenty years, the Council must have taken much longer than nine months, and that as the first thesis in the *Kathāvatthu* concerns the *puggala*, the question of paramount importance to be discussed must have been that of *attan* versus *an-attan*. The "drastic expulsion of ordained monks" can only have been carried through after the Council, not before, as the Chronicles say. In fact, the Council was a Congress, and every fact about it was different from what is recorded.[2]

To attain a certain conclusion where the data are like this is obviously impossible, but even if we could be sure that a Dhamma-council was held under Asoka, we get no help in determining anything definite about the history of Buddhism. All we are told is that a work called the *Kathāvatthu*, "subjects of discussion," was spoken there, and we have good reasons for holding that it was not the work which now exists in the Pāli Canon. The work which now exists is of great importance for the growth of doctrine, but we do not reach more credible results by assuming that it was either composed or recited at a third Council.

There is an excellent translation of the *Kathāvatthu* with extracts from the commentary by Mr. Shwe Zan Aung and Mrs. Rhys Davids. But the unfortunate result of this useful piece of work has been an astonishing amount of mistaken assumptions and slipshod inferences by scholars who have never taken the trouble to look at the text or to distinguish between the text and commentary. It was asserted that Tissa "composed" the work, though the Pāli authorities do not say so, and, as Mrs. Rhys Davids has pointed out,

[1] The number eight is said to have a precedent because there were eight at the second Council. But these eight had nothing to do with the Dhamma; they were the eight referees for the ten disputed Vinaya rules, and the Vinaya account knows nothing of Dhamma revision at the second Council.

[2] The view of the *Cambridge Hist. of India* (i, 498) is that "in the Kathāvatthu, composed at the time by Upagupta, we have a full record of the divergencies of opinion which led to its convention". The story of the Council is thus inserted in the Upagupta story, which knows nothing of the Council.

it could not have been composed by one man. It was also assumed that it mentions the sects that held the heretical doctrines which it refutes. If this were so, we should have fairly early evidence for the teachings of these schools. But, in fact, no names of schools are given in it.

Where we find the names is in a commentary certainly several centuries later than the Council. This commentary is occupied not in specifying the doctrines of the seventeen schools, but in expounding the refutations of doctrines mentioned in the text and in stating what schools hold or have held them. Nine out of the seventeen are not mentioned at all, while some doctrines, indeed, whole sections of the work, are attributed to later schools not among the seventeen. Only three of the original seventeen are mentioned as " now " holding certain doctrines. As Mrs. Rhys Davids points out, the work probably grew gradually. Its " patchwork-quilt appearance " shows its slow growth, for any new heresy could be added and refuted as required.[1]

The Schools

It is during the first three centuries of Buddhism that the community is said to have split into seventeen or, including the original body, eighteen schools. There are several lists of the schools in existence.[2]

That given by the Ceylon Chronicles is doubtless the oldest, but as it has been preserved by a school out of direct contact with India several of the names have been corrupted. There are also several lists coming from Sanskrit sources, but they all vary so much that it is impossible to suppose that we can form a chronological scheme of the growth of the divisions. They were naturally all drawn up long after the schools originated, and represent the attempts of the scholiasts to construct a history. They do, however, allow us to draw several important conclusions. The Chronicles call the schools *ācariyavāda*, " schools of teachers," and this suggests one cause of the origin of sects, that is, the rise of prominent teachers who were able to impose their views on certain communities. A number of the names are formed from personal names, those of the *ācariyas*, the teachers of

[1] *Points of Controversy*, p. xxxi. [2] See Appendix II.

the respective schools. Other names are place names, suggesting the development of schools in special localities, and some are formed from the peculiar doctrine of the school.

The real value of the lists is in giving us an approximate view as to what at various periods the various communities were held to be. From this point of view the list in the *Mahāvyutpatti* (275) is one of the most important. It is also of special interest in giving one of the few references in Sanskrit Buddhism to the schools of Ceylon. It is a Sarvāstivādin list, and may have been drawn up in the fifth or sixth century A.D.,[1] but it evidently contains older elements.

The arrangement is not, as in the other lists, chronological, but the schools are arranged in four groups :

1. *Sarvāstivādas :* Mūla-Sarvāstivādas, Kāśyapīyas, Mahīśāsakas, Dharmaguptas, Bahuśrutīyas, Tāmraśāṭīyas, Vibhajyavādins.
2. *Sammatīyas :* Kaurukullakas, Āvantakas, Vātsīputrīyas.
3. *Mahāsanghikas :* Pūrvaśailas, Aparaśailas, Haimavatas, Lokottaravādins, Prajñaptivādins.
4. *Sthaviras :* Mahāvihāravāsins, Jetavanīyas, Abhayagirivāsins.

A few of these schools are mere names, but each of the groups is significant as being historically important for its doctrines.[2]

The Sarvāstivādins and Theravādins (Skt. Sthaviravādins) each have Scriptures which show that they developed in close connection. Both Canons were originally in a Prakrit dialect and compiled on a common plan. But they were for

[1] The date of this list is, of course, independent of the question of the date of *Mvyut.*

[2] The geographical distribution of the chief schools also throws light on their development. Magadha and Kosala, the primitive sphere of Buddhism, had become the Maurya empire, which extended more and more to the north-west. In this direction the Sarvāstivādins spread, their chief seat being at Mathurā (Muttra in the United Provinces) among the Sūrasenas. The Mūla-Sarvāstivādins were chiefly in Kashmir. Further south, on the Jumna, was Kosambī in the region of the Vatsas (Pāli, Vaṃsas), probably the seat of the Vātsīputrīyas. Still further west were the Avantis, with capital Ujjenī. Franke has shown that linguistically Pāli belongs to the Ujjenī region, but it does not follow that the existing Pāli literature developed there. It is certain that South India became an important centre of literary activity, as Dr. B. C. Law has shown. See Bibliography. Addenda.

long preserved by memory, and the mere local separation of the various communities is enough to explain how differences of classification arose and grew. No doubt other differences began early, as we find at the second Council references to monks of the east and monks of the west. But it is not certain that the two schools considered themselves distinct even as late as the time of Asoka. The Chronicles appear to have put the separation before Asoka, Vasumitra puts it after. As there was no violent secession, it is not easy to see how the date of separation could be determined, especially as the two schools continued to live together for centuries.

In the above list the term Sarvāstivāda is a general one covering seven groups. The Chinese Canon, however, includes a Vinaya of this name, as well as one of the Mūla-Sarvāstivādins.[1] One branch here given is that of the Vibhajyavādins. The term means one who distinguishes or discriminates, referring specially to a method of philosophical discussion. It is the same term by which the Theravādins are said to have described themselves to Asoka. If there is a basis of fact to this story, it may imply that the word had not yet become a party term, for it is one that no Buddhist would have disclaimed in its plain meaning.

Among the Sammatīya group we find the Āvantakas, i.e. people of Avanti in the western district with the chief city Ujjenī. The term Vātsīputrīya suggests a connection with another western district, that of the Vatsas (Pāli, Vaṃsas). The name Vātsīputrīyas has never been explained. In form it means the followers of Vatsīputra[2] or the Vatsīputras, the Vatsa people. This school, though only known from the statements of opponents, is important for its peculiar doctrine of *pudgalavāda*, the theory that the individual is something more than the sum of the constituents of which he is composed. The name Kaurukullaka is of interest as the survival of an early School of which nothing is really

[1] *Mūla* = "root". That this sect really was, as it claimed to be, the original one need not be assumed, any more than in the case of modern sects that describe themselves as primitive or apostolical.

[2] Lit. "son of the Vatsa woman". Such personal names are common, like Ajātasattu's name Vedehīputta, "son of the Videha woman." Vatsīputra is conceivably the name of the ācariya who founded the school. In the Chronicles the sect name is Vajjiputtaka. It occurs twice over, first as the name of the originators of the first schism, the Mahāsanghikas, or, as *Dpvs*. calls them, the Mahāsangītikas, and again as a sect that split off later with the Mahimsāsakas. The latter are the Vātsīputrīyas. The Pali term is a corruption, unless *Vajji* is here = *Vṛji* = *Vraja*, the district near Mathurā.

known. Even the name is uncertain, as it occurs in at least four forms, and the Chronicles class it with the next group.

Of the Mahāsanghikas the only part of their Canon which has survived is that of the Lokottaravādin branch in the *Mahāvastu.* This school held a docetic theory of the nature of a Buddha, very important for Mahāyāna developments, and so also, according to the *Kathāvatthu* commentary, did the Pūrvaśailas and Aparaśailas, established in South India. The Haimavatas, says Vasumitra, were really Sthaviras (Theravādins) who had changed their name. It is likely enough that in his time there were no Theravādins in India except certain sects like the Haimavatas, who laid claim to the name. The same may be concluded from what Hiuen Tsiang reports of the Sthaviras in India in the seventh century. He describes most of them as being of the Mahāyāna sect. This group, in fact, includes those that were or became Mahāyānists.

The Sthaviras are the Pāli Theras, " elders," the members of the Theravāda, " the school of the Elders." Here we find all the three Theravāda schools established in Ceylon and divided just as described in the Ceylon Chronicles.[1]

The Mahāvihāravāsins, " inhabitants of the Great Vihāra," claimed to be the orthodox Theravādins established by Mahinda at Anurādhapura at the time of the official introduction of Buddhism into Ceylon under Asoka when the Mahavihāra was built. From the *Mahāvaṃsa* we learn that two centuries later under king Vaṭṭagāmaṇi (29 B.C.) the Abhayagiri vihāra was built, and soon afterwards a schism resulted. This is evidently the school of the Abhayagirivāsins, the inhabitants of the Abhayagiri vihāra, also at Anuradhapura. According to the *Sāsanavaṃsa* (24) they were known as the Dhammarucis. The Jetavanīya school arose in the reign of Mahāsena (A.D. 325–352), when the Jetavana vihāra was built. The *Sāsanavaṃsa* identifies it with the Sāgaliya school.

The remarkable fact about the *Mahāvyutpatti* list is the extent to which it is corroborated by the Chronicles. The list in the latter is doubtless old, but besides the eighteen schools it records later ones, six in India and two in Ceylon. The *Mahāvyutpatti* has dropped seven that had become obsolete and meaningless, and has placed five of the additional

[1] *Mhvs.*, xv, xxxiii, 80–3 ; xxxvii, 32–9. Cf. *Dpvs.*, xix, 14 ; xii, 70–5.

schools among the eighteen. Only two of its names are not found in the Chronicles, and it has the three Theravādin schools of Ceylon, the orthodox Theravādins, the Dhammarucis, and the Sāgaliyas. Its grouping of the schools also allows us to see the main lines of development. The most widely extended school was the Sarvāstivāda, which at first and for long must have been closely associated with the Theravāda. What particular school was represented by the mission of Mahinda to Ceylon we do not know. No written Scriptures were taken by this mission, as it was not till two centuries later that they are said to have been written down.[1] There may have been such an official recording, but what we possess are not the Scriptures as introduced in the third century B.C. It is the Canon as it existed in some school that claimed to be Theravādin, and had been turned into the dialect of the place from which it came, the dialect which we call Pāli.[2] Where this locality was is still disputed. Oldenberg thought it was probably in south India, in the kingdoms of Andhra or Kalinga, but from what we know of the schools of south India this is unlikely. The close connection with the Sarvāstivāda Canon makes it more likely that this Pāli school developed somewhere in the north. We find in it legends told with reference to great Buddhist settlements, but none referring to south India. Franke on philological grounds fixed the dialect in the region of Ujjenī. Walleser and Geiger for different and even contradictory reasons prefer Magadha. Grierson put it in the north-west, which was a stronghold of the Mūla-Sarvāstivādins.[3] In any case it is generally agreed that it is a form of Northern Buddhism, but owing to the fact that it has spread from Ceylon to Burma, Siam, and further India it has usually been termed Southern Buddhism.

The outstanding divisions in earlier Buddhism as determined by the literature are the schools of the Theravāda, Sarvāstivāda, and Mahāsanghika, the last represented by the Lokottaravāda of the *Mahāvastu*. It was within the last two that the new tendencies and theories arose which produced the Mahāyāna schools.

[1] *Mhvs.*, xxxiii, 100–1.

[2] The term Pāli as used by the Ceylon commentators means the text of the Scriptures as opposed to the commentaries. Western scholars have adopted it as the name of the language in which both text and commentary were written.

[3] Przyluski, *La légende de l'empéreur Açoka*, p. vi.

CHAPTER IV

EARLY DOCTRINE: YOGA

We have reason to believe that the rules of discipline go back to a very early period, and that the fundamental rules must go back to the beginnings of the Order.[1] All these rules were meant to make it possible for the individual to follow a way of life in which he could acquire the knowledge which the Master had realized for himself. The disciples held that this knowledge and the way to attain it had also been taught by the Master, and that in his utterances they possessed his teaching, the Dhamma as well as the Vinaya, which they preserved by memory. There can be no doubt that they did preserve such utterances, but they also possessed much more—discourses and commentaries of disciples, poems, legends, and stories, in which the Buddha-word might consist of not more than a single verse or sentence. It is not so easy, as in the case of the Vinaya, to distinguish what is truly original, but we possess lists and classifications which tell us what the earliest Buddhists held to be fundamental.

One list which remained unchanged, and was recognized in all schools, was that of the four Truths. To know these,

[1] From what has been said it will be seen that exact dates in the chronology of the different parts of the Canon are not to be attained. We may speak of an early and even a primitive nucleus, but except in the case of the early sections of the Pātimokkha we cannot point to it. We can often distinguish the relative age of different portions. Discussion has usually turned upon the question when the Pāli Canon received its present form. This has been said to be in the time of Asoka, because in the reign of this quite historical king the legend of one school tells that he held a Council. But even if the Council is historical, we know no detail about it except that the *Kathāvatthu* was recited at it. As we have no reason to think that the Canon was written down at that time, the view that it then assumed its present form is little more than a pious guess. The chief reason for thinking that the Vinaya rules and the four Āgamas had taken a definite shape even before Asoka is the fundamental correspondence between the Theravāda and Sarvāstivāda Canons. But their differences also show that they must have for long have floated only in the memory of those who learnt them by heart. The forms that we know are those which they had when they were written down, and this means probably, as the Theravāda holds, in the first century B.C. But the Sarvāstivāda Canon continued to grow for centuries.

not to accept them by faith in another, but to realize their truth by an inner conviction, was the goal of the disciple. The list in its simplest form appears as: this is pain; this is the cause of pain; this is the cessation of pain; this is the way leading to the cessation of pain.[1] We may attempt to go further back and ask in what sense the formula was originally meant, but that in some sense is the fundamental teaching of Buddhism. It implies what is called a pessimistic view of life, for "this" is man's existence. It is not more pessimistic than other religions that have called life a vale of tears, and it is definitely optimistic in teaching that the cause of pain can be known, and that there is a way by which it can be removed. But in being pessimistic it is consistently so, and it requires that one who really knows that existence is pain shall devote all his efforts to stopping it, that is, to understand what the cause is, and then to remove himself from all contact with it. The ordinary man does not believe that existence is pain. Even when he despairs about ever attaining pleasurable ends, he is still under the impulse, the thirst for pleasure. Evidently such a one is incapable of admitting or understanding even the first Truth. He can only come to realize the Truths by a course of moral and intellectual training.

The practice of mental training has always been a part of the Buddhist system, always, that is, so far as the documents allow us to trace it back. But it appears in the earliest documents (see above, p. 17), and there is no reason to doubt that mental training was a pre-Buddhistic practice, and that some forms of it were adopted from other sects. The practice was already known in the Brahmin schools and probably in others by the name of yoga. The training consists in the "yoking" (as yoga literally means) of the mind by fixing it on one subject, and so controlling the attention that everything else is excluded.[2] It may become a form of self-hypnotization, and in itself has no moral character. There is a resulting state or series of states of mind as the concentration becomes more intense, and the

[1] *Dīgha*, i, 83.

[2] There is nothing in the word yoga to imply a religious experience, but as it was practised by sects as a means of attaining union with God, its sense of yoking or joining could naturally develop that meaning; but even then, as in the *Bhagavadgītā*, it is rather the process of attaining that union than the union itself.

methods of fixing the attention are described in detail by the Buddhist commentators.

But in order to practise concentration of mind (*samādhi*) rightly, and acquire the states of trance (*jhāna*) and higher attainments (*samāpatti*), training in morality is presupposed. This leads to the threefold division of the disciple's training into morality (*sīla*), concentration (*samādhi*), and full knowledge (*paññā*).[1] This is the scheme as we find it given repeatedly in the two most authoritative collections of the Doctrine, the first two Nikāyas or Āgamas. On these the following account is based.

Morality is more than the Vinaya rules, for these chiefly concern the behaviour of the monk as the member of a community, and the moral conceptions of Buddhism are admittedly the highest product of Indian ethical thought. They derive their convincing character from two doctrines which were already established in Hindu belief, karma, "action," i.e. the retribution of all deliberately willed actions, and the doctrine of continued rebirth. The latter made the doctrine of retribution seem real, for a single existence does not always appear to bear out the teaching that whatsoever a man sows he shall also reap. But the real greatness of Buddhist morality is in the truly ethical character of its teaching. In this it was helped by its rejection of brahminical ritual and sacrifice, and its principles apply equally to the life of the layman and the ascetic. The formulation of the moral training in the *Dīgha* is no doubt a scholastic production. The question is how far it was a correct presentation of the earliest teaching will be considered later.

A man born as a householder or in some other low family hears the doctrine of a Buddha and acquires faith in him. He reflects that it is not easy to practise *brahmacariya*[2] while living in a house, and decides to go forth to a houseless

[1] *Dīgha*, i, 63 ff. This triple division with further subdivisions runs through the *Dīgha* and *Majjhima*, and is found in Sarvāstivāda works (*Mvyut.*, iv, 36), showing the agreement of the schools on fundamentals. The three divisions are also called the accomplishments or attainments (*sampadā*) (1) of morality, (2) of the mind and heart, (3) of full knowledge. *Dīgha*, i, 172.

[2] This term, another example of one borrowed from other sects, meant originally the practice of a religious student before marriage during his study of the Vedas under a brahmin teacher, and implied strict continence. This is the special sense in which the Buddhists adopted it, for it is explained just below as "avoiding sex intercourse", not merely avoiding violating the ordinary moral rules, which is *kāmesu micchācāro* "wrong indulgence in the passions". But it is also used in a wider sense of the whole religious life of one who has taken these rules upon him.

life, cutting off his hair and beard, giving up any wealth he may have, and abandoning all his relatives. "Having thus left the world he dwells restrained with the restraint of the Pātimokkha, accomplished in the practice of good conduct, and seeing the danger of even minute faults. He adopts and becomes trained in the rules of training, exercising good action in body and speech, getting his livelihood by pure means, and having four special objects in view: being accomplished in morality, having the door of his senses guarded, being endowed with mindfulness and self-possession, and being content.

These four objects form the division of moral training. The first is expounded by giving a list of rules called the Moralities (*sīla*).[1]

1. He abandons the killing of living things, lays aside the use of a stick or a knife, and full of pity he dwells with compassion for the welfare of all living things.

He abandons the taking of what is not given, takes and expects only what is given, and lives without thieving.

He abandons incontinence and lives apart, avoiding sex intercourse.

He abandons falsehood, and speaks the truth.

He abandons slanderous speech, and does not tell what he has heard in one place to cause dissension elsewhere. He heals divisions and encourages friendships, delighting in concord and speaking what produces it.

He abandons harsh speech, his speech is blameless, pleasant to the ear, reaching the heart, urbane and attractive to the multitude.

He abandons frivolous language, speaks duly and truly and in accordance with the Dhamma and Vinaya. His speech is such as to be remembered, elegant, clear, and to the point.

Then follow a number of rules applying especially to his life as monk.

He abandons injuring seeds or plants.

He eats once at one meal-time, and not at all at night, avoiding unseasonable food.

He abandons the seeing of dancing, singing, music, and shows.

He abandons using and adorning himself with garlands, scents, and unguents.

He abandons the use of a high or big bed.

He abandons the accepting of gold and silver.

The other rules in this section specify the abandoning of various kinds of property, kinds of food (raw grain, raw meat), acting as a go-between, cheating, bribery, fraud, and various acts of violence.

2. The second section is mainly an amplification of the frivolous practices in the first list—injury to seedlings, use of kinds of food, seeing dances and shows, games, the use of luxurious furniture, scents and unguents, frivolous tales, wrangling about the Dhamma and Vinaya, acting as intermediary and diviner.

[1] *Dīgha*, i, 63. They are divided into three sections, Small, Medium and Great, but this refers merely to their length, as the most important section containing all the positive rules is the first.

3. The third section gives a list of the "base arts" by which ascetics and brahmins gain a wrong living, auguries, charms, astrological, medical, and surgical practices.[1]

Secondly, he keeps the door of his senses guarded. If he sees anything, he does not devote his attention to its characteristics or its details. As greed and dejection [2] and evil thoughts might flow into him if he did not restrain his sense of sight, he restrains and guards it, and so of the other five senses.[3] Thus, having this restraint of the senses, he feels an inner unmixed pleasure.

Next he becomes mindful and self-possessed by performing all the ordinary actions of life with conscious reflexion upon the proper way of doing each of them, and finally he finds contentment in being satisfied with robes for his body and alms-bowl for his sustenance. He takes them with him as a bird its wings.

It will be seen that there is no lack of confidence that the individual can come to perform all these rules. It is true that he has cut off many occasions of stumbling by renouncing household life and choosing to practise *brahmacariya* "wholly complete, wholly pure, polished as a pearl"; yet the need of some moral support did come to be seen, and was one of the causes of the development and popularity of the belief in bodhisattas, beings who devote themselves to saving their fellow men.

But he still has to expel those hindrances (*nīvaraṇa*), tendencies of mind which prevent him from attaining clear knowledge. He begins to meditate, and practises concentration. Going to a secluded spot, in the forest, at the root of a tree, on a hill, in a mountain cave or cemetery, after having begged his alms, he sits down cross-legged and upright, setting up mindfulness before him. He purifies his mind of the five hindrances: longing for the world, malice, sloth and torpor,

[1] An interesting point with regard to this list is its relation to the *Ten rules of training* (*Dasasikkhāpadāni*) which have to be learnt by the novice (*Vin.*, i, 83), nine of which occur in this list. The first four of the Ten rules are identical with the first four of the Moralities, and the last five are the same as the five rules beginning with the rule about eating, down to the non-acceptance of gold and silver. The fifth of the Ten rules forbidding intoxicants does not occur here, though it is in the *Pātimokkha*, *Pac.*, 51.

[2] These are the two attitudes of the sensual man towards life. An eagerness to indulge in pleasures and a feeling of disgust and revulsion on discovering the vanity of sensual indulgence.

[3] The sixth sense is the inner sense of mind, the objects of which are thoughts, ideas, or any inner experience.

distraction and agitation, and doubt. This is the beginning of the concentration of mind (*samādhi*) which leads him through four stages of trance [1] (*jhāna*, Skt. *dhyāna*).

When he sees in himself these five hindrances expelled, exultation arises, as he exults joy arises, as his mind feels joy his body becomes serene and feels pleasure, and as it feels pleasure his mind is concentrated. Free from the passions and evil thoughts he attains and abides in the first trance of pleasure with joy, which is accompanied by reasoning and investigation and arises from seclusion. He suffuses, fills, and permeates his body with the pleasure and joy arising from seclusion, and there is nothing in his body untouched by this pleasure and joy arising from seclusion.

Again, with the ceasing of reasoning and investigation, in a state of internal serenity, with his mind fixed on one point, he attains and abides in the second trance of pleasure with joy produced by concentration, without reasoning and investigation. He suffuses, fills, and permeates his body with the pleasure and joy produced by concentration, and there is nothing in his body untouched by it.

Again, with equanimity towards joy and aversion, he abides mindful and conscious, and experiences the pleasure that the noble ones call "dwelling with equanimity, mindful, and happy", and attains and abides in the third trance. He suffuses, fills, and permeates his body with pleasure, without joy, and there is nothing in his body untouched by it.

Again, abandoning pleasure and pain, even before the disappearance of elation and depression he attains and abides in the fourth trance, which is without pain and pleasure, and with the purity of mindfulness and equanimity. He sits permeating his body with mind purified and cleansed, and there is nothing in his body untouched by it.

The monk has now reached the stage where full knowledge (*paññā*) begins. He reflects on his body, produced by a father and mother, a collection of milk and gruel to which his consciousness is bound. He acquires the superhuman faculties mentioned in the Pātimokkha, false boasting about which involved exclusion from the Order. These include the ability to materialize a shape of himself and create a "mind-formed" body, which may appear in any place he wishes. By the power of *iddhi* he is able to rise in the air, duplicate himself, and other even grotesque attainments. In the legends Buddha is represented as discouraging them in his disciples. He also acquires a telepathic power of

[1] Strictly speaking the trance is the final state of which these are stages. Rhys Davids said "there is no suggestion of trance, but rather an enhanced vitality" (*Pali Dict.*, s.v.), evidently taking trance for a state of coma. But the trances of meditation do not imply a decreased vitality. The inner experience becomes more intense as attention is withdrawn from outer things, and the person may appear unconscious. Once during a great thunderstorm, when two farmers and four oxen were struck, Buddha was walking in the open air, but was so absorbed that he neither saw nor heard anything of it. Yet he was "conscious and awake" all the time. *Dīgha*, ii, 131.

hearing distant sounds and of being able to read the minds of individuals. He can perceive whether a person's mind is passionate or calm, angry or not, etc., just as one looking into a mirror or clear water at his face can see whether he has a mole on it or not.[1]

Having reached this stage he is in a position to develop the three knowledges (*vijjā*).

(1) He directs his mind to the knowledge of his former existences. He remembers one, two, three births, and so on up to a hundred thousand through many ages (*kalpa*) of the evolution and dissolution of the universe, thinking " in that one I had such a name, clan, caste, food, feeling such pleasure and pain, and having such an end. Passing away thence I was reborn in such a place. There, too, I had such a name, etc., and such an end ". It is as clear to him as if a man were to go from his own village to another, and were to reflect on what he said and did, and how he returned.

(2) He directs his mind to the knowledge of the passing away and rebirth of individuals. He acquires the divine eye, and can see beings passing away and being reborn in different states of existence, high or low, happy or miserable, in accordance with their deeds.

(3) Finally, he directs his mind to the knowledge of the destruction of the *āsavas*.[2] He duly understands, " this is pain," " this is the cause of pain," " this is the cessation of pain," " this is the way leading to the cessation of pain." He duly understands : " these are the āsavas," " this is the cause of the āsavas," " this is the cessation of the āsavas," " this is the way to the destruction of the āsavas." When he thus knows and thus perceives, his mind is released from the āsava of sensual desire, from the āsava of (desire for) existence, and from the āsava of ignorance. In the released is the knowledge of his release ; he understands that birth

[1] All these forms of *iddhi*, materialization, invisibility, thought transference, and others (anæsthesia, raising the bodily temperature), are still known and practised by the lamas of Tibet, according to Mme A. David-Neel, who believes that there is a basis of truth in them. See her articles, " Les phénomènes psychiques au Thibet," in *Rev. de Paris*, 1st December, 1929, p. 566, and " La Thibet mystique ", ibid., 15th February, 1928.

[2] This term literally means " flowing in ", and it still has that meaning with the Jains, who look upon karma as something material flowing into the individual. Probably when the Buddhists adopted it it had already acquired a special sense. It is unnecessary to speculate about its derivation, as we know exactly what the Buddhists understood by it, i.e. sensual desire (*kāma*), desire for existence (*bhava*), and ignorance (*avijjā*), to which was later added wrong views (*diṭṭhi*, *dṛshṭi*).

is destroyed, the religious life has been led, done is what was to be done, there is nothing further for this world.[1]

This is the state of *paññā*, the full, intuitive knowledge which brings about the state of the *arahat*,[2] who has done everything required to reach the goal of his training, "than which there is no visible fruit higher and more excellent."[3] This scheme claims to form a complete whole, and there can be no doubt that it did at one time form the sum of the disciple's training. But the possibilities of the psychological developments were not exhausted, and it will be seen how it became extended. The immediate points of interest are, what were the methods for securing the attention, and what did the disciple meditate on.

The Buddhist tradition was that Buddha used to give each disciple a subject for meditation in accordance with his disposition and afterwards question him about it. It was certainly the practice later on for monks to receive subjects of meditation (*kammaṭṭhāna*) from their teachers. Physical means were adopted for the preliminary fixing of the attention.[4] These are the *kasiṇas* (Skt. *kṛtsna*), devices for using physical objects, of which there were ten: earth, water, fire, wind, blue, yellow, red, white, light, and consciousness. The method of using them is described by Buddhaghosa in great detail.[5] The monk in a secluded place makes a circle of reddish clay on the ground, or he may make it on a piece of cloth kept flat by tying four sticks to it. The circle should be one span four fingers across. He sits on a couch conveniently near and looks at the circle, repeating some suitable phrase, such as "insatiable are lusts", sometimes closing his eyes until the "sign" arises. When he can see the sign (i.e. the after-image) with his eyes shut as well as open, the

[1] "Il n'y a plus autre chose pour l'état d'être ici." See La Vallée Poussin, *Le dogme et la philos. du Bouddh.*, p. 185.

[2] Skt. *arhat* "worthy"; the term is merely an honorific title, which was adopted by the Buddhists and applied exclusively to the perfected disciple.

[3] The six knowledges of magic power, the divine ear, knowledge of others' thoughts, remembrance of former existences, knowledge of the passing away and rebirth of beings, and knowledge of the destruction of the āsavas are the six *abhiññā* or higher knowledges, *Mvyut.*, 14. Buddhaghosa calls the first five secular, *Vism.*, 373.

[4] *Ang.*, i, 38; this passage gives the fullest list in the Scriptures of these methods and of subjects of meditation. The Sarvāstivāda lists are almost identical, *Mvyut.*, 67 ff.

[5] *Vism.*, ch. iii, iv. He replaces the consciousness device by the separated-space device, as it is in the Attainments (see below) that "consciousness is infinite" is made an object of thought. Sarvāstivāda list in *Mvyut.*, 74.

required sign has come about. He then returns and with the sign begins his meditation proper, but if it disappears he must go back and recover it. The other devices are essentially the same. The water-device is done with a bowl of water, and the fire-device is done by making a hole in a rush-mat or piece of cloth and putting it before a blazing fire so that a bright circle appears. By these devices various stages of trance are attained and the possibility of performing special kinds of exercises.

Besides the four trances other methods are given. These are not necessarily later, but their place in the Buddhist system of training appears to be subordinate, and an attempt has been made to co-ordinate them with the trances. They are classified in accordance with Buddhist cosmology, which divides existence into three planes, the world of sense, the world of form, and the formless world up to the limit of existence (*bhavāgra*). The most important are the four (sometimes five) Attainments, which added to the trances make a series of eight or nine, as described below.

The four Brahma-vihāras (Brahma-abodes) show direct connection with brahminical practices, as they occur in the *Yoga-sūtras* (i, 33). This does not necessarily prove borrowing on the part of the Buddhists, but the Scriptures do recognize them as a non-Buddhist practice, and give a legend of Makhādeva, an ancient king of Mithilā, who practised them and who in consequence was reborn in the Brahma-world.[1] They are, in fact, there depreciated, for though it is possible to attain trance through them, they do not tend to " aversion, absence of passion, cessation, peace, higher knowledge, enlightenment, Nirvāṇa ". They are thus described:

" The monk abides pervading one quarter having his mind accompanied by love, likewise the second, third, and fourth. Thus above, below, around, everywhere, he abides pervading the entire world with his mind accompanied by love, with abundant, great immeasurable freedom from hatred and malice." In the three other vihāras the monk

[1] *Majjh.*, ii, 76. This shows that the name Brahmā was understood literally. In Buddhist cosmology the Brahma-world belonged to the world of form above the world of sense to which the earth and the lower heavens belong. But " brahma " is also used in the sense of " excellent " and Buddhaghosa admits that sense here. *Vism.*, 320.

in the same way pervades the world with compassion, sympathy, and equanimity.[1]

There are two other schemes of meditation, which were also used for concentrating the attention. They are almost ignored by Buddhaghosa in his treatment of subjects for meditation, but the second is important in showing how the stages of trance came to be extended, for the trances were enlarged to eight and sometimes nine by taking stages from this scheme and making them extensions of the four trances. The first is the eight Stages of Mastery (*abhibhāyatana*) [2]:

1. Perceiving forms (material shapes) internally he sees forms externally, limited, fair in colour or foul; having mastered them (thinking) " I know, I see ", thus perceiving, this is the first stage of mastery.
2. Perceiving forms internally he sees forms externally, unlimited, fair in colour or foul; having mastered them (thinking) " I know, I see ", thus perceiving, this is the second stage.
3. Not perceiving forms internally he sees forms externally, limited, fair in colour or foul; having mastered them (thinking) " I know, I see ", thus perceiving, this is the third stage.

In the fourth stage he sees the same forms as unlimited. In the fifth he perceives forms as blue, and in the rest he perceives them as yellow, red, and white respectively.

The interpretation of Mr. Woodward [3] appears to explain its significance. It is to attain the form-world by cultivating the path thereto. The form-world to the Buddhist was a reality—a stage of the universe above this world of the five senses, in which material shapes existed, but not the senses of touch, smell, and taste. He was supposed actually

[1] *Dīgha*, i, 250; *Mvyut.*, 69; they are also known as the four Immeasurables (*appamaññā*) *Dīgha*, iii, 223; cf. *Vism.*, pp. 295 ff., where Buddhaghosa has some practical remarks. The monk should not start by trying to love his enemy or he will get tired. Nor is it easy to practise equanimity, perfect balance of feelings, towards a dear friend. Love for all includes love for oneself, and with love for himself as being the easiest he should start. Buddhism did not make the modern opposition between self-love and altruistic love. It is self-love that justifies love to all. See the stories of King Pasenadi, whose wife refused to say that there was anyone dearer to her than herself. *Saṃy.*, i, 74.

[2] *Dīgha*, ii, 110; *Mvyut.*, 71.

[3] *Gradual Sayings*, i, 36. Rhys Davids thought that its purpose was " to get rid of the delusion that what one sees and feels is real and permanent ". *Dial.*, ii, 118.

to go there by such training, and psychologically the effect was so to concentrate his mind that he became fit for existence in that world.

The eight Stages of Release (*vimokkha*) are also a mode of concentration by which one became trained in stages for still higher worlds—from the formless world above the world of form up to the limit of existence. It still remains in the lists of exercises, but its original use has been modified by taking the fourth to the seventh stages and making them extensions of the four trances. These four are known as the Attainments (*samāpatti*), but they are also treated with the four trances, so that the whole becomes a series of eight. Sometimes the last release is added making nine stages.[1]

1. Possessing form (material shape) he sees forms.
2. Not perceiving forms internally he sees forms.
3. He is intent only on the thought " it is well ".
4. Passing entirely beyond perceptions of form, with the disappearance of perceptions of resistance, not attending to perceptions of diversity, (he perceives) " space is infinite ", and attains and abides in the stage of the infinity of space.
5. Passing entirely beyond the stage of the infinity of space, (he perceives) " consciousness is infinite ", and attains and abides in the stage of the infinity of consciousness.
6. Passing entirely beyond the stage of the infinity of consciousness, (he perceives) " there is nothing ", and attains and abides in the stage of nothingness.
7. Passing entirely beyond the stage of nothingness, he attains and abides in the stage of neither consciousness nor non-consciousness.
8. Passing entirely beyond the stage of neither consciousness nor non-consciousness, he attains and abides in the stage of the cessation of perception and feeling.

The disciple might get a particular subject of meditation from his teacher, but there is a standing list of subjects from which the teacher might choose according to the pupil's disposition.

(1) Four contemplations (*satipaṭṭhāna*) on the body, feelings, the mind, and thoughts, in which " he dwells ardent, conscious, mindful, dispelling his greed and dejection towards the world ". This is really a complete scheme of training, as will be seen below from the scheme of the four Contemplations.

(2) Four right efforts (*padhāna*). He exercises will, strives, puts forth energy, applies his mind—(*a*) to preventing the rising of evil, unprofitable thoughts ; (*b*) to dispelling evil, unprofitable thoughts that have arisen ; (*c*) to causing the rise of good thoughts ; (*d*) to establishing, clearing, improving, increasing, cultivating, and completing good thoughts that have arisen.

(3) Four bases of magic power, practised with the effort of concentration and combined respectively with will, thought, energy, and investigation.

[1] *Dīgha*, ii, 111, 156 ; *Mvyut.*, 70.

(4) Five faculties (*indriya*) are practised: faith, energy, mindfulness, concentration, and full knowledge. These, and also the powers, are said to be practised in each of the four trances.

(5) Five powers (*bala*) are practised, of the same names as the faculties. They are powers in the sense of being unshakable, says the commentary. The more elaborate analysis of the *Abhidharmakośa* (vi, 70) explains that the indriyas, which in the previous stage were predominant, can as *balas* never be crushed by the passions.

(6) Seven parts or limbs (*anga*) of enlightenment (*bodhi*) are practised: mindfulness, investigation of the doctrine, energy, joy (zest), calmness, concentration, equanimity.

(7) The eightfold Path: right views, right resolve, right speech, right action, right livelihood, right effort, right mindfulness, right concentration.[1]

The first of these, the four Contemplations, forms the subject of an important sutta,[2] and it is said to be "the one way for the purification of beings, for passing beyond grief and lamentation, for the ending of pain and misery, for the attaining of right method, and for the realizing of Nirvāna". It forms, as will be seen, an important part of the evidence for determining how the Buddhists conceived the nature and organization of the individual.

The monk goes to the forest or the root of a tree or an empty house, sitting cross-legged and upright, and setting up mindfulness (*sati*) before him. He begins his contemplation of the body. This portion consists of fourteen reflections, each with the same refrain. He breathes conscious of each breath. "He practises, 'conscious of my whole body I will breathe in'; he practises, 'conscious of my whole body I will breathe out'; he practises, 'calming my bodily organism I will breathe in'; he practises, 'calming my bodily organism I will breathe out'." He contemplates the body as something that arises, then as something that passes away, then as something that both arises and passes away. "His mindfulness becomes established with the thought, 'here is the body,' so far as required for knowledge and self-reflection. He abides independent, and grasps at nothing in the world. Even so the monk abides reflecting on the body."

Again the monk when walking reflects: "I walk," or when standing, "I stand," and in the same way when sitting or lying down; and he practises the same reflection

[1] This eightfold division in *Majjh.*, i, 301, is equated with the triple division; morality = right speech, action, and livelihood; concentration = right effort, mindfulness, and concentration; full knowledge = right views and right resolve.

[2] *Mahā-satipaṭṭhāna-sutta*. *Dīgha*, ii, 290.

for each. In all the actions of life he acts conscious of what he is doing.

Next he reflects on his body from the sole of his foot to the crown of his head as something enclosed in skin full of various kinds of impurity. A list of thirty-two items is given to be repeated : hair, nails, teeth, etc., which recur in other places.

He then contemplates the body as composed of the four elements, repeating the same reflections.

Again, the monk, as if he had seen a corpse in a cemetery dead for one, two, or three days, swollen, discoloured, and decomposed, reflects, and so applies it to his own body ; then as if he had seen it eaten by crows, vultures, dogs, and other creatures ; then as reduced to a scattered collection of bones, and, lastly, as whitened bones the colour of a shell, or reduced to powder ; and in each case he reflects as before. This portion was later developed into the ten *asubha*, in which there are ten stages of decomposition.[1]

The second contemplation is on the feelings, i.e. pleasant, unpleasant, and neutral sensations. " So he abides contemplating the feelings internally, or externally, or internally and externally. He abides contemplating the feelings as things that arise, then as things that pass away, and then as things that both arise and pass away." He again establishes mindfulness with the same formula as when contemplating the body.

Thirdly, he contemplates his states of mind (*citta*). He knows if it is in a state of lust or free from lust. A state of hatred or free from hatred, and so of dullness, distraction, exaltation, loftiness, concentration, or liberation. His contemplation is as before.

Lastly, he contemplates his thoughts (*dhamma*). *Dhamma* may mean " thing " in general, but here it is used of the things in the mind, thoughts, or ideas. Mind is treated as one of the senses, the sixth internal sense, and dhammas are its object, just as sights and sounds are objects of other senses. He contemplates thoughts which are the five hindrances. He knows that he has or has not sensual desire. He knows how there is the origin of sensual desire which had not yet arisen, how there is the putting away of sensual desire which

[1] *Ang.*, i, 43, calls them perceptions (*saññā*) and makes five of them. Buddhaghosa, *Vism.*, 110, gives ten.

has arisen, and how there is the non-arising of sensual desire which has been put away.

The other hindrances are treated in the same way: malice, sloth and torpor, distraction and agitation, and doubt.

The monk has now contemplated himself as analysed into body, feelings, mind, and thoughts. What follows is said to be still contemplation on thoughts, but it is done by introducing another analysis of the individual into five parts, the well-known groups of grasping (*upādānakkhandha*), the body, feeling, perception, the aggregates, and consciousness. Evidently this classification existed when the sutta was composed. Each of the five is reflected on in the same way, its rise, its passing away, and both its rise and passing away.

Then follows the reflection on the six internal and six external "spheres" (*āyatana*). These are the six senses or faculties of sight, hearing, touch, smell, taste, and mind, and the corresponding six objects. He reflects on each as rising and passing away. He understands any fetter that arises on account of both sense and object, how there is the arising of a fetter not arisen before, how there is the putting away of a fetter that has arisen, and how there is no arising in the future of a fetter that has been put away.

The seven parts of enlightenment (*bojjhanga*) are then reflected on. He is aware of each, whether it is present or absent, how it arises, and how by practice it is fully developed.

Finally, he reflects on the four noble truths, and Buddha declares that "for anyone who should practise these four contemplations for seven years, one of two fruits may be looked for: either full knowledge in this present life, or if there is a remainder leading to rebirth (*upādi*), the state of one who does not return." Or it may be for six years, and the possible time is gradually reduced to seven days.

This scheme, which now forms the first part of the thirty-seven qualities of enlightenment, thus appears here as an independent method of training sufficient in itself for attaining enlightenment. The fact that it contains classified psychological terms makes it probable that it is later than the scheme described above (p. 47), which proceeds by way of the four trances.

The seven groups of the *bodhipakkhikā dhammā*, from the four Contemplations to the Eightfold Path, form a whole of thirty-seven items, and they for long remained a summary of the positive aspect of the doctrine. In the story of Buddha's death they are said to have formed his last discourse to the monks.[1] Rhys Davids, apparently assuming that the details are historical, said, "it is of great interest to notice what are the points upon which Gotama, in this last address to his disciples, and at the solemn time when death was so near at hand, is reported to have laid such emphatic stress. . . . This summary of the Buddha's last address may fairly be taken as a summary of Buddhism, which thus appears to be simply a system of earnest self-culture and self-control."[2] Its importance does not lie in the supposition that it may contain a nucleus of truth about a quite legendary period, but in the fact that it was accepted by the chief schools as constituting the essentials of the doctrine. As thus stated it gives good grounds for those scholars like La Vallée Poussin, who refuse to call it a religion. It does not deny the gods, but it recommends remembrance[3] of them only in order to recognize that they have reached their respective heavens by means of such faith, morality, and other virtues as the disciple himself possesses. They are not worshipped, they are not the basis of morality, nor are they the bestowers of happiness.

The question about the term religion is largely verbal. Buddhism, like the religions amongst which it originated, formed a positive conception of the universe. Its cosmology and theory of recurring cycles were fundamentally the same as the brahminical. Certain problems about the universe and the individual arose, which were put aside as useless, but never considered unknowable or unthinkable. The Buddhist was convinced that he knew or could come to know

[1] Both the Pāli and Sanskrit forms of the legend contain them—*Dīgha*, ii, 120; *Divy.*, 200—showing that they formed a generally recognized summary of the positive side of the Doctrine.

[2] *Dial.*, ii, 128–9. They are later known as the *bodhipakkhikā dhammā*, the qualities or principles constituting enlightenment. They remain thirty-seven in Sanskrit works, *Mvyut.*, 38–44, *Dharmasang.*, 43, *Lal.*, 8, and even in definitely Mahāyāna works, *Lotus*, 458. It is the *Netti* (112), a Pāli work, which increases the number to forty-three, apparently by adding six of the perceptions (*saññā*).

[3] *Angut.*, iii, 287. This is one of the subjects of meditations called the six remembrances (*anussati*)—Buddha, the Doctrine, the Order, morality, liberality, and the gods. Four others were afterwards added—on death, the body, breathing, and calm. A set of twenty perceptions (*saññā*) also occurs in *Angut.*, i, 40. It contains five of the meditations on a corpse, but it appears to have been given up for later classifications. Buddhaghosa recognizes only one—perception of the repulsiveness of food.

quite enough about the universe in order to understand his relation to it, and what he must do in order to attain final happiness. His conception of it gave him the peace and confidence that others claimed as the boon of their own religion, but which he found only in his own. For him it was more truly a religion than any other.

It is notorious that Buddhism was far from being " simply a system of earnest self-culture and self-control ". Some of its presuppositions are already implied in the above scheme—a universe into any part of which a being might be born, and ruled by an inexorable law which determined him to be reborn according to his actions. It is still disputed whether original Buddhism was " nothing but vulgar magic and thaumaturgy coupled with hypnotic practices ", or whether Buddha was a " follower of some philosophic system in the genre of Patanjali's "—to take two extreme views. It is certain that the philosophic system came to exist, with theories of the nature of the individual, his career according to a law of causation, and the doctrine of his final destiny; and then with the Mahāyāna movement a transformation of all the problems through a new theory of reality and a conception of the Enlightened One which made him indistinguishable from the highest conceptions of Hindu deity.

CHAPTER V

CAUSATION

ONE of the most discussed doctrines of Buddhism is the Formula of causal origin, the so-called Chain of Causation, the *paṭicca-samuppāda*, Skt. *pratītya-samutpāda*. The Formula is held to expound the two truths of the origin of pain and the cessation of pain. It was apparently Burnouf who first called it a chain, *enchaînement*, but this is a question-begging term, for the name merely means " arising or coming into existence causally ", and there are Buddhists who deny that it should be understood as a continuous chain. The term usually translated " link " is *nidāna*, " cause," but each link is said to arise by having the previous one as cause (*paccaya*). There is an abundance of terms for cause which are never strictly distinguished. Another point which has not always been recognized is that the scheme with twelve " links " is only the stereotyped form which it finally assumed. There are several other shorter variants in the Canon, and they raise the question whether they are adapted from the longer form, or whether the longer is an inorganic combination of independent elements.[1] It will be convenient to give first the classical form in which the Formula is best known. This is found in the description of the attainment of arahatship, when the disciple having passed through the stages of morality and concentration reaches the knowledge of the destruction of the āsavas, and knows pain, its cause, its cessation, and the Way leading thereto. In what is probably the oldest form of this description [2] there is no mention of the Chain, but merely the statement that the truths are known. But we also find this statement expanded by the insertion of the Formula of causal origin, and its

[1] This latter is the view of Senart, *Apropos de la théorie bouddhique des douze nidānas*, *Mélanges de C. Harlez*, p. 281. Leyde, 1896. It makes superfluous the attempts of Western scholars to find in it a rational contribution to philosophic thought.

[2] *Dīgha*, i, 83, above, p. 48 ; the enlightenment of Buddha himself is described in the same terms, also without the Chain, in *Majjh*, i, 249. In a form with ten links it is given in the account of the enlightenment of Vipassin Buddha, *Dīgha*, ii, 30, and repeated in *Saṃy*, ii, 7, with twelve links.

repetition, in which each item is stated positively as a cause, is said to explain the cause of pain, and its repetition negatively, in which each item is said not to exist, explains the cessation of pain. The following is the Formula in the *Lalita-vistara*,[1] where after telling of the rebirth of beings it continues :

" So the Bodhisattva, with his mind concentrated, purified, cleansed, luminous, spotless, with the defilements gone, mild, dexterous, firm and impassible, in the last watch of the night at dawn . . . directed his mind to the passing away of the cause of pain. He thought : wretched is it that this world has come about, namely, is born, grows old, dies, passes away, is reborn. And thus one knows no escape from this whole mass of pain. Alas ! no means of ending all this great mass of pain is known, this old age, sickness, death, and so forth. Then, again, the Bodhisattva thought : when what exists do old age and death come to be, and what is the cause of old age and death ? He thought : When birth exists, old age and death arise, for old age and death have birth as their cause."

In the same way birth has coming into existence (*bhava*) as its cause ; coming into existence has grasping (*upādāna*) as its cause ; grasping has craving (*tṛshṇā*) as its cause ; craving has sensation (*vedanā*) as its cause ; sensation has contact (*sparśa*) as its cause ; contact has the six sense-organs (*ṣaḍāyatana*) as its cause ; the six sense-organs have mind and body (*nāma-rūpa*) as their cause ; mind and body have consciousness (*vijñāna*) as their cause ; consciousness has the aggregates (*saṃskārāḥ*) as its cause ; the aggregates have ignorance (*avidyā*) as their cause.

This is called the repetition in reverse order (*pratiloma*). The Bodhisattva then repeats it in direct order (*anuloma*). " When what exists do the aggregates come to be ? And what is the cause of the aggregates ? Then he thought : when ignorance exists, the aggregates come to be, for the aggregates have ignorance as a cause," and so on down to " with birth as cause old age, death, grief, lamentation, pain, misery, and despair come to be. Even so the origin of all this great mass of pain comes to be, the origin ! Thus as the Bodhisattva duly reflected repeatedly on these things

[1] 441 (345) ; *Mvst.*, ii, 285, is more verbose, but is essentially the same. The fullest treatment in the Pāli is *Saṃy.*, ii, 144.

unheard before, knowing arose, vision arose, knowledge arose, intelligence arose, full knowledge arose, light appeared."

He then repeats it backwards and forwards negatively: when what does not exist do old age and death not come to be? Or on the cessation of what is there the cessation of old age and death, ending with "even so is the cessation of all this great mass of pain", and knowledge of the cessation of pain arises. "At that time I duly knew: 'this is pain, this is the cause of the āsravas, this is the cessation of the āsravas, this is the path leading to the cessation of the āsravas.'" [1]

The differences of view as to the interpretation of this Formula turn on two points, whether it describes different stages of each individual who is involved in this mass of pain, or whether it has a cosmological significance, and depends upon speculations concerning the origin and passing away of the universe.[2] In the *Dīgha* itself it is called "profound, even in its appearance profound", and Ānanda is reproved for saying that it is extremely clear.[3] From this it is probable that at an early period there were disputes about its meaning, and that a need was early felt for its interpretation. This is shown still more in the commentarial explanations, and though the very fact that explanation was required prevents us from assuming that they give the primitive sense, they cannot be ignored if we are to decide what the Buddhists meant by it. There can be no doubt about its purpose when it was inserted in the above context. It was there understood as the knowledge of the nature and cause of pain attained by the individual which leads to escape from rebirth.

There are several terms occurring in it which also occur

[1] It may be noticed that there is a still later addition to the Formula. Sometimes there is prefixed to it the words "when this exists, that exists; with the arising of this that arises"; and to the negative form "when this does not exist, that does not exist; with the cessation of this that ceases". Here the causal law is stated generally, but it is interpreted in terms of the Formula; cf. *Udāna*, i, 1, and *Vin.*, i, 1.

[2] It is unnecessary to consider the older attempts of Western scholars at exegesis, which proceeded without regard to the interpretations actually adopted in the Scriptures and the commentaries. They are discussed in Oltramare, *La Formule des douze causes*, Genève, 1909; cf. A. B. Keith, *Buddh. phil.*, p. 106; L. de la Vallée Poussin, *Théorie des douze causes*, Gand, 1913. The theories of Jacobi and Schayer will be considered in connection with the question of Buddhist borrowings, Ch. VI.

[3] *Mahānidāna-sutta*, *Dīgha*, ii, 55; in this sutta the first two links and the fifth (six sense-organs) are omitted.

in another formula, the five groups (*khandhas*) which make up the individual. In the legend of Māgandiya (*Majjh.*, i, 511) Buddha says to him: "If I were to teach you the doctrine as to what health and Nirvāṇa are, and you were to come to know what health is and to see Nirvāṇa, then when vision arose you would cast away your passion for the five groups of grasping, and you would think, 'long indeed have I been cheated, deceived, and deluded by this my mind in that I went on grasping at body (*rūpa*), sensation (*vedanā*), perception (*saññā*), the aggregates (*sankhārā*), and consciousness (*viññāṇa*). On account of my grasping (*upādāna*) coming to be (*bhava*) arises, birth, old age, grief, lamentation, pain, dejection, and despair arise. Even thus is the origin of this whole mass of pain.'"

Here we have the well-known analysis of the individual into the material part, the body, and four divisions of the spiritual part. The only term here needing separate comment is *sankhāra*. The aggregates evidently form one of the groups of the spiritual part, and the scholastics explain them as "the mental concomitants or adjuncts which come or tend to come into consciousness at the uprising of a *citta* (thought)." [1] They include everything that may come into the mind, permanent qualities like memory, ideas, good and bad impulses or dispositions, as well as unconscious habits. It is evident that in the above legend they are supposed to explain one part of the constituents of the individual man. Māgandiya had just before congratulated himself on his perfect health, and Buddha here points out that it ends in old age and death. It is this grasping after the things of the body which results in coming to be, i.e. passing into a new existence. Rebirth is a term here out of place, birth is a stage, but the new existence, the coming to be, begins not with birth but with conception. The next stages of birth, old age, and death are clear.

In the stages here given, from grasping to old age and death, we have the last four links of the Chain, but nothing needs to be added to make them intelligible in this passage,

[1] Rh. Davids, *Pāli Dict.*, s.v. One analysis of the aggregates makes about fifty separate items. They appear to have been compiled in order to include every mental phenomenon, and the *Dhammasangaṇi* makes sure of this by adding "and any other non-material things that have arisen causally". The Pāli and Sanskrit lists largely agree, but are not identical. *Abhk.*, ii, 23; *Mvyut.*, 154. There is a simpler and probably earlier analysis of the aggregates into sankhāras of body, speech, and mind.

nor does their causal connection need explaining. The sequences are of every-day experience. It is the same in the *Sutta of grasping*,[1] where the sequence starts with craving (*taṇhā*):

> In one who abides surveying the enjoyment in things that make for grasping craving increases. Grasping is caused by craving, coming into existence by grasping, birth by coming into existence, and old age and death by birth. . . . Just as if a great mass of fire were burning of ten, twenty, thirty, or forty loads of faggots, and a man from time to time were to throw on it dry grasses, dry cow-dung, and dry faggots; even so a great mass of fire with that feeding and that fuel would burn for a long time. . . .
>
> In one who abides surveying the misery in things that make for grasping, craving ceases. With the ceasing of craving grasping ceases, with the ceasing of grasping coming into existence ceases, with the ceasing of coming into existence, birth ceases, and with the ceasing of birth old age and death cease. Grief, lamentation, pain, dejection, and despair cease. Even so is the cessation of all this mass of pain.

Here again it is the existence of an individual that is spoken of. The teaching is the doctrine of pain and putting an end to pain, which is caused by craving and the consequent grasping or clinging to things that lead to continuous existence.

The series in the two previous examples are only a part of the Chain of Causation. Unless the Chain can be proved to be part of the earliest teaching the question whether it was compounded of earlier separate portions is not very important. It occurs in the *Dīgha* (ii, 30) with the omission of the first two links, and again with the omission of the six sense-organs as well (ii, 55). This seems to show that it did not originally form a fixed sequence. Its entire omission in the earliest accounts of the enlightenment suggests that it was not then even invented. Someone evidently put it together, and the main point of interest is its philosophic significance. It implies a theory of causality, but we find cause understood in different senses. Ignorance is the cause of consciousness. Consciousness is here understood as rebirth-consciousness, the state in which the individual exists at the moment of conception. It is clear that ignorance in the Buddhist sense, ignorance of the truth of pain, will lead to rebirth, for the ignorant individual cannot take the only course which, according to Buddhist doctrine, would prevent it.

[1] *Upādāna-sutta, Saṃy.*, ii, 84. *Upādāna* also means "fuel", that which the fire grasps to maintain its existence.

Here we have an intelligible sense in which ignorance may be called a cause. Thus if one goes to a wrong village, it is because he was ignorant of the right way. But this is quite different from the sense in which contact (of the sense organs) is a cause of sensation. In this case we have an efficient cause. Again birth is the cause of old age. This appears to be like calling day the cause of the night.

The Buddhist commentators, however, have succeeded in interpreting the series as the different stages, or the essential factors of the stages, which an individual assumes during his existence in the world of change. Buddhaghosa makes it a theory of the causes of rebirth in any part of the universe.[1] For him the whole universe is divided into three planes, of which the lowest, the world of sensual desire from the deepest hells up to the heavens of sensual pleasures, is inhabited by beings with their six senses. Above these is the world of form, in which the senses of taste, smell, and touch are absent. In the formless world only mind exists. It is inhabited by beings who have practised the four Attainments of non-form.

"Ignorance is non-knowledge of pain, etc. In coming to be in the world of sense-desire ignorance is the cause of the aggregates of that world, and so in the world of form and the formless world. In the world of sense-desire the aggregates are the cause of rebirth-consciousness in that world, and so of the other worlds. In the world of sense-desire rebirth-consciousness is the cause of mind and body, and so in the world of form. In the formless world it is the cause of mind only. In the world of sense-desire mind and body (*nāma-rūpa*, the concrete individual) are the cause of the six organs of sense, in the world of form they are the cause of three organs of sense (sight, hearing, and mind), and in the formless world of one (mind). In the world of sense-desire the six organs of sense are the cause of six-fold contact, in the world of form of three contacts, and in the formless world the mind-organ is the cause of one contact. In the world of sense-desire the six contacts are the cause of the six senses, in the world of form three contacts are likewise the cause of three senses, and in the formless world one is the cause of one sense. In the world of sense-desire the six senses

[1] The following is from *Vism.*, 198 ff.; he gives a fuller exposition under *paññā*, pp. 517 ff., in which state the whole Chain is supposed to be fully understood.

are the cause of six groups of craving, likewise three senses in the world of form and one sense in the formless world. In this and that existence this and that craving is the cause of this and that grasping. Grasping, etc., is the cause of the various forms of coming to be. How ? Here one person thinks he will enjoy sense-pleasures, and commits misconduct with body, speech, or mind on account of his grasping at sense-pleasures, and through the fullness of his misconduct he is reborn in a state of unhappiness. There his karma which is the cause of his rebirth is karma-becoming. Rebirth-becoming consists of the khandhas (the five groups constituting the individual) due to his karma. The arising of these groups is birth, their ripening is old age, and their break-up is death. Another person thinks he will enjoy the happiness of heaven, so he practises good conduct, and through the fullness of his good conduct is born in heaven. There his karma is as before. Still another thinks he will enjoy the happiness of the Brahma-world, and through his grasping after sense-desires he practises friendliness, compassion, sympathy, and equanimity, and through the fullness of this practice he is born in the Brahma-world. There his karma is as before. Still another thinks he will enjoy happiness in the formless world . . . and so on as with the explanations based upon the remaining forms of grasping . . .

"Now ignorance and the aggregates form one group; consciousness, mind and body, the six sense-organs, contact, and the senses another; craving, grasping, and becoming another. The first group belongs to past existence, the two middle ones to the present, and the last to the future."

The last paragraph shows that Buddhaghosa divides the career of the individual who is transmigrating into three parts. Consciousness is birth-consciousness, the first two links belong to a past existence, and at the third he is reborn, but the actual point of passing to another existence is not birth but conception. Thereupon he develops into the khandhas, the material khandha of body (*rūpa*) with the four immaterial khandhas included in *nāma*, the immaterial part. These develop sense-organs, which with contact (i.e. stimulus of any one of the sense-organs) result in any of the six senses. From these develops the craving for satisfaction, the craving leads to grasping at anything that will satisfy them, and the grasping leads to *bhava*, coming to be, i.e. a new conception followed by birth, old age and death, and another future existence. So the sequence goes on. It is not referred to as a wheel in the older texts, but it is not easy to see how with this interpretation it could be considered in any other way. Each link mentioned does not express the whole of what exists at any given stage, but only that which is causal at that stage. With *nāma-rūpa* there is a complete being. It develops the six sense-organs, i.e. a complete being with sense-organs. But these organs are the cause, i.e. render possible the contacts, the exercise of each sense, which in their turn give rise to sensations, and so on.

The division into three existences, past, present, and future, is not peculiar to Pāli Buddhism. It is found in Nāgārjuna's *Friendly Epistle* and it belongs also to Sarvāstivāda, as seen in Vasubandhu's *Abhidharmakośa* (iii, 20), which makes a triple division in time, and in the purely Mahāyāna *Daśabhūmika-sūtra*,[1] though it is not quite the same division. The latter says: "what is said of the saṃskāras having ignorance as cause refers to the past; consciousness to feeling refers to the present; craving to becoming refers to the future, and so it goes on again." Its interpretation as individual development is still more clearly brought out in the *ṭīkā* on the *Bodhicaryāvatāra* (ix, 73), where it says, "through the union of mother and father at the seasonal concourse the seed of consciousness fettered by enjoyment and arising here or there produces in the mother's womb the germ of mind and body."

It is clear that this interpretation was a widely spread one, for it continued in Theravāda and Sarvāstivāda teaching, and is found even in Tantric Buddhism.[2] As Keith says,

[1] *Friendly Ep. JPTS.* 1886, p.30; *Abhk*, ii p. 62; G. Tucci, "A fragment from the Pratītyasamutpādavyākhyā of Vasubandhu," *JRAS.*, 1930, 611; *Daśabhumika-sūtra*, ed. Rahder, p. 51; the common Buddhist doctrine of the process of conception as described above is thus given in Divy., i, 442: "Now through the meeting of three circumstances sons and daughters are born. What are the three? When the mother and father being in love come together, the mother is at the due season, and the gandharva (the being to be reborn) is present." This appears not to be a peculiar Buddhist theory, but the usual view of conception accepted without question by the Buddhists. In the Pāli the same statement is put into the mouth of Buddha, and is also represented as being held by brahmins (*Majjh.*, i, 266; ii, 157).

[2] *Caṇḍamahāroṣaṇa-tantra*, ch. xvi, publ. by L. de la Vallée Poussin, *JRAS.*, 1897, p. 467; this work, in explaining rebirth, gives particular physiological details of the process of conception. It appears to hold that the first ten terms from ignorance to becoming (conception) are pre-natal. La Vallée Poussin, *Deux notes sur le Pratītyasamutpāda*, 14th Internat. Congress of Orientalists, Algiers, 1905.

it does not impose itself as necessarily representing the intention of its creators, but he declares that no other traditional interpretation has any chance of being original.[1] However, Buddhaghosa refers to another when he compares the scheme to a wheel, but not a revolving wheel as in the usual interpretation of the Chain. The nave is ignorance and the rim old age and death. The other ten links form ten spokes. Thus each of the ten arises directly from ignorance and ends in old age and death. There is, in fact, a sutta which explains pain in this way.[2] Pain is said in turn to be due to upadhi (the khandhas), to ignorance, etc. Sixteen items are spoken of, each directly the cause of pain. Among them eight of the links of the Formula occur, but the six sense-organs, becoming, birth, old age and death are omitted. It remains an isolated interpretation, and suggests that pain was once explained from different and independent causes without any order, and that the causal Formula might have been an attempt to co-ordinate them into a series and make one item dependent on another. Such an attempt from the heterogeneous nature of the items could never be made perfectly consistent, and the idea that behind the logical weakness of the current interpretation must lie a perfectly cogent one may be an illusion, and is certainly a mere surmise.

No perfectly logical interpretation has been found, and even if it were it would have no significance unless it could be shown that the Buddhists originally held it. How differently it may be conceived can be seen from Mr. Matsumoto's interpretation.[3]

For Mr. Matsumoto the Chain is part of the original teaching of Buddha. But the essential, he holds, does not rest upon the number of twelve links nor upon their order. In that case, how far does it remain a formula ? It is said to be only an attempt to explain the thought contained in it—that everything arises in mutual dependence. Of course it is possible, he says, to apply this to everything and make it the starting point of a world-picture. But this is not the meaning that Gautama Buddha applied to it. " For him after long striving the doctrine of causal origination resulted

[1] *Buddh. philos.*, p. 106.
[2] *Dvayatānupassana-sutta* " consideration of the dyads ", *Sn.*, pp. 724 ff.
[3] *Die Prajñāpāramitā-lit.*, p. 28.

as the final possibility of explaining human life as it presented itself to him. Concentration on this thought, the spiritual insight thereby brought about into the inner connection of the life-process, and the resulting knowledge of its unreality was for him at the same time emancipation, a state which must be looked upon as complete Nirvāna." The interpretation of the formula as a theory of temporal causality, according to Mr. Matsumoto, was a change brought about by the Sarvāstivādins, a change, that is, from "original Buddhism" and the meaning that Gautama Buddha applied to it. Mr. Matsumoto is quite certain what Buddha's original meaning was, and he finds it in the system of the *Prajñāpāramitā*, the Scripture of one of the schools of Mahāyāna. The significance of this must be considered later. He considers that the original meaning was perverted by the Sarvāstivāda Abhidhamma into a theory of the process of transmigration; but this is scarcely exact, for it occurs in the Canon itself in what is probably the oldest interpretation that we possess. This is the *Mahānidāna-sutta* (*Dīgha*, ii, 55), in which the first two links and the fifth do not appear. There it is said, "if consciousness did not descend into the womb of the mother, would mind and body become constituted therein? No, Lord. If the consciousness of one while yet young, whether of a boy or a girl, were to disappear, would the mind and body proceed to growth, increase, and development? No, Lord."

This is how the "inner connection of the life-process" presented itself to the earliest interpreters of the formula. Rhys Davids found in the sutta much more, for he held that it expressed the process of origination and cessation as a natural and universal law. "Events came impelled by preceding conditions, causes that man could by intelligence and good will study and govern, suspend, or intensify." Yet it is this very sutta which after closing the series with "mind and body have consciousness as a cause", adds, "consciousness has mind and body as a cause." We scarcely find here "the significance of the law of universal causation, breaking in on a great mind with a flash of intuition", nor was any application made of it as a universal law.

It is no wonder that the later Buddhists by coming to deny any real connection between each link, and even the natural causal sequence between contact and sensation, birth and old age, have deprived the formula of any meaning as a theory of causation. They have put in its place the Mahāyāna doctrine of interdependent relation, in which the causality held by the older schools becomes an illusion. We find that all the oldest interpretations do, in fact, treat it as a causal chain. They show us the attempts to make it a consistent account of the stages of the individual as he transmigrates. There is nothing to show that it ever had a more consistent meaning or why, if it had, the interpreters should have lost it.

An important question that remains is whether the formula has been borrowed from another system or suggested by similar sequences. It would be no surprising thing to find an originally logical scheme perverted by an adaptation to another set of principles. This will be more suitably discussed in connection with the relation of Buddhist doctrines to other Indian systems.

Note on the Wheel of Becoming

The Causal Formula does not appear to have been at first conceived as a wheel but as a line in the series of transmigrations of unknown beginning. But it easily lent itself to such a presentation. In the *Divyāvadāna* (300) Buddha, after hearing from Ānanda the merits of Maudgalyāyana (Moggallāna) as a teacher, says that there will not always be one like him, and orders the Five-spoked Wheel to be inscribed over the gateway of the Veluvana monastery at Rājagaha. He describes how it is to be made : " The five-spoked Wheel . . . is to be made with the five destinies (*gati*), the hells, animals, pretas (ghosts), gods, and human beings. Therein the hells are to be made at the bottom, the animals and ghosts above ; then gods and human beings ; the four continents, Pūrvavideha, Aparagodānīya, Uttarakuru, and Jambudvīpa. In the middle (the nave) passion, hatred, and stupidity are to be represented, passion in the form of a dove, hatred in the form of a snake, and stupidity in the form of a pig. An image of Buddha is to be made pointing out the circle of Nirvāṇa. Apparitional beings are to be represented by means of a windlass as passing away and being reborn. All round is to be represented the twelvefold Causal Origination in direct and reverse order. The

THE WHEEL OF BECOMING

[*face p.* 68

whole is to be represented as swallowed by Impermanence (*anityatā*), and two verses are to be written:

Make a beginning, renounce your home,
To the Buddha-teaching apply yourselves;
Smite away the army of Death,
As an elephant a house of reeds.

Who in this Law and Discipline
Shall vigilantly lead his life,
Abandoning the round of birth,
Shall verily make an end of pain.[1]

Among the cave paintings of Ajanta (ascribed to the 7th century A.D.) is a pictorial representation, which has been identified with the Wheel of Becoming (*bhavacakra*), but it is too fragmentary for making comparisons.[2] The form usually represented in Tibet has six spokes, as in that reproduced by Dr. Waddell. The five destinies have been increased to six by making the asuras, the rebel gods, a separate career. In the *Kathāvatthu* (viii, 1) the doctrine of six destinies is opposed. The upper sector represents the gods, who at the right are seen fighting under Indra (Śakra) against the Asuras, who are attacking them in the next sector. To the left other heavens are visible. The seated figure is Mahābrahmā, of whose four faces three can be seen in the original.

In the next sector are the Asuras, and at the foot of Mount Meru the wishing tree, Cittapāṭalī, which here extends into Indra's heaven of the thirty-three gods. In Indra's heaven is said to be the tree Pārijātaka (Pāli, Pāricchattaka), and here there may be some confusion or special legend about the two. Indra's heaven is properly on the top of Mount Meru, but the circular arrangement of the picture has probably prevented exact representation.

Below comes the realm of animals and fish. At the bottom of the ocean is the palace of the Nāgas, serpents who can assume human form.

In the lowest sector are the hells. In the upper part Yama

[1] The verses occur in *Saṃy.*, i, 156, and elsewhere.

[2] It was identified as such by Dr. L. A. Waddell, *Journ. As. Soc. Bengal*, 1893, vol. lxi, pt. 1, p. 133; *JRAS.*, 1894, p. 367; *The Buddhism of Tibet*, pp. 105 ff., where reproductions of this and the Tibetan form are given. He also attempted an interpretation of the Wheel, with analogies from Schopenhauer, Hartmann, and Spinoza. A satisfactory explanation based upon the evidence of the Sanskrit Buddhists was given by L. de la Vallée Poussin at the 14th International Congress of Orientalists (Algiers) in 1905 (*Actes*, 1e partie, § 1, p. 193).

is judging the sinners, and in the lower part are the hot hells on the left and the cold hells on the right.

Next is the realm of the pretas, beings with large bellies and very small mouths, always tortured with hunger and thirst. The remaining sector is that of human beings. In each sector is a figure of Avalokiteśvara, who visits all realms in fulfilment of his vow to save the world.

The Twelve nidānas running along the rim in direct order (clockwise direction) from the top are:

1. *Avidyā*, ignorance: blind man with a stick.
2. *Saṃskārāḥ*, lit. aggregates, compounds: potter with wheel and pots.
3. *Vijñāna*, consciousness: monkey climbing a tree with flowers.
4. *Nāmarūpa*, name and form, mind and body: a ship (the body) with four passengers representing *nāma*, i.e. the four immaterial skandhas: feeling, perception, saṃskāras, and consciousness. Consciousness is steering.
5. *Śaḍāyatanāni*, six sense-organs: an empty house.
6. *Sparśa*, contact: man and woman embracing. (6 and 7 are misplaced in the figure.)
7. *Vedanā*, feeling: man with an arrow in his eye.
8. *Tṛṣṇā*, thirst, craving: woman offering drink to a seated man.
9. *Upādāna*, grasping: man gathering fruit from a tree.
10. *Bhava*, becoming (conception): woman with child.
11. *Jāti*, birth: woman in childbirth.
12. *Jarāmaraṇa*, old age and death: man carrying a corpse to the cemetery.

It will be seen that the figures are merely illustrations of states in each stage, and sometimes only allegorical representations, as in the case of the potter and the ship. They do not throw much light on the theory of the wheel, but they show an interpretation which agrees in general with the view that it represents different stages in the transmigration of the individual.

CHAPTER VI

THE BACKGROUND OF BUDDHISM

THE training of the disciple through the stages of morality, concentration, full knowledge, and release shows little of any metaphysical considerations. But such principles are implicit in certain doctrines assumed, doctrines already established in popular beliefs—a theory of the structure of the universe, the belief that the individual transmigrates through it unceasingly unless he wins knowledge, and that his life is happy or wretched in his various existences according to the sum of his previous actions. These are general Indian beliefs which Buddhism accepted, while systematizing and generalizing them, and which are presupposed in all its peculiar dogmas. The fact that these theories underlie the special dogmatic and philosophical superstructure of Buddhism makes it necessary to consider both the antecedents of Buddhism as well as the state of contemporary thought at the time when the new religion was becoming established. The questions are more easily asked than answered, for the evidence at hand is both incomplete and to a great extent indirect.

For the early relations of Buddhism to Brahminism we have the ancient ritual and speculative works known as the Brāhmaṇas and the Upanishads. But as will be seen, the difficulty is to prove that early Buddhism had any direct contact with these works. The problem is not lessened by the fact that the Brahminism referred to in the Buddhist records belongs to a different region from that described in the ritual works. The first question is the relation of Buddhism to the contemporary rival schools, and for this we are limited, except in the case of Jainism, to Buddhist accounts, which are in all cases legendary. They are stereotyped accounts of doctrines, attributed in some cases to particular leaders, but no more historical than the early legends of Buddha himself. Doubtless there is a historical basis, but we learn little about the holders of these doctrines, the so-called six heretics, beyond the statements of their teaching. These statements, however, have a great importance in the development of Buddhist thought, for each heretic became distinguished as the holder of a characteristic doctrine, the denial of karma, and so on, and these doctrines are the leading ideas against which Buddhism for centuries directed its arguments.

The views of the six heretics are stated in their most picturesque form in the *Sāmaññaphala-sutta*, the " discourse on the fruit of being an ascetic (*samaṇa*) " in the sense of a Buddhist monk.[1] It consists of a legend recording king Ajātasattu's visit to Buddha. The king points out that there are all sorts of trades and occupations, and those who follow them have evident " fruit " therefrom. They live with their families and friends in comfort, give gifts to brahmins, and the result is happiness with the prospect of rebirth in heaven. Can Buddha show any such visible fruit for one who is an ascetic ? The king admits that he has put the same question to other ascetics and brahmins, and proceeds to give the answers which he has received.

He had first asked Pūraṇa Kassapa, who declared that whatever a man's actions were, the greatest crimes would not result in guilt or increase of guilt nor meritorious deeds in merit. This is the doctrine of *akiriyavāda* " non-action," which denies that karma has any results. Such a reply, said Ajātasattu, was like asking for a mango and getting a bread-fruit, and so were all the other replies. Next he asked Makkhalin Gosāla, who described an elaborate and fantastic system of births, conduct, and karma, but denied all responsibility for actions. Everything is fated, and when beings have run through their course of transmigrations they make an end of pain.

The king next inquired of Ajita Kesakambalin, who was a materialist. There is no karma. " A man consists of the four elements, and when he dies and is cremated the elements return to their places. Both fools and sages with the dissolution of the body are cut off and destroyed, and after death they are not." This is the doctrine of *ucchedavāda*, " cutting off," annihilation.

The fourth sage was Pakudha Kaccāyana, who explained that there were seven indestructible bodies : earth, water,

[1] *Dīgha*, i, 47 ; the teachings of the first four without names being mentioned are given in *Majjh.*, i, 513, and the other two occur in a further list of four.

fire, air, happiness, pain, and life or soul. There is no slayer or causer of slaying, no hearer, knower or causer of knowing. One who splits a head with a sword does not kill anyone. He merely makes a hole with a sword between the seven indestructible bodies. The next sage was Nigaṇṭha Nātaputta, the Jain, who explained his fourfold vow, but as it is agreed that both text and commentator misunderstand it, it need not be discussed. The last was Sanjaya Belaṭṭhiputta, who refused to make a positive or negative statement on the above points or on any others.

It is probable that all these names are real,[1] but hardly likely that the descriptions of the doctrines give us a fair picture of the state of thought in early Buddhist times. Two of the names are known from Jain works, Nātaputta and Gosāla, and the latter in those works is called an Ājīvika. This name is said to mean one who gets his livelihood from his profession of ascetic, and to be a name given by opponents. Hence it is not certain that the name was applied only to one peculiar sect. The Ājīvikas are mentioned by the Buddhists, but they never apply the name to Gosāla. According to the Jains, Gosāla joined the Jain leader, but quarrelled with him and they separated. For the Buddhists he is the representative teacher of fatalism. The best known of the six is the Nigaṇṭha Nātaputta, known to the Jains as Mahāvīra, their last leader. The obscurity of the present passage is the more remarkable as the Jains, known to the Buddhists as Nigaṇṭhas,[2] are mentioned frequently in the Scriptures, and one of their chief doctrines, *kiriyavāda*, the doctrine of action, is fairly discussed.

The rest stand merely as the representatives of certain doctrines, Pūraṇa of the denial of moral action, Ajita of materialism and a denial of the survival of the individual, and Pakudha of another kind of denial of moral action. Sanjaya is a mere caricature of shallow irresolution. No doubt there was materialism at all times. The Hindu philosophical systems mention the Chārvākas as such a school, but all that we know of them is much later than early Buddhism. Among the six the system of Pakudha, with its seven indestructible elements, most resembles a tendency of Indian

[1] The six were also well-known to the Sarvāstivādins; *Divy*, 143; *Av-Śat.*, 134.

[2] Skt. *nirgrantha* "free from bonds"; the name Jain, properly Jaina, "followers of the conqueror," is a derivative from *jina* "conqueror".

thought—the attempt to find something ultimately real behind the phenomena rather than in co-ordinating experience and interpreting it as the real. But nothing like this actual system is elsewhere found.[1]

The conclusion of the dialogue is of peculiar interest. What did the compiler think was the right attitude to take with regard to these questions of moral action and reward, materialism and fatalism ? They are not the " undetermined questions " which Buddha refused to answer, yet the rest of the dialogue ignores them. The Buddhist answer to the question of the fruits of samanaship is to ignore all these problems of morals and metaphysics, and to give a description of the career of the disciple—his course of moral training, the system of concentration, and the attainment of full knowledge. It maintains the same position as the previous discourse, the *Brahmajāla-sutta*, which concludes that beyond any speculations are " things profound, hard to see, hard to understand, calm and excellent, beyond the region of logic, subtle, comprehensible only to the wise, which the Tathāgata, having comprehended and realized, proclaims."

The *Brahmajāla-sutta* itself contains the fullest account of theories supposed to have been held by other schools, and it is in these that attempts have been made to find points of contact with the orthodox philosophical systems. It is called " the net of Brahma " (*brahma-jāla*), and claims to include in its list all possible views. " All those ascetics and brahmins who construct systems about the past or the future, or both, who hold theories about both, and who make various assertions about the past and future, are all caught in this net of sixty-two subjects. There they are, though they plunge and plunge about. There they are caught in the net, though they plunge and plunge about." The apparent elaborateness of the scheme becomes clearer when it is analysed. The views fall into two classes, speculations about the past and about the future :

I. There are those who hold views about the beginnings of things in eighteen ways :

(1) Some hold in four ways[2] that the self or soul (*ātman*) and the universe (*loka*) are eternal.

[1] Unless we refer to Empedocles. It is free from the objection which Aristotle brought against the early Greek theorists, that they assumed principles which explained only material existence.

[2] The four ways merely refer to the number of existences remembered, so that it is unnecessary to discuss them separately.

(2) Some hold in four ways that the self and universe are in some respects eternal and in some not.

(3) Some hold that the universe is finite, or infinite, or finite and infinite, or neither finite nor infinite.

(4) Some wriggle like eels in four ways, and refuse a clear answer.

(5) Some assert in two ways that the self and universe have arisen without a cause.

II. Some hold views about the future in forty-four ways :

(1) They hold in sixteen ways that the self exists as conscious after death.

(2) In eight ways that it exists as unconscious after death.

(3) In eight ways that it is neither conscious nor unconscious after death.

(4) They hold in seven ways the annihilation of the individual.

(5) They hold that Nirvāṇa consists in the enjoyment of this life in five ways, either in the pleasures of sense or in one of the four trances.

Some of these views are cosmological and do not need discussion, as they are not characteristic of any particular school. The first doctrine set forth is that the self and the universe are eternal (*sassatavāda*). It takes for granted that the universe passes through ages of disintegration and renewal, a point which the Buddhist does not dispute. An ascetic or brahmin who practises concentration remembers many of his past existences, and comes to the conclusion that " the self and the universe are eternal, barren (i.e. not producing anything new), standing as on a mountain peak, fixed as a firm pillar ; and these beings are reborn, transmigrate, arise and pass away, but (self and universe) are eternal." Here we have the important word *attā* (Skt. *ātman*) " self "[1]; no difficulty is made about it. The only question is whether it is eternal or not. We shall later find a different point of view implied in the word *ātmavāda*, the doctrine that a self or soul exists. We do not find it expressly stated that the self is not eternal, but only that a yogi has remembered such an enormous number of his existences that he infers that self and world are eternal. When we come to the doctrine that everything compound is transitory, then we shall find a positive argument against the eternal existence of the soul.

The second class of doctrines deals with the nature of the gods, and while not denying their existence sets out a theory which unceremoniously deprives the conception

[1] There is no reason why it should not be called " soul ", except that that word is generally associated with the related doctrines of Christian theology.

of deity of any value. The great Brahmā himself is reborn like any other being. He is the first to be born at the beginning of a new age, and imagines himself to be god (*issara*), as indeed he is for the time being. Other beings are born later, and he imagines that they have come into being at his wish, because he wished for them. And the other beings who meditate about it imagine that he is their maker, and that they themselves are impermanent and short-lived.

Brahmā is thus held by the theorizer to be eternal and the rest not. Another form of this class is to hold that the eye, ear, nose, tongue, and body are impermanent, but that thought, mind, or consciousness is permanent and eternal.

The next three cases do not call for any remark, as they do not describe any recognizable systems.

So far the questions have been concerning the origin of the soul. The rest deal with its future destiny. The next two classes are not clear as they stand. It is said that the self if conscious after death may have form, be finite, have one mode of consciousness, be happy or miserable, or it may be without form, etc., and varied in other ways. If the self is unconscious, it may have form or not form, and be varied in eight ways. Buddhaghosa takes these cases to refer to the supposed state of the liberated self as held by certain theorists, and explains some of the alternatives as being held by the Ājīvikas, Jains, and others. The third class is only a logical refinement. The fourth is the annihilation doctrine of Ajita, but it is elaborated by stating that extinction may take place (1) with the death of the body according to the materialistic view, or (2) with the death of a "divine self" in the world of sense, or (3) in the world of form, or (4–7) in one of the stages of the formless world. The last class (Nirvāṇa in this life) looks at first like the doctrine held both by Buddhists and brahmin schools that release may be attained in this life. But here the Nirvāṇa meant is the full enjoyment of the pleasures of sense, not the bliss attained by complete separation from them, or rejecting such sensualism the heretic thinks to find it in one of the four trances.

The apparent multiplicity of doctrines in the *Brahmajāla-sutta* is due to their being treated from every point of view, positively, negatively, and both. They are not actually denied, but are treated as containing the whole of what it is possible to assert concerning the self and the universe.

It cannot be doubted that many of them were never doctrines actually held, but only possibilities added to make the net complete. Still it is remarkable to find that not one of the doctrines mentioned can be certainly identified with those of brahmin schools. An exception possibly exists in the case of the first doctrine mentioned, that self and universe are eternal. Oldenberg held that in this passage the Sānkhya dualism of eternal spirit and eternal nature appear to be unmistakable.[1] Sānkhya uses the simile of " standing on a mountain peak ", but applies it only to the purusha (*ātman*), which remains unmoved against the evolution of the universe. He thus has to admit that the Buddhist account is inexact, as it often is in referring to the doctrines of other schools. Another place where he sees a reference to Sānkhya is where it is said that the eye, ear, nose, tongue, and body are impermanent, but that thought, mind, or consciousness is permanent and eternal. This, too, is inexact, for in Sānkhya not only the five senses but also the group to which mind belongs stands on the side of material nature. But even if the references are to Sānkhya, they do not show Sānkhya influencing Buddhism or imparting its principles. Both passages speak of doctrines that were rejected, and rejected even without being understood. Their importance is rather with regard to the history of Sānkhya and the possible changes that it may have undergone before it assumed its classical form.

An extensive influence of Sānkhya on Buddhism was held by Jacobi, who derived the Chain of Causation from the series found in the Sānkhya system in its classical form.[2] This system, as is well known, explains the evolution of the universe from a primitive undifferentiated matter called *prakṛti* (nature). This Nature has three constituents (*guṇa*) in perfect equilibrium, and it is the upsetting of this equilibrium and the consequent elaboration of the constituents in different proportions which constitute the actual world both material and spiritual. The constituents, which appear in matter as lightness, movement, and heaviness, appear in mental phenomena as goodness, passion, and dullness. Behind all this is the *purusha,* the permanent ātman.

[1] *Lehre der Upan.*, p. 295.

[2] *Der Ursprung des Buddhismus aus dem Sānkhya-yoga. Nachr. v.d.k. Ges. der Wiss. zu Göttingen, phil.-hist. Kl.*, 1896.

The first evolute of Nature is *buddhi* (intellect), which becomes individualized as *ahaṃkāra* (egoity). This is said to be parallel to the Buddhist *vijñāna* (consciousness) as cause of *nāma-rūpa* (name and form, individuality). Then, " from egoity proceed the ten organs, *indriya*, with the inner sense *manas*, and the five subtle elements, *tanmātras*." This is said to be quite similar to the procession of the six sense-organs from name and form. However, the Buddhist sense-organs really are organs, and it is from them that the actual faculties of sense proceed through the mediation of contact. The *indriyas* of Sānkhya are faculties, and there are eleven of them, for besides manas and the five corresponding to the five sense-organs there are five others corresponding to five external organs (voice, hand, etc.). Further there are the five subtle elements, i.e. the elements each in their purity, from which proceed the five gross elements, the elements as we perceive them in a state of mixture. These are said to correspond to the *dharmas* of the Buddhists, which are actually existing " things ", whether external objects or internal as thoughts and cognitions. The Buddhist dharmas, phenomena, Jacobi continues, correspond practically to the outer world, which is contained in the *mahābhūta*, the gross elements of Sānkhya-Yoga. According to Sānkhya, the gross elements proceed as a particular creation from the tanmātras. On the other hand, according to Buddhist doctrine they stand on the same line with them.

Here we have the fundamental problem for the interpretation of the Chain. The Sānkhya series is a cosmogony, explaining the evolution and structure of the universe. Jacobi has never raised the question whether the same interpretation is possible for the Buddhist series. The dharmas, the constituents of the universe, do not proceed from any subtle elements, nor are they ever found as a link in the Chain. The Chain is never interpreted as a cosmogony, but only as a series of states of the individual. If it ever was so interpreted, or if that was the original meaning intended, it had been entirely forgotten. But while we find stages and conceptions in the Sānkhya series which do not fit into the Buddhist Chain, how are craving, grasping, becoming, birth, and death to be fitted into the Sānkhya scheme ? They do not fit. Jacobi says that birth and death need no explanations ; that in all Indian philosophemes which assume rebirth, birth is a consequence of saṃsāra, and birth has old age and death as result.

This does not seem to touch the question of explaining them as members of a series. Birth, old age, and death belong to that part of the Formula which is most easily explained as describing the temporal career of an individual, and they do not occur in the ontological Sānkhya formula at all. Nor does the terminology make it more probable that one is dependent on the other. Viññāṇa is said to correspond with *buddhi*, *nāma-rūpa* with *ahaṃkāra*, *saḷāyatana* with the ten *indriyas*, the *manas*, and the five *tanmātras*, *tṛṣṇā* with *abhiniveśa* or *āśis*, *upādāna* is analogous to *dharmādharmau*.[1] *Prakṛti* [2] and the *guṇas*, the most fundamental principles of the Sānkhya construction, are nowhere found in Buddhism. How far such parallels are convincing may be left to the reader. In any case the Sānkhya scheme does not explain how the Buddhists understood their own formula, even if it may have given hints to the elaborator of the twelvefold Chain.

Jacobi's conclusions, which were accepted by Pischel [3] but rejected by Oldenberg,[4] have been extended by Dr. Schayer,[5] who holds that the Chain is a " kosmische Emanationsformel ". He thinks that the Buddhists did not understand their own formula. Native exegesis transforms the meaning into a " primitive Biologie ", and he finds this unsatisfactory, first because it compels us to the nonsensical placing of craving and grasping in the embryo stage, and secondly because to interpret *nāma-rūpa* as the psycho-physical being does not correspond to its original meaning and is a makeshift of later scholasticism. It will be seen that Dr. Schayer assumes that all the stages from *nāma-rūpa* to *bhava* take place in the embryo stage. But this cannot fairly be charged against the Pāli exegetes. They might fairly be blamed for omitting to mention birth after the stage of *nāma-rūpa* at conception, but the next causal state is held to be the formation of the six sense-organs, and the

[1] Jacobi, loc. cit., pp. 49 ff.

[2] Buddhaghosa uses it when he speaks of the holders of Sānkhya as pakativādins. *Vism.*, 525.

[3] *Leben und Lehre des Buddha*; " Wir wissen, dass der theoretische Buddhismus ganz auf dem Sāṃkhya-Yoga beruht," p. 61.

[4] *Die Lehre der Upan.*, p. 357.

[5] *Vorarbeiten z. Gesch. der mahāyānistischen Erlösungslehren, Untersuch. z. Gesch. des Buddhismus*, v, 235.

event of birth is not mentioned. But the exegetes never doubted that it took place. *Nāma-rūpa* is an upanishadic term, and will be more conveniently considered later.

There is, however, a further problem concerning the relation of Buddhism to Sānkhya. The system of the Yoga philosophy [1] has most of its leading conceptions identical with Sānkhya. It differs by introducing the concept of a God and by making yoga-practices an essential part of its training. Did Buddhism get its notions of Sānkhya through the Yoga philosophy? The historical facts are very slender. The legend tells us that Buddha before his enlightenment practised yoga under two teachers. It is not likely that exact details have been preserved and, in fact, the legend describes the teaching in purely Buddhistic terms. Āḷāra Kālāma is said to have practised the third Attainment of the state of nothingness, and Uddaka the fourth, the Attainment of the state of neither consciousness nor non-consciousness. This is what we are also told by Aśvaghosha in his life of Buddha,[2] a poem of the first or second century A.D. Here he follows the canonical account, but he also gives an account of Āḷāra's philosophy, and this has some resemblance to the Sānkhya philosophy. It is not identical with it, and it cannot be said to be probable that Aśvaghosha had any real knowledge of the philosophy of a teacher who had died some six centuries before, and some time before Buddha began to preach. But the resemblances between the yoga-practices and the terminology of Buddhism and Yoga are unmistakable.

We have found reason for believing that yoga-practices were an essential part of primitive Buddhism, and the Buddhist tradition repeatedly recognizes such practices in other schools. Yet when the actual documents are examined, difficulties arise. The fullest examination has been made by Senart.[3] He finds that the most certain parallelisms are crossed by evident discordances. The resemblances suddenly stop short without any evident cause. Similar nomenclatures are worked up differently. Classifications have the same numeration and similar meanings, and yet singly they do not correspond. Two reasons may be adduced to account for this. We do not know what was the actual form of Yoga

[1] It is important to distinguish yoga in the sense of yoga-practices from yoga in the sense of the philosophical system which chiefly practised them.

[2] *Buddhacarita*, xii, 17 ff.

[3] " Bouddhisme et Yoga " in *Revue de l'histoire des religions*, 1900, p. 345.

teaching in vogue when Buddha first learnt it, nor do we know what actual changes he may have made in it for his own purpose.

It is not possible to reach any positive conclusion without separating the borrowing that may have taken place during the constructive period of Buddhism from the borrowings that may have gone on when Yoga and Buddhism were two established systems. In the former case we can admit that yoga-practices are earlier than Buddhism, and that borrowing from some form of Yoga took place. But neither system now exists in its primitive form, and what we find in the actual documents of each system are resemblances in which there is the possibility of borrowing from either side. Such is the case with the four Brahma-vihāras, which appear to be late in Buddhism and a direct borrowing from Yoga. But the latter question is far less important, as it does not affect the question of the fundamentals of either system. The purpose of yoga-practices in each was different, and remained different and independent in each.

Comparison with Yoga does not appear to throw any more light on the origin of the Causal Formula. While there are resemblances in Buddhist terminology to Yoga terms, the Formula remains with striking unlikenesses both in terminology and purpose to either Sānkhya or Yoga. The one explains the genesis of the individual, and the other is an emanation formula explaining the genesis of the universe. However much the Formula as a scheme of individual genesis shows weaknesses, it shows still more when interpreted as an emanation formula. That the Buddhists ever understood it in this sense is a gratuitous assumption.

CHAPTER VII

BRAHMINISM AND THE UPANISHADS

SO far little has been said of the brahmins. Among the six schools brought forward by Ajātasattu there is no mention of one representing the brahmins, and among the sixty-two doctrines in the *Brahmajāla-sutta* it is difficult to recognize any as being held in the form stated by one of the orthodox schools. Yet the brahmins play a large part in Buddhist polemics, though it is as priests, not as mystics or philosophers. Their claim to be the highest caste, and to be the only caste able to perform the sacrifices and ceremonies necessary for men even to exist as a member of society, had led to protests. Buddhism was only one of these movements, which, as we have seen, were led by ascetics seeking, not a reformed state of worldly society, but an explanation of the ills of life and an escape from them.

A frequent term in the Scriptures is *samaṇa-brāhmaṇa*, ascetics and brahmins. Here the samaṇas are doubtless those who have permanently abandoned a household life, and may include brahmins who have adopted an ascetic life, for the brahmins proper are treated as householders, But the term samaṇa-brāhmaṇa is always used quite generally for those religious leaders who are mentioned as teaching doctrines in rivalry with the Buddhists. In the *Sāmaññaphala-sutta*, it is applied by Ajātasattu to the six teachers, who cannot all have been brahmins.

There is a great difference from what we know of the brahmins directly from their sacred literature and the picture we find of them in the Buddhist Scriptures. The brahmin literature with which we are concerned consists firstly of the Brāhmaṇas, extensive prose works expounding the hymns of the Vedas,[1] theorizing about the ritual of the sacrifice, and developing speculations about its meaning. These extend into cosmogonic theories, for the sacrifice had come to be

[1] The Buddhists speak only of three Vedas, the Rigveda, Sāmaveda, and Yajurveda. The fourth, the Atharvaveda, was known, though it was not yet recognized as a Veda by the other schools.

conceived as a ritual which keeps the whole universe going on in its due course. Appended to a Brāhmaṇa is usually an Āraṇyaka, " forest treatise," and added to this or forming part of it is an Upanishad, a work of " secret teaching ". All these works were secret or esoteric in the sense that they were confined to the brahmin schools, and as they were unwritten they could only be learnt by an initiated member of the school. But the Upanishads developed theories of the world and the soul going far beyond the teaching of the Vedas. They were the secret teaching in a special sense. These speculations led to new upanishads being composed, and though they are all said to belong to one or other of the Vedas, they are mostly quite independent works. We are here concerned only with those supposed to be early enough to be independent of Buddhist influence. The most important of these are the Bṛhadāraṇyaka and Chāndogya Upanishads.[1]

The warrior caste figures largely in the dialogues of the Upanishads, so much so that it has been held that the characteristic doctrines originated with this class. Whatever be their origin, they had become the possession of the brahmins, and although any of the three higher castes might devote themselves to Vedic study, we have the striking fact that the kshatriyas described in the Buddhist records show no trace of upanishadic teaching. The original centre of brahmin culture was far from the cradle of Buddhism. This centre was in the West, chiefly in the region between the Ganges and the Jumna. It gradually permeated the East of India, but there are indications to show that the East, and Magadha especially, were long considered unfit for the habitation of brahmins. But at least as a sacrificial system Brahminism had established itself there before the development of Buddhism. There was not the same reason why the study of the secret doctrine should have spread as early as the brahmin cult, which performed the sacred rites for individuals at every stage of life.

Controversy between brahmins and the Buddhists turns upon caste, sacrifice, and the possession of the sacred lore,

[1] In the list of upanishads in the *Muktikā Up.* the first ten are still recognized as belonging to the oldest class :—

Īśa, Kena, Kaṭha, Praśna,
Muṇḍaka, Māṇḍūkya, Taittirīya,
With Aitareya, Chāndogya,
And likewise Bṛhadāraṇyaka.

the three Vedas. The brahmins are represented as saying "the brahmin is the best colour (caste), the other colour is base; the brahmin is the white colour, the other colour is black; the brahmins are purified,[1] not non-brahmins. The brahmins are the true sons of Brahma, born from his mouth, Brahma-born, Brahma-created, heirs of Brahma".[2] The word for colour here is *vaṇṇa* (*varṇa*), and is the same word which means "caste" in the sense of the four classes of mankind held to be the four primitive castes produced in the beginning, from which the others have originated by intermixture. Another statement attributed to a brahmin is, "there are these four castes, kshatriyas (warriors), brahmins (priests), vaiśyas (traders and farmers), and śūdras (serfs). Of these four the three castes of kshatriyas, vaiśyas, and śūdras are really but attendants on the brahmins."

A number of suttas are devoted to refuting the brahmin claims, but they do not read like actual discussions. They are mostly in the form of legends, and the stereotyped arguments are repeated over and over again. We are told of a conversation between Buddha and the brahmin Soṇadaṇḍa. Soṇadaṇḍa declared that there are five things that constitute a brahmin: he is well born on both sides for seven generations; he knows the mantras, the three Vedas, and accessory sciences; he is handsome and fair in colour; he is virtuous; he is learned and the first or second of those who hold out the spoon at the sacrifice. Buddha asked if any of the five qualifications might be omitted. Soṇadaṇḍa at once admitted that colour might be omitted, then that knowing the mantras did not matter, nor birth if he is virtuous and learned. There is no real discussion, and what we have comes to be merely an assertion of the Buddhist position that virtue and wisdom are the highest things in the world. The same description of the brahmin is given by king Avantiputta of Madhurā (Mathurā) to the elder Mahā-Kaccāna.[3] The elder shows that a wealthy kshatriya can have one of the other castes to minister to him. If a brahmin were a thief or adulterer, he would be punished like any other. If a man, no matter what his caste, were to adopt the ascetic life, he

[1] Purified is often used in Buddhist phraseology of final release; so in the title of Buddhaghosa's great work, *Visuddhi-magga*, "the way of purity."

[2] *Majjh.*, ii, 84; *Dīgha*, ii, 81.

[3] *Majjh.*, iii, 83.

would be honoured as a recluse. The same argument is brought forward against the brahmin Assalāyana,[1] and countries life those of the Yonas and Kambojas [2] are pointed out where there are only two castes, noble and slave, and these may change places. If there were two brahmin brothers, one learned and one not, the former would be received first as a guest, but if the learned one were wicked and the other virtuous, then the latter would receive honour. Brahmins are also made to admit that as a matter of fact they are unable to be sure that their descent has been kept pure for seven generations. Esukāri [3] offers another mark of the brahmin caste: a brahmin may be served by any of the four castes, a kshatriya by any of the three lower, a vaiśya by the two lowest, and a śūdra only by a śūdra. But Buddha replies that it is merely the brahmin view, and says that not all service should be undertaken or rejected. That which makes a man better and not worse should be undertaken. He is not better or worse through high birth, high caste, or great wealth. Even if of high birth he may be either criminal or virtuous, and he is rewarded according to his actions, not according to his caste. Again, the castes are said to be distinguished by their sources of wealth, the brahmin by living on alms, the kshatriya by his bow and arrows, the vaiśya by farming and cattle-rearing, and the śūdra by his sickle and carrying-pole; but the four classes are mere designations according as a man happens to be born, just as a fire that burns logs is a wood fire, or a fire that burns straw a straw fire. True wealth, Buddha proclaims, is the noble transcendent Doctrine. Anyone, whatever his caste is, may practise this and develop the thought of love and freedom from enmity.

The brahmins are also attacked as being degenerate. They are contrasted with their ancient ancestors, who kept their own caste laws. They did not seek to be well groomed and adorned, nor did they live on rich food and enjoy luxurious palaces and chariots.[4] Usually the discussions

[1] *Ibid.*, ii, 147.

[2] These are the names of two peoples mentioned by Asoka in his inscriptions (Rock Edict) as being within his realm. There is no reason to connect the Yonas directly with the Greeks, though the name (Yavana) is the name by which the Persians knew them.

[3] *Majjh.*, ii, 177.

[4] *Dīgha*, i, 104; *Sn.*, 284–315. The attacks on caste were long continued. In the *Lalita-vistāra* (159) the Bodhisattva chooses his wife for her good

are described with great urbanity, but there is a certain animus in the description of five ancient brahmin practices which are said to be not now found among brahmins but are still found among dogs.[1] A still more disparaging reference occurs in the *Majjhima* (iii, 167), where certain people are said to be " running like brahmins at the smell of a sacrifice ". The brahmins are never referred to as living an ascetic life. Yet this is taught in the Upanishads. " Brahmins who have come to know this ātman rise beyond desire for sons, desire for wealth, and desire for worlds, and practice living on alms . . . Therefore, let a brahmin, becoming disgusted with learning, desire to abide in a state of ignorance. When disgusted with both the state of learning and ignorance then he becomes a recluse." [2] But the ancient ideal state of the brahmins as described by the Buddhists is that of the householder. The life of the brahmin philosopher appears to be unknown.

Where the discussions touch most closely upon positive Buddhist doctrines is in the treatment of the way of salvation and in cosmogony, the theory of the origin of the universe. But what we find are the peculiar Buddhist theories, stated without any distinct recognition of the different conceptions of brahminism, and in no case with any allusion or quotation referring to an upanishad. On the one hand there was the view of the brahmin priests that by due performance of the sacrifices and other duties of life rebirth in heaven might be won, and on the other the secret doctrine of the brahmin recluses that freedom from rebirth might be won by attaining a certain knowledge. It is only the first that we find discussed by the Buddhists. The *Tevijja-sutta*, the discourse on the three-fold knowledge, the Vedas, undertakes to discuss the value of sacrifice, and the brahmins are represented as holding that it leads to life in the Brahma-world. But the Brahma-world as described belongs purely to the Buddhist conception of the universe. It is a definite region above the heavens of sense-pleasures, and is ruled by Mahā-Brahmā, the god who thinks he has created the universe, and every inhabitant

qualities from a number of ladies of all castes. The *Vajrasūci* sometimes attributed to Aśvaghosha (first cent. A.D.) uses brahmin works to enforce its refutation.

[1] Union of a brahmin only with a brahmin woman ; seasonal intercourse ; not buying and selling ; not storing up wealth ; begging only in the morning and evening ; not to any amount or after a good meal. *Angut.*, iii, 221.

[2] *Bṛhad. Up.*, iii, 5.

of that heaven is called a Brahmā. To reach that heaven is called attaining to the companionship of Brahmā. The view that the ancient Vedic sages knew the way to attain it is refuted by asking if they have ever seen Brahmā. It turns out that they have never seen him, nor do they know where he is. They are like a string of blind men led by a blind man. They indulge in the pleasures of the five senses, and this, even if they indulge in them quite lawfully, can only (on Buddhist theory) result in rebirth in one of the heavens of sense pleasures, not in the heaven of Brahmā.

What is expounded here is not the brahmin theory at all, but the possibility of attaining to the Brahma-world as the Buddhists conceived it to exist, that is, by the practice of the Brahma-vihāras. The brahmin view is refuted only in the sense that it must be false if the Buddhist conception is true. But all this, whether understood according to brahmin or Buddhist theories, has nothing to do with the upanishadic teaching about union with Brahma. Even the name is not the same, for the Buddhist Brahmā is a personal god who is also recognized by the Brahmins. But he, like the other Vedic gods, is only a manifestation of the ultimate reality Brahma.[1] This neuter Brahma is never mentioned by the Buddhists, nor do they ever discuss the upanishadic doctrine of attaining to this Brahma or becoming identified with it. Salvation for the teachers of the upanishads consisted in knowing that the individual self was identical with Brahma. This doctrine, though utterly opposed to Buddhist teaching, is never referred to in the Scriptures, though if it had been known it would have been the one most in need of refutation. It is possibly alluded to in the passage where the doctrine that the world is the self is mentioned (p. 102).

Questions of cosmogony are much older than the Upanishads. In the Vedic hymns we find the universe conceived as a sacrifice performed by the gods. Once it is even represented as a human sacrifice, in which the four classes of society proceed from different parts of the primeval man.[2] Or it is an egg. The Brāhmaṇas and Upanishads go on multiplying these myths. The favourite ideas are emanation, in which a primeval being emits everything from

[1] Brahmā (masc.) as a god is not known to the Vedic hymns. He appears later and is mentioned in the Upanishads, but the chief conception there is the neuter *brahma*.

[2] *Rigveda*, x, 90.

himself,[1] or production by the magic means of austerities (*tapas*). "Verily in the beginning there was nothing here. This (world) was covered over with Death, with hunger; for hunger is Death. He formed the thought, 'would that I might have a self.'"[2] Most of these myths are attempts to find an absolute beginning, for neither the doctrine of recurrent cycles nor rebirth is yet found, and it is against such vain attempts that the attacks of the *Brahmajāla-sutta* are directed.[3] But another principle was also involved. An origin implies an originator. The Buddhists opposed this in two ways. As we have seen, they explained away Brahmā the creator as being an individual who arose first at the beginning of a new cycle, and imagined that he had created all the rest as it arose out of the chaotic state between two cycles. He is represented as declaring, "I am Brahmā, the great Brahmā, the subduer, the unsubdued, the beholder of all, the subjector, god, maker, former, the chief appointer, the controller, the father of those that have been and shall be." Besides thus explaining away the creator, the Buddhists invented a creation myth of their own.[4] As the doctrine of recurrent cycles was assumed, it was not necessary to ask about an absolute beginning. There is no destruction of the whole universe, but only up to the world of Brahmā.

When the world begins to re-evolve in a new cycle, beings are reborn in it from a still higher world (Ābhassara, the Radiant world). At that time all was water and complete darkness. Here we have the nearest approach to a beginning as represented in the Brāhmaṇas. There was no sun or moon, no distinction of seasons, of male and female. Beings consisted of mind, feeding on joy, self-luminous, passing through the air, and abiding in glory. After a long time edible earth appeared on the water like scum on boiled milk. One of the beings becoming greedy tasted it, and other beings followed his example. Their luminousness disappeared, and moon and sun arose. Further stages are described, the disappearance of the edible earth, the growth of plants, until rice appeared. Greed and violence arose, sex and sex customs which were

[1] *Kaushītaki Br.*, vi, 10.
[2] *Bṛhad. Up.*, i, 2, 1.
[3] Above, p. .
[4] *Aggaññā-sutta*, *Dīgha*, iii, 80. It occurs also in Sanskrit forms showing that it belonged to the common tradition of early Buddhism. *Mvst.*, i, 338. It was originally one of the Vinaya legends. *Rockhill*, pp. 1 ff.

held to be wicked, and houses were built for concealment. Stealing, lying, and punishment arose, until the people went to the handsomest and ablest of the beings and asked him to administer justice. As he was authorized (*sammata*) by the people, he was known as Mahāsammata, the Great authorized One. He was the first king and first kshatriya, the origin of the warrior caste. Some of the beings decided to put away evil practices. They lived in leaf-huts, meditating, and begging their food. Some of these not being able to meditate compiled books [1] (the three Vedas, says the commentary). This was the origin of the brahmins. Others who adopted trades became the vaiśyas, and those who took to hunting śūdras. The discussion has thus come round again to the significance of caste.

There is no implication here that caste is indifferent. It is admitted that the four divisions are the normal state of society, and the warrior caste is made the chief. It was natural that a movement originating in opposition to brahminism should emphasize its own pretensions and in particular the descent of its founder as a member of the warrior caste. His ancestry is traced back to Mahāsammata, and the legend says that the founders of his clan, the sons of king Okkāka, who became the Sakyas, were so jealous of their purity of blood that they married their own sisters. But caste is put on a moral basis. A man of whatever caste, if he does wrong in deed, word, or thought, will after death go to hell or to some unhappy state; if he does right, to happiness and the world of heaven. For those who abandon the world caste disappears. Out of these four groups is formed the group of ascetics (*samaṇa*). " Anyone in these four castes who becomes a monk, an arahat, who has destroyed the āsavas, who has done what had to be done, who has laid down the burden, who has accomplished his purpose, who has destroyed the fetter of coming to be and is emancipated by full knowledge, he is declared to be chief among these (four) through his dhamma (his prescribed course of action),[2] not through

[1] *Gantha*, something tied together, i.e. the bundle of palm-leaves forming a book. Apart from the anachronism of thus describing the Vedas, it is an indication of the late origin of the legend itself.

[2] Franke translates " seinem Wesen nach ", Mrs. Rhys Davids " in virtue of a norm ". The *dhamma* of any particular class is that course of action which is right in accordance with the duties peculiar to that class. Here the *dhamma* of the arahat coincides with the doctrine, the word of Buddha which teaches the whole career of the arahat.

that which is not." The idea of the true brahmin is finally entirely moralized. The name brahmin is used over and over again for the perfected disciple, the arahat.

The relations of the upanishadic literature to Buddhism have been most fully studied by Oldenberg.[1] He points out the widely separated geographical position and the considerably later form of the buddhistic literature as shown in language, metre, the development of continuous thought, and management of dialogue. Another distinction is that the upanishads give us a picture only of village life, while the suttas show us city life, highly developed trade, and luxurious habits of living. The last point, however, is not very significant. We can speak of a literature contemporary with Buddha, but we find it embedded in a mass of legends which may be two centuries or more later. The memorizers who invented or adopted these legends had no historic sense to preserve the archaic features of previous centuries. They described the towns, the social life, the courtesans and traders of their own time as they knew them, and what they tell us of them is not, nor was it ever meant to be, the word of Buddha.

The idea of Brahma (neuter) in the old upanishads is said to have become hypostatized in Buddhism into a personal god Brahmā. But this rather implies that the older philosophic idea had been known to the Buddhists and then had become transformed into a much less philosophic conception. We have no evidence that early Buddhism ever knew it. It moves on the lines of the popular polytheism, which had never known the secret lore of the sages.

There can be no doubt, says Oldenberg, about the chronological conclusions. Buddhist literature is later than the Bṛhadāraṇyaka or Chāndogya Upanishad, and it is unthinkable that it should be the immediate successor of those works. Here Oldenberg is in opposition to scholars like Hopkins, who cannot believe that even the oldest upanishads "go back of the sixth century".[2] But it is surely a great assumption to speak of succession at all. We do not know that the upanishads had any connection with the region or social

[1] *Die Lehre der Upanishaden und die Anfänge des Buddhismus*, Göttingen, 1915.

[2] Hopkins, in *JAOS.*, xxii, 336.

conditions in which Buddhism originated.[1] They may have been going on in the seclusion of their hermitages at the very time when the Buddhists were attacking the brahmin pretensions in Magadha.

When we come to the question of the actual doctrines which may have been borrowed, we find that they are claimed to be not in the Upanishads, but in the philosophical schools of Yoga and Sānkhya. In the case of Yoga, as we have seen, it is rather a method of training which is in question. Some form of Yoga no doubt preceded Buddhism, and some of the particular methods may have been borrowed, but as the Buddhist system continued to grow we can in no case be sure that these belonged to original Buddhism. We have seen what is supposed to have been borrowed from Sānkhya. Even if the evidence for the borrowing of the Causal Formula were more cogent, we should have no reason to think that the Formula formed one of the foundations of the original system.[2]

The polemics of Buddhism help to show the kind of intellectual world in which its early expounders moved, but do not tell us of the fundamental beliefs which led its followers to abandon household life and undertake a long course of training. Buddhism rejected the worship of gods and the celebration of sacrifices as a means to final happiness. It rejected speculations about ultimate beginnings, especially about whether the self and the world were eternal, and a number of speculations about the ultimate state of the self in the future. What the Buddhist theories were as to the nature of this self and the ultimate state called Nirvāṇa are still matters of discussion.

[1] Oldenberg himself refused to see the supposed references to several Upanishads, which Walleser finds in an old Buddhist text; cf. Walleser, *Philos. Grundlage des älteren Buddhismus*, p. 67. Oldenberg (*Zur Gesch. des altind. Prosa*, p. 40) held that the *Sāmaññaphala-sutta* was a direct imitation of a dialogue in *Bṛhad. Up.*, iv, 1. In both cases there is a question between a king and a sage; in both the king tells what others have said; and in both cases these are six teachers. This has nothing to do with the origin of Buddhism, but with the literary form in which the editors put the dialogue. At that time literary contact may well have taken place.

[2] A question which cannot be discussed here is whether classical Sānkhya was earlier than Buddhism. Garbe and Jacobi held that it was, and if so their view of borrowing would be thereby strengthened. But even then we could not infer that it was primitive Buddhism that borrowed it.

CHAPTER VIII

DOGMA AND PHILOSOPHY: THE SOUL

RELIGION, said Schopenhauer, is the philosophy of the people. On the other hand, as La Vallée Poussin remarks, "on ne doit confondre le dogme ou la religion avec le 'système' ou la philosophie."[1] In one respect there is certainly a great difference. Philosophy aims to be "the complete interpretation of experience". Religion is not interested in completeness. It is interested in a few facts of experience to which it attributes an absolute truth and value. Its interpretations of these are called dogmas. Whether they can be interpreted in harmony with all the rest of experience is secondary. At first it is not even recognized that there may be contradictions. If the disciple is ever brought to see an apparent contradiction, he may say that what he holds is fundamental, whatever else is true. In that case he remains purely at the standpoint of religion. Or he may proceed to show that the contradictions are not real. He then assumes the standpoint of philosophy, and the final result of his thought is a natural theology or a philosophy of religion. It is still not quite what the philosophers call philosophy, for it retains those fundamentals which religion started with, but which philosophy could never have found out for itself.

Buddhism, in accordance with this distinction, began by being a religion. It is needless to dispute about the term religion. If it necessarily implies an intelligent and almighty entity as the ultimate explanation and the ultimate goal of things, then Buddhism is not a religion. We may prefer to say that the fundamental dogmas of Buddhism differ so much from the dogmas of religious systems that they cannot be brought under one definition. But Buddhism in one respect was at first rather on the side of religion than of philosophy in that it started with fundamental convictions, which only became a philosophical system when they had to be made consistent and defended against rival views.

[1] *Le dogme et la philos. du Bouddhisme*, p. 205.

It is probable that every dogma when followed out in all its implications would be found to involve universal principles, and hence the question of its relation to other principles would sooner or later arise. This is what has happened in Buddhism. The distinct and formal expression of a principle has more than once brought to light a consequence, and the principle has had to be reformulated, or the consequence has become an additional principle.

We have seen what the dogmatic position of the earliest ascertainable form of Buddhism was. There was a teacher revivifying the moral consciousness of his contemporaries, and with the insight of a prophet preaching an ethical doctrine that swept away much of the old ritualism. There was the new conception of the destiny of man, which promised a happiness not to be found in the weary round of earthly or heavenly existences, and there was the teaching of the Way, a definite course of life which, if followed out, led to escape, liberation. Not liberation in a distant future, but, as is said over and over again, a state to be realized *diṭṭhe dhamme*, in this actual life, by the disciple. Its fundamental dogma, the fact of pain, was put forward not as a theory to be considered, but as an actual fact, which only needed a right understanding to be accepted; and escape from pain was to be won by a method, the Noble Eightfold Way. This method does not seem to leave much room for theorizing, nor do we find any in the earliest description of the disciple's training. But theory lay dormant in the doctrines of the nature and destiny of man.

The question of the nature of man centres in the doctrine of the soul. Soul has been defined as the principle of thought and action in man, or as that which thinks, wills, and feels, conceived as a perdurable entity and a subject of conscious spiritual experience. But definition is of little use. As that which thinks, wills, and feels it is the direct experience of everyone. But the term soul, or the corresponding word for *anima* in the West, has strong religious associations, and its use generally implies further theories, such as the existence of soul as a substance independent of the body, its immateriality and immortality, theories which reach far beyond the range of direct experience. The closest Indian term corresponding to soul is *ātman* (Pāli *attā*) yet the result of comparison is mere confusion unless the significance of the term is determined quite independently of the associations lying in the word soul. It is in the Upanishads where we find a new doctrine of the soul formulated which has ever since remained fundamental in Indian thought, and it is this which needs to be examined in considering the Buddhist doctrine of the self.

The word *ātman* is found in the earliest Vedic hymns. The derivation of the word is uncertain. It is sometimes held to have meant " breath ", but it had already acquired a more special meaning. It is breath in the sense of " life ". The soma drink is said to be the ātman of the sacrifice. The sun is called the ātman of all that moves and stands. The commonest meaning is that of " self ", a use which is still found in the modern Indian languages. These meanings were probably not distinctly separated. This life or self was something which could leave the body and return. As such it is spoken of in the Rigveda as *manas*.[1] Such conceptions coming down from what are called primitive times are continued in the Upanishads. There is the self, the size of a thumb, which abides in the heart. From the heart pass a hundred and one channels, from which the ātman may issue. From one passage at the top of the head it may pass to immortality. It may leave the body in sleep. " Therefore let not one wake him suddenly, they say; for hard is the healing of one to whom he does not return." [2] But a deeper conception is expressed, that the ātman is that which is most real. " This person consists of the essence of food. This is his head, this is his right side, this is his left side, this is his ātman, this is his lower part, the base." [3] Here the body is being described, and the ātman appears to be the trunk of the body. But the passage goes on to say that besides this ātman consisting of food there is another ātman consisting of breath, and its ātman is space; behind this is another consisting of mind, and its ātman is instruction (the Vedas); behind this is another consisting of knowledge, and its ātman is yoga; behind this is another consisting of bliss, and its ātman is bliss.

The Upanishads retain much of the early imagery and

[1] E.g. *RV.*, x, 58, which is a charm for bringing back the spirit of an unconscious person to the body; cf. P. Tuxen, *Forestillingen om Sjælen i Rigveda*, Copenhagen, 1919.
[2] *Bṛhad. Up.*, iv, 3, 13.
[3] *Taitt. Up.*, ii, 1–5.

conceptions of the hymns and Brāhmaṇas, and they might have gone on refining these notions of the self as a small entity within the body, and of the world as generated by a primeval being, without reaching an essentially different standpoint. But new teaching came, which was looked upon as a revelation and taught as a secret. This was that the world not merely originated from one: it is one. It is Brahma, and Brahma is the self. When the pupil Śvetaketu had returned from twelve years' study of the Vedas and thought himself learned, his father removed his conceit, and taught him the Great Utterance: *thou art that.* " The voice of a person, my dear, when dying goes to the mind; his mind to breath; his breath to heat; heat to the highest divinity. That which is the most minute, this universe has it as its ātman. That is the real. That is the ātman. That thou art, O Śvetaketu." [1] The doctrine of Śāṇḍilya is: " this my ātman within my heart, more minute than a grain of rice or barley or millet or the kernel of a grain of millet—this my ātman in my heart is greater than the earth, greater than the space of air, greater than the sky, greater than these worlds. Consisting of all actions, all desires, all odours, all tastes, embracing this all, this my ātman in my heart—this is Brahma." [2]

We see here the difficulty of rising beyond the old conception which expressed everything in spatial terms. Plato having described the soul as something entirely different from anything perceptible to the senses was able to reach the concept of something to which spatial terms do not apply. To speak of the size of the soul is meaningless. The Upanishads are feeling after this, but have to express it in contradictory terms: " more minute than the minute, greater than the great, is the ātman placed in the cavity (of the heart) of the creature." In the same way the imagery of going to the world of Brahma is continued. The emancipated one is a river entering the ocean:

> Like as rivers flowing into the ocean
> Disappear, abandoning name and form,
> So he that knows, being freed from name and form,
> Attains to the divine person, beyond the beyond.[3]

[1] *Chānd. Up.*, vi, 8, 6.
[2] Ibid., III, 143.
[3] *Muṇḍ. Up.*, iii, 2, 8.

But to know Brahma and the ātman is to have attained release :

> The one controller, the inner ātman of all beings,
> Who makes his one form to be manifold,
> The wise who perceive him abiding in the self (ātman),
> To them is eternal happiness not to others.[1]

Can we think that this doctrine was known to Buddha and that he rejected it ? Buddhism makes no mention of Brahma (neuter) as the one reality, or of any identity of this with the ātman. The Brahmā that we find so often mentioned in Buddhist writings is a personal god ruling over a separate region of the universe, and born and reborn as inevitably as any other being. But this Brahmā is never brought into relation with the Buddhist theory of the self.

The Buddhist conception of the individual, the person consisting of a material and immaterial part, is a quite definite theory, which at first appears without any polemics. It is expressed in different ways but all essentially the same. In the four contemplations, as we have seen (p. 53), the individual meditates on himself as compounded of body, sensations, mind, and thought. Another form of expression occurs in the system of the four trances (p. 47) when the stage of full knowledge begins and the individual begins to perceive everything as it really is. He first directs his attention to his body. " With mind concentrated, purified, cleansed, spotless, with the defilements gone, supple, ready to act, firm and impassible, he turns and directs his mind to knowledge and insight. He thus understands : this is my body, possessing form (material shape), originating from the four great elements, produced by a mother and father, a collection of milk and gruel, subject to rubbing, pounding, breaking, and dissolution ; and this is my consciousness, on this body it rests, to this it is bound." Here the individual consists of body and consciousness. Either we have here a more rudimentary analysis or the sensations and thoughts are taken as implicit in consciousness.[2]

[1] *Kaṭha Up.*, v, 12.

[2] The terms are not all identical in the different formulæ. *Citta* (thought), *mano* (mind), and *viññāṇa* (consciousness) are often equated, but they are not quite identical in meaning. *Citta* often implies feeling, and may mean heart. *Viññāṇa* may imply understanding. But when coupled with body all three express the same fact, the immaterial part of the individual. Similarly *rūpa* when applied to the body is the same as *kāya*.

Besides these we have the more usual division according to the five khandhas or skandhas (masses, groups): body, feeling, perception, the aggregates, and consciousness. There is also the term *nāma-rūpa*, "name and form," occurring in the Causal Formula. It is equated to the khandhas by making *nāma* correspond to the four immaterial khandhas, but in the *Sammādiṭṭhi-sutta* (*Majjh.*, i, 53), where there is an exposition of the terms of the Causal Formula, *nāma* is said to consist of feeling, perception, volition (*cetanā*), contact, and attention, and *rūpa* to consist of the four great elements and what is included in them. Here we have two more analyses of the individual. *Nāma-rūpa* is a term found in the Upanishads, but never in the specially Buddhist sense. It is used there with its absolutely literal meaning, as when the rivers are said to lose their name and form on entering the ocean,[1] and then it comes to mean individual existence. Both here and in Buddhism it appears to have been adopted from popular usage. It was the analysis into khandhas which became the established form for the analysis of the individual, and underwent further elaboration and comment. Can it be said to be primitive? Did Buddha himself express himself in such a way? Unless we are to suppose that Buddhism was indeed originally nothing more than "vulgar magic and thaumaturgy coupled with hypnotic practices", we should expect to find it constructive on the intellectual as well as the moral side. We do in fact find schemes for practising a way of life. We also find as part of them three or more descriptions of the nature and constitution of man. We are not bound to say that the scheme of the five khandhas was the earliest or was primitive. But when we find several such schemes all agreeing in essentials, and no rival doctrines claiming a place, we are entitled to hold that this way of describing the individual by enumerating all the characteristic features was original. All the different modes may be due to Buddha for, as Mrs. Rhys Davids says, "he would be simply unable to repeat himself." This appears to be the case also with the Causal Formula. There are some half-dozen forms of the causal sequence, and it

[1] *Muṇd.*, 3, 2, 8; *Praśna*, 6, 5. It is curious that the same simile of the rivers entering the ocean occurs in *Udāna*, v, 5, but there the term used is *nāma-gotra* "names and clans", and it refers there not to loss of individuality but to the literal loss of secular name and clan by one who abandons the world and becomes a son of the Sakyan.

is not till we get to the much elaborated *Saṃyutta-nikāya* that we find the regular twelvefold form treated as a standard. Similarly the five khandhas have become a standard form. The forms which have survived in the description of the monk's progress through the four trances (p. 47), and in the four contemplations (p. 53) are probably older. They became neglected when with the growth of Abhidhamma such standard lists became compiled and commented on.

What is the relation of the individual constituted by the five khandhas to the ātman ? In the oldest texts there is none. In the sense of self, and as opposed to another (*para-*), ātman is frequent enough.[1] But even in the *Brahmajāla-sutta*, where all the heresies are supposed to be included, there is no denial of an ātman. We are there told of some who say that the self is eternal, we are told of Brahmā, who thinks himself eternal and other beings not, of others who hold that thought (*citta*), or mind (*mano*), or consciousness (*viññāṇa*) is eternal, of the eel-wriggler who refuses to say whether a Tathāgata, an emancipated one, exists after death, of those who hold that the self possessing form or in some other mode exists after death, and of those who hold that the self, whether the bodily self consisting of the four elements or a finer mental self, perishes at death. No question is raised as to whether the ātman exists or not but whether in some way or other it is eternal.

The first place where we find the express denial of an ātman mentioned is in an analysis of *upādāna*, grasping. Upādāna is divided into four kinds, (1) the grasping of sensual desire (*kāma*), (2) of heresy (*diṭṭhi*), (3) of mere moral practice and rites (*sīlabbata*), and (4) of the doctrine of an ātman (*attavāda*).[2] This shows that when this formula was made, the doctrine of an ātman was expressly taught, but it tells us nothing about the school that held it, and as there is little trace of upanishadic doctrine it is unlikely this was being opposed. It is more likely to imply opposition to Mīmāṃsā as held by the descendants of the class of brahmins whom Buddha opposed. Their position later on is represented by Kumārila, who has a long section in defence of ātmavāda.[3]

[1] Another late term is *attabhāva*, lit. self-existence, an actually existent individual; *Majjh.*, ii, 181; *Angut.*, i, 134; *Dhsang.*, 597. In Buddhist Sanskrit it means the self.

[2] *Dīgha*, iii, 230; *Majjh.*, i, 66; *Saṃy.*, ii, 3, etc.

[3] *Mīmāṃsaślokavārttika*, v. 18, transl. by G. Jha, Calcutta, 1907.

There is a possible reference to upanishadic doctrine where self and world are identified (p. 102), but even here there is no reference to Brahma. The *Mahāniddesa*[1] speaks of the "heresy of ātman" (*attadiṭṭhi*) and the "misconception of ātman" (*attagāha*). Both these are late terms and forms of expression which are quite unlike the formulation of the problem as we find it in the scheme of the five khandhas or in the parallel expressions for the union of mind and body.

But though the mere scheme of the khandhas as constituting the individual is implicitly the denial of something else called an ātman, there is nothing to make it probable that the doctrine was at first termed *anattavāda*. Aung and Walleser say, "there can be no doubt that Buddha himself preached the doctrine of *anattavāda* as one of the most important doctrines, if one only recognizes that the doctrine laid down in the suttas was his own." If only! and yet after having posed this if, they leave it in the air and slip from the question as to what is in the suttas and what Buddha himself taught to the harmless statement that "for Buddhism no acting subject besides action exists and nothing that perceives besides perception."[2]

It is an illusion to suppose that we can prove that Buddha taught the doctrine of non-self in so many words, though it can be deduced, as the Buddhists themselves deduced it, from the doctrine of the khandhas and the other formulæ in which the individual is analysed into his elements. The term *anattavāda* has no meaning without stating what theory of the ātman was denied. It shows that some form of ātman-belief came to be rejected, and that this also included a belief in its eternity, but what philosophical system was opposed when the term was invented remains a mere supposition.

The introduction of the terms *attavāda*, *attadiṭṭhi*, implies a new point of view: it was the self conceived as something more than the self of direct experience. Such a doctrine did arise among the Buddhists, but not by attempting to

[1] Although this is a commentary on the *Suttanipāta*, there is no reference to *attavāda* in the *Suttanipāta* itself. The phrase *attaṃ pahāya* (800) is being commented on. This means "having rejected what has been seized", and so it is understood by the commentary *Paramatthajotika*, where *attaṃ* (*āptaṃ*) = *gahītaṃ*. The *Niddesa* is against both sense and grammar, but it is evidence for the existence of the doctrine in its own period.

[2] *Dogmatik des mod. süd. Buddhismus*, p. 16.

introduce ātmavāda. They never thought of calling this something the ātman, but started from a fresh point of view, and spoke of the individual (*puggala*, Skt. *pudgala*). This doctrine (*pudgalavāda*) is the first of the rejected doctrines in the *Kathāvatthu*: that the individual exists in the sense of being real or true in the highest sense. The commentator attributes the theory to the Vātsīputrīyas and the Sammitiyas, and to followers of non-Buddhist schools. The holders of the doctrine tried to be orthodox for, as it was explained, they held an ātman called pudgala, which was different and not different from the skandhas (*Bodhicaryāv.*, ix, 60 *com.*). The *Abhidharmakośa* devotes a whole chapter to its refutation.

There is a sutta called the *Burden-sutta* (*Saṃy.*, iii, 25) which has been held to support the doctrine. "The burden, O monks, I will teach you, the taking of the burden, the grasping of the burden, and the laying down of the burden." It is then explained that the five khandhas are the load. "The burden-taking is the individual; any elder of such a name and such a clan." The grasping of the burden is "that craving which tends to re-birth, accompanied by delight and passion, taking delight here and there, namely the craving for sensual pleasure, for existence, for non-existence". The laying down of the burden is the cessation of craving without a trace, its relinquishment, and release. Then follow two stanzas which are the real sutta, for the preceding prose is only a comment on it:

> The burdens verily are the five khandhas,
> The burden-taking is the individual;
> Grasping the khandhas is pain in the world,
> Laying down the burden is happiness.
> When he has laid the heavy burden down,
> And has not taken up another burden,
> And has drawn out craving with its root,
> Free from hunger he has won Nirvāṇa.

Here we have three parallel expressions: the taking of the burden (*bhāra-hāra*), the grasping after it, and the laying it down. There is no doubt that *bhāra-hāra* means "burden-taking", but it has been translated "burden-bearer". The point is not very important, for in any case it is interpreted as being the individual. The laying down of the burden is by rooting out craving and thus attaining Nirvāṇa. But we are as far off as ever from proving by this single text that the individual is to be understood as a permanent entity and real or true in the highest sense.

The doctrine of *pudgalavāda* does not appear to have spread among the Buddhist schools, and the rejection of the doctrine of an ātman (*ātmavāda*) became more intense with the growth of controversy. Yet the attempt has been made to find an ātman doctrine directly taught by Buddha. In the Vinaya account of the first conversions made by Buddha we are told that he found a party of thirty wealthy young men who had been sporting with their wives in a grove. One of them who had no wife had brought a courtesan, and when they were not noticing she had taken their things and made off. While seeking her they came across Buddha, and asked if he had seen a woman. Buddha replied, "What do you think, young men, which is better, for you to go in search of a woman, or to go in search of yourselves?" "It is better, Lord, for us to go in search of ourselves (*attānaṃ*)." The word for "self" is the same as the word for "soul", and we are asked to believe that Buddha was advising them to go in search of their souls.

This scarcely needs serious discussion, but there is a standing formula in describing the khandhas, which does not indeed teach an ātman directly, but which is supposed to leave a loophole that implies it. Usually it occurs as a mere formula, but there is a sutta where it is brought into connection with the general doctrine of the khandhas. It is attributed to Sāriputta, so that it may be taken as the form in which the developed doctrine had become established.[1]

Body (*rūpa*) consists of the four great elements and what is included in them. Earth is either external (i.e. solid matter) or internal forming the parts of the body: hair, nails, teeth, and the rest of the individual. Water is either external or internal as the various liquids of the body. Internal heat is heat which produces digestion and so on. Internal air is the various breaths and winds of the body. After each of these comes the formula, "this is not mine, I am not this, this is not my self; even so, should it rightly be regarded and considered." In the well-known *Anattalakkhaṇa-sutta*,[2]

[1] *Majjh.*, i, 184.

[2] *Saṃy.*, iii, 66. This is the sutta which, according to the Vinaya (i, 14), was the second discourse of Buddha preached to the first five disciples. *Anattalakkhaṇa* means "not having the marks of a self or soul". As the sutta shows, it is merely a denial that the khandhas were *ātman*, whatever that term means.

and repeatedly in other places, all the khandhas are treated in the same way, ending with consciousness. " Is it fitting to consider what is impermanent, painful, and subject to change as ' this is mine, I am this, this is my self ' ? No, Lord. Therefore, monks, whatever consciousness, past, future, or present, internal or external, gross or subtle, low or eminent, far or near, all this consciousness is not mine, I am not this, this is not my self."

But if we translate *na m'eso attā* (this is not my self) as " this is not my soul ", there is the possibility of supposing that Buddha implied that there was a permanent soul somewhere else, even if not in the five khandhas. Such a translation is perfectly arbitrary, and that sense would only have plausibility if we could suppose that the later community had suppressed the ātman doctrine so effectually from the rest of his forty-five years of teaching that no one remembered anything of it. Yet although at his death his teaching was preserved in the minds of thousands of disciples (and indeed nowhere else) we find no trace of it even as a heresy among the Buddhists. If a trace had survived, we should have expected the Vātsīputrīyas to have appealed to it when they started their doctrine of an individual *plus* the five khandhas. But in fact they started from a quite independent point of view, and there is nothing to show that they thought they were contradicting the teaching about the self.[1]

The *sutta of the simile of the snake* (*Majjh*, i, 133) repeats the argument against an ātman being found in the five khandhas, and also explicitly denies an ātman. It cannot be taken as a primitive expression of the Buddhist position, so that it does not do more than illustrate the attitude as it became finally formulated.

An ignorant, untrained man considers body and the other khandhas, and thinks, " this is mine, I am this, this is my self," and forms the heresy, " the world is the self. Hereafter I shall become permanent, stable, eternal, unchangeable, and so I shall stay for ever. This is mine, this am I, this is my self." The enlightened disciple says, " This is not mine,

[1] What there is that is permanent is stated in the Sarvāstivāda form of the *Anattalakkhaṇa-sutta*, which begins : " Form has the nature of the destructible, and with its cessation is Nirvāṇa, which is of indestructible nature. Feeling, perception, the aggregates, consciousness, are of destructible nature, and with the cessation of each is Nirvāṇa, of indestructible nature." *Av. Śat.*, ii, 169.

I am not this, this is not my self," and does not worry about what does not exist. A monk may hold this heresy, and then hear a Buddha or a disciple of his preaching the doctrine directed to the destruction of heresies, the quieting of all the aggregates, the giving up of all material of rebirth, the annihilation of craving, to cessation and Nirvāṇa. Then he thinks he will be cut off and annihilated. One who does not hold that heresy never thinks whether he will be annihilated or not, and does not lament. If there were an ātman, there would be something of mine belonging to an ātman; but as an ātman and something belonging to an ātman do not exist in truth and reality, this view that the world is the ātman is simply and entirely the doctrine of fools. Buddha is then represented as replying to the charge that his doctrine implies the annihilation, destruction, and non-existence of an existent being. "In the past and now I teach pain and the cessation of pain. If herein others abuse, revile, and annoy the Tathāgata, the Tathāgata does not feel anger, displeasure, or discontent of mind. And if others honour, revere, exalt, and worship the Tathāgata, he does not feel joy, happiness, and exultation of mind. He thinks, 'it is on account of what I came to comprehend long ago that such things are done.'"

This sutta appears to be a still later formulation of the argument against the ātman doctrine. Here the heresy usually stated as "the world and self are eternal" is converted into the doctrine that the world is the self and that both are eternal. There may be here some reference to upanishadic doctrine, though it is still not the identity of self and Brahma. The strongly polemical passages in which Buddha is made to defend himself against the falsehoods and misrepresentations of opponents appear like the wrangling of schools. The whole standpoint is different from that of the discussions in the *Dīgha*. There it is not the question of the existence of an *ātman*, but of its eternity or annihilation; here the doctrine of the assertion of an ātman is denied.

Another way of finding a permanent substrate is to identify consciousness itself with the ātman. This is treated in the legend of the monk Sāti (*Majjh.*, i, 256), who formed the evil view that consciousness is something which remains consciousness, and as such passes from birth to birth. The whole refutation rests upon the twelvefold Causal Formula. "Consciousness originates from a cause and without a cause there is no arising of consciousness." It manifests itself through each of the six senses. "Through whatever cause consciousness arises it gets its name from that cause. Through the eye and visible forms consciousness arises, and is known as eye-consciousness." Consciousness through the other senses is explained in the same way. Here it is not the birth-consciousness of the Causal Formula that is being explained, but the rise of a particular conscious state by stimulus of a sense-organ.

The individual is then analysed according to the constituents of which he is compounded and which sustain him. These are said to be the four foods (*āhāra*): material food, contact, cogitation (*manosañcetana*), and consciousness. These are all produced by craving, craving by feeling, feeling by contact, contact by the six sense-organs, the six sense-organs by name and form, name and form by (birth-) consciousness, consciousness by the aggregates, and the aggregates by ignorance. Here the origin of the living individual as actually constituted of foods or sustenances is explained. It is followed by still another variant of the Causal Formula, in which the origin of the individual from the stage of birth-consciousness is traced as against the view that consciousness persists as such through all stages. Birth-consciousness is identified with the embryo (*gabbha*). When three conditions are present there is entry or descent of the embryo: when mother and father come together, when the mother is of child-bearing age, and when the gandhabba (the being to be reborn) is present. When the boy is born [1] he develops his faculties, he experiences feeling through each of the senses, he delights in them, and delight (*nandī*) arises. This delight in the senses is grasping, on account of grasping becoming, on account of becoming birth, on account of birth old age and death arise. Even so is the origin of all this mass of pain. This is still another form of the Causal Formula, and one which shows that it was understood as stages of the individual. Craving (*taṇhā*) is not mentioned, but delight (*nandī*), a word sometimes treated as a synonym

[1] It is expressly said that his mother gives birth to him and feeds him with milk, so that the view of Dr. Schayer that the stages down to grasping are pre-natal will not hold here. If that view could be adopted, we should have a more consistent description of one life from conception to death.

of craving, takes its place. It is hardly likely that this could have arisen after the form with twelve links had become fixed.

Such is the way in which the difficulty of Sāti is explained—consciousness is not something permanent which persists unchanged from birth to birth, but one form which the individual assumes at one stage of his existence. Conception consists in "the descent of the embryo". This statement is opposed to the view of Childers that it is only karma which transmigrates, but no evidence has ever been given for his view. The descent of the embryo is called the descent of consciousness or cognition in the *Mahānidāna-sutta* (above p. 67). Yet Rhys Davids when translating the very words of that sutta, *viññāṇaṃ va hi mātu kucchiṃ okkamitvā*, as "were cognition after having descended into the mother's womb" (*Dial.*, ii, 60), adds a note to say, "there is no conception of cognition, as a unity, descending from outside into the womb like a ball into a bag." Even if it were only karma which were transmigrating, one would have thought that it must come from outside.

In one sense karma transmigrates, because the individual which transmigrates is loaded with karma in every stage. The groups of which he consists are always changing, but it is because they are not wholly dispersed that he continues to be reborn. Freedom from re-birth is exactly the final dispersion of all the khandhas, and this takes place with the destruction of craving. But until this happens the individual is a being with a definite past, which with the proper training he can remember. This is not a mere concession to popular ideas, for apart from the fact that no other teaching is mentioned, we find the remembrance of former births continually referred to as one of the acquirements of the disciple under training.

Although the Buddhist believed in the survival of the individual in the next existence as firmly as any Christian, it may be asked whether his theory of the khandhas justified him in doing so. No explanation is ever given why the khandhas should be always combined in separate personalities. There is no principle of individuation, nor even any recognition of what Kant called the synthetic unity of apperception. It is probable that the opponents of the theory of khandhas-only were feeling after some such principle, and there is no doubt that the orthodox Hindu theories of the ātman depended on more than the instinctive rejection of the thought of personal annihilation. But this principle was never separated out from dogmatic concepts of the soul, and it was always possible to reject these and at the same time to neglect the principle of truth which they contained. In any case the doctrines of immortality (eternal life as distinct from mere survival after death), the existence of a permanent spiritual substance, and of a being thinking and feeling apart from material conditions, did not come within the range of evidence recognized by the Buddhists. The critical question for the Buddhists was not the survival of the individual at death, which they held and defended against the doctrine of annihilation (*ucchedavāda*), but the existence of the individual when the aggregation of the khandhas has finally ceased. That question depends upon the much disputed meaning of Nirvāṇa.

CHAPTER IX

KARMA

JUST as the conception of an ātman in brahminical speculation can be traced from the notion of a small entity residing in the heart to that of the universal reality of all things, so the doctrine of karma, " action," develops until it becomes a universal principle of ethics. Any act as judged by its results may be good or bad. This is a far wider conception than the question of right and wrong. Early man's welfare depended on his being able to discover from his experience what actions were advantageous and what injurious. He had to form theories. Two of these are the belief in magic and the belief in divine beings. How these beliefs began is not our present concern, for the earliest Indian societies were far from being primitive in the sense of being near the actual beginnings of human development.

Magic is the belief that by the performance of certain prescribed actions and the repetition of formulas certain desired results will follow. It has been held to have been an attempt at natural science, for early man would have no means of distinguishing the working of a rainmaking-spell from the equally mysterious production of fire by the use of the fire-drill. But whatever its origin, magic came to be an independent science or pseudo-science based on the ritual performance of certain actions. Its growth was favoured by its connection with an elaborate mythology which helped to make it plausible, and by the desire to believe the wonderful results promised and no doubt often achieved.

Ritual is found in sacrifice as well as in magic, but in India we find sacrifice, at least in the earliest period, existing quite distinct from the rites of magic. Along with sacrifice there was the belief in gods, personal beings who were the authors of many events beyond human control. The gods might be influenced, especially by being placated with offerings that served them as food. They came down to receive it, and grass was strewn at the sacrifice for them to sit on. Thus they were benefited, and the worshipper offered his sacrifice expecting a fair return.

The sacrifice thus looked upon as an appeal to the gods to be gracious is entirely different from a magical ceremony, in which a result follows merely from the performance of a prescribed act. Yet the belief became established that if the sacrifice were duly performed a certain result would inevitably follow. The performance alone produced the result, not the favour of a divine being. To the extent to which this idea predominates, the ritual of sacrifice becomes indistinguishable from that of magic. This appears as the prevailing notion in the later Vedic period of the Brāhmaṇas. In the Brāhmaṇa of the Hundred Paths rules are given for the proper building of the altar. To get the desired result the altar must be of a prescribed size, and this is explained by the myth of the gods who were instructed by the god Prajāpati how to build an altar.

> The gods performed these sacrifices: the Fire sacrifice, the New and Full Moon sacrifices, the Four-monthly sacrifices, the Animal sacrifice, the Soma sacrifice. They sacrificing with these sacrifices did not obtain immortality. . . .
>
> Then went on praising and performing austerity, desiring to obtain immortality. Prajāpati addressed them: ye do not put down my forms; ye either leave out or carry out too fully, therefore ye do not become immortal.
>
> They said: Tell us this, how we may put down all thy forms. He said: Sixty and three hundred enclosing stones lay down, and sixty and three hundred yajushmati-bricks, also six and thirty; of lokampṛṇa-bricks put down ten thousand and eight hundred; thus ye will put down all my forms, and will become immortal. The gods thus put them down. Thence the gods were immortal.
>
> Death spoke to the gods: surely thus all men will become immortal. Now what shall be my share? They said: henceforth no other shall be immortal with his body, but only when thou shalt have taken that body as thy share. Thus having parted with his body he shall be immortal who is to be immortal through knowledge or karma. Now in that they said this: through knowledge or karma, it is this fire-altar that is the knowledge, and this fire-altar that is the karma.
>
> So they who know this, or they who do this karma, having died are born again, thus being born again they are born again to immortality. Thus they who do not know, or they who do not know this karma, on dying are born again, they become the food of Death again and again.[1]

The karma and the knowledge here spoken of is that required for the due performance of the sacrifice. Doubtless the idea of action as moral action already existed. Moral rules grow up inevitably in a society in accordance with the actual social conditions. But in India we find a wider conception than karma. It is dharma, thought of as a universal

[1] *Śatapatha Br.*, x, 4, 3, 4–10.

law of action. It appears in the Vedas expressed by *ṛta* "law", the law that everything in the universe has a prescribed course, from the path of the sun to the duties of each individual according to his own caste. Law or dharma thus universalized the conception of karma. It naturally included ritual actions, involving both what we call religious injunctions as well as morality. But in the Upanishads we find a clear distinction arising between mere ritualism and ethical action. Brahma, after having created the castes, is said to have created dharma. "He further created a better form. That was dharma, the power of the power (*kshatra*) which is dharma. Therefore, there is nothing beyond dharma. Hence a weaker man prevails over a stronger as though by a king. Even so that which is dharma is truth. Therefore, of one who speaks truth they say he speaks dharma, or of one who speaks dharma they say he speaks truth. Both indeed are one and the same."[1] And again: "According as one acts, according as one conducts himself, so does he become. He that does good becomes good; he that does evil becomes evil. One becomes virtuous by virtuous karma, bad by bad karma."[2]

The above Brāhmaṇa passage is also the first in which we hear of rebirth. It was a novelty in brahminism, for there is no trace of it in the Vedas. There we find in one of the funeral hymns the dead person thus addressed:

> Go forth, go forth, along the paths, where fathers
> Of ours before have travelled on aforetime;
> Both kings exulting in their own oblations
> God Varuṇa shalt thou behold and Yama.
>
> Come with the fathers, come along with Yama,
> With gifts and offerings in the highest heaven;
> Come home again, leaving behind all evil,
> Come with thy body, full of life and vigour.[3]

The son of the departed was required to make periodical offerings at the grave, as indeed he is still. At some not very ancient period we find the idea of reincarnation coming to hold a definite place in Indian belief. Death is not final repose. Yet when the idea of reincarnation is introduced, the reason for such periodical ceremonies would seem to be removed. The departed person is called *preta* (lit. departed), and he remains such until the funeral rites are

[1] *Bṛhad. Up.*, 1, 4, 14. [2] Ibid., 4, 4, 5. [3] *Rigveda*, x, 14, 7–8.

performed. The old practice of periodical funeral offerings was continued after the rise of the new doctrine, and it is found also among the Buddhist laity, though with a transformed significance.

In the Upanishads, the reincarnation doctrine is fully developed, but that it could not be very old is shown by the fact that the older idea that the father is reborn in his son also occurs there (*Kaush. Up.*, 2,15). But superseding this we find the doctrine of rebirth as another being: "He is born again here as a worm, or as a moth, or as a bird, or as a tiger, or as a lion, or as a fish, or as a boar, or as a man, or as some other being in these states, according to his karma, according to his knowledge." [1]

The upanishadic teaching, however, did nothing to alter the sacrificial system. It remained the valid and the only valid course for the uninitiated. Buddhism challenged the whole of it in principle. Naturally in the life of the laity much of the older beliefs remained. It was only the monk who could discard his "name and clan" and ignore all the ceremonial practices necessary for social life. That caste and caste distinctions remained among the Buddhist laity is shown in the legend of the five dreams of Buddha on the night before his enlightenment. The fourth of these dreams was that four birds of different colours came from the four quarters and, falling at Buddha's feet, became entirely white. They are interpreted as laymen of the four castes, who abandon a household life and become enlightened disciples.[2]

Several modifications were introduced by the Buddhists into the Hindu doctrine of reincarnation. The term *preta* (*peta*) was retained, and was applied not to the transitory stage of the departed before the performance of the funeral rites, but was made one of the five possible careers of existence (*gati*) for beings that are reborn. These are (1) hell, (2) birth as an animal, (3) birth as a preta, (4) birth as a man, (5) birth as a god. The first three are specially states of punishment.[3] The pretas are ghosts with small mouths and big bellies, tortured by hunger and thirst. They correspond to the homeless ghosts of brahminical belief, who wander as such because the funeral rites have not been performed. But

[1] *Kaush. Up.*, i, 2.

[2] *Ang.*, iii, 240; *Mvst.*, ii, 136.

[3] A fourth unhappy state (*apāya*) was later added, that of the asuras, the rebel gods. *Khuddakap. Com.*, 189.

for the Buddhists they are beings in a definite existence, into which they are born in accordance with the karma to be expiated. The *Petavatthu* (stories of petas) is a work in the *Khuddaka-nikāya*, which represents the ghosts as returning to their old homes and depending for their food on what is set out for them by their still living relatives —evidently a reminiscence or continuation of the old practice of libations to the dead.

The Buddhists also modified the conception of Yama. In the Vedas he is king of the dead in the happy world of the fathers, i.e. the deceased ancestors. For the Buddhists he is still king of the dead, but of those dead who are condemned to a period in hell (niraya), and he is in charge of the tortures inflicted there.

The five or six possible careers of existence cover the whole universe. We also find the range of existence divided into the nine abodes of beings (*āvāsā*). There are three planes :

(i) *Kāmāvacara*, the plane in which there is enjoyment of the five senses, corresponds to the first abode inhabited by beings with variety of body and variety of perceptions. It includes human beings, some gods, and some beings in the three states of punishment : (*a*) the hells, of which there are eight hot hells, the lowest being *Avīci*.[1] Besides these are eight cold hells and other minor hells, which are probably a later addition ; (*b*) The sphere of the pretas ; (*c*) the world of men ; (*d*) the lower heavens, including the heaven of the four Great Kings, of the Thirty-three gods, ruled by Śakra or Indra, the Yāma gods, Nirmāṇarati gods (delighting in transformation), and the Paranirmitavaśavartin gods (having power over the transformation of others).

(ii) In *Rūpāvacara*, the world of form, the senses of taste, smell, and touch are absent. It includes four abodes, the (*a*) Brahmā-world (which later is subdivided into four); (*b*) the Ābhāsvara gods ; (*c*) the Śubhakṛtsnas, the wholly bright gods, and (*d*) the Asaṃjñisattvas, beings without perception. Further subdivisions are also found.

(iii) *Arūpāvacara* is the formless world, in which there is only the sense of mind. The four abodes are the stages of

[1] This term is interpreted uncertainly by the commentators. Literally it is " without a wave ", i.e. with continuous flame, but Kern has shown that it is probably for *avācī* " below ", and corrupted through analogy with *udīcī* " above ". For the whole of this cosmology see *State of the Dead* in Hastings, *ERE*.

the four Attainments : (*a*) in which there is the perception, "space is infinite" ; (*b*) in which there is the perception, "consciousness is infinite" ; (*c*) in which there is the perception, "there is nothing" ; (*d*) the fourth is the stage of neither consciousness nor non-consciousness. It reaches to the limit of existence (*bhavāgra*), through which a being may transmigrate.

It is a Buddhist doctrine that the next state of a being to be reborn is determined by the last wish. Buddhaghosa gives examples of it in discussing the Causal Formula (p. 64). There is no necessary violation of the law of karma in this, for whatever that state is, the individual's karma will begin to take effect in it. Nor can an individual at the end of a life make an arbitrary wish. It is really determined by the life he has led, by the character which he has come to be. We find a parallel to this in the modern parable of Dr. Jekyll and Mr. Hyde. Dr. Jekyll did not wish to cease to be Mr. Hyde. His accumulated karma had converted into a Mr. Hyde, and he wished to practise the life of a Mr. Hyde more than ever. What he did not wish was the unpleasant consequences.

None of the practices of training in themselves produce final release. So far as they train the mind in turning it from contact with the things of sense they form stages in coming to a realization of the Truths. But the direct result is only to bring about rebirth in the appropriate abode. In all of them there is the fetter of the desire for existence in some form. To practise friendliness is a means of being born in the Brahma-world, and the practice of the highest contemplations, the Attainments, in itself leads only to rebirth in the Formless world. They bring the disciple nearer the goal by the breaking one after another of the fetters.

The operation of karma was worked out in detail by the scholastics. Actions have a ripening (*vipāka*), and a fruit (*phala*). There are certain crimes which bring their punishment in this present life (*ānantariya*): murder of a mother, a father, an arahat, shedding the blood of a Buddha, and schism. Karma may be black, white, mixed, or neither black nor white.

(1) If a man produces injurious aggregations of body, speech, and mind, he is reborn in an injurious world. There he is affected by injurious impressions, and feels injurious feelings extremely painful,

such as do those who are beings in hell. Thus the rebirth of a creature is due to the creature. It is through what he does that he is reborn. Thus beings are the heirs of their karma.

(2) If a man produces a non-injurious aggregation of body, speech, and mind, he is reborn in a non-injurious world. There he is affected by non-injurious impressions, and feels non-injurious feelings extremely pleasant, such as do the Wholly-bright gods.

(3) If a man produces an injurious and non-injurious aggregation of body, speech, and mind, he is reborn in a world both injurious and non-injurious. He is affected by both kinds of impressions and feelings, such as human beings, some gods, and some beings in states of punishment.

(4) When the intention is directed to the abandonment of black karma with black ripening, of white karma with white ripening, and of black-white karma with black-white ripening, this is called neither black nor white, producing neither black nor white karma. It tends to the destruction of karma.[1]

The different kinds of fruit are also specified according to the character of the deeds. The woman or man who kills or sheds blood is reborn in hell, or if the person attains human form she or he is short-lived. Those who have compassion for the welfare of all living beings are reborn in heaven, or if as human beings they are long-lived. For crimes of violence the fruit is sickness, for anger ugliness, for desiring honour and lordship weakness, for miserliness poverty, for pride and insolence low birth, for not resorting to ascetics and brahmins and asking what is good and what should be done stupidity.[2] These things are known because, as we are told, " some ascetic or brahmin by means of austerity, effort, application, and attention produces such concentration of mind that with concentrated mind and purified divine eye surpassing human vision he sees a certain man practising murder, theft, adultery, lying, malicious and harsh speech, frivolous talk, greed, malevolence, false views. He sees the man after death born in an unhappy state or in hell. He says, ' surely there are evil karmas and ripening of misdeeds, for I have seen such a man born in hell.' And he says, ' surely he who commits such crimes is born in hell. They who know thus know rightly ; the knowledge of those who know otherwise is false.' "[3]

The *Sutta of Death's messengers* pictures the arrival of the sinner in hell. King Yama questions him about the first messenger. " Hallo, man, when you were among mankind did you not see the first messenger of Death ? " " I did not,

[1] *Majjh.*, i, 389. [2] *Majjh.*, iii, 202. [3] *Majjh.*, iii, 210.

sir."[1] "Did you not see a woman or a man of eighty, ninety, or a hundred years, bent with age, leaning on a stick, shaking wretchedly, greyhaired or bald, and with discoloured body?" "I did, sir." "Did you not, when you got intelligence and grew up, think, 'I, too, am liable to old age, I must surely do good in deed, word, and thought?'" "I could not, sir, I was careless." "Through carelessness you did no good in deed, word, or thought. Verily, they shall deal with you according to your carelessness. Your evil karma was not done by your mother or father or brother or sister, not by your friends and companions, not by kinsmen and relations or the gods or ascetics and brahmins. Verily, you did the evil karma, and it is you who will suffer the ripening."

Yama then questions him about the second messenger, the sight of a sick man, and about the third, the sight of a corpse. "Then the guardians of hell take the fivefold bonds, they put a hot iron stake through one hand and one through the other, one through each foot, and another through his breast. Thus he suffers pain, sharp, keen, piercing torture, nor does he die until his evil karma comes to an end."[2]

Even after the criminal has exhausted his karma in hell it is very difficult for him to be born again as a man. If there were a yoke with one hole in it floating on the ocean and borne about by the four winds, it would be easier for a one-eyed turtle rising to the surface once in a hundred years to put its head through the hole than for such a being to attain man's estate. Even when he does so, he is born as an outcast, or in some low rank of life. Rhys Davids preferred to call hell purgatory, but the Buddhist hells are anything but a preparation and purification for a life of bliss. The being, unless there is some still unripened good karma, must start at the end of the scale again.

It has been said that the annihilation of karma is the aim of the disciple, and that this constitutes salvation. This is only indirectly true in the sense that karma is produced by craving or by craving in the three forms of greed, hatred, and stupidity.[3] The mere absence or neutralizing of karma without the destruction of its cause is vain. On this point

[1] These messengers were also the first three of the four signs sent by the gods to Gotama while at the height of his glory to remind him of his destiny. The fourth sign was a man who had renounced the world. *Jāt.*, i, 59.

[2] *Ang.*, i, 138.

[3] *Ang.*, i, 134; they are called the three roots of demerit.

Buddhism was in direct opposition to Jainism. The actual historical relations of Buddhism to Jainism do not here concern us. We find certain doctrines discussed and opposed, but the actual historical statements are due to a later tradition, and their interpretation is a matter of dispute. We find the Jains, under the name of Nigaṇṭhas, represented as holding the doctrines of the omniscience of their leader and of the annihilation of karma as the means of obtaining release. But the Achelakas, the naked ascetics, are also opposed, and their practices of austerity are much the same as what we know of the Jains. There is a sutta in which a Nigaṇṭha gives a list of these practices, but he attributes them to other teachers. Jacobi consequently held that the original Nigaṇṭhas were the followers of Pārśva, the predecessor of Mahāvīra, and that Mahāvīra, the Jain leader, probably borrowed the rigid rules from the Achelakas or Ājīvikas, the followers of Gosāla.[1] Here the naked ascetics concern us only as the representatives of a rival way of salvation.

One way of regarding the performance of austerities is to consider it as the heaping up of good karma or as neutralizing bad, but the list of the naked ascetic's practices is considered from a different point of view, in their possessing value as a means of training the mind. In the *Kassapasīhanāda-sutta* (*Dīgha*, i, 161) the question raised is, "among those things which are bad and accounted bad, blameworthy, to be shunned, ignoble and wicked, and accounted such, who is there who has put them utterly away, is it the ascetic Gotama or other reverend leaders of schools ?" It is Gotama, and it is by means of the Noble Eightfold Path. That is the true meaning of becoming an ascetic and brahmin. The naked ascetic replies by giving a long list of repulsive practices in begging, eating, and sleeping.[2] They are rejected by Buddha because "unless the attainments of morality, mental training, and full knowledge have been practised and realized he is far from being an ascetic, far from being a brahmin. It is in so far as a monk practises the thought of friendliness without hatred or ill-will, and with the destruction of the āsavas (lust, desire for existence, false views), and abides in this actual life having himself grasped and realized

[1] *Jaina Sūtras*, transl. by H. Jacobi, vol. ii.
[2] In *Majjh.*, i, 77, Buddha is said to have formerly practised them himself.

emancipation of mind and emancipation of knowledge, that freed from the āsavas he is a (true) ascetic and brahmin ".

These practices and other frightful kinds of self-mortification are also discussed from the point of view of their value in the training of mind and body. The *Mahā-Saccaka-sutta* (*Majjh.*, i, 237) represents austerities as being practised by Gotama during his six years' search for the right method. A man is trained in body when, if pleasant feelings arise, they do not overpower his mind, and he is trained in mind when his mind is not overpowered by painful feelings. Since the time when Gotama left his home and donned the yellow dress, on no occasion did pleasant or painful feeling overpower his mind. He found that only those ascetics and brahmins in whom sensual passions are calmed are capable of knowledge and highest enlightenment. Without his mind being once overcome by painful feeling he practised stoppage of breathing until the gods thought he was dead; he took less and less food until he was reduced to a skeleton; but he found that with the sharpest austerities he could not reach superhuman truly noble knowledge and insight. Then he remembered how once when his father was working he sat under the shade of a rose-apple tree and attained the first trance.[1] Perhaps that was the way to enlightenment. Thinking that there was no danger in the pleasure that was without sensual desires and without evil ideas he took solid food again. His five followers then left him, but he went on to practise the four trances, and found that the pleasant feeling which arose did not overpower his mind. The rest of the sutta is the description of attaining enlightenment in the same words as are used of every disciple who attains it, as described above (p. 47). The only difference is that Buddha was the discoverer of the method.

The view that extinction of pain is brought about by the exhaustion of karma is attributed to the Nigaṇṭhas. It is the most extreme form of the doctrine of action (*kiriyavāda*). Karma is conceived as something flowing into the individual. An action produces so much karma, whether it was intended or not. As represented by the Buddhists, the Nigaṇṭhas hold that " whatever an individual experiences, whether

[1] The Pāli commentary places this event in early childhood, but it is explained in three other ways in Sanskrit works: cf. *The Life of Buddha*, p. 44; below, p. 136.

GOTAMA PRACTISING AUSTERITIES

[*face p.* 116

pleasurable, painful, or indifferent, is all the effect of his previous karma, and that so by the extinction of old karmas through austerity and by the non-performance of new karmas there is no outflow in the future, and that through there being no outflow in the future there will be destruction of karma, through destruction of karma destruction of pain, through the destruction of pain destruction of feeling, and through destruction of feeling all pain will be exhausted". The view that an act of killing, even if unintentional, involved retribution is rejected in *Kathāvatthu*, xx, 1. The Jains are charged with holding it in *Abhk.*, iv, 73; cf. *Jaina Sūtras*.

Buddhism by making the ethical character of an action depend upon the motive and not upon the external performance transformed the doctrine of karma. The aim was no longer to attend to external actions, but to the motives that inspire them. As Buddhaghosa puts it, the Buddhas are like lions which when shot attack the hunter; they make the pain to cease and teach the cessation of pain by referring to the cause. The heretics are like dogs which attack the stick that hit them; they teach the cessation of pain by teaching the application of self-mortification and such things; they refer to the effect, not the cause.[1] Doubtless this teaching was not entirely new. We find truly ethical concepts in the Upanishads. But it was an important protest against a rival view of karma, which was carried to its extreme by the Jains.

The whole scheme of Buddhist training came to be arranged in four stages of the Noble Eightfold Path. Even those who do not go beyond faith and love towards Buddha are destined to heaven. They whose practice is in accordance with the Doctrine and faith are destined to enlightenment. To enter on the Path requires an intellectual change.

They who have cast off the three fetters of belief in a permanent individuality (*sakkāya*), doubt, and belief in mere morality and rites are those who have reached the first stage of Entering the stream (*sotāpatti*). They are not liable to be reborn in an unhappy existence, and are destined to enlightenment. They who have cast off the three fetters and weakened the bonds of passion, hatred, and stupidity have reached the second stage of the Once-returner (*sakadāgāmin*). They will return once to this world before making an end of pain.

[1] Vism., 507.

They who have cast off the five lower fetters (the three above with sensual passion and malice), and who arise by apparitional birth [1] in a higher stage of existence, and there attain Nirvāṇa, without returning to this world, have reached the third stage of the Non-returner (*anāgāmin*).

They who are arahats have destroyed the āsavas (lust, desire for existence, ignorance), they have completed what was to be done, they have laid down the burden, obtained their end, and with the destruction of the fetter of desire for existence are liberated with complete knowledge. Their course cannot be pointed out.[2]

This scheme is not a course of training, like the four contemplations or the three stages of morality, concentration, and full knowledge, but it is a scholastic elaboration of the stages attained by liberation from the ten fetters. Each stage is also subdivided into the path and the fruit. It depends upon the training, not upon any external act, for a man may enter the Order and yet be far from entering the stream. We are told of a learned disciple who had learnt the three Piṭakas and expounded them to five hundred disciples. He was able to answer Buddha's questions about the Trances and the Attainments, but he was put to shame by an ignorant monk who had won insight, for he was unable to answer a question about Entering the stream.[3]

[1] There are four kinds of birth—oviparous, viviparous, birth from moisture (as insects), and apparitional (*opapātika*), which takes place in the higher planes of existence without any physiological process, and the individual reborn (as a god or still higher being) simply appears there.

[2] *Majjh.*, i, 141.

[3] *Dhp. com.*, i, 154.

CHAPTER X

RELEASE AND NIRVĀṆA

THE prevalence in Indian religions of a doctrine of release (*moksha, vimukti*) from the ills of existence was a natural result of the conception of the universe as a world of change and rebirth. Each school had its own special teaching, and the Buddhist doctrine stands out in its originality and in the ethical character of the whole scheme. The disciple advances not by accumulating good deeds, but by quenching those tendencies which lead him to do evil. The perfected monk reaches a stage not beyond good and evil, but a state in which his moral training is so perfected that it is impossible for him to commit murder, theft, lying, and other sins.[1] Its greatest contrast is perhaps with Jainism, to which in externals it has many resemblances. The Jain doctrine, says Jacobi, is that " liberated souls will be embodied no more ; they have accomplished absolute purity ; they dwell in the state of perfection at the top of the universe, and have no more to do with worldly affairs ; they have reached *nirvāṇa* (*nivṛti*, or *mukti*). Metaphysically the difference between the mundane (the still transmigrating) and the liberated soul consists in this, that the former is entirely filled with subtle matter, as a bag is filled with sand, while the latter is absolutely pure and free from any material alloy." [2]

The Buddhist view has rather a resemblance to the doctrine of the Upanishads in that release depends upon a certain kind of knowledge. But in the Upanishads it is the knowledge of an existing fact, the fact, expressed in the most varied ways that the self is identical with Brahma. The Brahma-knowers become " plunged in Brahma ", " the self enters the Brahma-abode ", or " enters the all " ; " it becomes one in the imperishable," and " goes to the divine Person ". When in Buddhism the doctrine that the world and the self are the same is touched upon, it is not rejected as false, but put aside as a useless view.

In some respects Buddhism has a closer relation to the

[1] *Dīgha*, iii, 235. [2] *ERE.*, vii, 468.

doctrine of Sānkhya and Yoga. Sānkhya, like Buddhism, emphasizes the existence of pain, and teaches that release from pain is brought about by dissociation from any contact with the world of change. This is produced by knowledge, but it is the knowledge that the purusha, the imperishable self, is already absolutely distinct and separate.

For Buddhism final release is brought about by a process of training of the self, in which it is released by stages from the bonds or fetters that hinder complete insight. The disciple, when he begins to meditate (p. 46), devotes himself to purifying his mind from the five hindrances, sensual passion or longing for the world, malice, sloth and torpor, distraction and agitation, and doubt. He is like a man freed from a debt, or recovered from sickness, or loosed from the bonds of prison, or as a freed slave. There is also a list of ten fetters, which are fitted into the scheme of the four stages of the Path. The first five are the lower fetters: belief in a permanent individuality, doubt, belief in mere morality and rites, sensual passion, malice; and the five higher: desire for existence in the world of form (which here includes everything below the formless world), desire for existence in the formless world, pride, distraction, and ignorance.[1] Other forms of the ten fetters exist, and they appear to be a later formulation than the fundamental division of the three āsavas: sensual desire, desire for existence (two forms of craving or grasping), and ignorance. Still another arrangement of those qualities of character which have to be eradicated exists in the certainly later list of the *kilesas*, usually translated depravities: greed, hatred, stupidity, pride, false views, doubt, sloth, distraction, shamelessness, recklessness.[2] The first three also occur independently as the three roots of demerit or bad action. Greed (*lobha*) is a positive form of craving and is correlative to hatred (*dosa*), the hostility to what is unpleasant. Stupidity or dullness of mind (*moha*) equally leads to unmeritorious actions. It is these roots that have to be destroyed, not the mere avoidance of bad karma which they produce.

[1] *Dīgha*, iii, 234; another list at *Dhsang.*, 1113; in the latter the sixth and seventh are combined in *bhavarāga*, desire for existence in any form. This is really the second āsava.

[2] *Dhsang.*, 1548; a list of eight, *Mahānidd.*, 258; of twelve 386; of six *Dhsang.*, 67.

With the destruction of all these, whether called fetters, depravities, or āsavas, the disciple is released (*vimutta*). He is released with complete freedom from grasping, knowing that all compounds are impermanent, all compounds are painful, all things are without a self, and that everything which has an origin has also a cessation."[1] This is the emancipation of full knowledge (*paññā*), in which with the destruction of the āsavas all false views are destroyed, and with the knowledge of the Truths he has come to know things as they are. He is also said to be emancipated with release of heart or mind.[2] This is the actual experience of release obtained by the attainment of the trances or the eight releases. He is then said to be released in two ways (*ubhato-bhāgavimutta*), with the actual knowledge of his state, and with the ecstatic experience of being free from all bonds.[3]

The counterpart of full knowledge is release, and the counterpart of release is *nibbāna*, Nirvāṇa. This is said to have been the answer given by the nun Dhammadinnā to the layman Visākha (*Majjh.*, i, 304). When he asked what was the counterpart to Nirvāṇa, she said, " you push your questions too far, Visākha. The religious life is plunged in Nirvāṇa, its aim is Nirvāṇa, its end is Nirvāṇa. If you wish, go and ask the Lord, and as he explains it, thus bear it in mind." The layman did so, and the Lord replied, " the nun Dhammadinnā is learned, she is of great wisdom. If you had asked me the question, I should have explained it as she did. That, indeed, is the answer. Thus bear it in mind."

Nirvāṇa is the final state that the disciple reaches with the completion of the course of his training:

> The bhikkhu, filled with wisdom here,
> In lust, desire, delighting not,
> Repose, the immortal, has attained,
> The unchangeable Nirvāṇa-state.

The term *nirvāṇa*[4] was correctly explained by Colebrooke

[1] *Mahānidd.*, 283.

[2] *Ceto*; this includes the emotions, but does not, like " heart ", exclude the intellect.

[3] *Majjh.*, i, 477; *Pugg.*, 14. The fall of Godhika from his state of " temporary release " is said to have been the fall from this ecstatic state; see p. 131.

[4] A misconception (not found in Childers) has arisen about the distinction between *nirvāṇa* and *parinirvāṇa*. The latter is supposed to be the nirvāṇa reached at death, " complete nirvāṇa." But there is not the slightest evidence for this distinction. It has already been explained from the grammatical point of view (I think by E. Kuhn). *Pari-* compounded with a verb converts

a century ago: "Both these sects (Buddhists and Jains) propose, for the grand object to which man should aspire, the attainment of a final happy state, from which there is no return. All concur in assigning to its attainment the same term, *mukti*, or *moksha*, with some shades of difference in the interpretation of the word: as emancipation, deliverance from evil; liberation from worldly bonds; relief from further transmigration, etc. . . .

"The term which the *Bauddhas*, as well as *Jainas*, more particularly affect, and which, however, is also used by the rest, is *nirvāṇa*, profound calm. In its ordinary acceptation, as an adjective, it signifies extinct, as a fire which is gone out; set, as a luminary which has gone down; defunct, as a saint who has passed away; its etymology is from *vā*, to blow as wind, with the preposition *nir* used in a negative sense: it means calm and unruffled. The notion which is attached to the word, in the acceptation now under consideration, is that of perfect apathy . . . Perpetual uninterrupted apathy can hardly be said to differ from eternal sleep. The notion of it as of a happy condition seems to be derived from the experience of ecstacies, or from that of profound sleep from which a person awakes refreshed. The pleasant feeling is referred back to the period of actual repose . . . the *vedānta* considers the individual soul to be temporarily, during the period of profound sleep, in the like condition of reunion with the Supreme, which it permanently arrives at on its final emancipation from body.

"This doctrine is not that of the *Jainas* nor *Bauddhas*. But neither do they consider the endless repose allotted to their perfect saints as attended with a discontinuance of individuality. It is not annihilation, but unceasing apathy,

the verb from the expression of a state to the expression of the achievement of an action: *nirvāṇa* is the state of release; *parinirvāṇa* is the attaining of that state. The monk *parinirvāti* "attains Nirvāna" at the time of enlightenment as well as at death. The *P.T.S. Dictionary* defines *parinibbāna* as "complete Nirvāna", but immediately goes on to show that the same term is used of both kinds. Nirvāṇa at death is when a Buddha or an arahat *anupādisesāya nibbānadhātuyā parinibbāyati* "attains nirvāna with the nirvāna-element which is without a substrate of rebirth" (*Dīgha*, ii, 136). The word *nibbāna* is used in this definition of "final Nirvāṇa". The nirvāṇa attained during life (at enlightenment) is defined in the same words except that *saupādisesāya* is used, "he attains nirvāṇa with the nirvāṇa-element which is with a substrate of rebirth." When Buddha's attainment of nirvāṇa is referred to, especially in the later literature, the nirvāṇa at death is generally meant, but if the distinction is expressed it is always by *saupādisesa* and *anupādisesa* (Skt. *sopadhiśeṣa* and *nirupadhiśeṣa*). See p. 131.

which they understand to be the extinction (*nirvāṇa*) of their saints." [1]

It need not be said that the etymological analysis of a word common to several religions will not decide its meaning for Buddhism. Even if the idea of annihilation is present in *nirvāṇa,* there is nothing to imply the annihilation of the individual, and it is used by sects for whom this meaning would be impossible. It is not found in the early Upanishads, and probably did not originate in brahminical circles. In Jainism it is the usual word for the state of the released disciple, who is in no wise annihilated. As Jainism is older than Buddhism, it is unlikely that the word was borrowed from the latter, and the Buddhists may have taken it over from the Jains with the already established meaning of final release.

Colebrooke's view was first discussed by Burnouf,[2] but as he had to depend chiefly on Tibetan translations the question was not much advanced. He assumed that extinction meant the extinction of the individual. The problem has been much discussed since, sometimes with an evident bias showing the influence of the writer's own views of the nature of human destiny. Another unfortunate fact has been the habit of speaking of the passages in the Scriptures as the *ipsissima verba* of Buddha without testing the assumption, in spite of the emphatic words of Franke that " it is given as yet to no mortal man to demonstrate that any one Buddhist sentence was spoken during the lifetime of the Founder." [3]

Oldenberg found a large number of passages bearing on the subject, but the most decisive of these are attributed to disciples, not to Buddha himself. They are interpretations which even his followers did not venture to ascribe to the Master. What we learn from them in the first place is the doctrine which had become established in the community. Whether it was the original doctrine, or whether the disciples had forgotten or actually effaced an earlier teaching rests on complex considerations.

The literal meaning of *nirvāṇa* does not help us. It means " blowing out " as of a lamp, and the verb is used literally

[1] *Trans. RAS.*, 1827, p. 566. (*Misc. Essays*, ed. 1873, p. 424.)

[2] *Introd.*, pp. 18, 589.

[3] " The Buddhist Councils at Rājagaha and Vesālī," transl. by Mrs. Rhys Davids, *JPTS.*, 1908, p. 20.

of the extinguishing of a light, but this is not a prominent notion in the treatment of the subject, and the meaning has been modified by its being connected with another verb, for the participle is formed from *nir-vṛ* or *ni-vṛ*, meaning tranquil, happy, ceased, and *parinirvṛta* in its technical sense is " having attained nirvāṇa ". In any case it does not assert the annihilation of the individual. Buddhist polemics are continually directed against two views, that of permanence (*sassatā*) and that of annihilation (*uccheda*). They are prominent in the *Brahmajāla-sutta*, and are elsewhere attributed to the teachers Pakudha and Ajita Kesakambalin respectively (pp. 72, 73). The Buddhist attitude to these views is expressed in the list of undetermined questions (*avyākṛtavastūni*) :

(1) Whether the universe is eternal or not.

(2) Whether the universe is finite or not.

(3) Whether that which is the vital principle (*jīva*) is the body.

(4) Whether after death a Tathāgata (a released person) exists or not, whether he exists and does not exist, whether he is neither existent nor non-existent.[1]

The first two of these views are given in the *Brahmajāla-sutta*, and the first is there combined with the doctrine that also the self is eternal. In this list the question about the self is included in the third and fourth views, but is stated in quite different language. The assertion that the vital principle is the same as the body would involve the doctrine of annihilation as stated by Ajita, that both fools and wise at the dissolution of the body are cut off and destroyed. But here the word for body is neither the usual *kāya* nor *rūpa*, but *sarīra*. The word for the spiritual part is also different, *jīva* merely meaning life. The phrase *taṃ jīvaṃ taṃ sarīraṃ* looks like the statement of a tenet expressed in the words of the teacher who held it. It occurs separately in the *Jāliya-sutta* (*Dīgha*, i, 159), where it was put as a question to Buddha by two wandering ascetics. Their purpose, according to Buddhaghosa, was to get either a positive or a negative answer, and thus to accuse him of annihilationism or eternalism. His reply is to describe the attaining of the

[1] *Majjh.*, i, 157, etc. ; *Mvyut.*, 206 ; *Dhs.*, 137 ; they are four in number, but with their different modes of stating them they amount to fourteen.

four trances and enlightenment, and to conclude that for one who thus knows and thus perceives it is not fitting for him to say either.

The doctrine of annihilationism as put by Ajita implies annihilation at death, but other forms of the doctrine in the *Brahmajāla-sutta* admit the existence of a finer self, which yet is finally annihilated. For Buddhism neither of these points is fundamental. Perhaps more than any other Indian religion it held views about the departed resembling those of the modern spiritualists. The Scriptures are full of stories of the materialization of dead persons, and of individuals with special powers of communicating with them. And if these stories do not belong to the earliest stages of the Doctrine, it is all the more clear that they were told by the same persons who refused to recognize the eternity of the self. The fundamental question is whether a Tathāgata [1] exists after death ; and that is put aside in the fourth undetermined question : every possible way of asserting it or denying it is stated and rejected.

It is evident from the *Sutta of the simile of the snake* (*Majjh.*, i, 139) that the Buddhists were accused of nihilism, not merely on account of any denial like that of Ajita's, but because their doctrine of release was held to imply it. Buddha is there made to say that not all the gods with Indra, Brahmā, and Pajāpati are able to track out a monk with mind released and say, "there rests the consciousness of a Tathāgata." Then follows a repudiation of the charge of annihilationism : "some ascetics and brahmins accuse me wrongly, baselessly, falsely, and groundlessly, saying that the ascetic Gotama is a nihilist, and preaches the annihilation, destruction, and non-existence of an existent being. That is what I am not and do not affirm. Both previously and now I preach pain and the cessation of pain."

Here the charge of annihilationism is simply denied. In a discourse attributed to Sāriputta it is discussed and refuted. The elder Yamaka had formed the view, "thus do I understand the doctrine taught by the Lord, that a monk in whom the āsavas are destroyed is annihilated and destroyed with the dissolution of the body, and does not exist after death." Yamaka is made to admit that the body and all

[1] It is clear that this term here applies not merely to a Buddha, but to anyone who has attained final release. Buddhaghosa commenting on *Dīgha*, i, 27, takes *Tathāgata* in the sense of *satta*.

the other constituents of the individual are impermanent, and that, therefore, he cannot say of any one of them, " this is mine, I am this, this is my self." " What do you think, friend Yamaka, is a Tathāgata the body ? " " No, friend." (And so of feeling, perception, the aggregates, and consciousness.) " Do you look on a Tathāgata as existing in body, etc. ? " " No, friend." " Do you look on a Tathāgata as existing apart from body, etc.—or as consisting of them—or as existing without any of them ? " To all these questions Yamaka answers no. No loophole is left for asserting the existence of a self either within or beyond the five constituents. The conclusion is that " a Tathāgata cannot be held to be perceived as existing even in this life in truth and reality." [1]

The undetermined questions are often made the basis of a discourse, in which Buddha gives reasons for refusing to answer them. He declares that it is not on the truth of any of these alternatives that the practice of the religious life depends. " There is still birth, there is old age, there is death, grief, lamentation, suffering, sorrow, and despair, of which I preach the destruction even in this present life. Therefore, bear in mind what I have not determined as being undetermined . . . And why have I not determined them ? Because they are not useful, do not belong to the principle of the religious life, and do not tend to revulsion, absence of passion, cessation, tranquillity, insight, enlightenment, Nirvāṇa." [2]

When the wanderer Vacchagotta asks where a monk whose mind is released is reborn, and declares himself dissatisfied with the reply that it does not fit the case to say that he is reborn or not reborn, or both reborn and not reborn, or neither reborn nor not reborn, Buddha declares : " profound is this Doctrine, hard to see, hard to comprehend, calm, excellent, beyond the sphere of reasoning, subtle, intelligible only to the wise. For you it is hard to understand, who hold other views, another faith, other inclinations, another discipline, and another teacher. Therefore, I will question you in turn, and do you answer as you think fit. If a fire were burning before you, would you know it ? I should. If one asked you on account of what the fire burns what would you answer ? I should say the fire burns on account of the fuel of grass and sticks. If the fire were

[1] *Saṃy.*, iii, 109. [2] *Majjh.*, i, 431.

extinguished, would you know it was extinguished ? I should. If one asked you in what direction it had gone, east, west, north, or south, what would you answer ? It does not fit the case, for the fire was burning on account of the fuel of grass and sticks, and through consuming this it is without food, and is what is called extinct. Even so, Vacchagotta, the body (with feeling, perception, aggregates, and consciousness) by which one might define a Tathāgata is passed away, cut off at the root, uprooted like a palm-tree, made non-existent, not liable to arise again in the future. A Tathāgata released from what is called body, etc., is profound, immeasurable, hard to fathom, like the great ocean. It does not fit the case to say that he is reborn or not reborn or reborn and not reborn or neither reborn nor not reborn." [1]

In spite of this repeated refusal to make any assertion one way or the other, Oldenberg came to the conclusion that it was a mere shirking of the question in order not to shock a weak-minded hearer.[2] He quoted another legend of Vacchagotta, who came and asked Buddha whether the ātman exists, and then whether it is non-existent. In each case Buddha remained silent. After Vacchagotta had gone, Ānanda asked Buddha why he did not reply. "If, Ānanda, when Vacchagotta asked, 'is there an ātman ?' I had said, 'there is an ātman,' then I should have been one of those ascetics and brahmins who hold the doctrine of eternalism. But if I had replied 'there is no ātman', then I should have been one of those who hold the doctrine of annihilation. And if, when Vacchagotta asked 'is there an ātman' ? I had replied, 'there is an ātman,' would it have been in accordance with the knowledge that all things are without ātman ?" "No, Lord." "If I had said, 'there is no ātman,' the bewildered Vacchagotta would have become still more bewildered, thinking, 'then did my ātman exist before, and now it does not exist ?' " [3]

Oldenberg's conclusion was, "through the shirking of the question as to the existence or non-existence of the ego, is heard the answer, to which the premises of the Buddhist teaching tended : The ego is not. Or, what is equivalent : The Nirvâna is annihilation."

[1] *Majjh.*, i, 486.
[2] *Buddha*, 1st ed., Engl. tr., p. 272.
[3] *Saṃy.*, iv, 400.

It is certain, however, that this is a conclusion which the Buddhists never drew. In this very sutta annihilationism is rejected. It is not really to the point to say that the Buddhist premises tended to this conclusion. The only real question is what conclusion did the Buddhists draw and what for them was the logical inference. Existence (*bhava*) for them depended upon knowledge obtained through the six senses, except the knowledge of the permanent attained at enlightenment. They recognized the individual as consisting of elements perceptible to the senses. They had before them the question as to what becomes of him when everything that can be predicated of him is withdrawn. What the clairvoyants and spiritualists can tell us of discarnate spirits is of no help here. That is merely about existence in another plane of the universe. The Buddhists had reached the conception of a state of which neither existence nor non-existence as we know it could be asserted. They were not left in suspense that the answer might be one way or the other. The question was put in such a way that they rested certain that an answer was neither useful nor possible.

This state is described with a wealth of epithets as, "the harbour of refuge, the cool cave, the island amidst the floods, the place of bliss, emancipation, liberation, safety, the supreme, the transcendental, the uncreated, the tranquil, the home of ease, the calm, the end of suffering, the medicine for all evil, the unshaken, the ambrosia, the immaterial, the imperishable, the abiding, the further shore, the unending, the bliss of effort, the supreme joy, the ineffable, the detachment, the holy city." [1] These are names of Nirvāṇa used by those who have realized it in this life, and in whom there is still a "substratum of existence" as we know it. What when that substratum is withdrawn? Then everything is withdrawn by which anything can be asserted. He who is released is "profound, immeasurable, hard to fathom, like the great ocean". And if the disciples refused to assert anything, they were not agnostics or eel-wrigglers, but were merely thinking clearly and refusing to express the inexpressible. It does not fit the case to assert existence or non-existence when its object has been explained as being of quite a different kind from that about which assertion is possible.

[1] Rhys Davids, *Early Buddhism*, p. 72.

There are two collections of verses attributed to several hundreds of monks and nuns, all of whom were held to have attained enlightenment. They contain no more guessing or theorizing about the ineffable and inexpressible than the words attributed to Buddha himself. As Mrs. Rhys Davids says of the nuns, "their verses do not seem to betray anything that can be construed as a consciousness that hidden glories, more wonderful than the brief span of 'cool' and calm that they now know as Arahants, are awaiting them." [1]

Two of the "fervent utterances" in the *Udāna* (viii, 1–3) have been held to be assertions of such hidden glories after death:

> There is the stage (*āyatana*), where there is neither earth nor water, nor fire, nor wind, nor the stage of the infinity of space, nor the stage of nothingness, nor the stage of neither consciousness nor non-consciousness, neither this world, nor the other world, nor sun and moon. There, monks, I say there is neither coming nor going, nor staying nor passing away, nor arising; without support or going on or basis is it. This is the end of pain.
>
> There is an unborn, an unbecome, an unmade, an uncompounded; if there were not, there would not be an escape from the born, the become, the made, the compounded. But because there is an unborn, an unbecome, an unmade, an uncompounded, therefore there is an escape from the born, the become, the made, and the compounded.

This is a description in entirely negative terms of the Nirvāṇa which every arahat attained, an emphatic assertion of what was to him the only reality. But of the state that the arahat may reach after death there is not a word.

Oldenberg's view may be taken as representative of those investigators who would commit the Buddhists, in spite of all their efforts, to a one-sided dogmatism, and make them assert not what they themselves inferred, but what others thought they should do.[2] But Oldenberg later came to a different conclusion. He pointed out that there is a change of standpoint from the view that the question *ought* not to be answered to the view that it *could* not be answered. (This merely means that different disciples discussed it in different ways.) The nun Khemā (again a disciple is expounding) says that the Lord has not explained it, just as no one can measure the water of the ocean, for, "freed from the designation of body (and the other constituents)

[1] *Psalms of the Sisters*, Introd., xxxi.

[2] The chief representatives of the annihilation view are Childers (*Pāli Dict.*, s.v.) and J. D'Alwis, *Buddhist Nirvāna*, Colombo, 1871.

a Tathāgata is profound, immeasurable, hard to fathom, like the great ocean."[1] Does the idea, says Oldenberg, which Buddhism had about that Beyond imply an absolutizing of individual being as in later Sānkhya, or had they floating in their minds a universal, absolute being in which the secret of achievement is realized ? " From the way in which Buddhism treats this class of problems, or rather refuses to treat them, it follows that the ideas here in question can only be traced through a haze. But the traces that can be made out indicate rather that a universal being reaching far beyond the limits of the individual floated in their minds : an absolute, naturally not as *Weltgrund*, because in fact they had no impulse to ask about a *Weltgrund*, either openly or covertly, but an absolute as final highest goal." This is a withdrawal of the charge that if Buddha had drawn the last conclusion of his own principles, he would have arrived at annihilation.

Dr. F. O. Schrader has attacked " the nihilistic conception of Parinibbānam " and defended " the assertion to the contrary ", but without stating clearly what he means by this.[2] He says quite naively, " I cannot here explain the reasons why, to my way of thinking, philosophy is forced to accept the metaphysical conception of the Absolute One." Not only that, but he is also certain that Buddha accepted it. " It was the Buddha, without any doubt, who banished out of the world the last glitter of immutability, and liberated, on the other hand, from the last terrestrial feature it still possessed, viz. consciousness, the notion of the Absolute." With such premises much can be proved.

One of Dr. Schrader's conclusions is that " it is beyond doubt that in Buddha's opinion there rests of the *parinibbuto* (one who has attained Nirvāṇa) not the slightest shade of individuality ". It need hardly be said that this is only Dr. Schrader's " way of thinking ", but it does involve a question more than once touched upon by the commentators. Already in the Upanishads it was a problem whether the liberated ātman knew that it was liberated. Indra was told that when one is asleep, composed, and knows no dream, that is the ātman. With this answer he was dissatisfied, for " such a one does not know with the thought, ' I am he,'

[1] *Lehre der Up.*, p. 309.
[2] " On the problem of Nirvāṇa," *JPTS.*, 1905, p. 157.

so that he becomes one who has gone to destruction ". He went back to know more, but after five more years of study all he learnt was that while one is in the body there is no freedom from pleasure and pain; when he is without the body he is not touched by pleasure and pain.[1]

Buddhism makes no such confident assertion as this, nor any positive statement at all about the final state of the released. The commentators, however, speak of the last consciousness and the last thought. It is in the form of consciousness that the individual exists when transmigration takes place. The story is told of Godhika (*Saṃy.*, i, 109), who attained temporary release [2] six times, but fell away. On attaining it the seventh time he cut his throat. When Buddha and his monks came to see him, a dark cloud was moving in all directions. "That," said Buddha, "is Māra the wicked looking to see where Godhika's consciousness has become established; but Godhika has attained Nirvāṇa with consciousness not established anywhere." This does not tell anything positive about the state of Nirvāṇa, but it illustrates the doctrine that consciousness with all the other constituents of the individual "stops" (*nirujjhati*) with the death of the arahat.

Psychological theorizings such as these do not tell us anything more about the fundamental question. The list of undetermined questions remained established like a creed throughout the history of Buddhism. The distinction of two kinds of Nirvāṇa is probably such a development. It is one which would raise itself as a problem after Buddha's death. In *Dhammapada* 89 there is a reference to "those who have attained Nirvāṇa in the world with the destruction of the āsavas ".[3] The commentator here explains "attained Nirvāṇa" as attained by the two attainings of Nirvāṇa (*dvīhi parinibbānehi*), (1) that which is with a remainder of substrate of rebirth after reaching arahatship and getting rid of the course of the depravities, and (2) that which is

[1] *Chānd. Up.*, viii, 11, 12.

[2] *Samayavimutti*, *Kathāv*, i, 86; *Mvyut.*, 46; this, according to the commentators, was release of mind obtained by practice of the trances, and Godhika, through sickness, could not maintain his state of trance. The *Abhidharmakośa* (vi, 58) also discusses the case of Godhika, and says that, although he fell from his state of temporary release, he did not fall from his state of arahat.

[3] *Khīṇāsavā . . . loke parinibbutā*; here, again, the word supposed to describe final Nirvāṇa is used of the living monk.

without a remainder of substrate of rebirth with the cessation of the last thought and getting rid of the course of the khandhas. What is to be understood by this substrate of rebirth has been disputed, for in Pāli the term is *upādi* and in Sanskrit *upadhi*.[1] It is now generally agreed to be a collective name for the khandhas, the elements constituting the individual, which at death, unless dispersed by knowledge of the truths, continue their existence in a new birth. The form that they have at the moment of conception is consciousness (*viññāṇa, citta*), and with enlightenment it is said to cease. It is not said to be annihilated, but it stops or ceases (*nirujjhati*) to transmigrate. What that implies may be still further argued, but it is known only to the arahat.

In these discussions by Sāriputta, Dhammadinnā, Khemā, and other disciples is it possible to distinguish any primitive teaching? They had before them a conception clearly separated out from two rival theories, the theory that there was something in the world of sense absolutely permanent and eternal, which they found to be contradicted by experience, and on the other hand the theory of annihilation, which contradicted their own theory of moral equity. Between these two they were not in a position of suspense. They knew that there was a state to be attained, which they defined only negatively, the goal of the Eightfold Path, the end of the disciple's training in morality, concentration, and full knowledge.

Doubtless all this was not explicit in the earliest teaching. We have the direct evidence of the various efforts of disciples to state it convincingly, and to restate it in opposition to rival theories. But even the earliest teaching about the self was subordinate to the teaching about the final end. Rival theories of the self were rejected because they were in conflict with the ideal of the goal. This ideal involved a system of discipline differing from all other Indian systems, and evidently due to the genius of one man. On this was based a system of moral and mental training directed to one goal. The teaching about that goal, we also have reason to believe, was due to one mind, the mind that taught the way to it.

[1] See *PTS. Dict.*, s.v., and H. O. Lovejoy, "The Buddhist technical terms *upādāna* and *upādisesa*," *JAOS.*, 1898, pt. ii, p. 126.

CHAPTER XI

BUDDHA

BUDDHA was not only "the teacher of the Way" and "the producer of the unproduced Path": he was for the Buddhist the actuality of the central doctrine, the one who had lived it and reached the goal. Hence everything that we learn in the Scriptures about his personal history is coloured by dogmatic views concerning the nature and destiny of a Buddha and of those acts which were essential steps in his career. The records of personal details which we find in the Scriptures are generally not the Buddha-word but additions due mainly to classes of reciters (*bhāṇaka*) of the discourses. The two most important classes were the reciters of the Dīgha and the reciters of the Majjhima, and it is easy to see that they possessed traditions which sometimes became incorporated in the text. We also find divergent traditions, for the Jātaka commentator after telling how the four signs, which appeared to Gotama just before he left the world, occurred on different days, adds, "the Dīgha-reciters, however, say that they happened on the same day."[1] Evidently unwritten divergent traditions existed.

This is most obvious in the case of the statements attached to each discourse saying where and on what occasion it was given.[2] Some of these may be genuine records, but the fact that in the case of every discourse the same kind of statement is given makes it probable that many of them rest on surmise. Besides such formal statements we often find complete legends. These are most frequent in the Vinaya, where each rule is furnished with an account of the event which led to its promulgation; but legends of the same kind occur in the suttas, their insertion there being

[1] *Jāt.*, i, 59.

[2] These statements are called *nidānas*, and sometimes are merely indicated, e.g. *Sāvatthī nidānaṃ* "occasion at Sāvatthī", or merely "Sāvatthī", meaning that the whole usual statement about Buddha staying there is to be repeated. The commentator on the *Buddhavaṃsa* draws attention to the fact that this work begins without a nidāna.

justified by the Buddha-word which they contain. Passages like these make it probable that they were part of a complete legend, but a continuous life of Buddha, except in a very concise form, is not found until long after the close of the Pāli Canon. In several schools the separate legends of the Vinaya were collected to form an avadāna, a complete account of the " heroic deeds " of the Master. In the Mahāsanghika school it was the *Mahāvastu.* From Chinese sources we hear of several Sarvāstivāda schools which had such a biography, and the *Lalita-vistara* is probably a Mahāyāna elaboration of a Sarvāstivāda avadāna. All these works conclude with the Enlightenment and the immediately following events of " setting in motion the Wheel of the Doctrine ".

The Pāli Canon has no such work, but in several commentaries biographical accounts are found. Of these the most important is the Introduction to the *Jātaka,* the *Nidāna-kathā.* Its account of Buddha's previous existences is based on the *Buddhavaṃsa,* and the story of his last existence is taken from the commentaries and the Canon. Its special importance is that it shows a definite stage in the growth of the Buddha doctrine, as it can be compared both with what we find in other schools and with the statements in the Canon. Its chief difference from earlier accounts lies in its developed doctrine of the Bodhisatta and his ten Perfections, the ten virtues which he practises during his preparation for Buddhahood. They are mentioned only in the two latest books of the Sutta-piṭaka.

The author divides his account into three parts, nidānas, the " occasions " or causes which led to the events recorded in the tales. The first is the " distant occasion ", the whole period from the time when Gotama as the ascetic Sumedha saw Dīpankara Buddha, and made the resolution that he would not there and then realize the Doctrine, but would put that aim deliberately aside, and first win omniscience and become a Buddha. He resolved that after having done so he would " embark on the ship of the Doctrine, and take great multitudes across the ocean of transmigration, and then attain Nirvāṇa ". He meditated on the eight conditions for attaining Buddhahood, and especially on the ten Perfections, the ten virtues which Bodhisattas perfectly attain during their career—almsgiving, morality, renunciation, wisdom, exertion, patience, truth, resolution, friendliness, equanimity. Dīpankara prophesied that his vow would be fulfilled, and so did all the succeeding Buddhas, under all of whom he repeated his vow, until he was born as a god in the Tusita heaven.

Then the second nidāna, "the non-distant," begins with his last birth up to his attaining of enlightenment. When the time for his last birth came, he made five great surveys (*vilokana*), and reflected on (1) the right time, when the age of men is neither too long nor too short for them to reflect on old age and death; (2) the continent, Jambudīpa (India), for only there are Buddhas born; (3) the country, which was the Middle District, and in it was Kapilavatthu; (4) the family, and he chose a kshatriya family, as that was then in greater honour than the brahmin caste, and king Suddhodana would be his father; (5) the mother, queen Māyā, because she was sober and had kept the five lay precepts from her birth.

But Suddhodana was his father only in a legal sense.[1] At the midsummer festival queen Māyā took the eight Uposatha vows of abstinence, and entering her chamber fell asleep and dreamt a dream. In her dream the Bodhisatta in the form of a white elephant appeared to enter her right side. Her dream was interpreted by the brahmins, who said that she would have a son destined to be either a universal king or a Buddha. When the time of his birth drew near, she wished to go to her parents' home, but on the way she alighted to sport in the Lumbinī grove, and there the Bodhisatta was born. Four Great Brahmās received him in a golden net, and from them the four Great Kings received him and gave him to human beings. Standing on the ground he faced the east, advanced seven steps, and said, "I am the chief in the world."

In the heaven of the Thirty-three the gods were rejoicing at the news. An ascetic named Kāladevala (or Asita), who had acquired the eight Attainments, went up to this heaven and learnt the cause of their rejoicing. Coming down he went to the king's abode and asked to see the child. The boy was presented to him, and the ascetic, who could

[1] Though the queen was not a virgin, this is what is generally understood by the term virgin birth. Both in the *Mahāvastu* (ii, 5) and *Lalitavistara* (46) she asks the king's permission to spend the night alone. It is also implied in the Pāli by the fact of her taking the vows.

remember the future as well as the past, perceived that his own death would take place before the boy became a Buddha. So he smiled and then wept, but he assured the people that it was on account of his own loss.[1] Five days afterwards the name-giving ceremony took place, and the brahmins again prophesied that the child would become either a universal king or a Buddha.[2] But one of them, Koṇḍañña, prophesied his buddhahood without a doubt. It was he who was the first to be converted by Buddha. The king was told that his son would abandon the world on seeing the four signs: an old man, a sick man, a corpse, and a man who had renounced the world, so he set guards to ward off such omens.

The rest of this first period consists of his life in his three palaces, his marriage (at the age of sixteen), and his skill and achievements in the arts. The most interesting incident is that of the ploughing festival. While his father with a golden plough was performing the ceremony, the nurses placed him under a canopy beneath a rose-apple tree. They left him, and he immediately sat up cross-legged and attained the first trance. When the nurses returned they found that the shadows of the other trees had moved, but that of the rose-apple tree had stayed. This event is based on a phrase in the Canon (*Majjh.*, i, 246), but other accounts place it much later, and one of them puts it on the day before the great Renunciation.

When the gods thought that the time of his enlightenment was drawing near, they sent the four signs. At the sight of the first three he was much agitated in heart, but at the sight of the ascetic he decided to leave the world that very day. On returning from the park in his chariot his father sent the message that a son was born to him. He replied, " Rāhula is born, a fetter is born," and Rāhula became his son's name. He passed in his glory through the city, and a maiden named

[1] The resemblances of this story to that of Simeon in Luke, ii, 22 ff., have often been pointed out. It is generally admitted to be the most striking of the parallels in the legends to stories in the Gospels. If there is more than a parallel and actual borrowing on the part of the evangelist, the differences need explaining as well as the resemblances—why the ascetic wept and Simeon departed in peace, why the ascetic, who heard the news from the gods in heaven, should have been replaced by shepherds, and why Simeon is only introduced six weeks later, and then not at the child's house.

[2] The name, not mentioned here, was Siddhattha, " he whose aim is accomplished."

Kisāgotamī, seeing him from the palace roof, in joy uttered this *udāna* :

> Happy indeed is the mother,
> Happy indeed is the father,
> Happy indeed is the wife,
> Who has such a husband as he.

The Bodhisatta heard, and thought of the word " happy " (*nibbuta*, which also means " extinguished "). He thought, " when the fire of passion is extinguished, the heart is happy ; when the fire of hate, the fire of stupidity are extinguished, it is happy ; with the extinction of pride, false views, and all the depravities and pains, it is what is called *nibbutaṃ*, happy." He sent her a precious pearl necklace for having taught him a good lesson.

In the night he awoke to find his dancing girls sleeping round him in disgusting attitudes, and filled with loathing he ordered his charioteer to saddle his horse. He thought he would look at his son, but fearing to awaken his wife, stopped, and left the palace. With his charioteer behind him he fled, crossing three kingdoms until he reached the river Anomā. On the way he rejected the temptation of Māra, who promised him that in seven days he should be a universal king.

He sent his charioteer back with his ornaments and the horse, but the horse died of grief. Cutting off his hair and beard, he received the eight requisites of a monk [1] from a Mahābrahmā god, and went on to Rājagaha. There king Bimbisāra was so pleased at his behaviour that he offered him entire sovereignty. The Bodhisatta refused, but promised that when he had attained Buddhahood he would come first to Bimbisāra's kingdom. He then joined Āḷāra Kālāma, but was not satisfied with his method of practising the attainments (of yoga) nor with that of Uddaka Rāmaputta, so he left them, and began to " strive the great striving ", the practice of austerities, which he continued for six years. Having carried this out to the uttermost he concluded that austerities were not the way to enlightenment, and began to take solid food again. Then the five monks who had joined him lost faith in him and left him.

Sujātā, the daughter of a landowner, had vowed to make a thankoffering to a certain god of a banyan tree. That

[1] Three robes, bowl, razor, needle, girdle, and water-strainer ; cf. p. 19.

night the Bodhisatta had dreamt five dreams, from which he knew that he would that day win enlightenment. He went and sat under the tree, and Sujātā, thinking he was the tree god, gave him the offering in a golden bowl. This is described in great detail, for it was the only food that he received during the next forty-nine days. After eating it he took the golden bowl (his own had miraculously vanished) and set it floating on the river, saying, "if to-day I shall be able to become a Buddha, let this bowl go up stream; if not, let it go down stream." It went up, sank in a whirlpool, and struck the bowls of the three previous Buddhas.

Then he went in the direction of the Bodhi tree. On the way a grass-cutter gave him eight handfuls of grass for the seat. He sat down facing the east with the words, "may skin, sinew, and bone dry up as it will, my flesh and blood grow dry in my body; but without attaining complete enlightenment I will not leave this seat." At that time the god Māra, thinking "Prince Siddhattha wants to escape from my realm, now I will not let him escape", advanced from the north with his army, which stretched out to the mountains encircling the world. All the gods fled, but the Bodhisatta protected himself by thinking of the ten perfections, which in past lives he had perfectly practised. Māra sent storms of wind, rain, rocks, blazing weapons, charcoal, ashes, sand, and mud, but in vain. Māra then said, "Siddhattha, get up from that seat, it does not belong to you, it belongs to me." The Bodhisatta replied, "Māra, you have not fulfilled the ten Perfections, nor the minor Perfections, nor the supreme Perfections, nor even the five great Renunciations, and other practices. This seat does not belong to you, it belongs to me." Māra in rage then hurled his wheel weapon, but it became a canopy of flowers, and the Bodhisatta said, "Māra, who is your witness that you have given alms?" A shout burst forth from Māra's host, "I am witness, I am witness." Then Māra said, "Siddhattha, who is your witness that you have given alms?" The Bodhisatta had no living witness, but with his right hand he touched the earth and said, "of my great gift of the seven hundreds in my birth as Vessantara are you witness or not witness?" And the great earth with a roar surpassing the roar of Māra's hosts, said, "I was then your witness." When Māra's elephant heard the words, "you gave,

Siddhattha, the great gift, the highest gift," he fell on his knees, and the host fled in all directions. The gods returned and sang a song of victory.

It was while the sun was still over the horizon that the host was put to flight. In the first watch of the night the Bodhisatta attained the knowledge of his former existences, in the second the divine eye, and in the last the knowledge of Causal Origination. At dawn he penetrated the knowledge of omniscience, and the whole ten thousand world system was illuminated. Amid the wonders that appear when all Buddhas penetrate omniscience he uttered this *udāna*:

> Through worldly round of many births
> I ran my course, but did not find,
> Seeking the builder of the house;
> Painful is birth again and again.
> House-builder! I behold thee now,
> Again a house thou shalt not build;
> All thy rafters are broken now,
> The ridge-pole also is destroyed;
> My mind, its elements dissolved,
> The end of cravings has attained.[1]

The last epoch, "the present occasion," now begins. The next seven weeks were spent by the now Enlightened One (*buddha*) at or near the Bodhi tree. During the fifth week he sat under the goatherd's banyan tree, where he was tempted by the three daughters of Māra, Craving, Hate, and Lust, but in vain. In the sixth week a storm arose, and a nāga (snake-king) protected him with his hood. On the forty-ninth day Sakka brought him a fruit and water, and two merchants, Tapassu and Bhalluka, who were passing, brought him food. But he had no bowl, so the four Great Kings brought four sapphire bowls, which he rejected, then four stone ones, which he accepted, and fitted them together so that they miraculously became one. And the two merchants took refuge in Buddha and the Doctrine.

Going to the goatherd's banyan tree Buddha deliberated whether he should teach the doctrine to others. Then Brahmā Sahampati, thinking that the world would be destroyed, came with a train of gods and implored him to teach. He promised,

[1] This is *Dhp.*, 153, 154, and according to this tradition they are the first words of the Buddha-utterance. In the *Vinaya*, i, 2, another set of verses is given. The commentators record both traditions. Sanskrit accounts give still others.

and thought first of going to his old teacher Āḷāra, but on applying his mind saw that he had died a week before. Then he thought of Uddaka, but he had died the evening before, so thinking of the five disciples who had left him he knew that they were in the deer park of Benares, and decided to "set turning the Wheel of the Doctrine" there. When the disciples saw him coming, they decided to pay him no reverence beyond offering him a seat. But Buddha knowing their thoughts pervaded them with love, so that they could not keep their resolve, but showed him all respect. They addressed him by name or as friend, but he explained that he was *Sammāsambuddha*, the fully enlightened. Then he preached the *Dhammacakkappavattana-sutta*, the discourse of setting in motion the Wheel of the Doctrine. Koṇḍañña at once attained the fruit of entering the stream, and the other four on each of the following days. On the fifth day he preached the *Anattalakkhaṇa-sutta*, on the marks of non-soul, and all attained arahatship.

Afterwards he converted Yasa, a wealthy young man of Benares, and then his fifty-four companions, and when he had passed the period of Retreat, he sent the whole sixty out in different directions on alms pilgrimage.[1] He himself went on to Uruvelā, converting thirty noble youths on the way, whom he also sent on pilgrimage. At Uruvelā he converted the three brothers Kassapa, matted-haired ascetics, with their followers, and took them with him to Rājagaha. There he was honourably received by Bimbisāra, who presented a park called the Veluvana (bamboo grove) near Rājagaha for a monastery of the Order. At that time Sāriputta and Moggallāna, two friends who had left the world, were converted, and became the two chief disciples.[2]

The next spring he visited his father at Kapilavatthu. He was well received, but had to work a miracle in order to

[1] It does not here actually say preach, but in *Vin.*, i, 21, the words are "teach the doctrine, good in the beginning, good in the middle, good in the end in the spirit and the letter; preach an entirely complete and purified religious life (*brahmacariya*)".

[2] Their conversion was due to Assaji, one of the five monks, who repeated to Sāriputta the verse :—

> Of things that proceed from a cause
> Their cause the Tathāgata has told,
> And also their cessation ;
> Thus teaches the great ascetic.

This is the famous verse which has been found inscribed in many places in North India.

make the proud Sakyas do obeisance to him. He converted his father and Mahāpajāpatī his aunt; but his wife, who like him had adopted the ascetic dress, refused to go to see him. She said, "if I have any excellence, my master will come himself to my presence, and when he comes, I will reverence him." Buddha approved of her wish, went to see her, and she came swiftly, clasped his ankles, placed his feet round her head, and did reverence to him according to her desire. He also converted his half-brother, Nanda, son of Mahāpajāpatī, against his will, and his son Rāhula, and returned to Rājagaha.

At that time a merchant of Sāvatthī, Sudatta, known by his title Anāthapiṇḍika (giver of alms to the unprotected), visited Rājagaha. He was converted, and invited Buddha to Sāvatthī. Then he presented the Order with the monastery of the Jetavana (grove of Jeta) which he purchased by covering the ground with gold pieces.[1]

Here the *Jātaka* account ends. The commentary on the *Buddhavaṃsa*, commenting on the life of Gotama, gives in almost the same words an account of the period from his decision to be born down to the first sermon, and in the introduction an account of the events from the Renunciation down to his promise to Brahmā that he would preach. Its most important contribution to the legend is the list of places where Buddha stayed on his alms pilgrimages during the first twenty years of his preaching. After that time he stayed at Sāvatthī, either at the Jetavana or at the monastery built by the great lay woman Visākhā in the Eastern Park (Pubbārāma). The importance of this list is that it helps to date a number of legends that occur in the Canon and the commentaries. They have been woven into a continuous legend in the *Mālālankāravatthu*.[2] But as the legends, when they occur in the Canon, are without any indication of date, the probability is that their chronological arrangement is due to the author of that list, and that the dates are merely the result of inference. There is a similar Tibetan chronology, but it takes no notice of the permanent residence at Sāvatthī, and the places mentioned show no sort of correspondence.

[1] According to *Vin.*, ii, 154, a small portion remained uncovered, and was completed by Prince Jeta, from whom the ground had been bought.

[2] This has been translated from the Burmese by C. Bennett (*JAOS.*, 1853) as "Life of Gaudama", and by Bishop Bigandet as *The Life or Legend of Gaudama*, 4th ed., 1911.

The importance of these commentarial accounts is due to the fact that we are able to compare them with the Canon, both with regard to the development of the legendary and historical portion, and also (much more important for our present purpose) with regard to the doctrine of the nature of a Buddha.

It is naturally in the distinctly legendary portion of the Canon that we chiefly find biographical matter. The *Ambaṭṭha-sutta* (*Dīgha*, i) gives the story of the founding of the Sakya clan by the sons of king Okkāka. The *Mahāvastu* (i, 348) also gives it, and continues it down to Suddhodana. This continuation occurs in the Pāli only in the commentaries, but it forms a continuous legend, and the portion in the *Dīgha* appears to be a piece of the legend inserted by the Dīgha-reciters. When we come to the birth of Buddha we find, at least in some portions of the Canon, a Bodhisatta doctrine. The *Mahāpadāna-sutta* (*Dīgha*, ii, 1) tells of six previous Buddhas and of the marvellous events at the birth of a Bodhisatta. These events are also recounted of Gotama himself in the "Sutta of the marvellous and wondrous events" (*Majjh.*, iii, 118). The Bodhisatta descends "mindful and conscious" from the Tusita heaven, he stays visible as a thread through a precious stone, is received by the gods at his birth, and his mother dies after seven days. The *Mahāpadāna-sutta* also gives the names of his caste, gotra, age, tree of enlightenment, two chief disciples, the number of his disciples, the names of his chief attendant, his father, mother, and city.

In the *Suttanipāta* several ballads occur, which were the common property of different schools, the story of the sage Asita's visit, Gotama's meeting with Bimbisāra after leaving his home, and his temptation by Māra while practising austerities. This is not the story of the great contest, though this is referred to in the poem. These ballads imply a further extension of literary activity, as they appear to be based on the prose legends already existing in the nidānas of the reciters.

Another incident connected with his birth is the list of the thirty-two auspicious marks on the body. These are given in several suttas. They are said to indicate that their owner will become either a universal king or a Buddha, and they are evidently a case of the widely spread art of fortune-telling by bodily marks, *angavijjā*, which is deprecated in the *Brahmajāla-sutta.*

There is one reference to Gotama's luxurious life in his three palaces and a description of his renunciation stated so vaguely that it seems to imply no knowledge of the well-known picturesque legend :

Now before my enlightenment, while yet a bodhisatta and not yet fully enlightened, I thought, oppressive is life in a house, a place of dust. In the free air is abandonment of the world. Not easy is it for him who dwells in a house to practise a completely full, completely pure, and perfect religious life. What if I remove my hair and beard, and putting on yellow robes go forth from a house to a houseless life.

Now at another time, while yet a boy, a black-haired lad in the prime of youth, in the first stage of life, while my unwilling mother and father wept with tear-stained faces, I cut off my hair and beard, and putting on yellow robes went forth from a house to a houseless life.[1]

Two accounts seem to be here combined, and the latter is not even in harmony with the legend. However, the main dates are given in a verse quoted both by Theravādins and Sarvāstivādins :

At nine and twenty years of age, Subhadra,
I left the world, my search for the good pursuing ;
Now fifty years and one year more are over,
Since I went forth and left the world, Subhadra.
Morality, concentration have I practised,
And knowledge, too, with single mind attentive,
Preaching the limits of the noble doctrine ;
Outside the range thereof is no ascetic.[2]

The attaining of enlightenment is told several times in the actual words of the attaining of the four trances and the destruction of the āsavas, as in the *Sāmaññaphala-sutta* (p. 47). It is quite abstractly put, and neither the fight with Māra nor even the tree is mentioned. But in the *Ariyapariyesana-sutta* (*Majjh.*, i, 160) there is a long piece of narrative, telling how he left his weeping parents, how he visited Āḷāra and Uddaka and left them dissatisfied, and how he sought for the peace of Nirvāṇa and attained it. No details of the Enlightenment are given here. The narrative continues with his doubt whether to preach the doctrine, and his consent, which he gave when Brahmā came and implored him, next his intention to preach first to his old teachers, and his visit to Benares, where he found the five

[1] *Majjh.*, i, 240.

[2] *Av. Śat.*, ii, 231 ; *Dīgha*, ii, 151. The Pāli is corrupt and omits lines 5 and 6.

disciples, and convinced them that he was an arahat and fully enlightened, but there is no mention here of the so-called First Sermon.

Much of this narrative also occurs in the Vinaya, but there it is in the third person. The Vinaya quotes many sutta passages verbally, and it is unlikely that it would alter the words of the sacred text. It is thus more probable that the story existed first as part of the tradition of the reciters, from where it was inserted both in the Vinaya and the sutta, but in the latter was changed to the first person. Another *Majjhima* passage gives an account of the extreme austerities before enlightenment, which appears to have once formed part of the same narrative or the same collection of traditions.[1]

The legend is continued in the Vinaya in connection with the rules for admission to the Order, the conversion of Yasa and his companions, the three Kassapas, Bimbisāra, and the two chief disciples; the visit to Kapilavatthu and the conversion of his family. The most significant of later events are the schism of Devadatta (see p. 24) and the admission of women. In the fifth year Suddhodana died, and his widow Mahāpajāpatī asked permission to enter the Order. Buddha with great reluctance consented, but prophesied that the good doctrine would last only five hundred years, otherwise it would have lasted a thousand.[2]

All the Vinaya narratives are pure legend except where suttas happen to be quoted. The most extensive of the narratives is the *Mahāparinibbāna-sutta* (*Dīgha*, ii, 72). This is properly a legend, not a discourse at all. The only reason why it is among the suttas is that so many discourses in it are given as being uttered by Buddha at different stages of his journey.[3] As has been pointed out (p. 29), M. Finot considers it to have been continuous with the legend of the first two Councils in the appendix to the Vinaya.[4] It tells of Buddha's journey from Rājagaha to Vesālī and his keeping Retreat there. At the end of Retreat (i.e. in October after the rains) he prophesied his attainment of Nirvāṇa in three

[1] *Majjh.*, i, 240; *Lal.*, 314 (250), gives essentially the same account.

[2] *Vin.*, ii, 253; this occurs also *Ang.*, iv, 274; another case of legends common to sutta and Vinaya.

[3] They have been identified by Rhys Davids in *Dial.*, ii, 72.

[4] This has been practically proved by Dr. Obermiller, who has shown that the two are actually combined in the Tibetan *Vinaya-kshudraka*. *IHQ.*, 1932, p. 781.

months. He then went on by stages to Kusinārā,[1] where his death took place between two sāla trees. These data imply that it took place at the end of December, and this agrees with the statement that the sāla trees were in flower out of season. Later tradition, however, places the day on the full-moon day of the month Vesākha (April–May), which was also the day of his birth and enlightenment.

The *Mahāparinibbāna-sutta* underwent much elaboration in other schools. Several forms of it exist in Tibetan and Chinese. The latter have been discussed by Dr. Przyluski without reaching any definite conclusion as to the historicity.[2] A shorter form occurs in the Canon itself (*Saṃy.*, i, 157), but this may be an extract and not an earlier form. That the Pāli cannot be an early record is shown by the references to the practice of pilgrimages to the places of Buddha's birth, his enlightenment, his first preaching, and his complete Nirvāṇa.

These passages show us that when the Canon was closed there was in existence a legend whose main outlines were fixed much in the same form as we now know it. It is unnecessary here to discuss the details of the history. The early period is one which would naturally be less if at all known to the early disciples, and would also lend itself to the activities of devout imagination. For the later period there was continuous memory and tradition, which point to the work and activity of a great religious genius.

There is one legend which has received a quite disproportionate amount of attention, the contest with Māra. In itself it is an important mythological legend, but it is never told in the Scriptures, and is never there connected with any point of doctrine. Even in its developed form, as in the Jātaka, it has no doctrinal significance. Gotama there goes to the tree to win enlightenment, and Māra tries to drive him away because the seat is his. He fails to do so because Gotama has kept certain virtues in perfection, and Māra's host flees. Then Gotama proceeds to meditate and attain complete knowledge. Thus in between the story of his visiting other teachers in his search for the right method with his years of striving and just before his enlightenment comes the fight with Māra without any organic

[1] It was identified by Cunningham with Kasia in the Gorakhpur District.
[2] "Le Parinirvāṇa et les funérailles du Buddha," *JA.*, 1918, i, 485.

connection. There can be little doubt that the figure of Māra the wicked (*Māro pāpimā*) comes from the brahmanic legend of Death the wicked (*Mṛtyuḥ pāpmā*).[1] If we knew more of the origin of this legend, the origin of the myth would no doubt be clear. There are other brahmanic legends of fights with monsters, such as Indra with Namuci, and Māra is once actually called Namuci (*Sn.*, 439). Whether it was originally a sun myth or a myth of the fight for the tree of immortality is a question for the comparative mythologists.[2] It is not now the fashion to assume that all the stories told by primitive peoples, which we call myths, were nature-myths.

There is no evidence that the Buddhists understood it in either sense. They have preserved the story of the fight for the place under the tree, but have not made it an essential part of the story. The figure of Māra was adopted, but his character was changed. He is not merely the god of death, but lord of the realm of sense. That is where the story is made to fit into the Buddhist plan of salvation. Māra says, "prince Siddhattha wants to escape from my realm." As a personification of lust or craving he appears in the Scriptures repeatedly. The figures in his army are Lusts, Aversion, Hunger and Thirst, Craving, Sloth and Indolence, Cowardice, Doubt, Hypocrisy, and Stupidity (*Sn.*, 436). Here we have the personified fetters that every disciple must break in his fight with Māra, lord of the senses. They appear again as the three daughters of Māra: Craving, Aversion, and Lust. In this character Māra appears as the tempter, asking Buddha both before and after his enlightenment to attain temporal dominion or to rely on good works. There is a whole section in the *Saṃyutta*, where Māra appears as the tempter of Buddha and the disciples. In scholastic Buddhism he is identified with the fetters and depravities. When the *Dhammapada* (40) says "fight Māra with the weapon of wisdom", the commentator explains, "repel *kilesamāra*," Māra of the depravities, and repeatedly in Abhidhamma greed appears as Māra's share, Māra's fish-hook, Māra's realm. The four Māras of scholasticism are

[1] J. Scheftelowitz, "Neues Material über die manichäische Urseele und die Entstehung des Zarvanismus," *Z. f. Indol.*, 1926, 317.

[2] J. H. C. Kern, *Geschiedenis van het Buddhisme* for the former theory. E. Senart, *Essai sur la légende de Buddha* for the latter. See also art. "Māra" in *ERE*. For the brahminical legend see Scheftelowitz.

(1) the khandhas, (2) the depravities, (3) the god Māra, (4) death.

As may be seen from the biographical details mentioned in the Scriptures, the Buddhists are more interested in those events of Buddha's life that have a doctrinal significance than in those which appeal to the historian. A whole sutta is devoted to his conception and prenatal existence, and nothing further except the visit of Asita is told until he left the world. But not all these details can be referred to the state of the legend at one time. When we find him mentioned in some discourses as a great ascetic and teacher without any reference to a former existence or former Buddhas, we seem to have an earlier stage of tradition than that which puts him in the succession of former teachers. This is borne out by the fact that in the four Nikāyas only six previous Buddhas are mentioned. Even this does not appear primitive, but the names are common to all schools. In the *Buddhavaṃsa*, one of the latest works in the Canon, a list of twenty-seven is given, and under Buddha Dīpankara, the twenty-fourth before Gotama, Gotama is said to have first made his vow to become Buddha. The other schools also mention Dīpankara, but the numbers and names of the others vary considerably. This implies a later and independent growth of the legend.

We do not know enough of the historical background of Buddhism to be able to say how the conception of a bodhisatta, a being predestined to buddhahood, began. With the belief in reincarnation the conception may well have originated among the Buddhists independently. But the Jains also have a list of twenty-three leaders preceding Mahāvīra, their last teacher. It is probable also that Mahāvīra's predecessor, Pārśva, was a historical personage, so that for the Jains there was a starting point for the formation of a series. As both these leaders were earlier than Buddha, there was here also a starting point for a rival series by the Buddhists. It is, of course, possible to suppose that even before Buddha there were traditions of earlier Buddhas, but there is nothing in the texts to support this. The fact that there were stupas to earlier Buddhas in Asoka's time proves nothing, for the doctrine of earlier Buddhas was then established. The doctrine of a Bodhisatta as a being who acquires six or ten perfect virtues in order to attain

Buddhahood is certainly later than the bulk of the Canon. Even the Abhidhamma work *Puggala-paññatti*, which describes different characters from that of the vicious man up to the perfect Buddha, makes no mention of the Bodhisatta.

We find descriptions of Buddha in the Scriptures which describe him merely as a great teacher. Not even his royal descent is there mentioned. He is described as one who has abandoned a great family circle, and has gone forth from a wealthy kshatriya family. He is beautiful and virtuous and a great teacher. In the words of the formula to be used when meditating on Buddha he is " the Lord, the Arahat, the fully enlightened, endowed with knowledge and conduct, the Sugata (he who has well gone), knower of the world, the supreme charioteer of men to be tamed, the Buddha, the Lord ". This is not the humanized portrait of a divine being, but an expression of the belief in an historical being, a belief which remained in spite of all the growth in the wonderful qualities that became attributed to him. In the description in the *Majjhima* of his attaining enlightenment he is spoken of as acquiring those qualities which any arahat attains. But as Buddha he differs by being the discoverer of this attainment, and the attainment itself implies the possession of marvellous powers far beyond those of ordinary men. The qualities of a Buddha became an increasing list of powers possessed by him alone.

Already the Jains claimed omniscience for their leader. They are said to have held that he was " omniscient, all-seeing, and possessed complete knowledge and insight; that whether walking or standing, asleep or awake, knowledge and insight were continually present ". This claim is ridiculed by the Buddhists, and the omniscient teacher is described as so ignorant that he goes for alms to a house not knowing that it is empty, or as having to ask his way to a village. Buddha is represented as denying that he claims such omniscience.[1] What he claims is the three knowledges, (1) that he remembers numberless past existences, as far back as he wishes, (2) that with his divine eye he can see beings passing away and being reborn according to their karma, (3) that with the destruction of the āsavas he has of himself attained and realized release of mind and knowledge in this life and abides in it.

[1] *Majjh.*, i, 482.

These are the knowledges attained by all arhats, differing only in the length of time that they can remember. The question is raised in *Majjhima*, iii, 8, whether there is a monk endowed in every way with the qualities that the Lord possesses. The only difference there mentioned is that the Lord was the originator of the Path, the knower of the unknown Path, and the preacher of the Path that had not been preached. There we find the person of Buddha simply described in a way which is sometimes supposed to be a modern rationalized portrait. The special qualities and marvellous powers of Buddha are many, but we can see their growth from simple beginnings. The superhuman qualities ascribed to the arahat were enough to give them a start. We find them already developed in the ten powers (*bala*) of a Buddha:

(1) He knows what is possible as possible, and what is impossible as impossible.

(2) He knows the ripening of karmas, past, present, and future.

(3) He knows whither all paths (of conduct) lead.

(4) He knows the many and various elements or factors of the world (existence).

(5) He knows the various intentions of individuals.

(6) He knows the faculties of other beings, whether quick or slow, etc.

(7) He knows the impurity, purity, and growth of the trances, releases, concentrations, and attainments.

(8) He knows numberless former existences.

(9) With his divine eye he sees beings passing away and being reborn according to their karma.

(10) With the destruction of the āsavas he has of himself attained and realized release of mind and knowledge in this life and abides in it.[1]

The last three of these are the three knowledges of the arhat and are those which Buddha was said to claim when he was asked if he was omniscient (p. 148). Apparently when that sutta was compiled there was no claim to omniscience.

But this quality came to be attributed to him, though not in the form adopted by the Jains. It is found in the latest parts of the Canon, and appears to be a development of the

[1] *Majjh.*, i, 69; *Dhs.*, 76; *Mvyut.*, 7; commentary in *Vibhanga*, 335–344.

doctrine of the ten powers. How omniscience differs from the knowledge involved in the ten powers is discussed by Buddhaghosa in commenting on the above passage. Other schools, he says, say that the knowledge of the ten powers is not knowledge of particulars, while omniscience is. But Buddhaghosa points out that this is not the principle of division. Through the ten powers Buddha knows each one's particular duty, and omniscience is everything beyond this. It is ordinary human knowledge infinitely extended, but it is not the knowledge which produces release. By it one might know the trances or the magic powers, but not be able to perform them. One might know the Path, but could not thereby get rid of the depravities. That belongs to the three knowledges of the Path. They are intuitive and direct, and have to be realized.

The omniscience attributed to Buddha is not what the Jains claimed for their leader, the view that complete knowledge is continually present, but that Buddha can so direct his attention that anything can come within the "knowledge net" (*ñāṇajāla*), the range of his knowledge. Still further classification is found in the scholastic list of the five eyes of Buddha: (1) the eye of flesh, which is keen enough to see to the distance of a league; (2) the divine eye (ninth power); (3) the eye of wisdom (*paññā*), which he possesses as the discoverer of the Path; (4) the Buddha-eye, by which he knows the hearts and intentions of individuals (sixth power); (5) the universal eye, or omniscience.[1]

The attributes of Buddha go on increasing, but the development is modified by the rise of the bodhisatta doctrine, so that the whole doctrine is one of the development of an individual from the time when he makes the vow and practises and cultivates for ages all the qualities that finally result in Buddhahood. The further development of the Buddha doctrine must, therefore, be considered along with the teaching concerning a predestined Buddha.

The names and titles of Buddha are many. The *Mahāvyutpatti* has a list of eighty-one, many of them being merely poetical epithets. The best known of these is *Śākyamuni*, "the recluse of the Śākyas." His personal name, not found in the Scriptures, is given as Siddhattha (Skt. Siddhārtha), "he whose aim is accomplished." The

[1] *Mahānidd.*, 355.

name Gotama (Skt. Gautama) is not a personal name, but the name of his clan or gotra, and practically corresponds to a surname. As the Gautamas were a brahmin clan, it has been surmised that in this case the gotra was really that of the brahmin through whom brahmin rites were introduced, just as the neighbouring tribe of Mallas were called Vāsishṭhas from another brahmin gotra. The clan name was the usual name of address, unless a title was used, and hence brahmins are represented as addressing him as Gotama. The title used by disciples is Bhagavat, " Lord," a term used also by the Jains and various Hindu sects for their special deity. The translation " Blessed One " is a mere transference from Christian hagiology.

The essential name is Buddha, " the enlightened." Jina, " conqueror," is also found, but the Jains have adopted it as the special title of their own leaders. The name Tathāgata occurs as the name by which Buddha refers to himself. The derivation is not quite certain, for it might mean either " thus gone " (*tathā-gata*) or " thus come " (*tathā-āgata*), but similar compounds like *su-gata* (well-gone) and *samyag-gata* (duly gone) make the former the more probable. The word is quite clear in its literal meaning of " having arrived at such a state ". *Patiṃ dṛstvā tathāgataṃ*, " having seen her husband reduced to such a condition," is said of Damayantī in the *Mahābhārata*. Buddhaghosa analyses the word in both ways, and explains it as " having come (and having gone) like the former Buddhas ", i.e. having acquired the same qualities and performed the same essential actions. But Buddhaghosa goes on to take another meaning of *tathā*. If a thing is thus or so, it is opposed to what is not so, what is wrong, or perverse, *vitatha*. Hence an adjective *tatha*, " true," has been evolved, and Buddhaghosa, starting from this, finds six other meanings in it. There is no doubt that for the devout Buddhist all the meanings are there. We can, therefore, admit that " he who has won truth " fairly represents one meaning which the later Buddhists found in it, but this meaning has been deduced from *tatha-gata*, and it cannot be proved that this, and not *tathāgata*, was the original form.[1] There is no doubt that the *Mahāvastu*

[1] See Lord Chalmers, *JRAS.*, 1898, p. 113 ; Mrs. Rhys Davids, translation of *Dhammasangaṇi*, p. 294. Buddhaghosa's *tatha-āgata* is grammatically better, but not more probable.

(ii, 266) understood it in its primary meaning, where it makes Kāla, the Nāga king, thus address Gotama on the day of his enlightenment :

> Even as Krakucchanda goes,
> Konākamuni, and Kāśyapa,
> So dost thou go (*tathā gacchasi*), O great hero,
> Buddha to-day wilt thou become.

CHAPTER XII

DEVELOPMENTS IN ABHIDHAMMA

WITH Asoka in the middle of the third century B.C. Buddhism comes into the light of secular history. Both Pāli and Sanskrit schools possess legends about Asoka, and we have the contemporary evidence of his edicts.[1] The legends, as we have seen (ch. III), are late traditions, and the most important event for the history of Buddhism, the third Council, is unknown to the Sanskrit tradition and ignored in the edicts. But, even if the Council really took place, we learn nothing about the state of the Canon as a whole, for it was still unwritten, nor do we know what took place at the Council beyond the fact that the work the *Kathāvatthu* is said to have been spoken at it.

The edicts of Asoka are found in various places from the extreme north-west of India to as far south as Mysore. There is a set of fourteen rock inscriptions, which are found repeated in various places, six pillar-edicts, and a number of minor inscriptions. Two of the rock-edicts are dated in the twelfth year of Asoka's consecration, which would make their date about 253 B.C.

Among the references of religious interest is the statement in Rock-Edict XIII, that he has won the victory of *dhamma* (religion) " among all his borderers, even to the extent of six hundred yojanas, where (is) the Yona king Antiyoga [Antiochus II of Syria], and beyond this Antiyoga, (where are ruling) four kings Tulamaya [Ptolemy II of Egypt], Antekina [Antigonus Gonatas of Macedonia], Makā [Magas of Cyrene], and Alikyashudala [Alexander of Epirus or of Corinth], and likewise to the south the Choḍa-paṃḍiyā

[1] Pāli story of Asoka in *Mhvs.*, v, ff., and the commentaries on the Scriptures. Much of the Sanskrit story is extant in *Divy.* It has been dealt with more fully from Chinese sources by J. Przyluski in *La légende de l'empereur Aśoka.* The text and translation of the edicts in E. Hultzsch, *Inscriptions of Asoka*, Oxford, 1925, and also in R. Mookerji's *Asoka*, London, 1928. D. R. Bhandarkar's *Asoka*, Calcutta, 1925, also gives translations. Both these books deal ably with the historical problems. V. A. Smith has treated the subject in his *Asoka* and *The early history of India.*

[Cholas and Pāṇḍyas] as far as Tambapaṃni [Tāmraparṇī]; likewise here in the king's dominion among the Yonas and Kambojas, among the Nābhakas and Nābhapaṃtis, among the Bhojas and Pitinikyas, the Andhras and Pāladas, everywhere (people) are following Devānampiya's instruction in *dhamma* . . ."

From this we see that Asoka's empire extended to the extreme north of India, where it included part of what is now Afghanistan and Baluchistan, and bordered on the Syrian Empire of Antiochus; to the south the bounds of his empire are shown by the mention of the Cholas and Pāṇḍyas at the end of the peninsula, and also Tambapaṃni. But where is Tambapaṃni? It is a well-known name of Ceylon, which the Greeks spoke of as Taprobane. But Hultzsch records the fact that it is also the name of a small river in the Tinnevelly District. This inscription hardly allows us to decide which of the two was meant, but the name also occurs in Rock Edict II, among the names of peoples, the Cholas, Pāṇḍyas and others, where it cannot be taken as indicating a boundary.[1] It is thus more likely that the name refers to Ceylon, but these two references are all the information that we get from the inscriptions about Asoka's relation with the Sinhalese. The story of the introduction of Buddhism into Ceylon by Asoka's son Mahinda belongs only to the Chronicles, and does not really add to our historical information. Asoka's own account of his missionary efforts in so many directions makes it probable that he did not omit Ceylon, but what form the Scriptures had when they were introduced into the island is not known. Those now existing in Ceylon belong to a recension which was probably edited in the west of India, and there is nothing to connect them directly with Asoka's mission.

What Asoka meant by religion or morality (*dhamma*) doubtless varied in the course of his life. We find that he bitterly regretted the slaughter involved in his conquest of the Kalingas, and he appears to have undergone a conversion. He speaks of having for more than two years not exerted himself well as a lay disciple, but that afterwards he exerted himself greatly. He undertook religious tours, and he

[1] V. A. Smith mistranslated it, and made it mean "as far as Tambapaṇṇi", but, as Hultzsch and Mookerji show, it means "what is (known as) Tambapaṇṇi".

mentions his going to the Bodhi tree (*sambodhi*).[1] He teaches respect to parents and teachers and forbids the slaying of living creatures. There is no doubt that he was a Buddhist, but other sects were honoured by him, so that the dhamma which he fostered must have been chiefly the rules of morality. It has even been held that in his time Buddhism consisted of nothing but moral rules, and that the edicts show us an earlier stage of Buddhism, "une doctrine toute morale," as Senart says. This theory implies not only that Buddhism was such in its first beginnings, but also that it was nothing more than that a century or two later. So that we are asked to suppose that not merely the doctrine of the Path was an invention of monks, but that it had not even been invented in the time of Asoka. One thing supposed to show this is that his edicts do not mention Nirvāṇa. He speaks of wishing to make all living beings happy in this world in order that in the other world they may attain heaven (R.E., vi), and again says that the practice of dhamma produces endless merit in the world beyond (R.E., ix). But this is merely ordinary teaching. To preach Nirvāṇa as a reward to people living in the world would be an absurdity. To preach heaven as a reward for good deeds is Buddha's own doctrine. As Dr. Bhandarkar says, if it is once grasped that Asoka was himself a lay follower of Buddhism and preached to the householders, and that his teaching was based on what that religion ordained for its laity, there is nothing surprising in the fact that he makes no mention of Nirvāṇa or the Eightfold Way in his edicts, but on the contrary speaks of heaven, and holds it up as the reward of dhamma in the next life.[2]

Yet Asoka did recognize something more. He also addressed the Order, and to them he did not speak of heaven. In what is known as the Bhabru or Bairat No. 2 Rock Edict (now at Calcutta) he specifies a number of scriptural passages to be listened to and learnt. They show that he thought of the doctrine as something much more than purely moral rules. The whole inscription is as follows:

[1] Dr. D. R. Bhandarkar, I think, first pointed this out. It used to be translated "set out for enlightenment", or even "arrivé à la vraie intelligence"; cf. Przyluski, *Le Bouddhisme*, p. 25. The inscriptions recording Asoka's visit to Buddha's birthplace and to the stupa of the previous Buddha Konākamana are extant, but as they were "discovered" by the forger A. Führer, they are suspect. Führer also claimed to have discovered the stupa itself, but no one else has ever seen it.

[2] *Asoka*, p. 123; see also his essay in *Buddhistic Studies*, p. 619.

"Priyadasi, the Magadha king, having saluted the Order speaks (to them the wish of) health and comfortable life. It is known to you, reverend ones, how great is my reverence and good will to Buddha, the Doctrine, and the Order. Whatever, reverend ones, has been spoken by the Lord Buddha, all that has been well spoken. But as for what, reverend ones, would appear to me that 'thus the good Doctrine will be of long duration', that I undertake to say. These expositions of the Doctrine, reverend ones: (1) *Vinaya-samukasa*, (2) *Aliya-vasāni*, (3) *Anāgata-bhayāni*, (4) *Muni-gāthā*, (5) *Moneya-sūta*, (6) *Upatisa-pasina*, and (7) *Lāghulovāda*, which was spoken by the Lord Buddha about falsehood—these expositions of the Doctrine I desire, reverend ones, that many groups of monks and nuns may repeatedly hear and bear in mind, and likewise laymen and laywomen. For this purpose, reverend ones, I am causing this to be inscribed, that they may know my intention".

Here seven passages appear to be mentioned. The first two are unknown, and much trouble has been taken in "identifying" them with passages with other names, and thus giving more or less likely guesses. Dr. Walleser explains them as not being titles at all.[1] The others have been identified with more plausibility.[2] They are all addressed to monks, and they teach, not heaven as the goal, but, although never neglecting moral action, inculcate the doctrine of release and enlightenment.

Dr. Mookerji says that this edict throws great light upon the history of the Buddhist canonical literature, but it is difficult to see in what way. It may be supposed that Asoka chose those passages which had impressed him and which he thought suitable for the monks. There is no mention in them of the Vinaya itself (even the word *vinaya* in *vinaya-samukasa* is disputed by Walleser) nor of the Abhidhamma, and only one or possibly two passages are in the four Nikāyas.

About the state of the Canon in the time of Asoka neither

[1] *Das Edikt von Bhabra*, 1923; *Nochmals das Edikt von Bhabra*, 1925.

[2] *Anāgata-bhayāni* "dangers in the future". There are four suttas discussing this subject. *Angut.*, iii, 100–110; *Munigāthā* "verses on the recluse" = *Munisutta*, *Sn.* i, 12; *Moneya-sūta*, "sutta on the state of a recluse" = *Nālaka-sutta*, *Sn.* iii, 11; *Upatisa-pasina* "question of Upatissa" = *Sāriputta-sutta*, *Sn.* iv, 16; *Lāghulovāda* "exhortation to Rāhula" = *Majjh.*, i, 414. (4) and (5) occur partly in *Mahāvastu*, iii, 110, 386. Cf. Hultzsch for earlier identifications, and D. Kosambi, *Ind. Ant.*, xli, 40.

the Edicts nor the Chronicles tell us anything positive, but much can be concluded from a comparison of the existing recensions. We have seen that the structure of the Vinaya must have been by this time already fixed, and this harmonizes with the importance attributed to the Sangha by Asoka. But the legendary portion of the Vinaya was always liable to addition. Any rule could be expounded by adding a story to explain its origin. This went much further in the Sarvāstivāda Vinayas than in the Pāli.[1] In Ceylon, on the other hand, the Vinaya seems to have more early become a closed text, probably when it was introduced into the island in a written form. It contains no legends, or legends disguised as prophecies, referring to the period of Asoka.

The arrangement of the four Nikāyas or Āgamas must also have originated before sectarian differences became acute. The same principle of division is found in all schools: one collection of long suttas, one collection of medium long, one of groups of connected subjects, and a numerical group. As there is no doubt that this grouping was earlier than the committing of the discourses to writing, it is easy to see how the same material might be grouped differently by different schools, though the collection of long suttas is nearly the same in all. Before the adoption of this arrangement there must have been much opportunity for the introduction of unauthorized material, but there was an evident desire to keep the text pure, and the elaborate subdivisions of the Nikāyas were a help in preventing the introduction of arbitrary additions. Not only was the matter in each group determined to some extent by its special character, but each group was subdivided into smaller groups and again into series (*vaggas*) of about ten each. At the end of each series the titles of each sutta were recorded in a memorial verse. There was the less temptation to introduce spurious passages owing to the fact that no attempt was made to include within the four Nikāyas everything that might claim to be the Buddha-word. When the four Nikāyas were organized, it would be natural that there should be some works which could not be included in the scheme, or which were suspect. A number of such unclassified passages are, in fact, found in most schools. In the Pāli and some other schools they

[1] This can be seen from Rockhill's *Life of the Buddha*, which consists chiefly of Vinaya extracts.

have been formed into a fifth Nikāya, but even in the Pāli, which has carried systematization furthest, there has been no general agreement as to what should be admitted. In this group we have the Buddhist Apocrypha. Its very existence was likely to preserve the older collections from accretions, as it remained a repository for doubtful works. This does not take us back to a primitive tradition, but only to a stage when the recorded Buddha-word was classified and edited.

The scepticism which sometimes exists with regard to the antiquity of these collections often results from a shallow analogy with theories of Biblical tradition. The Buddhist Scriptures do not as a whole form a sacrosanct entity. It is true, as Asoka said, that whatever has been spoken by Buddha has been well spoken, but that does not make the whole Canon verbally inspired. This was fully recognized by the old commentators, who knew quite well that much of it was spoken by disciples. We find them from time to time pointing out that certain passages were added later, as they say, by the *saṅgītikāras*, the holders of the Councils. A modern critical analysis, even if it could be convincingly achieved, would doubtless go further. For our present purpose it is only necessary to recognize a body of ancient tradition common to all the older schools, which contains traces of development, but no evidence of violation of the primitive teaching.

Development, however, did take place, and we find it in the Abhidhamma. The time of the growth and establishment of Abhidhamma may be placed between Asoka in the third century B.C. and Kanishka in the first century A.D. Of actual history in this period we know practically nothing, but before the end of it we find the Pāli Scriptures established in Ceylon, and, as the Ceylon tradition says, committed to writing by the end of the first century B.C. It is also this period which saw the rise of the Mahāyāna movement. We thus have the consolidating of the doctrine in the schools of Abhidhamma and the rise of new conceptions, new ontological theories, and a transformation of the Buddha doctrine, which can be seen already influencing or developing out of the Sarvāstivāda and Mahāsanghika schools.

The Buddhist monasteries became places of education. What we actually know of them is the late reports of the

Chinese pilgrims, but we can see in Abhidhamma a system of instruction which must have begun much earlier. Abhidhamma, "special dhamma," appears to have first meant a method of discussion and development of the principles of the Dhamma. Hence we find it recognized by different schools, but the works that have developed out of the study are sectarian and not common to all the schools. They all recognize a system of logical analysis, *paṭisambhidā* or *pratisaṃvit*.[1] This is divided into (1) analysis of the meaning (*attha*) of terms (or of things, for the terms define things), (2) analysis of *dhamma*, which the *Vibhanga* and Buddhaghosa explain as the knowledge of the causes of things, (3) analysis of grammar (*nirutti*), (4) analysis of *paṭibhāṇa*, the power of ready exposition.[2] These terms do not seem to have been always interpreted in the same way. According to the Chinese work *Tsa-tsi*,[3] *attha* is the knowledge of proper and common characters, *dharma* the knowledge of synonyms.

This method of study is illustrated in the *Niddesa*, a work in the Canon attributed to Sāriputta. There we find words interpreted by giving long lists of synonyms (*dhamma*), others have ordinary definitions (*attha*), as when a seat (*āsana*) is said to be " where people sit ", and is then followed by a list of eight synonyms. These lists of synonyms formed a rudimentary dictionary, which developed into *kośas*, the usual Indian dictionaries of synonyms. Dialect forms and unusual constructions also needed explanation. This is the *nirutti*. Besides this there is the interpretation of the doctrinal matter. For this the power of exposition (*paṭibhāṇa*) was wanted. Mr. P. Maung Tin calls it " ready wit ".

The whole of this method occurs in Abhidhamma works proper. The synonyms were applied in any context and used for any exposition, and we find much of the material repeated in various places in the Abhidhamma books.[4] Some of it also occurs in the old verbal commentary on the *Sutta-vibhanga* in the Vinaya, evidently in an earlier stage, for there the definitions, which sometimes correspond with those

[1] *Vibhanga*, 293 ; *Mvyut.*, 13 ; *Dhs.*, 51 ; *Mvastu.*, iii, 321.
[2] This is according to *Vibhanga* and *Vism.*, 440 ; see also Mr. Aung's valuable notes in *Points of Controversy* for modern Burmese views.
[3] Quoted by L. de la Vallée Poussin in *Vijñaptimātratāsiddhi*, 652.
[4] See " Buddhist Education in Pāli and Sanskrit Schools " in *Buddhist Studies*, ed. by Dr. B. C. Law.

in the *Niddesa,* explain the words in their context without lists of synonyms.[1]

In the sense of a method and a body of traditional material Abhidhamma is no doubt much older than the existing works of that name. Some of the classified lists occur in the suttas, and seem to imply that the method was already in existence when those suttas were revised. One case is of special interest as showing a direct connection between the Abhidhamma of Theravādins and of Sarvāstivādins. The *Saṅgīti-sutta* of *Dīgha,* iii, 207, is a purely Abhidhamma list of items or principles beginning with a class of ones up to a class of tens. It is a different recension of the *Saṅgīti-paryāya,* which is the second of the Sarvāstivāda books of Abhidhamma. The Theravādins appear to have put it among the suttas before there was a distinct Abhidhamma section. Both schools attribute it to Sāriputta. It was probably intended to be recited in chorus (*saṅgīti*) as the name implies.

The actual Abhidhamma works were evidently compiled separately in the different schools, but based on common material. Those of the Theravādins do not give us a picture of the whole doctrine, nor, except in the case of the *Kathā-vatthu* and *Puggalapaññatti,* do they show the development of new theories. They analyse the Dhamma, and starting from a psychological basis they discuss ethical and logical questions from this standpoint. What Mrs. Rhys Davids says of the first Abhidhamma work, the *Dhammasaṅgaṇi* applies to most of the other Pāli books in showing their standpoint, "the method of the book is explicative, deductive; its object was, not to add to the Dhamma, but to unfold the orthodox import of terms in use among the body of the faithful, and, by organizing and systematizing the aggregate of doctrinal concepts, to render the learner's intellect both clear and efficient." [2]

Abhidhamma is thus only indirectly psychological, but it involves much psychological analysis. Every study of the mind has to begin by dealing with the popular terms which already exist, and these furnish the categories according to which the science is likely to develop. The terms at hand were those of common experience, and they never acquired

[1] The *Kathāvatthu,* v, 5, rejects the doctrine that all knowledge consists of such analysis. This would be to ignore higher intuitive knowledge.

[2] *Dhammasang.,* transl., p. xvi.

the scientific precision of Western psychology. Cognition, will or conation, and feeling have been in modern times made entirely distinct elements or aspects of mental states, but they never appear alone. The Buddhists never tried to treat them alone. Their classifications are classes of states in which one or other of these aspects are prominent. Will (*cetanā*) is an actual state, and hence a state of consciousness in which conation is predominant. Feeling (*vedanā*) is distinguished as pleasant, painful and non-pleasant, and non-painful. But it expresses not merely the three emotional aspects ; it also implies three conscious states of feeling, so that it could also be distinguished according to the six senses. It is in consciousness that any actual state of feeling exists, and thus feeling was also classified according to the particular sense through which it was manifested.

Materialism never became a serious problem in India. The few systems known survive only in refutations of their opponents. Its growth seems to have been prevented by the very abundance of terms for the non-material aspect of the individual. The terms were there, thought (*citta*), mind (*mano*), consciousness (*viññāṇa*), and heart (*hadaya*). All these occur in a list of synonyms of mind, and naturally have different shades of meaning. The difficulty was rather to deal with the superabundance of terms, and in spite of the tendency to assume that for a separate word there must be a corresponding separate thing, it is to the credit of Buddhist psychology that it did not unduly multiply entities. But it did classify. That is perhaps the chief feature of Abhidhamma psychology, and it is a further proof of the identity of method in the different schools that these methods and classifications correspond.

Buddhaghosa's *Way of Purity* shows in its third part the conclusions which Abhidhamma study reached in the Theravāda school. He is not directly interested in the problems of Abhidhamma, but, as his title implies, in the Way. The fullest and most systematic exposition of Abhidhamma is the *Abhidharma-kośa* of Vasubandhu with his own commentary (*bhāshya*) and the supercommentary (*vyākhyā*) of Yaśomitra. It chiefly represents the Sarvāstivāda standpoint and also gives the views of other schools.

Throughout the Abhidharma schools the same general conception prevails that existence does not consist of a primary substance, whether material or spiritual, but of a number of elements, *dharmas*. The classification of these and the problems of their interrelations form the primary question. The same material is classified in different ways from different points of view. The dharmas, of which there are seventy-five in Vasubandhu's scheme, are either compounded or uncompounded. The uncompounded are three, space and two nirodhas or cessations, (1) cessation by comprehension of the truths, (2) cessation not through knowledge, but by extinction of the cause, as when a fire goes out. This distinction was denied by the Theravādins on the ground that it made two Nirvāṇas (*Kathāv.*, ii, 11).

The other seventy-two dharmas are compounded, i.e. not permanent elements, but liable to change. These are also classified according to the five groups, *skandhas* (*khandhas*):—

1. *Body* or matter (*rūpa*) with eleven divisions: the five sense-organs, their five objects, and also an interesting psychological concept called *avijñapti*, which may be called unmanifested action. A case of manifested action would be the taking of the vows. But a man who has taken the vows has produced a certain result, though he may not always be thinking of it. Through this *avijñapti* or subconscious effect his avoidance of a sinful action is a different thing from its casual avoidance by an ordinary man.[1]

2. *Feeling* (*vedanā*).

3. *Perception* (*saṃjñā*).

4. The *saṃskāras*. This important group has a name which, whether translated aggregates, syntheses, or compounds, gives no idea of the meaning. The list itself makes it clear. The saṃskāras are chiefly conscious and unconscious manifestations of will. They were probably intended to include all the states of mind distinct from the other khandhas as well as forces or traits of the individual outside consciousness. They are consequently divided into (1) saṃskāras associated with consciousness, (2) those not associated with consciousness. Vasubandhu classifies them as follows[2]:—

(i) Saṃskāras associated with consciousness:—

(1) Ten generally present in consciousness: feeling, perception, will, contact (immediate sensation), desire, understanding, memory, attention, inclination, concentration.

[1] See La Vallée Poussin, *The Way to Nirvāṇa*, p. 71; *Abhk.*, i, 11.
[2] Stcherbatsky, *Central Conception*, p. 100; *Abhk.*, ii, 23.

(2) Ten generally good: faith, courage, equanimity, modesty, disgust at things objectionable, absence of greed, of hatred, of desire to harm, dexterity of thought, zeal.

(3) Six generally bad or indifferent: dullness, carelessness, clumsiness of thought, disbelief, sloth, excitement.

(4) Two generally bad: immodesty and not feeling disgust at things objectionable.

(5) Ten bad, of limited occurrence: anger, hypocrisy, envy, jealousy, approval of objectionable things, causing harm, unfriendliness, deceit, trickery, exhilaration.

(6) Eight undetermined: remorse, torpor, reasoning, reflexion, passion, hatred, pride, doubt.

(ii) The second group of fourteen saṃskāras are immaterial elements, but not associated with consciousness: acquisition (*prāpti*), a force which keeps together the elements of one stream of consciousness, non-acquisition (*aprāpti*), a force which keeps some of these elements in abeyance, allotment of groups (*nikāyasabhāga*), a force producing general classes, three forces which produce respectively unconsciousness (*āsaṃjñika*), the attainment of the unconscious, and the attainment of cessation, life force (*jīvita*), origination (*jāti*), continuance (*sthiti*), decay (*jarā*), impermanence (*anityatā*), the three forces giving signification to words (*nāma*), sentences (*pada*), and syllables (*vyañjana*).

5. The remaining skandha of consciousness (*vijñāna*).

In this classification, which is largely made up by the enumeration of empirical items, it is not surprising that there was not perfect agreement in different schools. Even the Sarvāstivādins had variant lists of the saṃskāras.[1] There is a Theravādin list of fifty-one in *Dhammasangaṇi*, but it does not entirely correspond to the forty-six of Vasubandhu, as it contains several of the group of those not associated with consciousness. The *Kathāvatthu* discusses several doctrines, which show other differences in detail. It rejects the view that there are still other uncompounded elements, such as the four Truths, and the Causal Formula (vi, 1), the view that there are no mental states other than mind (vii, 3), and that morality belongs to the non-conscious (x, 7). These instances show to what a large extent the doctrines discussed by the *Kathāvatthu* are of a minor character, and such as might be held within the same school. On all fundamental

[1] See the lists in *Mvyut.*, 104; *Dharmasang.*, 31, 32.

questions Theravādins and Sarvāstivādins were agreed. Throughout the whole work there are only three distinct doctrines said to be held by the Sarvāstivādins against the Theravādins, and only one of these affects the doctrine of the Path. It is the question of the falling back of an arhat (p. 131). New doctrines, it will be seen, do make their appearance, but they are intrusions arising out of the buddhological speculations of certain schools, not out of Abhidhamma.

The doctrine which has given the Sarvāstivādins their name is the theory that "everything exists" (*sarvam asti*). As being an ontological doctrine it does not essentially affect the teaching about the Way. It is an attempt to solve the problem of time. The *Kathāvatthu* (i, 6) refutes it by taking a number of instances and showing the absurdity of asserting that they are existent both in the present, the past, and the future. Professor Stcherbatsky, however, says: "When the principle 'everything exists' is set forth, it has a meaning that nothing but the twelve bases of cognition are existent. An object which cannot be viewed as a *separate* object of cognition or a *separate* faculty of cognition is unreal, as e.g. the soul, or the personality. Being a congeries of separate elements, it is declared to be a name and not a reality, not a *dharma*." This interpretation is entirely unlike that of the *Kathāvatthu*. It would make the problem not the problem of the nature of time, but of the reality of certain concepts according as they come within the scheme of the "bases of cognition", the āyatanas.

The twelve āyatanas are also, like the scheme of the khandhas, a means of classifying everything. They consist of the six senses: sight, hearing, smell, taste, touch, and mind or consciousness, and of the six objects of the senses: body, sound, odour, objects of taste, tangibles, objects of consciousness. "Everything" is thus classified under the six channels of knowledge and their objects, but in whatever way everything is classed, the essential question is how it exists. The Theravādins understood it to mean that the Sarvāstivādins asserted that "the past exists, the future exists, the present exists".[1] As O. Rosenberg said, the name of the school means the view which says that everything is, in which "everything" does not refer to all dharmas,

[1] *Points of Controversy*, p. 85.

in the sense of dharmas of every kind, but to the dharmas of all the three times.[1]

We have here two distinct interpretations of the Scripture utterance, *sarvam asti*. As the *āyatanas* (bases of cognition) form a classification of everything knowable grouped under the separate senses, the statement asserts that everything which really exists must come under one of the senses, and it implies that anything which cannot be so included is unreal. This is the sense in which it is taken by Stcherbatsky, and hence does not refer to the problem of time. But there were Sarvāstivādins who asserted the existence of past, present, and future as real things (*dravyatā*). This is the sense which is rejected by the *Kathāvatthu*. Both views are discussed in the *Abhidharmakośa*, iv, 27, and there the former interpretation is called the good Sarvāstivādin doctrine. It is in fact a doctrine in which all Buddhists agreed, but it does not solve the problem of time raised by the second interpretation.

Another attempt to solve the problem of time was the doctrine of momentariness (*kshanikavāda*). It was a remarkable application of the atomic theory to time. Time was reduced to a series of atomic moments, and the only actually existent time was the present moment. Its origin is unknown, but it is late, and we know most about it from the prominence which is given to its refutation in brahmin and Jain works. The *Kathāvatthu* (xxii, 8) in one of its latest sections attributes it to some South Indian schools, and states the doctrine in the form, " all things are momentary units of consciousness." This, as well as the atomic theory developed by some schools, belongs rather to the history of Indian logic and natural science than to the history of Buddhism.

[1] *Probleme*, p. 249.

CHAPTER XIII

DEVELOPMENT OF THE DOCTRINE : THE BUDDHAS

THE psychology of the Abhidhamma books shows the basis from which later developments in the doctrine started, but in itself it was merely the systematizing of the older theories. It remained unchanged to such an extent that Vasubandhu's great work became a "treasury" of the Mahāyāna schools. In Abhidhamma the question of an ātman or soul was not prominent. As a modern psychologist says, in words that a Buddhist might have used: "To the psychologist the conception of a soul is not helpful. He has no independent means of knowing anything about it which could be useful to him. For him the term 'soul' is virtually only another name for the total system of psychical dispositions and psychical processes." [1]

Yet some of the Buddhists came to see that the totality of dispositions and processes does not express the whole matter. This totality is arranged in groups called individuals. If one of these groups is nothing more than these dispositions and processes, how is he distinguished from any other group? Why should there be groups at all? Hence the doctrine of *pudgalavāda*, the view that the individual is an entity plus the skandhas of which he is composed. This is not the ātman-doctrine, though that doctrine would be one possible solution of the problem.[2] The ātman-doctrine, however, as formulated by the opponents of the Buddhists, was always rejected, and the upholders of the pudgala-doctrine guarded themselves against it by maintaining that the individual is neither the same as the elements which constitute him nor different from them.[3]

The most important developments of doctrine which took place between the time of Asoka and the beginning of the

[1] G. F. Stout, *Groundwork of Psychology*, p. 8.

[2] The sutta arguments against an ātman are all reproduced in the refutation of the pudgala in *Kathāv.*, i, 1.

[3] *Abhk.*, ix, p. 232. Besides psychology and logic there is classification of much more in Abhidhamma, but they do not represent a progress in thought. They can be best studied in the *Abhidharmakośa*.

Christian era were concerned with the nature of a Buddha. It was also within this period that the new metaphysical speculations must have begun, but these form a separate problem. The chief schools that have to be considered in connection with the new buddhological doctrines are the Theravādins, the Mahāsanghikas, and the Sarvāstivādins. Of these the Sarvāstivādins are the most important. Their chief seat was at Mathurā, but they extended up to the northwest as far as Kashmir. They broke up into schools, all closely related, and their differences appear to have been mainly due to the development of slightly varying traditions in the separate centres of their activity. The Theravādins, so far as they are known in India, must have existed in Magadha, and probably also along the route to the south past Kosambī (the capital of the Vatsas or Vaṃsas), and Ujjenī. The Mahāsanghikas also existed in Magadha, but when we come down to the historical period, we find the holders of their doctrines established in South India. Mr. Matsumoto treats the Sarvāstivādins as a mere branch of the Theravādins, and it is certain that at some period this must have been the case. But separation by mere extent of distance made independent growth inevitable. Their study of Abhidharma was systematized in their own compositions, and they developed the rest of their Scriptures independently in their Vinaya legends and avadānas. It is here that we find the new doctrines appearing which were to transform the older ideal of arahatship, and were to form the central motive for later theories concerning Buddhas and aspirants to Buddhahood. The Mahāsanghikas developed another side of buddhology which led to a kind of docetism.

We have seen what the conception of the nature of a Buddha was as developed in the suttas (p. 149). The great transformation that took place was that everyone might seek not merely to win salvation, but might aim at becoming a Buddha. Such a person is a *bodhisatta* (Skt. *bodhisattva*).[1] The doctrine that Buddhahood is a possible goal for everyone never appears in the suttas, but the term bodhisattva does. There it means

[1] The Sanskrit form has no doubt been formed from the Pāli or Prākrit *bodhisatta*, which is ambiguous. It may mean a " being (*sattva*) of enlightenment " ; but it may also mean " attached (*sakta*) to enlightenment ". The latter interpretation is adopted by the commentator of *Ang.*, i, 258, and is more probably the original one. But the Sarvāstivādins understood it in the other way, as the later Pāli authors did.

the state of a Buddha (Gotama or one of his predecessors) before his enlightenment. We also find in the latest suttas a list of six previous Buddhas, Vipassin (Vipaśyin), Sikhin (Śikhin). Vessabhū (Viśvabhuk or Viśvabhū), Kakusandha (Krakucchanda), Konāgamana (Kanakamuni), and Kassapa (Kāśyapa).[1] These names agree in all the schools, though there is evidently some corruption in the forms. A number of still earlier Buddhas have been added, but they vary in the different schools and appear to be inventions later than the sutta period.[2] They all contain the name of Dīpankara, the Buddha under whom Gotama first made the vow to attain complete enlightenment. As a part of this doctrine of a succession of Buddhas arose the belief in a future Buddha, Metteyya, or Maitreya.[3] Gotama Buddha both in the *Dīgha* (iii, 76) and in the *Mahāvastu* (iii, 240) prophesies Metteyya's future coming. These quasi-historical Buddhas do not play a large part in later doctrine, as they were overshadowed by the bodhisatta-doctrine and the innumerable Buddhas to which this doctrine gave rise.

This is the extent to which we find the Buddha doctrine developed by the Theravādins in their Scriptures. There was some further development, which is found in the commentaries, but this, as will be seen, was probably due to external influences. The insignificance of the bodhisatta doctrine for the Theravādins may be gathered from the fact that it is practically absent from the Abhidhamma. Even in the *Puggalapaññatti*, which gives a classification of different types of individuals, it is not mentioned. In this work there is some development of the Buddha doctrine, for a Buddha is said to be omniscient, and another kind of Buddha is also described, the *paccekabuddha* (*pratyekabuddha*), "independent or separate Buddha." He is said to differ from the complete Buddha (*sammāsambuddha*) in not being omniscient and in not having mastery of the fruits of complete buddhahood.[4] Unlike the arhat, he has attained enlightenment independently and without the help of a Buddha's teaching, but he is not able to preach it like a complete Buddha. This

[1] *Mahāpadāna-sutta* (*Dīgha*, ii, 1), where the life of each is given. The story of Vipassin is also given in great detail largely in the same words as in the account of Gotama's birth and enlightenment in *Majjh.*, iii, 120 ; i, 167 ; *Vin.*, i, 1.

[2] *Buddhavaṃsa* ; *Lal.*, 5 ; *Mvst.*, iii, 230 ff. ; longer *Sukhāvatī-vyūha*, § 3.

[3] E. Abegg, *Der Messias-glaube in Indien und Iran.*

[4] *Pugg.*, i, 28, 29.

conception of a private Buddha winning the truth merely for himself remained one of the Theravāda doctrines, and is also found in other schools, but it never had any historical importance. Legends of such beings are frequent in the commentaries and later literature.

It is in the avadānas of the Sarvāstivādins that we first find the bodhisattva ideal. There we read that Buddha preached so that " in some the roots of goodness that form a part of release were produced, in some those (four) roots that form a part of penetration, in some the fruit of Entering the Stream was realized, in some the fruit of the Once-returner, in some the fruit of the Non-returner, in some arhatship with the abandonment of all the vices was realized, in some the thought of (attaining) the disciple's enlightenment was produced, in some the thought of a pratyekabuddha's enlightenment, and in some the thought of complete enlightenment was produced."[1] Here the different stages of the disciple's career are described as we find it in the suttas, but it is preceded by preparatory stages, and there is added to them the thought of becoming a pratyekabuddha as well as the career of a bodhisattva, the thought which arises in him when he decides to win the enlightenment of a complete Buddha. It is sometimes said that this is a borrowing from Mahāyāna. For this, whether true or not, there is no evidence. We do not know how the earliest schools of Mahāyāna began, but we do know that they must have begun amongst the Sarvāstivādins. In the Sarvāstivāda schools there were all the conditions for the rise of such a doctrine. There was the belief in one particular human being who had attained such enlightenment, the belief that he was only one among previous beings who had done so, and also (with the doctrine of rebirth) the belief that he had gradually prepared himself for the great attainment. It is thus clear how the belief might arise that other beings might do the same. Buddha was already preached as the great being who had for cycles of ages undertaken this task for the good of all beings. That others should also undertake the task and, instead of merely winning their own release work also for the release of others, was a new and greater ideal. We know that this new ideal did originate, but we know nothing about its actual origin. To say that the Sarvāstivādins borrowed it from Mahāyāna

[1] *Divy.*, 50, 209, etc.

schools explains nothing. The Mahāyāna schools themselves were originally Sarvāstivādin, so that in any case the doctrine arose in Sarvāstivādin schools.

The doctrine would not at first produce a schism. We actually find it in Sarvāstivāda works held along with the teaching of the older ideal of arhatship. It would only lead to the rise of a new sect when the older ideal was rejected as a low career (*hīna-yāna*) and the actual consequences of the new doctrine were developed. In any case the oldest form in which we find it expressed is in Sarvāstivāda works. It finds another expression in the *Avadāna-śataka*, in a story repeated in different forms of a king in the far past who was visited by a Buddha. The king was delighted by the Buddha's description of the qualities that produce enlightenment, and made the vow to win supreme enlightenment. That king, we are told, was the individual who became Gotama Buddha. He thus as a layman put aside the thought of winning the truths under that Buddha in order after repeated rebirths to win all the qualities of a Buddha.

Although we are unable to point to the actual place or the particular school in which the doctrine arose, we thus find all the conditions for its origination among the Sarvāstivādins. We can speak of Mahāyāna doctrine when it began to be cultivated as the sole or only worthy ideal. As the Mahāyānists existed at the time when the extant Sarvāstivāda documents were compiled, it is possible that reciprocal Mahāyāna influences may be found in them, but it is in these documents that we find the earliest form of the bodhisattva doctrine.

The above list of stages speaks of three enlightenments, that of the disciples (*śrāvaka*), that of the pratyekabuddhas, and the complete enlightenment of a Buddha. These are the three careers (*yāna*) spoken of in Mahāyāna works, but here they are not yet placed in opposition to one another. The career of a disciple ending with the state of arahat is that described in the suttas. It has been extended by the Sarvāstivādins by making seven preliminary stages in which the faculties are produced and trained.[1]

(1) The first is that of the beginner (*ādikarmika*) in which the " roots of goodness " are first produced by meditation

[1] *Abhk.*, vi, 15–33, 70 ; cf. *Divy.*, 80, 240.

on the body, etc.[1] Then follow four stages called roots that belong to the penetration of the truths (*nirvedhabhāgīya*):

(2) *Ushmagata,* "state of heat," in which the disciple meditates on the four truths under sixteen aspects.[2]

(3) *Murdhānaḥ,* "heads," so-called because they are the tops of the roots of goodness from which fall is possible. The meditation is as before.

(4) *Kshānti,* "patience," but here rather in the sense of the pleasurable acceptance of the truths. Here the disciple increases the faculties of faith, courage, etc., so that he cannot fall back.

(5) *Laukikāgradharmāḥ,* "supreme secular qualities." Here the faculties become powers (*bala*), for they cannot be crushed by the passions.

Through the knowledges thus acquired he enters on

(6) *Bhāvanamārga,* the way of meditation, and

(7) *Darśanamārga,* the way of insight.

When the disciple has entered the fourth stage he cannot fall back, so that he is destined to become an arhat and attain Nirvāṇa. Hence the candidate for bodhisattvaship and Buddhahood does not enter that stage.[3]

There is a bodhisattva doctrine also in Theravāda works. It first appears in the two latest books of the Canon, the *Buddhavaṃsa* and the *Cariyāpiṭaka.* The differences from the Sarvāstivāda doctrine are striking. It is never looked upon as an alternative to arhatship, but is applied only to Gotama Buddha. Yet it is explained in such a way as to make it appear as if it were a possible career for others. In a memorial verse eight conditions are stated as necessary in order that the wish to attain Buddhahood may be realized: the candidate must be (1) a human being, (2) a male, (3) he must have the capacity to attain arhatship, (4) he must have made his wish in the presence of living Buddhas, (5) he must have left the world and not be a householder when he makes the wish, (6) he must be in possession of the five higher knowledges (*abhiññā*) and the eight attainments,

[1] The Theravādins also developed a preliminary stage, *gotrabhū* "one who belongs to the clan (of disciples)". La Vallée Poussin says it corresponds to the stage of laukikāgradharmas. *Abhk.*, vi, 20.

[2] *Mvyut.*, 54.

[3] The *Kathāv.*, iv, 8, treats as a heresy the view that Gotama reached the stage of the determination (*niyama*) of his career under the previous Buddha Kassapa.

(7) he must have undertaken to sacrifice his life for the Buddhas, and (8) he must have great desire and strength and exertion for the purpose of the qualities that make a Buddha.[1] He is further credited not only with six perfections of virtue (*pāramitā, pāramī*), but four more are added, making a list of ten.

The developed state of the bodhisattva doctrine in Therāvāda, with its entire absence in the earlier literature, makes it appear as if it had been introduced from another school. The *Buddhavaṃsa* existed in a Sanskrit form, and it is probable that the doctrine in this developed form was introduced along with this work. It was explained in such a way that it could be held in an orthodox manner in harmony with earlier doctrine, for it was never applied to any other individual than the historical Buddha or his predecessors. The *Buddhavaṃsa* was evidently known to the compiler of the *Mahāvastu*, and in this work the Bodhisatta doctrine, though more developed, is essentially like that in the *Buddhavaṃsa*.

It is the *Kathāvatthu* which chiefly allows us to see the relation of the Theravādins to other schools. The Sarvāstivādins are mentioned by the commentary only three or four times, evidently because there was little matter of dispute between these schools. Other doctrines chiefly of psychological and ethical import are mentioned, which although not attributed to the Sarvāstivādins belong to the problem of the classification of dharmas or mental factors as elaborated in the Abhidharma schools. There are three questions concerning Bodhisattas, but only in one case, and that only in the commentary, can any reference to the career of the bodhisattva be seen. There it is said (xiii, 4) that Buddhas by the power of their knowledge have prophesied that " this person in the future will attain enlightenment ". This rather resembles the Sarvāstivāda doctrine than that of the Theravādins and Mahāsanghikas, who represent Buddha as prophesying only of his successor Metteyya.

The most important part of the *Kathāvatthu* doctrinally is that which deals with the views of the Pubbaseliyas and Aparaseliyas, related schools of south India, who are referred to collectively as the Andhakas. The commentary does not reckon them among the eighteen sects, but it gives them a very important share in the points discussed. They are

[1] *Buddhavaṃsa*, ii, 59 ; com. in *Jāt.*, i, 14.

evidently the same as the three schools of Caityaśailas, Aparaśailas, and Uttaraśailas mentioned by Vasumitra [1] as branches of the Mahāsanghikas. We may put aside what is said of the Mahāsanghikas in the Ceylon Chronicles. There we are told that this school formed a great Council after being defeated at the second Council on ten points of discipline. Bhavya, however, says that the dispute was on five doctrinal points. These points are given by Vasumitra as (*a*) arahats can be tempted by others, (*b*) they have still ignorance, (*c*) and doubt, (*d*) they gain enlightenment through the other (i.e. a teacher), (*e*) the path is realized by utterance (by uttering an exclamation). These five points occur in the *Kathāvatthu* (ii, 1–6) almost in this form, where they are attributed to the Pubbaseliyas, etc.[2]

Evidently these schools belong to the southern group which in addition to these doctrines developed a docetic theory of the nature of a Buddha. The theory is best known in literature from the *Mahāvastu*, which expressly claims to be drawn from the Vinaya of the Lokottaravādins, a branch of the Mahāsanghikas. The tendencies of this group of schools can be well seen in the *Kathāvatthu*. The commentator puts most of the group in south India, and he is probably speaking of contemporary circumstances with which he was in close contact. The chief principle is that a Buddha is supramundane (*lokottara*), above the laws and conditions of ordinary human existence. Hence his behaviour as a human being was merely a convention. It should not even be said that he abode in the world of men and taught the doctrine. It was only a mind-formed image of him which appeared in the world. These schools also exalted the powers of the great disciples by holding that they had acquired the powers of a Buddha, and that they as well as a Buddha could work miracles in the true sense.[3]

The teaching of the *Mahāvastu* is essentially the same. "Nothing in the fully enlightened Buddhas is comparable

[1] *Masuda*, p. 15.

[2] La Vallée Poussin, "The five points of Mahādeva," *JRAS.*, 1910, 413. Whether these points were actually discussed at the second Council is not important. The historical fact is that they were held by the Mahāsanghikas along with their buddhological theories.

[3] The magic powers (*iddhi*) acquired by an arhat are held to be normal processes for anyone who applies the means necessary for acquiring them. This heresy consisted in holding that by a mere act of will such things as the creation of food or stopping the process of decay might be produced.

to anything in the world, but everything connected with these great sages is supramundane " (i, 159). When a Buddha is born from the side of his mother, she is uninjured, for he has a mind-formed body. He is, however, not really born from a mother and father at all, but arises as an apparitional being by the force of his own qualities (i, 145). The Sarvāstivādins, on the other hand, emphasized the human character of Buddha. Their Vinaya even speaks of the union of his parents at his conception.[1] The *Lalitavistara* (100), in a passage which probably preserves Sarvāstivāda doctrine, says that unbelievers will arise who will refuse to believe in Buddha's birth from a mother, but that it was not as a god that he turned the Wheel of the Doctrine, for then human beings would be discouraged, thinking, " we are mere men and unable to reach the state of a god." But it also has docetic passages, pointing out that Buddha acts like a human being in order to conform to the custom of the world. It was for that reason that he allowed himself as an infant to be taken to the temple, though he pointed out that he had already been addressed as *devātideva*, god surpassing the gods.[2] So when he first saw the signs of old age, sickness, and death, of which he had been kept in ignorance, he asked his charioteer what they meant. But the sūtra says that he asked " although he knew ".

We find these tendencies at work before the period at which Mahāyāna can be called a separate system. The earlier Mahāyāna sūtras lay stress on the nature of a Buddha and his qualities. Later on the career of the Bodhisattva becomes prominent. But this career ends in Buddhahood, so that it becomes impossible to separate the Buddha doctrine from the theory of his existence as a mere human being, who rises by a long course of training practised for ages until he becomes an omniscient Tathāgata.

The chronology of this period, which may be said to extend from Asoka, circa 250 B.C. to the beginning of the first century A.D., contains some interesting problems. The most significant event is the Council said to have been held under the Kushāna king Kanishka. In the first century B.C. the Yue-chi Tatars had invaded India, and the tribe of the Kushānas formed an empire extending from Afghanistan to the Panjab.

[1] Foucaux, *Rgya tch'er rol pa*, ii, p. xxi.
[2] *Lal.*, 134 (119) ; the term is also found in Pāli, *Niddesa*, ii, 307.

The names of the first three rulers are given as Kujula Kadphises, V'ima Kadphises, and Kanishka, but it is not agreed whether Kanishka came first or third.[1] If he came first, his reign would have begun in the first century B.C., but the archæological discoveries of Sir John Marshall have led Professor Rapson to conclude that he succeeded the other two, and that the Śaka era which began in A.D. 77–8 was the date of Kanishka's accession. This at present appears to be the most probable opinion. It is in his reign that we hear of a Buddhist Council being held, and according to this scheme of chronology the most likely date for it would be about A.D. 100. For the Sarvāstivādins it is the third Buddhist Council. The earliest account of it is found in Hiuen Tsiang, about five centuries later.[2]

Kanishka is looked upon as a second Asoka. Hiuen Tsiang tells us that he found the views of different schools so contradictory that he decided to arrange the teaching of the three Piṭakas according to the various schools, and summoned a Council for the purpose. So many men appeared that a selection had to be made, and finally there remained 499 arhats, exactly as at the first Council. The venerable Vasumitra was not among them because he was not an arhat, but, like Ānanda at the first Council, he proved his fitness by a miracle, and was admitted. Then the Council under Vasumitra's guidance composed three commentaries, the *Upadeśa-śāstra* to explain the Sūtra-piṭaka, the *Vinaya-vibhāshā-śāstra* for the Vinaya, and the *Abhidharma-vibhāshā-śāstra* for the Abhidharma. Kanishka ordered them to be engraved on sheets of copper and enclosed in a stupa with the Scriptures in the middle. The details do not look very credible, and in fact the whole account only proves that five centuries later the existence of the Council was believed in. La Vallée Poussin calls the account "an apologetic quasi-invention", and points out that the *Abhidharmakośa* does not appear to make any mention of it. "The narratives of this Council are to some extent dogmatic legends, and seem only to bear witness to the literary activity of the Sarvāstivādins." [3]

[1] O. Franke, *Beiträge aus chin. Quellen zur Kenntnis der Türkvölker und Skythen*, Berlin, 1904; H. Oldenberg, "The era of Kanishka," *JPTS.*, 1912; E. J. Rapson in *CHI.*, vol. i, ch. xxiii.

[2] Beal, i, 151 ff. Hiuen Tsiang does not say where it was held. It is usually assumed to have been at Jālandhara.

[3] "Councils," in *ERE.*

The commentaries (which in any case were not composed at the Council) really existed. Two commentaries on the Abhidharma still exist in Chinese, the *Vibhāshā* and the *Mahāvibhāshā*.[1] On the basis of these Vasubandhu is said to have compiled his *Abhidharmakośa*. He belongs to the second half of the fifth century A.D.,[2] but even without the guarantee that the Council was a reality we can place the doctrine expounded in the first century B.C. The language of the Vibhāshās was almost certainly Sanskrit, and their existence implies that the Sarvāstivādin Canon had already been committed to writing. As the grammatical peculiarities of the Canon show clearly that it was previously existent in Prākrit, it is quite likely that its systematic committing to writing implied at the same time its translation into Sanskrit. The Vibhāshās were especially studied by the Sarvāstivādins of Kashmir, and hence their name of Vaibhāshikas. The story of the Council, and the Council itself, if it ever existed, belonged to the Sarvāstivādins. There is no reason for the supposition that the Mahāyānists had anything to do with it. Yet the Mahāyāna must have already been growing. It did not, however, start from Abhidharma. One impulse came from the religious enthusiasm of the bodhisattva ideal. Another lay in the new treatment of the ontological doctrines latent in the dogmas of impermanence and of the non-existence of a self.

[1] Takakusu, "The Sarvāstivādin Abhidharma books," *JPTS.*, 1905.

[2] *Indian studies in honor of C. R. Lanman*, Cambridge, Mass., 1929, where the question is discussed by three Japanese scholars.

CHAPTER XIV

THE LOTUS OF THE TRUE DOCTRINE

THE problems of the composition of the Mahāyāna Scriptures are much more complex than what we find in the eighteen schools. These schools had a body of Scripture which was essentially the same for all. Even the avadānas of the Sarvāstivādins were not an attempt to compile new suttas to be added to the original collection. But the Mahāyānists deliberately composed new discourses on the model of the old. These works begin with the same phraseology, " thus have I heard " (the words which Ānanda is held to have used when reciting the suttas at the first Council), and they continue with the statement that Buddha was dwelling at a certain place. Then follows a discourse very different from the matter of the old suttas. What view the authors held about historical facts is not clear. It may be that the structure of the discourse was considered a mere convention, and that enthusiasm for the truth of the doctrines expounded produced the conviction that it must have been the primitive teaching.

These works, which teach the " great career " (*mahāyāna*), are opposed to the " hearer's " or disciple's career (*śrāvaka-yāna*) and the pratyekabuddha's career. This last is not important except as being one of the possible means of winning enlightenment recognized by the older teaching. The disciple's career is that which aims at attaining arahatship and winning Nirvāṇa as in all the older schools, and these are usually grouped together and referred to as *Hīnayāna*. This is a term which has become popularized as the translation of a phrase used by the Chinese pilgrims, who seem to have known it as a convenient name for all schools which were not Mahāyāna. But this is not the way the term is used in the Sanskrit texts. The texts when referring to definite schools always speak of *śrāvaka-yāna* and *pratyekabuddha-yāna*, but *hīnayāna*, which very rarely occurs, is used generally for " low or base career ".[1]

[1] The material has been collected by S. C. Vidyābhūṣaṇa, *JRAS.*, 1900, 29.

"Career" is *yāna*. This was first pointed out by Dr. Dasgupta.[1] There is no reason to translate it "vehicle", merely because Burnouf did so nearly a century ago. The three careers happen to be mentioned in a simile of three chariots in chapter 3 of the *Lotus*, but as vehicles they are not called *yāna* but *ratha*, chariots.

The doctrine taught in the Mahāyāna discourses varies according to the different schools, and even in the same school according to the aspect prominent in the mind of the compiler. In the *Lotus* it is the omniscience of the Buddhas, and the doctrine that all beings may attain the state of Buddha. This state is obtained by becoming a bodhisattva, and the bodhisattvas come to be the chief objects of religious enthusiasm. They are individualized as half-mythical beings who undertake to save the world, and then the advantages of worshipping and winning the favour of these great beings is extolled rather than the gigantic labour of becoming such a saviour. The Buddhas and bodhisattvas are conceived as mighty beneficent beings rivalling the gods of the surrounding Hinduism. They may not have been conceived as gods in the sense of the ultimate reality of things, but popular thought was not concerned with such problems. It sought objects of worship, and it found them in the Buddhas and bodhisattvas who became little else than the gods of the old polytheism under other names. The element of devotion (*bhakti*) was thus introduced into Buddhism. "Several scholars," says La Vallée Poussin, "regard the origin of the devotion to the Buddhas as a real puzzle (Max Müller) and believe that it is to be found in the influence of the 'barbarians', notably the Mazdaeans—an influence which was exercised especially in Northern India, the Panjab, and Kashmir, where religious statuary reached such high development."[2] There is no doubt about Persian influence in India, but religious devotion is a psychical phenomenon. It is a natural tendency of the soul to seek an object of religious love and worship, and it appears in any state of society when a suitable object for its exercise appears or is conceived. To imagine that the Buddhists were not devotional until Mazdaean influence penetrated

[1] *Hist. Indian Philos.*, i, 125; see also J. Rahder, *Daśabhūmika-sūtra*, pref., p. xx.
[2] *Mahāyāna* in *ERE.*

India seems to be superfluous. They were surrounded by religions of devotional enthusiasm, and all that was needed was a transference of Krishna-worship or Śiva-worship to these new deities, the bodhisattvas. What Mazdeism may conceivably have done was to introduce a knowledge of some of these beings. But even in the case of Amitābha, the Buddha of " infinite light ", who is sometimes supposed to be of Persian origin, there is no proof of borrowing. " The whole ' theology ' of the religion of Amitābha is Indian." The question of borrowing in fact only concerns details of archæology.

All this concerns the doctrine as apprehended by the layman, but there are also sūtras of a more philosophical character. They teach the doctrine of the Void, a theory of the nature of ultimate reality. It appears to have no connection with the religious teaching about bodhisattvas, but we find it taken for granted in the most devotional type of sūtras. It was a development of the ancient teaching which analysed the supposed reality of the self into separate elements, and it is represented by two chief schools, the Mādhyamika and the Vijñānavāda.

It was, however, the conception of Buddhism as a religion, a career in which the destiny of the individual could be realized, that formed the moving spirit of the new conceptions. It will be more profitable, instead of stating these doctrines in the abstract, to begin by analysing one of the most important of the Mahāyāna sūtras, the *Lotus of the true Doctrine* (*Saddharmapuṇḍarīka*). It shows us an early stage, in which the teaching is still defending itself in opposition to the older schools. It also shows the bodhisattva doctrine as subordinate to the teaching about the nature of a Buddha. It has been said to display Mahāyāna Buddhism with all its characteristic traits and all its excellences and defects, but that is saying too much. It presents only the popular side of the bodhisattva doctrine, and it has nothing to tell about the revolution in metaphysical thought achieved by the new movement. Though it mentions and takes for granted the doctrine of the Void, it is devoted to expounding the new doctrine of the nature of a Buddha, and in explaining away the pratyekabuddha and the career of a disciple or arhatship as errors or mere temporary expedients.

As in the case of many other Mahāyāna sūtras there are

peculiar problems connected with its composition. It consists largely of verse, but these passages are embedded in prose, which often repeats the matter of the verses. Evidently it does not now exist in its earliest form. Winternitz puts it in its primitive state at about A.D. 200. But the Mahāyāna movement was much earlier than this. The *Lotus*, however, is one of the earliest extant sūtras which deal with the bodhisattva doctrine and the new mythology of Buddha belief.

The sūtra begins by stating in exactly the same phraseology as the oldest discourses that the Lord was staying at Vulture hill with twelve hundred arhats. But instead of the two or three who are usually mentioned, the names of nearly thirty are given. They are the most famous personages in the older legend, and the first five are the five disciples. Here is already a great difference from the Pāli suttas, for in these the five never appear as hearers. What we have here is a deliberate use of legend. The fact that the names are never so used in the Pāli suttas implies that in these suttas there was a real tradition. They did not deliberately manufacture history. If there had been a tendency to invention, the five would have been the first to be introduced.

But here the list of hearers continues for several pages. There is Buddha's foster-mother at the head of six thousand nuns, among whom is his wife Yaśodharā. Then follows what is the most important item in these sūtras, a group of 80,000 bodhisattvas, twenty-five of whom are named, and among them the two famous ones, Mañjuśrī and Avalokiteśvara. Enormous numbers of gods appear, those led by Śakra and Brahmā, hundreds of thousands of myriads of ten millions of nāgas, kinnaras, gandharvas, asuras, and garuḍas. The Lord is said to have just given a great exposition, and he enters a state of concentration. A ray of light bursts from the circle of hair between his eyes [1] and illuminates 18,000 other Buddha-fields, and there is an earthquake. Mañjuśrī at great length explains to Maitreya (the future Buddha, who is here as a bodhisattva) that the Lord is going to begin a discourse (ch. 1).

The Lord tells Śāriputra that only Buddhas [2] can explain

[1] This circle is one of the thirty-two marks of a Buddha.
[2] The word is *tathāgata*, and is here generally used when referring to buddhas in general.

things. His knowledge surpasses that of all other beings, and he declares that he addresses all the disciples and pratyekabuddhas, all those who have been established in Nirvāṇa and have been released from the series of pains. This is a direct challenge to the older teaching, and the arhats present are puzzled. Śāriputra asks the Lord to explain himself, and the proud arhats get up and leave the assembly. It is the kind of thing that might quite well have happened at a Mahāyāna meeting in which there were some Sarvāstivādins present. Buddha declares that the meeting has been cleared of rubbish and that it is well that the proud ones are gone. The sole aim why a perfect Buddha appears in the world is to show to all beings the Tathāgata-knowledge. "By means of only one career I teach beings the doctrine, namely, the Buddha-career. No second or third career exists." But the Buddhas are skilful in devices, and at the decay of a cycle, when the roots of goodness are small they expound the Buddha-career by teaching it as being threefold. They show Nirvāṇa to those of low dispositions, but this is a device to save those who might not believe if they were told that they will become Buddhas (ch. 2).

Śāriputra, who has already reached Nirvāṇa, is astonished at the teaching, and fears that it may be Māra speaking, but soon recognizes that he will become a Buddha. The Lord revives in him the knowledge that he once made the vow of a bodhisattva, and promises its fulfilment. Śāriputra wishes the error of his own disciples to be removed, but the Lord says that he uses different devices according to different temperaments. Just as a man, if his children were in a burning house, might tempt them to come out by offering them different kinds of toys, bullock-chariots, goat-chariots, and deer-chariots, but when he has enticed them out he gives all of them splendid bullock-chariots; so Buddha offers the three careers with the degrees of concentration and release, and other methods of the disciples, but they are all superseded by the Buddha-career. Those who despise the teaching of this sūtra will be reborn in hell and other places of suffering. The sūtra is not to be recited to foolish people, but only to those who are striving for complete enlightenment (ch. 3). It is thus useless for the disciples of the older teaching to protest and say that the Nirvāṇa ideal was taught by Buddha. Their opponents admit that it was, but only to people too foolish to understand the higher doctrine.

Three other disciples come and express their astonishment on finding that after having attained Nirvāṇa they are destined to complete enlightenment. They say they are like a son who leaves his father's house and returns after many years. He goes and works for pay in his father's house, not knowing that his father has secretly recognized him. Even when his father falls sick and offers him his wealth he refuses it, and continues as a servant. His father at his death acknowledges his son, and leaves him all his wealth. Even so are these disciples the sons of Buddha who have received Nirvāṇa as pay, though the jewel of omniscience is their inheritance (ch. 4).

Buddha tells them that although the rain is the same that falls on all plants, yet according to their dispositions they respond differently. So there is only one career, but there are beings who act differently. The attitude of disciples is explained by a parable. A man who is born blind thinks that there are no visible objects. He is like beings living in the world of ignorance. A great physician (Buddha) cures his blindness, and he thinks he can use his eyesight properly until he is taught better by certain sages. He is like the disciples who think they know everything until they are taught the true way of enlightenment by the bodhisattvas (ch. 5). The Lord then prophesies the careers of his hearers as future Buddhas, but they will still have to pay reverence first to many millions of Buddhas (ch. 6). He tells them of an ancient Buddha whom he remembers whose life was 5,400,000 myriads of ten millions of cycles. This is one example of the figures frequent in these sūtras. The life of this Buddha with some other exaggerations is based on that of the historical Buddha. After winning enlightenment he recited this *Lotus of the true doctrine* for eight thousand cycles. His sixteen sons, who all became Buddhas, continued to repeat it, and the last was Śākyamuni, who is repeating it now. It is when a Buddha is going to attain final Nirvāṇa that he explains that there is only one career. He is like a guide leading a company of men to Ratnadvīpa (jewel-island), who on the way become wearied and want to turn back. He creates a magic city, where they rest, and are then willing to go on to their true destination. So Buddha draws beings on with the illusory idea of Nirvāṇa, and then shows them the true goal of omniscience (ch. 7).

The sūtra continues to make havoc of the older doctrine by telling of the conversion to the Buddha-career of all the other great disciples who are present, Pūrṇa, the chief of preachers of the doctrine, Kauṇḍinya, the first of the five disciples, Ānanda, Buddha's attendant, his son Rāhula, and the rest of the arhats (chs. 8, 9). Then turning to the bodhisattvas present, he tells the great value of this sūtra for their career. Those who hear only a single verse are sure of complete enlightenment. To utter a single harsh word against it is a worse sin than speaking evil in the face of the Tathāgata. A bodhisattva who preaches it should enter the abode of the Tathāgata, wear his robe, and sit on the seat of the doctrine. The abode is the abiding in friendliness to all beings, the robe is great patience and meekness, and the seat is entrance into the voidness of all things. Here the reference to the Void is one of the few cases which show that a philosophical doctrine was in existence at the time (ch. 10).

The discourse now becomes fantastic, but it is important in showing what the popular conception of a Buddha had become. A stupa of jewels appears, and a voice comes from it praising Buddha for uttering this sūtra. It is the stupa containing the body of the past Buddha Prabhūtaratna, which this Buddha wished to be present whenever the *Lotus* was being recited, and the Tathāgatas from other Buddha-fields are to be present as well. Buddha, therefore, darts a ray which makes millions of worlds visible in all directions with Buddhas preaching the Doctrine in each. They arrive in numbers like the sands of the Ganges, so that there is no room for any gods, and ask Buddha to open the stupa. He does so, Prabhūtaratna is seen sitting cross-legged within, and Buddha sits down by him on half the seat. The rest of the sūtra is a eulogy on its merits.

Buddha tells how when he was a king he passed a thousand years as servant to a monk in order to learn the *Lotus*. This monk was Devadatta, and it was in his service that Buddha acquired the Perfections. Therefore, some day Devadatta will become a Buddha. Mañjuśrī comes from the ocean, where he has been converting numberless beings. A nāga girl of eight years appears, she is ready for enlightenment, but cannot attain it because of her sex. Then she presents a jewel to Buddha, her sex changes, she becomes a bodhisattva, and goes away to the south to preach (ch. 11).

Innumerable bodhisattvas come and offer to preach the sūtra and Maitreya in astonishment asks how Buddha could have taught so many beings in the forty years that have passed since his enlightenment (ch. 12–14). The answer shows the Mahāyāna position both with regard to Buddha doctrine and metaphysics. Buddha indeed began to teach forty years ago, but that was a device ; in reality he is eternal. If people should think he was always here, they would become careless. As he explains :

> The Tathāgata, who was so long ago enlightened, is of unlimited length of life, and has always existed. Without having attained Nirvāṇa he makes a show of attaining Nirvāṇa for the sake of those who have to be trained. And not even to-day is my ancient course as bodhisattva completed, nor is the length of my life fulfilled, but even to-day twice as many ten million myriads of hundreds of thousands of cycles will be required for completing my length of life. Now again, though not attaining Nirvāṇa, I announce my attaining of Nirvāṇa. And why ? In this way I ripen beings, lest if I were to stay for a very long time, and through being often seen, beings with imperfect roots of goodness . . . if they saw that the Tathāgata stays, would get the idea that it is mere sport . . . they would not exercise energy to escape from the threefold world, and they would not get the idea that Tathāgatas are hard to obtain. Hence the Tathāgata through his skill in devices has said to those beings, " hard to obtain, O monks, is the appearing of a Tathāgata." [1]

All that the disciples of the older doctrine maintain about the historical Buddha is thus admitted, and yet the truth is quite otherwise.

> For the threefold world is seen by the Tathāgata as it really is : it is not born, it dies not, it passes not away, it arises not, it transmigrates not, it attains not Nirvāṇa. It is not real, not unreal, not existent, not non-existent, not thus, not otherwise, not false, not unfalse, not otherwise, not thus.

This is a bare statement of the fundamental doctrine of the Void. Its significance will be seen below in the light of the Perfection of Wisdom. Yet in the popular mode of expression the Tathāgata does manifest himself. He does so " when men have become unbelieving, unwise, ignorant, careless, fond of sensual pleasures ". In the same way the god Krishna in the *Bhagavadgītā* (iv, 7, 8) says, " whenever there is a decay of righteousness and a rising of unrighteousness, then I emanate myself. In order to save the good and

[1] *Lotus*, p. 319.

to destroy evil doers, to establish righteousness I am born from age to age." The actual historical relations between Buddhism and Krishnaism or Vaishnavism are not known, but here we have popular Mahāyāna Buddhism conforming exactly to the beliefs of contemporary Hinduism. The metaphysical basis of Buddhism, however, remains quite independent (ch. 15).

The following chapters extol the merits of preaching and hearing the sūtra (ch. 16–20), and tell of the great devotion shown by a number of bodhisattvas in worshipping it and preaching it (ch. 21–6). Before restoring the stupa to its place the two Buddhas, Śākyamuni and Prabhūtaratna, for 100,000 years put out their tongues, which reach to the world of Brahmā.[1]

It will be seen that the chief interest of the *Lotus* is devoted to Buddhas and their qualities. The bodhisattvas are quite subordinate to them except in chapters 22 to 26. The Buddha has become an eternal being and an object of worship not differing in powers or qualities from the gods of the rival religions. The religion is no monotheism, any more than popular Hinduism was.[2] Not only were there Buddhas at the ten points of space (the four quarters, the intermediate quarters, zenith, and nadir), but each world system had its corresponding Buddhas and bodhisattvas. The names and numbers of these Buddhas vary greatly. The short *Sukhāvatīvyūha* puts five or six at each point. The *Lotus* has a list of sixteen, two at each point, except that there is one at the N.E. and Śākyamuni in the centre. Two of them are otherwise famous: Akshobhya in the east and Amitābha in the west. It is easy to see how this type of Buddhism disappeared from India. As a form of worship it differed in the eyes of its devotees, who repeated charms and adorned the statues, by no more than the names of the deities. But for the ordained members of the Order, as well as for those of the laity to whom religion was more than ritual, the conception of a bodhisattva's career had a different interest. It was a beneficent ideal far surpassing the winning of Nirvāṇa

[1] Kern, who explained the imagery of the sūtra astronomically, said that Sākyamuni was the sun and Prabhūtaratna the moon in eclipse. The attendant bodhisattvas were the stars, and the Buddhas' tongues the sun's rays.

[2] Nevertheless, the logic of monotheism was applied. The *Mahāvastu* (i, 122) says that there is only one Buddha in each Buddha-field, otherwise it would imply that a Buddha was incapable of doing all his Buddha work.

for oneself. Yet it is not this conception which is prominent in the *Lotus*. It is still the popular conception of beings who are worthy of worship and who confer benefits on their clients. Then the bodhisattvas rather than the Buddhas become the chief objects of devotion. This is the point of view of the remaining chapters of the *Lotus*.

Note on Spells

Chapter 21 of the *Lotus* is entitled *Spells* (*dhāraṇī*). Spells form an important part of popular Buddhism, but they have nothing in themselves peculiarly characteristic of Buddhism. They are a form of sympathetic magic, which consists in asserting (along with certain ritual actions) that a certain wished for event is taking place, and by the power of the word it is supposed that if every detail is properly performed the event does happen. Spells are found in India as early as the Rig-veda, and the Atharva-veda is little more than a collection of such spells or charms. But the practice is much wider and no doubt much older than Vedism. Spells of the same type are existent in Old English, Old High German, and Keltic, to go no further.

Spells of this kind had already infected popular Buddhism, for there are several examples in the Pāli Canon. In the *Āṭānāṭiya-sutta* (*Dīgha*, iii, 194), the four Great Kings with their troops visit Buddha. Vessavana (*Kuvera*), Great King of the north, gives Buddha a form of " protection " (*rakkhā*) against evil-disposed non-human beings, yakshas, gandharvas, kumbhaṇḍas, and nāgas. These are the minor gods in the train of the four Kings, but many of them, says Vessavana, are well disposed to Buddha and, if monks, nuns, laymen, and lay women will repeat the spell, such beings will protect them. The spell itself is in verse and consists of homage to the seven Buddhas and to the four Great Kings. Buddha afterwards repeats it to his monks, so that it becomes part of the Buddha-word.[1] The general belief among Buddhists in such beings and their powers is apparent throughout. We are told that when Buddha goes into any village or town non-human beings do not injure men (*Dīgha*, i, 132).

The belief in the magic power of the word led to the view

[1] This occurs in a collection of spells chiefly from the Scriptures known as the *Pirita* (Pāli, *paritta*) " protection ", still used by the Buddhists of Ceylon and Further India. Buddhaghosa, commenting on the sutta, explains how the spell is to be performed.

that the words need not be intelligible. In Old English we find lists of corrupt Keltic words, which once had a meaning, but which came to be repeated merely as words having power. This has gone much further in India, where long lists of merely invented words are repeated. In the *Lotus* (ch. 21) the bodhisattva Bhaishajyarāja and others utter spells of protection for those who preserve the sūtra. They are lists of meaningless words, and usually end with the word *svāhā* (a Vedic term used in making oblations to the gods). An example of one of the shorter ones in the *Lotus* is *aṭṭe taṭṭe naṭṭe vanaṭṭe anaḍe nāḍi kunaḍi svāhā*. All the words are in the form of feminine vocatives, and appear to be modelled on spells addressed to female divinities. Spells of exactly the same type, and sometimes the identical spells, are also found in Hinduism. Female divinities in early Hinduism are almost non-existent, and there can be no doubt that both in Hinduism and Buddhism there has been a borrowing from non-Aryan sources.

One of the best known spells of this type is the well-known *oṃ maṇipadme hūṃ*. It has often been misunderstood, for it was first reported by travellers quite ignorant of the language.[1] This was even the case with Klaproth, who expounded it in 1831.[2] He did not see that *maṇi* is not a separate word, but only a stem. He thought it might be nominative or vocative, but if it were a word and vocative it would be *maṇe*, and if nominative *maṇiḥ*. Really *maṇipadme* is one word and a feminine vocative,[3] so that with the syllables of invocation *oṃ* and *hūṃ* it means "O Maṇipadmā". Maṇipadmā is "she who has a jewel-lotus". F. W. Thomas thinks that she was a female counterpart of Avalokiteśvara, but in the *Kāraṇḍavyūha*, where the spell is expounded, there is no trace of such a female being.

[1] The earliest appears to be the Franciscan, Willelm de Rubruk or Rubruquis, who was sent in 1253 to Tartary by Louis IX of France. He gives it in the form *ou mani hactain*, and, as one of the priests told him, says it means "Deus tu nosti". *Itinerarium* in *Recueil de voyages et de Mémoires publié par la Société de Géographie*, Paris, 1839.

[2] *JA.*, 1831, 185 ff. "Le sens de la phrase est très-claire. Lue *Om Maṇi Padma hoûm* elle signifie Oh ! précieux Lotus, Amen ; et si on lit *Om maṇi padme hoûm*, Oh ! le Joyau (est) dans le Lotus, Amen."

[3] This was pointed out by W. H. Mill in 1835, but his explanation made no impression. H. H. Wilson thought it was a locative, and hence invented the bodhisattva Maṇipadma. That is the only reason why this name occurs in the great St. Petersburg Lexicon. The whole matter was finally made grammatically clear by F. W. Thomas, *JRAS.*, 1906, 464, and A. H. Franke, *JRAS.*, 1915, 397 ff.

More probably it is constructed like the rest on the model of the Hindu spells.[1] Avalokiteśvara is represented with a lotus in his hand. Maṇipadma as an epithet does not appear to be applied to him, but he has epithets like *padmapāṇi* "having a lotus in his hand", *padmadhara* "bearing a lotus", and *śubhapadmahasta* "having a fair lotus in his hand". It is not certain, however, that the spell was originally connected with Avalokiteśvara. The "six-syllabled spell" is mentioned in *Divyāvadāna* (613), and probably refers to this spell. But there is no mention there of Avalokiteśvara. Also in the *Lotus*, although there is much about Avalokiteśvara and spells, there is no mention of this one.

Hundreds of dhāraṇīs exist, and they are not all mere gibberish. They are usually embodied in a sūtra as in the case of the *Āṭānāṭiya-sutta*. In the *Megha-sūtra*[2] Buddha gives spells to the Nāgas for rain-making, which are to be uttered by the reciters of the doctrine with particular ceremonies. The *Aparimitāyurjñāna-sūtra* has been translated into Tibetan, Chinese, and North Aryan.[3] It is a spell of 108 syllables for obtaining unlimited life. The great Mahāyāna sūtras, like the *Lotus* itself, come to be treated as magic objects bringing blessing to any who hear them, who read or write them, or cause them to be written. Of the *Lotus* itself it is said that "it is a saviour of all beings from all dangers, a releaser from all pains. It is like a pool for the thirsty, a fire for the cold, like a garment for the naked, a caravan leader for merchants, a mother for her children, a ship for those sailing across, a physician for the sick, a lamp for those wrapped in darkness, a jewel for the seekers of wealth, a universal king for princelets, an ocean for rivers, a torch for dispelling all darkness." Of Chapter 22 it is said that "it will be like medicine for the sick and suffering. On him who has heard this section of the doctrine no bodily pain will come, nor old age, nor untimely death".

[1] Female counterparts did come to be invented, but they are not found in the *Kāraṇḍavyūha*, nor the tantric sense which became attached to *maṇi* and *padma*.

[2] Edited by C. Bendall, *JRAS.*, 1880, 286, but he omits many of the spells as being "gibberish and mysticism".

[3] Ed. by Walleser, Heidelberg, 1916.

CHAPTER XV

POPULAR BODHISATTVA DOCTRINE

THE bodhisattva's career is one of long training, a progress rising in stages to Buddhahood. But in popular teaching its two prominent features are the enormous toils and sufferings that the aspirants have undergone, and the marvellous blessings that they confer on others. It is to these two qualities that the remaining chapters of the *Lotus* are devoted (ch. 22–6). Several bodhisattvas come before the two Buddhas in the stupa, but the outstanding one is Avalokiteśvara.[1] These chapters are probably later than the first part of the sūtra, and they show us another stage, but not the last, in the development of the religion of devotion or *bhakti* in Buddhism.

[1] The difficulty in interpreting this name lies in *avalokita*. The whole may mean either " Lord of *avalokita* " or " the Lord who is *avalokita* ". The former is the more probable judging by similar compounds—*Dharmeśvara* " Lord of the doctrine ", *Dharaṇīśvara* " Lord of the earth ", and another title of Avalokiteśvara, *Lokeśvara* " Lord of the world ". *Avalokita* comes from the verb *avalokayati* " to look at, to survey ". It does not mean " to look down at " (herabschauen). The latest discussion is by H. Zimmer, *Z. f. Indologie u. Ir.*, 1922, 73 ff. There is no doubt that *avalokitaṃ* can be used as a noun " Looking at or surveying." Zimmer says that it is not likely that Av. was so named from the activity of looking in general. That is so, but he has taken no notice of the fact that the verb in Pāli is frequently used of Buddha in a very special sense. In the Pāli commentaries he looks at the world, or surveys it, twice a day in order to see what beings need his help (*mahākaruṇā-samāpattito vuṭṭhāya lokaṃ volokento*, rising from the attainment of great compassion and surveying the world, *Dīgha com.*, 673). It is also used in *Mvst.* in the two *Avalokita-sūtras*, where he makes the " surveys " before deciding where and when to be born. Śāntideva quotes one of them as *Avalokana-sūtra*. *Vilokitaṃ* is also used in the same sense (*Mvst.*, ii, 1 ; *Lal.*, 21 ; but *olokitāni*, *Mvst.*, i, 142). Avalokiteśvara, just like Buddha, surveys the world in his compassion for all beings, and in this sense is " Lord of the survey ". The *Lotus* itself explains that he is so called because he will help anyone who hears his name or bears it in mind, and again in the verse portion (p. 451) says : " He having seen beings afflicted with many hundred pains, and, as he possesses the power of pure knowledge, having beheld (*vilokiyā*) those distressed with many pains, is therefore the saviour in the world including the gods." The same explanation was given by Burnouf (*Int.*, 226) on the authority of the *Guṇa-kāraṇḍavyūha*. It is probably the exigency of verse which has caused the compound with *vi-* rather than *ava-* to be used. Some of the Chinese translators read the name as *avalokita-svara*, and according to Giles (*Chin. Dict.*, 6363, 13,209) translated it as *kwan* " to gaze at ", " to view," *yin* " sound ". This is as meaningless in the Chinese as the Sanskrit, but the translators had to make it mean something, so they interpreted it, according to Giles, as " the hear-prayer Bodhisattva ". Other Chinese translators read the word correctly, and translated it " on-looking sovereign " Eitel, *Handbook of Chinese Buddhism*, s.v.

Avalokiteśvara in Chapter 24 is praised by Buddha for the benefits that he confers on all his worshippers. He saves from all sorts of misfortunes merely by the utterance, " reverence, reverence to the giver of safety, Avalokiteśvara, the bodhisattva, the great being." There is no reference to the six-syllabled spell. He saves from the passions of lust, hatred, and stupidity. He bestows offspring and other blessings. He assumes different forms in order to reach all beings, and appears as a Buddha or one of the Hindu gods, Brahma, Indra, Śiva. This is exactly the aspect under which he appears in the *Kāraṇḍavyūha,* a sūtra devoted expressly to him. This sūtra is still later than the *Lotus,* and shows bodhisattva worship at its height.[1]

In the *Kāraṇḍavyūha* there are no polemics against the śrāvakas. The " disciples " had probably lost any importance as rivals, and they are not mentioned as being present, but there are long lists of bodhisattvas, different classes of gods and goddesses, and many hundred thousands of laymen, laywomen, wanderers, and even Jains (*nirgranthas*). One curious feature is that although it is reckoned a late sūtra, it preserves some passages from Sarvāstivādin works, even preserving the arhat doctrine and a mention of their Scriptures, evidently when recording old legends. But all references to doctrine are quite perfunctory, except belief in the merits of Avalokiteśvara and the blessings that result from worshipping him.

Buddha was at Śrāvastī, and rays issued from Avīcī, the lowest hell, adorning and turning to gold the whole city. Buddha explained that it was due to the majesty of Avalokiteśvara, who had entered this hell. On his entrance the place became cool, the tortured beings were relieved, and Yama, king of the Dharma, praised him in a long eulogy. He then went to the city of ghosts (pretas). Water flowed from the pores of his skin, and the ghosts were freed from hunger and thirst. He then taught them this sūtra, their heresy of belief in a permanent entity [2] was destroyed, they attained to the happy world Sukhāvatī and became bodhisattvas.

Buddha then told of Avalokiteśvara's former merits.

[1] There is an elaboration of the sūtra in verse, *Guṇa-kāraṇḍavyūha,* which has been analysed by Burnouf, *Int.,* 220.

[2] *Satkāyadṛṣṭi* or *ātmātmīyagrāha.* This is belief in a self and not peculiar to Mahāyāna.

In the time of Vipaśvin Buddha he created the world. " From his eyes arose the moon and sun, from his forehead Maheśvara (Śiva), from his shoulders Brahmā and others, from his heart Nārāyaṇa (Vishṇu), from his teeth Sarasvatī, from his mouth the Wind, from his feet the Earth (*dharaṇī*), and from his belly Varuṇa. Then he said to Maheśvara, thou shalt be Maheśvara when the Kali age arises. Thou shalt be called the primal god (*ādideva*), creator and maker."

In the time of Śikhin Buddha he came with a message of greeting to Śikhin from Amitābha, the Buddha of Sukhāvatī, the Happy Land, in the western quarter. It is Avalokiteśvara's special function to take his worshippers there. " Robed in pure white, flying with the speed of the wind, they go to the region of Sukhāvatī to hear face to face the doctrine of Amitābha, and having heard the doctrine the pain of transmigration no longer torments their bodies, nor old age and death with lust, hate, and stupidity, nor the pain of hunger and thirst. They abide in that region as long as the firm promise of Avalokiteśvara is not fulfilled, until all beings are released from all pains, as long as they are not set in supreme perfect enlightenment," that is to say, until all become Buddhas. Even in this school the final end remains the same, the winning of Nirvāṇa.

He further teaches beings according to whatever discipline they follow. More catholic than in the *Lotus*, he assumes the form of a Buddha, a Pratyekabuddha, or an arhat in order to teach, and even takes the forms of the Hindu gods, Maheśvara, etc., and preaches according to the doctrine of each. In the time of Viśvabhū Buddha he went to the realm of the rebel gods, the asuras, and consoled and converted them, and then to the dark land of the monsters, the yakshas and rākshasas. At his preaching " some reached the fruit of Entering the Stream, some the fruit of Once-returner, some arhatship, some supreme enlightenment ". Then he went to the gods of the Pure Abode in the form of a brahmin, where, after working a miracle, he declared, " I am no god, but a man, and have become a bodhisattva, having compassion on the abandoned and wretched, and a teacher of the way of enlightenment."

He also went to Ceylon. Here we find several legends that belong to the older schools, and they have been inserted in the sūtra so mechanically that the older teaching has been preserved. Ceylon was formerly inhabited by female rākshasas, monsters who feed on human flesh. He changed himself into the lovely form of the god of Love. The monsters asked him to be their husband, and he promised, if they would do what he ordered. So he expounded to them the Noble Eightfold Path, the ten rules of good action, and taught them the four Āgamas. Some attained the fruit of Entering the Stream, or the fruit of Once-returner, of Non-returner, some arhatship, some Pratyekabuddhahood. This is the so-called Hīnayāna teaching as it probably stood in a sūtra used by the compiler of this work.

From Ceylon he went to Benares, where there were many thousands of worms. Taking the form of a bee he hummed the invocation to Buddha, the Doctrine, and the Order, which revived in them the memory of Buddha, so that they all reached Sukhāvatī and became bodhisattvas.

Thence he went to Magadha, where a famine had lasted for twenty years, and brought down showers of rain and food. An old man there explained to the astonished people that this could only be due to the virtues of Avalokiteśvara.

Buddha then tells of the innumerable samādhis attained by Avalokiteśvara (nearly seventy are named), and of his coming to save some shipwrecked merchants from the female rākshasas of Ceylon by appearing as a horse and taking them back to India.[1]

In each of the hair-pores of Avalokiteśvara is a world in which those dwell who know his six-syllabled spell, *oṃ maṇipadme hūṃ*, and they never again wander in transmigration.[2] Buddha himself after enormous toils obtained the spell from Padmottama Buddha, who had obtained it from Amitābha. Buddha, however, sends the bodhisattva who has asked him for it to a reciter of the Dharma at Benares to receive it. The bodhisattva does so, and when he asks for it, a voice from the sky orders the reciter to give it. The bodhisattva looks up and sees Avalokiteśvara with a lotus in his hand. He returns to Buddha and 770,000,000 Buddhas

[1] This is the well-known *Rākshasī-sūtra* (so called in *Divy.*, 524) given in full in *Mvst.*, iii, 67 ; cf. *Divy.*, 120 ; *Rom. Leg.*, 332, and a mutilated version in *Jāt.*, 196. In the earlier form of the story the horse was Buddha, but here Avalokiteśvara takes his place, and saves the caravan leader, who is Buddha in a previous birth.

[2] Rahder quotes from *Vimalakīrtinirdeśa*, "a bodhisattva can manifest in a single pore of his skin all the lands in all the ten quarters, even the sun, moon, and stars."

BUDDHA'S FIRST SERMON

PRESENTATION OF OM MAṆIPADME HŪM

[*face p.* 192

assemble and utter the spell, *oṃ cale cule cunye svāhā.* The acquiring of the great spell is a much greater matter than it might seem, as it should be inscribed in a circle (*maṇḍala*) made of certain substances with appropriate divisions and figures.

It is unnecessary to follow the sūtra quite to the end. Avalokiteśvara himself visits Buddha. Maheśvara (Śiva) comes with his consort Umā and asks for a prophecy. Avalokiteśvara prophesies that he will become the Buddha Bhasmeśvara,[1] and that Umā will change her sex and become the Buddha Umeśvara. This is one of the instances in this sūtra that show a connection with Śiva-worship, but there is no clear trace as yet of the development of the sexual symbolism and practices known as tantric, which came to infect both Śaivism and Buddhism.

It will be noticed that there is practically nothing of Mahāyāna doctrine proper beyond bodhisattva worship in these sūtras, but there are still other aspects of the belief to be considered. The happy land, Sukhāvatī, is merely one of the heavens of the Buddhas of the ten points of space, which has become important as being the heaven specially associated with Avalokiteśvara, the bodhisattva attendant on Amitābha. There are two sūtras called *Sukhāvatī-vyūha*, which lavish all their powers of description in portraying a heaven surpassing in bliss any of those of rival religions or even of rival Buddhas.

The longer *Sukhāvatī-vyūha* is in form much like the *Lotus*. It is chiefly the qualities of Tathāgatas that are eulogized. Buddha gives a list of eighty-one Buddhas, the last of whom was Lokeśvararāja. This Buddha described to his disciple Dharmākara the perfections of innumerable Buddha fields. The disciple took all these Buddha fields and conceived a field eighty-one times more excellent than all those which had been described. He vowed to become its Buddha, and now he dwells in it, the Happy Land Sukhāvatī, as Amitābha, the Buddha of immeasurable light and of immeasurable life (Amitāyus). The two chief bodhisattvas there are Avalokiteśvara and Mahāsthāmaprāpta. This is the only mention in the sūtra of Avalokiteśvara's importance. In the shorter *Sukhāvatīvyūha* he is not mentioned at all.

[1] "Lord of ashes" ; Śiva is known as *Bhasmaśuddhikara* "performing purification with ashes", and similar epithets.

Both here and in the *Lotus* the chief interest is confined to the nature of Tathāgatas and their worship. The great growth of bodhisattva worship appears to be later. This growth was a natural development in a country where *bhakti*, devotion to a personal god like Krishna and Śiva, had assumed such dimensions. Attempts have been made to explain the bodhisattvas as transformations of Hindu gods, but this appears to be a needless complication in stating the problem. There is no need to seek the personalities of the bodhisattvas in another religion. They already existed in great numbers as the product of free invention, and their worship was only an extension of Buddha worship, which was older even than the Mahāyāna movement. Bodhisattva worship was a rival movement rather than an imitation of Hindu forms of devotion. When a few of them had become popular, like Avalokiteśvara, Mañjuśrī, and Vajrapāṇi, it is not surprising if they took over some of the characteristic features of the rival deities. Avalokiteśvara has some of the features of Śiva. In the *Kāraṇḍavyūha* he even has the same title, Maheśvara. Yet he is quite distinct, and when the god Maheśvara is introduced it is as a disciple and worshipper of the great Lord Avalokiteśvara. Another bodhisattva in these sūtras is Mañjuśrī. He is here a great being, but not essentially different from the others. Later he becomes of very different significance, but we can see how he has developed from a simple bodhisattva. His origin needs no explaining, but once he existed and became popular, more and more virtues and powers could be claimed for him which, in the eyes of his worshippers, would make him outrival the gods of the other religions.

A very different way of considering Bodhisattvahood is that taken by the actual individuals who entered upon the career. This aspect, so far as it belongs to Mahāyāna, is still practically free from metaphysical questions. It is seen at its best in the works of Śāntideva, a poet and bodhisattva of the seventh century A.D. According to the Tibetan author, Tāranātha, he was born as a king's son in Surat. When he was to be chosen crown prince, he was persuaded by Mañjuśrī and Tārā in a dream to renounce the throne. Tāranātha also records his later life and seven of his miracles, which do not appear very credible.

Śāntideva has been called the Thomas à Kempis of

Buddhism. He was evidently a character who had a true vocation for the bodhisattva's ideal—the saving of all creatures. He might, like Abou ben Adhem, have said, " write me as one who loves his fellow-men." His *Śikshāsamuccaya* (collection of the rules of instruction) is a poem of twenty-seven verses, to which he has added a long commentary consisting chiefly of extracts from the Mahāyāna Scriptures. It is a book of moral rules for the bodhisattva who has made the vow and is beginning the training, and it forms a bodhisattva Vinaya, as it calls itself. He begins by emphasizing the importance of the thought of winning enlightenment. It is more important even than true doctrine, for the bodhisattva can still develop the qualities of a Buddha. All beings like himself shun dangers and pain, and there is no reason why he should preserve himself rather than others. He should make his vow of moral restraint in the presence of a Buddha or spiritual teacher, for in thinking of them he will be the less likely to break it. He must avoid evil ways, evil and frivolous company, and the special sins that beset the bodhisattva when he begins his career (*ādikarmika*). Of these there are eight: (1) discouraging hearers by preaching the doctrine in a way unsuited to their disposition, (2) persuading them to follow the Career of disciples or Pratyekabuddhas on the ground that the Perfections are too high for them, (3) teaching that the study of Mahāyāna makes it unnecessary to keep the Prātimoksha or the moral rules, (4) disparaging the Career of disciples, (5) speaking grudgingly of others and exalting oneself, (6) boasting of one's attainments for the sake of gain and glory, (7) when in the state of a king's priest or minister robbing and injuring the Order, (8) when in the state of a king causing corruption amongst the monks.

Śāntideva is throughout chiefly interested in the moral training of the bodhisattva, and has very little to say about the higher attainments. He gives the ten great vows according to the *Daśabhūmika-sūtra* (below, p. 206) and discusses the Causal Formula, but ends by saying " well, we know indeed that the compounded is very bad and evil, and we will make a cutting off of this combination and assemblage, but for the sake of the ripening of beings we will not proceed to a complete cessation of all compounded things ".

What Śāntideva tells us in this work is expressed chiefly

in extracts from Mahāyāna sūtras, and from these we gain a much more favourable impression of Mahāyāna literature than is afforded by such works as the *Lotus*. Śāntideva was no doubt an exceptional character, but the fact that such a man and such teaching could appear in the seventh century, and could obtain recognition as one of the most prominent teachers, shows that Buddhism was not in a general state of moral decadence. The degeneration which appeared affected certain schools, according as they suffered from the corruptions to which ascetic movements are always exposed, or as they adopted beliefs and practices foreign to Buddhism.

Śāntideva's *Bodhicaryāvatāra*, "entrance into training for enlightenment," has been called the finest poem in Buddhism. It is remarkable not merely as literature, but most of all in its personal aspect of the revelation of a deeply religious mind. He is filled with the thought that he must strive through unnumbered births to acquire the virtues through which in the presence of the Buddhas he prays to become a tranquillizer of all the pains of all beings. There is a system of worship for bodhisattvas on which his prayers seem to be based [1]: (1) Praise of the Buddhas, (2) acts of worship, (3) confession of sin, (4) praise of virtue, (5) exhorting Buddhas to preach and asking them to delay their Nirvāṇa, (6) rise of the thought of enlightenment, (7) transference of his own merits for the benefit of other beings. His confession thus begins :

> Whatever sin I have done or caused to be done in numberless births or in this, whatever through my delusion I have approved to my hurt, that I confess as misdeed, and now am tortured by remorse.
>
> Whatever sin I have committed against the three Jewels, against mother and father, or against teachers and others, in deed, word, and thought, with many vices and offences, O Guides, all that grievous sin I confess.
>
> And how may I escape it ? I am ever afflicted, O Guides, let not death come too soon upon me, ere my sin is destroyed.

His thought of enlightenment thus finds expression :

> Thus through all the good done by me may I become a tranquillizer of all the pains of all beings.
>
> May I become medicine for the sick and their physician, their support until sickness comes not again.
>
> Their pains of hunger and thirst may I quench with showers of food and drink ; in the famines at the end of an age may I become drink and nourishment.

[1] *Dhs.*, 14 ; cf. La Vallée Poussin, *Bouddhism e, études et mat.*, p. 106.

May I become an unfailing store for the wretched, and be first to supply them with the manifold things of their need.

My own self and my pleasures, all my righteousness, past, present, and future, I sacrifice without regard, in order to achieve the welfare of all beings.

For himself he has one consolation, the knowledge of the two truths, which he will one day reach in its perfection with the Perfection of Wisdom.

When to them that are burnt in the fire of pain shall I bring peace through my favours born from the rain-clouds of my merit? When shall I in reverence teach the Void to them that look upon things as real?

CHAPTER XVI

THE BODHISATTVA'S CAREER

TWO aspects of Mahāyāna doctrine, which seem to show no relation to each other, stand out in great contrast. There is the religious side of the worship of saintly beings with the ideal of a succession of lives of heroic virtues, and the philosophical side developing the boldest speculations in logic and epistemology. The cause of this contrast was inherent in Buddhism from the beginning—the division into the monastic order and the laity. The layman received instruction from the Order, " discourses about almsgiving, morality, heaven, the evils of lusts, the worthlessness of the defilements, and the blessing of renunciation," as a standing description expresses it. Only to those whose minds were disposed and who were ready to leave a household life were the four Truths taught.

The layman while in the world was a member of a society in which caste was not merely a religious belief but part of the structure of society. As a member of that society, however well disposed he was to the Order, he still had his caste duties to fulfil. From birth, and even before birth, ceremonies were performed for his well-being, and he remained subject to household rites and sacraments at every stage of life. Buddhism made no attempt to abolish the caste system. We find passages where rites and sacrifices are reinterpreted and moralized, but no condemnation of them as such.[1] It was only when a person entered the Order that his clan was merged in the clan of ascetics and he became a son of

[1] The *Sigālovāda-sutta*, *Dīgha*, iii, 180, is well known. It has been called the householder's book of discipline (*gihi-vinaya*). It is not in the ordinary sense a discourse, but consists of a poem of twenty-six verses with an introductory legend and a commentary. The question whether a layman can become an arhat is a perversity of expression. The real question is what are the conditions for becoming an arhat. If a layman can fulfil these conditions (and sudden conversion and insight are admitted), then, of course, he becomes an arhat. But in so doing he has cut off everything that binds him to the world, and even if he lives in a house he is exempt from the passions. The problem appears to have arisen from the fact that legends of the earliest period speak of laymen attaining arhatship at once. These do not belong to serious history.

Buddha. As a layman he kept the five moral precepts with three further rules of abstinence on the fast-days.

In the older literature the religion of the layman appears to be much as we find it in Hindu ritual books. Kings performed great sacrifices, and the ordinary layman his daily rites. This theory of the whole duty of man was comprehended for the Hindu in the Karma-mīmāṃsā system, which made salvation depend upon karma, this karma being the due performance of the sacrifices as understood by the brahmin priesthood. Upanishadic thought had already advanced beyond this point, but the teaching of the Upanishads was not intended for the ordinary layman, nor was it meant to make the sacrifices superfluous except for those who by following a special training had reached a higher stage.

But for the layman a new type of religion arose. It may in its origin not have been brahminical at all, but it finally became absorbed in Hinduism. In this type we find an exclusive devotion (*bhakti*) to one god, a personal being who promises salvation to all that faithfully worship him. The earliest literary example of this type is the *Bhagavadgītā*, the poem in which the god Krishna transforms the doctrine of karma by teaching that action should not be performed for the sake of the resulting merit or pleasure, but that salvation depends upon the god's power to save his devoted worshippers. The importance of the work here is only as one example of the emotional religions which permeated popular Hinduism. We have no evidence to place the contact of such religions with Buddhism earlier than the second century B.C.[1] It is from that period that we find archæological evidence for the existence of the religion of bhakti, and it is also from that time that the worship of bodhisattvas

[1] Krishna worship and the *Bhagavadgītā* may be much older than this. The poem is placed before the rise of Buddhism by Professor Belvalkar (*Shree Gopal Basu Mallik Lectures*, 1925) and Professor Dasgupta (*Hist. Ind. Philos.*, ii, 549). There is nothing in the history of Buddhism to disprove this. The poem arose in the west of India, and may well have existed there for a long time before coming into contact with Buddhism. Krishna is not mentioned in the Pāli suttas. In one of the latest books there are two references to the worship of Vāsudeva (*Mahānidd.*, i, 89, 92), but we do not know if this god was then identified with Krishna. The story of Krishna (with no reference to his divine character) occurs in *Jāt.*, 454. There is no reason why his character as a god should have been suppressed if it had been known, for the Buddhists were fond of making the Hindu gods supporters of Buddhism. Both Krishna and Śiva are found in later Buddhist works. Cf. R. G. Bhandarkar, *Vaiṣṇavism*; V. G. Bhat, *The Bhagavadgītā, a study*.

appears in Buddhism. The belief in bodhisattvas may well have developed naturally out of the story of the historical Buddha and his previous existences. The career which he undertook came to be looked upon as a possible career for all, and the inventiveness of the Mahāyānists supplied the names of numberless bodhisattvas. There can be little doubt that the bhakti worship which the Buddhist layman found all round him stimulated exactly the same kind of worship as we find in the popular bodhisattva doctrine.

Besides the worship of these great beings, there was a theoretical treatment of the stages of the bodhisattva's career by the various schools of Buddhist education. The earliest is in the *Mahāvastu*, where a list of ten stages is given. Here we meet the same problem as in the case of Sarvāstivāda doctrine, namely, as to whether this can be called a borrowing from Mahāyāna. It does not seem as if there is any one school which can be spoken of as the originator of this doctrine and as the source from which the rest have borrowed it. The conception of a Buddha as a man who strove through numberless births is wider than any school. When the Sarvāstivādins began to teach that anyone through Buddha's teaching might make the vow to become a Buddha, we have no reason to believe that there was a distinct Mahāyāna school from which they could have borrowed it. The reason why we are asked to consider the doctrine of a bodhisattva's career a borrowing from Mahāyāna is that the Pāli form of early Buddhism was once taken as a standard and compared with Mahāyāna. Everything not found in it was supposed to be Mahāyāna. But the main line of descent of Buddhist doctrine in India is through the Sarvastivādins and Mahāsanghikas. They continued their development long after the Theravādins had passed to Ceylon and disappeared from India. In India Sarvastivādins, Mahāsanghikas, and Mahāyānists remained in contact, living and teaching in the same monasteries. All sorts of borrowings would thus be possible, but we do not know enough of the origin of Mahāyāna to be able to say that the new doctrines started in a Mahāyāna school and then infected the older teaching. It was the making of these doctrines the exclusive teaching that constituted a new school, but still one in which the older teaching could be looked upon as a preliminary stage of the new. The real break comes with the doctrine of the Void, a break so violent that the teaching of two kinds of truth was needed to preserve the formulas of the old religion.

In the teaching of the Mahāsanghikas, as expressed in the *Mahāvastu*, the differences from Mahāyāna are still more distinct. The ten stages of the Bodhisattva's career are not the same as in Mahāyāna. The most that can be said is that they may have been elaborated in rivalry with some Mahāyāna school. The conception of the career in the *Mahāvastu* also shows more primitive features. It is described not as a career for any bodhisattva, but as having been the career of Śākyamuni and previous Buddhas. In this respect it agrees much with the Theravādin conception. Both omit the characteristic teaching of Mahāyāna that all may become Buddhas. There will be future Buddhas, but each is chosen by a Buddha to be his successor. The *Mahāvastu* teaches that one of the five necessary actions of a Buddha is to appoint a successor, a viceroy or crown prince (*yuvarājā*) who is to be consecrated. Śākyamuni himself appointed Ajita, the bodhisattva, who after him will become a Buddha named Ajita of the Maitreya gotra in the city of Bandhumā.[1]

The *Mahāvastu* is a long exposition of the career of the bodhisattva, but it always refers to the historical bodhisattva, Gotama, or as it usually calls him, Śākyamuni. It begins by explaining the four kinds of conduct of bodhisattvas, (1) their conduct as natural unconverted men (*prakṛticaryā*), when they follow the ordinary moral rules, pay reverence to Buddhas and their disciples, but do not produce the thought of attaining perfect enlightenment, (2) their conduct in making the vow (*praṇidhāna*) to become a Buddha, (3) their conduct in practising the ten stages leading to Buddhahood (*anulomacaryā*), (4) their reaching a stage from which there is no falling back (*avaivartacaryā*).

The stages (*bhūmi*) are ten, and are described in a chapter called the *Daśabhūmika* (i, 63–193).

The chapter begins by giving in verse the story of the elder Kāśyapa hearing of the death of Buddha, Buddha's funeral, and an account of the first Council. Kāśyapa then asks Kātyāyana to set forth the career of the Buddhas.

[1] i, 51 ; the other four actions are setting in motion the Wheel of the Doctrine, converting his mother, his father, and beings who are capable of becoming Buddhists.

(1) The first stage is *Durārohā*, " hard to reach." In this stage bodhisattvas are at first unconverted. They exercise the eight good qualities of liberality, compassion, zeal, unweariedness, absence of pride, study of all the śāstras, heroism, taking leave of the world, and steadfastness. Through certain vices (sensual pleasures, sloth, not practising the thought of impermanence), they may fail to reach the next stage. This means that they are reborn again and again in this stage till those vices are eradicated. Those who are to advance make the vow to attain perfect enlightenment. This produces greater merit than if they were to make a gift of the whole of India heaped up with jewels.

(2) Second stage, *Baddhamānā*, " bound." Here they have a dislike for existences. They have twenty special inclinations: good, kind, sweet, etc. On account of twenty-eight vices (love of gain and praise, etc.) they may fail to reach the next stage.

(3) Third stage, *Pushpamaṇḍitā*, " adorned with flowers." They sacrifice their wealth and themselves to obtain a single " well-spoken " verse of the Doctrine, and through fourteen vices may fail to reach the next stage.

(4) Fourth stage, *Rucirā*, " beautiful." The bodhisattvas avoid certain great crimes at this stage, and receive births as gods or in high positions. For sins such as corrupting nuns they may fail to reach the next stage.

(5) In the fifth stage, *Citravistarā*, "of varied expanse," they look on all existence as on fire with lust, hate, and delusion.

(6) They arrive at the sixth stage, *Rūpavatī*, " of fair form," with the thought, " few delights has this terrible whirlpool of the world." At this point it is explained that there are never two Buddhas in one Buddha-field, but there are innumerable Buddhas each in a separate field or universe. There are certain hindering vices mentioned here, but the passage is corrupt.

(7) Seventh stage, *Durjayā*, " hard to conquer." Their minds turn to self control. Through the thought of great compassion they pass to the next stage. The three last stages are arranged according to the stages of the life of a prince who becomes a universal monarch—his birth, appointment as viceroy, and consecration. Throughout these there is no turning back.

(8) Eighth stage, *Janmanideśa*, " discussion of birth." A list of Buddhas is given, under whom in the first seven

births Śākyamuni made the roots of goodness to grow and became a son of the Buddhas. In this stage bodhisattvas are to be looked upon as Buddhas. They are eloquent and great teachers.[1]

(9) Ninth stage, *Yauvarājya*, "viceroyship." The list of such Buddhas is continued. Some of them, as Dr. Rahder notes, are named from their eloquence.

(10) Tenth stage, *Abhisheka*, "consecration as king." The bodhisattvas are born in the Tushita heaven, and then have a desire for a human existence. Although they are spoken of in the plural, the individual described is always Śākyamuni. A long account is given of his conception and birth with the special doctrines of the Mahāsanghikas concerning the nature of bodhisattvas. The bodhisattvas are not really produced by parents. They arise of their own choice, and their birth is apparitional. When they are born they have the knowledge of all human arts. They do not indulge in sensual pleasures. Rāhula was not Buddha's son in the course of nature, but arose (as universal monarchs do) by apparitional birth. This is the logical result of the doctrine that the Buddhas have extinguished the passions and are undefiled by contact with the world. Although bodhisattvas develop into beings in whom human action is a mere appearance, yet they have begun as ordinary fallible creatures, and it is through their great compassion and desire to save all beings that they have arrived at a state beyond the world of impermanence, pain, and soullessness. This is unlike the gnostic docetism which represented the essentially divine as assuming the mere appearance of the human. Indian thought never conceived any fundamental difference in kind between the human and the divine. Whether as in Vedic thought they started with the One and reached the individual, or as in Buddhism extended the individual into a universal principle, the conception always resulted in pantheism or pancosmism according to the aspect emphasized.

This description of the bodhisattva's career has nothing essentially out of harmony with the older teaching. There is no bodhisattva-worship and the purpose of the whole scheme is to show how the worship culminates in attaining

[1] Dr. N. Dutt says that in the last four stages there is hardly anything more than a mere mention of Buddhas and Bodhisattvas who attained them, but he has overlooked a long description, especially of the eighth stage, pp. 105–6.

the nature of a Buddha. The bodhisattva in gradually getting rid of moral vices, of desire for existence, and false views, is following the training of the disciple. The difference comes when he decides not to realize the truths under another Buddha, but deliberately to submit himself to a further series of rebirths so that he can in time acquire the virtues and qualities that belong only to a Buddha and become a teacher of gods and men.

The Theravāda teaching is much the same, but, as has been pointed out (p. 171), the doctrine is discussed only in one Pāli work, the *Buddhavaṃsa.* This work is quoted in the *Mahāvastu,* so that it certainly existed in another school, and it is possible that it was adopted as it stood by the Theravādins. It shows considerable development of the doctrine, as in the clear statement made by the bodhisattva to postpone his Nirvāṇa, in the list of the eight qualities required to make a Buddha, and in the list of the ten Perfections. But there is no list of bhūmis, and the commentator on the *Jātaka* seems to have no notion of the significance of the Perfection of wisdom (*paññā*). For the Theravādins this is the full knowledge of the arhat, and for the Mahāyānists the apprehension of the highest Mahāyāna doctrine, but the commentator explains it by instancing some Jātakas in which the bodhisattva showed great intelligence and practical sense. This makes it appear as a fragment adopted from a school where the doctrine was much more complete and systematized.

The fullest Mahāyāna statement of the bodhisattva doctrine is in the *Daśabhūmika-sūtra.* Another scheme of ten stages appears here and is repeated with variations in other works. The stages of progress to arhatship already existed in the older doctrine, and they have been enlarged and adapted to the bodhisattva's career.[1] There can be no doubt that such schemes formed part of the regular oral

[1] Dr. N. Dutt speaks of " a list of ten Hīnayānic bhūmis " as occurring in the *Śatasāhasrikā,* a Mahāyāna work, but this is a misapprehension. It is not a single list, but the names of the three stages or goals attained by following the three yānas. The first seven are a list of the stages of the aspirant for arhatship. It ends with *kṛtāvī* " he who has done what he had to do ", i.e. the arhat. This list occurs separately in *Mvyut.,* 50, where it is expressly called the stages of the disciple. The eighth is the Pratyekabuddhabhūmi, which is also a separate career and stage and " hīnayānic ". The two last are Bodhisattvabhūmi and Buddhabhūmi, and are probably intended to be contrasted with the previous careers. Dr. Dutt, however, tries to equate the whole ten with the ten Mahāyāna stages ; *Aspects,* pp. 286–9.

teaching of the schools. The teaching would differ according to the school and the character of the individual teachers, for it is combined all through with the other doctrines prominent in each school. This rivalry and hostility is very clear in the *Bodhisattvabhūmi*, a work of the Yogāchāra school.

The general career of the bodhisattva is given in the *Caryāmārgabhūmisūtra*.[1] "A bodhisattva who practises the career progresses gradually and little by little till the moment when he arrives at supreme wisdom. By means of the six Perfections he discerns the practice of the Void. After having accumulated merits during innumerable cycles he acquires the career of a Buddha. Like a young soldier who advances, at first he is poor, but gradually he obtains great riches. By making efforts he is promoted to the grade of lieutenant; finally he becomes general. By degrees he is raised to the dignity of governor of a province, receiving 360,000 measures of rice as revenue. Successively he becomes minister of second rank, of first rank, universal monarch, king of the gods. Thus he who practises the stages of the career of the bodhisattvas produces the thought of enlightenment, fulfils (the Perfections of) almsgiving, morality, patience, heroism, meditation, and wisdom in succession. He vanquishes the six movements of the heart (contentment, anger, sadness, joy, love, hatred), rejects the three poisons (passions, hatred, stupidity) and the cover of the skandhas. He turns to the three modes of release, arrives at the condition of not turning back, and approaches the state of being bound to existence by only one birth. As in polishing a mirror the iron is washed, cleaned, and smoothed, so that it is thinned and at last reflects images, so the bodhisattva practises the six Perfections, and accumulates merits until the moment when he becomes a Buddha and saves the world. He cares for all beings as if they were his children. His gradual exercise of the career is like the waxing of the moon, the growth of plants, or the building of a house followed by the feast of inauguration."

The *Daśabhūmika-sūtra*[2] describes how the Lord was in

[1] Translated into Chinese, A.D. 284. The above passage is from Dr. Rahder's version given in his edition of *Daśabh.*, p. xxi.

[2] Rahder says that Paramārtha says that this sūtra belongs to the Mahāsanghikas. If this is correct, all that it means is that the sect which used this sūtra claimed to belong to that school. This is likely enough, but it was certainly not the sect that produced the *Mahāvastu*.

the heaven of the Paranirmitavaśavartin gods (the highest of the heavens of sense, next to the heaven of Brahmā). It was in the second week after he had attained enlightenment, and he was surrounded by bodhisattvas, first of whom was Vajragarbha, and by unspeakably numerous bodhisattvas from other buddha-fields. At that time Vajragarbha entered a form of concentration called Mahāyānaprabhāsa, "splendour of Mahāyāna." Thereupon a host of Tathāgatas from other universes, all called Vajragarbha, showed themselves and approved. They stroked Vajragarbha's head, and he rose up from the trance. Then he addressed the bodhisattvas about the stage of knowledge (*jñānabhūmi*) which all bodhisattvas enter, gave a list of the ten bodhisattva-stages, and became silent. The bodhisattva Vimukticandra implored him to expound them, and Vajragarbha replied that if they were to hear those inconceivable things, doubt and disputes might arise. Hence it was through compassion that he kept silent. All the bodhisattvas with one voice implored him, and then a ray of light issued from Śākyamuni's forehead illumining the ten quarters. It went round and formed in the air a cell like a shining cloud of rays, and from it, through the might of Buddha, came a voice telling him to utter his exposition by the power of the Buddhas. Vajragarbha consented, but begged their attention and reverence in listening to it.

> A thing most difficult in words to utter;
> But this immeasurable might of Buddha
> Has entered me, and these embodied rays,
> Through the great might whereof I have the power.

1. The first stage is *Pramuditā*, "joyous." Here the bodhisattva, who has formerly done good deeds and caused the roots of goodness to grow, produces the thought of enlightenment. He thus passes beyond the stage of the common man and enters the family of the Tathāgatas. He becomes joyful and cheerful, remembering the Buddhas and bodhisattvas and their achievements. As he has no thought or love of self, he is free from the five fears of not making a livelihood, of disgrace, of death, of an evil destiny, or timidity in assemblies. He has great compassion, and makes ten great vows: (1) in all realms and in all ways to perform great worship to Buddhas, (2) to preserve the teaching of all the Buddhas wherever and whenever it shall

appear, (3) to see the rising of Buddhas in all fields from the time when they leave the Tushita heaven down to their final Nirvāṇa, (4) to vow the thought of enlightenment for attaining all the Perfections and all the stages, (5) to ripen all beings in every form of birth and in all planes of the universe, and set them in omniscience, (6) to perceive all the differences that exist in all universes, (7) to purify all Buddha-fields and delight beings according to their dispositions, (8) to bring about one disposition in all bodhisattvas, to attain to each birth in his own body, to prevent interruption in the practice of a bodhisattva's career and attain the inconceivable Mahāyāna, (9) to practise the bodhisattva's career which is set going without turning back, to get a body like Bhaishajyarāja[1] or like a wishing gem, (10) to be enlightened with the highest perfect enlightenment in all worlds, to show forth the whole career of a Buddha from his state as a child and an ordinary man to his final nirvāṇa.

For the purifying of this stage he has ten qualities : faith, compassion, friendliness, liberality, endurance of weariness, knowledge of śāstras, knowledge of the world, modesty and shyness, firmness.

2. In the second stage, *Vimalā*, "pure," he avoids the ten sins of body, speech, and mind. Of the Ten Perfections morality is practised to the greatest extent but not the others.

3. By practising ten dispositions of mind he reaches the third stage, *Prabhākarī*, "luminous." He perceives impermanence in all compound things. He practises the eight stages of trance, the four brahmavihāras, the magic powers, and the five higher knowledges. He sees many Buddhas, the bonds of lust, of body, and of becoming are weakened, and the bonds of heresy are destroyed. His dispositions of gentleness, patience, etc., are purified, and he especially practises the Perfection of patience.

4. He passes to the fourth stage, *Arcishmatī*, "brilliant," by practising ten *dharmālokas*, lights of the Doctrine, examining the world of living beings, etc. He then practises ten qualities that ripen knowledge, the four contemplations, the five faculties of faith, etc., the bodhyangas, and the

[1] Here identified with Bhaishajyaguru, a Buddha who wished that his body should attain enlightenment shining like lapis lazuli, that his name should cure maladies and release prisoners. His heaven is in the eastern quarter, as Amitābha's is in the west. See Pelliot, *BEFEO.*, iii, 33, 1903.

eight-fold Way. His mind becomes more kindly and soft, doubts are cut off, his dispositions are purified. He renounces the world in the teaching of a Tathāgata, and practises the Perfection of heroism.

5. He passes to the fifth stage, *Sudurjayā*, "hard to conquer," by practising uniformity and purity of disposition with regard to ten matters: the doctrines of past, future, and present Buddhas, morality, etc. He understands the four Truths, becomes skilled in ten kinds of truth, relative, absolute, etc., and duly knows that all compounded things are unreal and vain. Out of compassion he learns secular arts which will be useful to all beings, mathematics, medicine, different forms of literature, knowledge of metals, astrology, interpretation of dreams, etc. Still more during his lives in this stage does he renounce the world and become a preacher. He specially practises the Perfection of dhyāna (meditation).

6. The sixth stage, *Abhimukhī*, "facing," is reached through the ten samenesses of things. This list is a statement of the Mahāyāna principle that all particular things are unreal, without a mark, without arising or origin, like the illusion of a dream, etc. But through his compassion he looks at the originating and passing away of the world as if it were real, and meditates on the twelvefold Causal Formula in ten different schemes. But reflecting that there is no self, no creature, no individual, he enters upon the three releases of voidness, signlessness, and aimlessness. These are the characteristics of things in reality, but he retains the ideas of self and other, doer and perceiver, existence and non-existence.

So far, it will be seen, he has practised all the stages that lead to arhatship. But now he turns away from the stages of disciple and pratyekabuddha. He has reached *prajñā* (*paññā*), which in the older teaching meant the full knowledge of the arhat. The term is still retained, but now it has the additional meaning which the Mahāyānists put into it—the knowledge of the truth of things as they understood it. In this sense, as the Perfection practised at this stage, it is usually called the Perfection of Wisdom.

7. In the seventh stage, *Dūrangamā*, "going far," he practises the Perfection of skill in expedients (*upāyakauśalya*). He also practises all the ten Perfections, (1) *giving*, by giving his root of virtue in his desire for buddha-knowledge,

(2) *morality*, in extinguishing all the defilements, (3) *patience*, in his pity and love for all beings, (4) *heroism*, in acts of extreme goodness, (5) *meditation*, in aiming at omniscience, (6) *wisdom*, in considering with approval the doctrine of the non-arising of all things, (7) *skill in expedients* (for converting beings), in his efforts for unlimited knowledge, (8) *the vow*, in his efforts to make the supremely highest vow, (9) *power*, in being able to change his form and teach beings of other careers according to their dispositions, (10) *knowledge* in acquiring the true knowledge of all things.

He practises in their fullness the four elements of popularity. These are, giving or liberality, pleasant speech, beneficent conduct, and impartiality. Like a skilled sailor who knows the nature of waves and currents and embarks on a great ship in the ocean but is not defiled by the filthy water, so the bodhisattva in the seventh stage has entered the great ocean of omniscience and has embarked on the great ship of the Perfections, but he does not yet realize cessation (Nirvāṇa). He has the knowledge of a Buddha and exercises to the full his task of saving all beings.

The eighth stage is *Acalā*, " immovable." He knows that things are non-existent, and he is beyond the pleasures of body, speech, and mind, like a man who has awakened from a dream and perceives that his dream experience was unreal. Buddhas then ask him to acquire the ten powers of a Tathāgata (above, p. 149) and the four subjects of confidence. He continues to preach and acquire further powers.

In the ninth stage, *Sādhumatī*, " the stage of the good," he understands still more the methods of converting beings. As a preacher of the Doctrine he develops the four methods of analysis of a bodhisattva (see p. 159), and preaches in all universes. The analysis here, however, is that of Mahāyāna doctrine.

The tenth stage, *Dharmameghā*, " cloud of dharmas," is also called *Abhisheka*, " consecration." The bodhisattva attains all forms of concentration. A vast lotus appears, and the bodhisattva sits on it in the concentration called the knowledge of the omniscient. Other lotuses appear, on which other bodhisattvas from the ten quarters sit and gaze at him. An earthquake shakes all the universes, and rays of light issue appeasing the pains of all creatures. Rays issue from the foreheads of the assembled Buddhas and rest on his head. He is thus consecrated (*abhishikta*, lit. sprinkled). and called a fully enlightened Buddha, just as a universal monarch takes his eldest son and " sprinkles " him as viceroy with water from the four oceans. The bodhisattva through his skill in remembering is able to take up and keep in mind all the clouds of dharmas showered on him by the buddhas in his presence, but he still has to be reborn once. Then when he descends from the Tushita heaven to this world, he is ready to undertake all the prescribed actions of a Buddha in saving creatures. It is easy to see, without a special theory of docetism, why such a being in his last existence acts by merely conforming to the custom of the world.

Other discussions of the bodhisattva's career are found, and it is clear that the subject was discussed and elaborated by different schools variously without any great changes in system or principle. The *Bodhisattvabhūmi* is a work of the Yogāchāra school, and goes into minute details. It begins by discussing the ten principles which belong to the career of a bodhisattva, and it adds two more stages. These are preliminary and previous to making the vow. (1) *Gotrabhūmi*, the stage in which the destined bodhisattva comes to belong to the clan or family of Buddhas. It corresponds to the *prakṛticaryā*, the " natural " conduct of the bodhisattva as given in the *Mahāvastu* (above p. 201). Five gotras are given in the *Mahāvyutpatti* (61), (*a*) that of the disciple's career, (*b*) pratyekabuddha's career, (*c*) tathāgata's career (which the bodhisattva follows), (*d*) undetermined gotra, (*e*) absence of gotra. The last not absolutely predestined destinies. Those whose gotra is undetermined or non-existent may in some instances originate roots of goodness through the teaching of bodhisattvas or Buddhas. The second preliminary stage is *Adhimukticaryābhūmi*, " stage of aspiration," in which the thought of enlightenment has been formed, but the vow has not yet been made.

Another classification of the bodhisattva's career made by the *Bodhisattvabhūmi*, a Yogāchāra elaboration, is the division into twelve (or including the Buddha stage) thirteen vihāras, " abodes." It is a scholastic addition which does not carry the conception any further.[1]

[1] The chapter on vihāras has been published by Rahder in the *Daśabhūmikasūtra*, and it has been analysed by La Vallée Poussin in *Vijñaptimātratāsiddhi*, p. 721. The first part of the work has been summarized in English by C. Bendall and La Vallée Poussin, *Muséon*, 1905–6.

Another classification which depended on the fancy of the scholastics is the list of six or ten virtues which the bodhisattva practises in perfection during his career, hence they are perfections, *pāramitā*. The list of the first six appears to be original, as it ends with the attainment of full knowledge or wisdom, *prajñā*. But the *Daśabhūmika-sūtra* has four more, which make a list fitting imperfectly with the ten stages. There are also ten in the *Buddhavaṃsa*, but the Pāli commentators do not seem to have known what to do with them. They also vary in name and in order. Of the first six Wisdom comes fourth, meditation (*dhyāna*) is omitted, and renunciation (*nekkhamma*) inserted. The rest are truth, resolution (*adhiṭṭhāna*, corresponding to *praṇidhāna*, "the vow"), love, and equanimity. The *Mahāvastu* almost ignores them, but in one place gives a list of the first six.

All through the career of the Bodhisattva run two motives, the aim of becoming a Buddha in order to save beings and the attainment of absolute truth in the Perfection of Wisdom. The two do not appear to be essentially related. Indeed, the bodhisattva has to avoid realizing the highest truth. When he meditates on the Causal Formula he has to take the view that particular things are real, and when he preaches to beings of other disciplines and religions he actually assumes the form of a teacher of those religions and sets forth relative truth. The reason of this combination was the existence of Buddhism as a great religion for the laity at the side of its existence in the schools as a carefully taught body of doctrine. Hence on the one hand the popular sūtras describing the marvellous achievements of Avalokiteśvara and the Land of Bliss promised to his worshippers, and on the other the philosophical sūtras which set forth a doctrine of the unreality of the world of experience, the doctrine of the Void. Even these latter sūtras have a popular character, as they state in oracular language (attributed to Buddha) the principles which were argued and maintained orally in the schools. Their full exposition is found not in these sūtras, but in the works of eminent doctors like Nāgārjuna, who expounded them in systematic treatises.

CHAPTER XVII

THE DOCTRINE OF THE VOID

THE bodhisattva doctrine arose out of the fact that Buddhism was at first a religion involving the teaching that an individual in order to win salvation must follow out a course of life directed to one end.[1] This was the career of the arhat, and it was this career which was remodelled and extended into the career of the bodhisattva. His career to enlightenment also meant grasping the truth of the new metaphysical theories. In the second and first centuries B.C. the prevailing schools of Buddhism in northern India were branches of the Sarvāstivādins, and somewhere within them the new developments arose. But these schools, which were large institutions of education in all branches of the doctrine, also developed their philosophical principles. From the beginning these principles involved metaphysical assumptions, whether they were recognized as assumptions or not. They certainly became recognized when they had to be defended against opponents.

There were internal disputes between the different schools, and probably rivalry with the orthodox philosophies. The result was a metaphysical system in conscious opposition to the older standpoint. Dr. Stcherbatsky thus describes it in rather highly coloured language: " When we see an atheistic, soul-denying, philosophic teaching of a path to

[1] The precariousness of the dating of the later period of Buddhism can be seen from Walleser's attempt to date the rise of the doctrine of the Void as seen in the Prajñāpāramitā literature. He says that it is fairly credibly recorded that the beginnings of Mahāyāna fall in the period immediately preceding the reign of Kanishka. This credible record is that of Tāranātha, a Tibetan author of the seventeenth century, and he only says that at the time of the third Council (i.e. of Kanishka) all sorts of Mahāyāna texts appeared. But we do not learn how long it had already existed in the oral teaching of the schools. The first systematic exposition of the doctrine of the Void was by Nāgārjuna, who is usually put in the second century A.D. There were already Prajñāparamitā sūtras in existence, works ascribed to Buddha and intended to give authority to doctrines already taught. They are probably among the earliest Mahāyāna works, and show close relation to the Sarvāstivādins both in literary resemblances and in their direct hostility to the older doctrine. We may place the doctrines and perhaps some of the sūtras as early as the first century B.C. Still earlier must be the period before the doctrines became the possession of a distinct school. Walleser, *Prajñāpāramitā*, p. 1; Stcherbatsky, *The Conception of Buddhist Nirvāṇa*, p. 66.

personal final deliverance, consisting in an absolute extinction of life and a simple worship of the memory of its human founder—when we see it superseded by a magnificent High Church with a supreme God, surrounded by a numerous pantheon and a host of saints, a religion highly devotional, highly ceremonious and clerical, with an ideal of universal salvation of all living creatures, a salvation by the divine grace of Buddhas and Bodhisattvas, a salvation not in annihilation but in eternal life—we are fully justified in maintaining that the history of religions has scarcely witnessed such a break between new and old within the pale of what nevertheless continues to claim common descent from the same religious founder."[1]

We find the first stage of the transformation of the metaphysical basis already completed in the doctrine of the Void. This doctrine belongs to several schools, but the earliest formulation found is the doctrine which came to be known as the Mādhyamika, the teaching of Nāgārjuna. We do not know the actual circumstances of the transformation, and it is useless to attempt to trace in the abstract the supposed course of this change. Such changes do not occur in the abstract. They are due to the intellectual ability of individuals, and there must have been many original minds in the Buddhist schools of the two or three centuries before the Christian era. But the last thing that such minds wanted was to appear original. What they claimed to be expounding was the teaching of Buddha, and that this was their teaching they always maintained. If it was pointed out that Buddha's discourses contained different teaching, then they explained it as teaching meant only for the simple, or they replied that the higher doctrine had been proclaimed by Buddha in one of the heavens and was intended to be promulgated later. They already had the example of the Abhidharma, which was first taught in this way. They were further enabled to justify their position by producing discourses in Buddha's actual words, which gave them a basis for all that they wished to say.

[1] *The Conception of Buddhist Nirvāṇa*, p. 36. How differently the matter can be conceived may be seen from Rosenberg's remark (*Probleme*, 226) that between Mahāyāna and Hīnāyana "es keinen Grundunterschied in der Weltanschauung gibt. Der Unterschied besteht nicht in der Theorie, sondern in der Praxis der Erlösung, in welcher das Mahāyāna eine grössere Anzahl von Wegen zulässt, die zum selben Ziele führen." This seems to underrate the importance of philosophical principles.

Perhaps the earliest class of such discourses is a number of sūtras known as *Prajñāpāramitā*, the Perfection of Wisdom. Some of them may be as early as the first century B.C., and we may take them as evidence that at the time when they appeared the new teaching was being systematically promulgated in the schools. The works of Nāgārjuna in the second century A.D. are the earliest written record of the reasoned out system which probably lay behind these sūtras from the beginning. There may be something in Nāgārjuna's work due to his own genius, but he was not professing to be original. His presentation of the system has made *Śūnyavāda*, the doctrine of the Void, one of the most important philosophical systems of India.

This, however, cannot be said of its presentation in the *Prajñāpāramitā* sūtras. There the doctrine is dogmatically stated, and it is put in such a form that it has been termed sheer nonsense.[1] In order to present this aspect it will be well to analyse one of the shorter forms, the *Vajracchedikā* (Diamond-cutter). Its teaching is that the senses give us only the experience of transient phenomena. No particular thing is real. At every moment it is passing into something else. And the conclusion is summed up in a verse, which says that as in the sky :

> The stars, as darkness, as a lamp,
> As Māyā,[2] as hoar frost, or a bubble,
> As dream, or as the lightning's flash,
> So should one look on compound things.

The sūtra begins in exactly the same way as the older sūtras, except that many bodhisattvas are said to be present with the monks, and it consists of a dialogue between Buddha and the elder Subhūti, one of the eighty great disciples.

A bodhisattva, says Buddha, must produce the thought that all beings in all forms of existence are to be placed by him in the Nirvāṇa which is without a remainder of element of rebirth (*upadhi*). Yet not one of them is placed in Nirvāṇa. If the idea of a being were to arise in the bodhisattva, he ought not to be called a bodhisattva. It is denied that a Tathāgata is to be perceived by his marks. The possession

[1] So Dr. Har Dayal, *The Bodhisattva doctrine*, who calls it puerile logomachy, p. 245, and this of a system represented by Nāgārjuna, whom Dr. Masuda calls the greatest Buddhist thinker since Buddha.

[2] *Māyā* is deception and, as other references show, here refers to the illusion produced by a magician or conjurer of things apparently real.

of marks spoken of by the Tathāgata is the possession of non-marks. A disciple who has attained the fruit of Entering the Stream does not think that he has attained it. He has attained no *dharma* or thing. If he were to think so, he would have the belief in a self (*ātman*) or living being or individual. This exposition of the doctrine is said to be inconceivable and incomparable. It cannot be listened to by beings of low disposition who believe in an ātman. Tathāgata is a name of true suchness (*bhūtatathatā*) it is a name of the law of non-arising, of the destruction of things, and of the utterly non-arisen. If one should say that the doctrine has been taught by the Tathāgata, he would speak falsely. " One who should say that belief in a self has been spoken by the Tathāgata would not speak truly, for the belief in a self spoken by the Tathāgata is a no-belief. Therefore it is called belief in a self. Thus all things are to be known and looked upon by one who does not rest upon the perception of things but of the perception of non-things. The perception of non-things has been called non-perception by the Tathāgata. Therefore it is called the non-perception of things."

There is no attempt here at explanation or proof. The assertions and denials are put dogmatically, and they are made about the most fundamental beliefs of a Buddhist, as if the author wished to shock his hearers. There is little doubt that this was one of his motives, for he taunts his opponents with the fact that the teaching is beyond the intelligence of beings of low disposition, and that it is to be understood only by those who have acquired bodhisattva knowledge. He speaks of hearers who are terrified at it. It is the confidence that he possesses this knowledge which makes him so ready to startle his opponents.

There are at least twelve sūtras which set forth the doctrine of the Void in this popular form. They belong to a school which expounded it as the Perfection of Wisdom. The best known is the *Ashṭasāhasrika-prajñāpāramitā-sūtra*.[1] This sūtra is free from the imaginative passages in some of the later works, which often run riot in describing the attendant hosts of gods. This probably indicates an early stage of

[1] i.e. the Perfection of Wisdom in 8,000 verses. It is in prose, but its length is calculated according to the number of syllables it would have if it were in verse.

Mahāyāna, when there was direct imitation of the sober style of the earlier sūtras. Not even bodhisattvas are present. Buddha asks the elder Subhūti to let a thought occur to him so that bodhisattvas may acquire the Perfection of Wisdom. The elder Śāriputra wonders whether Subhūti will do it by applying his own wisdom or through the might of Buddha. Subhūti, knowing his thought, replies that everything that disciples say is done through the virile force of the Tathāgata. " But (Subhūti continues) when the Lord says ' bodhisattva ', of what object is that the name ? I do not see the object named ' bodhisattva '. Further, I do not see the object named ' Perfection of Wisdom ' . . . What bodhisattva and in what Perfection of Wisdom shall I exhort and instruct ? But further, if at my speaking and teaching the mind of a bodhisattva does not sink, if he is not terrified [at the doctrine now set forth] even so is he to be instructed in the Perfection of Wisdom . . . The bodhisattva who is practising the Perfection of Wisdom must so learn that in learning he forms no imagination through the thought of enlightenment. And why ? Because his thought is non-thought. The nature of his thought is pure (i.e. free from any sense-element)."

Subhūti goes on to explain that in the state of non-thought there is neither existence nor non-existence. This state of non-thought is without change and without false imagination. Hence a bodhisattva is to be considered as not capable of turning back from enlightenment, and is to be looked upon as not deprived of the Perfection of Wisdom. This Perfection of Wisdom should be heard by those in the stage of disciple, by those in the stage of pratyekabuddha, and also by those in the stage of bodhisattva. For in the Perfection of Wisdom all the qualities of a bodhisattva are contained at length.

The first chapter is devoted to repeating in different ways that the bodhisattva wins complete enlightenment by not accepting any dharma as real. Form, feeling, all the skandhas are delusion (*māyā*). The actual nature of things (*dharmatā*) is dependent upon the nature of such delusion. Just as a clever conjurer may produce the illusion of a crowd of people, but when he makes them vanish he has not killed them, so a bodhisattva takes countless beings to Nirvāṇa, though there is no being who attains Nirvāṇa. The same teaching is given in the next chapter, where it is addressed to the gods. The gods are laymen, and it is clear that this is the popular form of the doctrine addressed to laymen.

The fundamental principle is expounded in the chapter on the Void. " 'Profound' is a name of the Void, of the signless, of the undetermined, of non-accumulating, of non-arising, of non-birth, of non-passion, of cessation, of Nirvāṇa, of departure." It is also a name for all things, and things that are void are also imperishable. The Void is the immeasurable. Hence in these things no distinction or plurality is found.

It is not surprising that a system expressed in such terms should have been called negativism or even nihilism.[1] It was even so-called by contemporary opponents, and Nāgārjuna's commentator Chandrakīrti had to deny that the Mādhyamikas were nihilists (*nāstika*, *nāsti*, " is not "). D. T. Suzuki says, " it simply means conditionality or transitoriness of all phenomenal existences." [2] Stcherbatsky translates *śūnya* (void) and *śūnyatā* (voidness) by " relativity ", and says, " we use the term 'relative' to express the fact that a thing can be identified only by mentioning its relations to something else, and becomes meaningless without these relations." [3] This explains the relative side, but says nothing about the positive. It is not the doctrine that all is relative, but that all is relative to an absolute.

It is clear that a term which has to be interpreted in such an apparently arbitrary way as by Suzuki and Stcherbatsky is not self-evident. The choice of the term was due to the practice of the early Mahāyānists of adopting certain established terms in a new sense.[4] They were thus enabled to find evidence in the Scriptures for their own doctrines. The term Void in the literal sense of emptiness is often found. There are two suttas on emptiness in the *Majjhima* (121, 122). The monk first meditates on the emptiness of an empty place, and then on the eight stages of concentration, each of which is empty with regard to the

[1] According to Walleser, Buddhism was at first " positivistisch ", and then turned to " den ausgesprochensten Negativismus ". According to O. Franke, nothing but negativism was ever taught in old Buddhism. *Festschrift E. Kuhn*, p. 336.

[2] *Outlines of Mahāyāna Buddhism*, p. 173.

[3] *Conc. of Nirv.*, p. 42.

[4] *Gambhīra*, *anutpāda*, *animitta*, *apraṇihita*, *virāga*, *nirodha*, *nirvāṇa*, all synonyms of the Void, are examples of such terms.

former, until he rests in signless (*animitta*) concentration of mind. Here the Void is purely psychological. The universe (*loka*) is also said to be void of a self or of anything belonging to a self,[1] and there is the same standpoint in *Sutta-nipāta*, 1119:

> As void one should look upon the world,
> O Mogharāja, being ever mindful;
> When he has destroyed the theory of a self,
> Then will he overcome Death.

Three of the most characteristic terms of the doctrine of the Void are also found applied to the sense-contact of one who rises from the Attainment of the cessation of perception and feeling: *suññata* (here an adjective, void), *animitta* (signless), and *appaṇihita* (undetermined, unapplied).[2] It may be asked whether we have in this case the intrusion of later doctrine, but the probability is that, as in several other cases, the terms have later been given a new sense in the doctrine of the Void.

The old doctrine that there was no entity in a self beyond the elements that compose it was extended to things in general (*dharmanairātmya*). Existence consists of dharmas, things or objects, but what can be said of these objects? They are all impermanent and changing, and nothing can be said of them at one moment which is not false the next. They are as unreal as the ātman itself.

The Buddhist thinkers had without realizing it stumbled upon the fact that the terms of ordinary language do not express the real facts of existence. Words are static, but not the objects to which they refer. The contradictions were attributed not to the defects of verbal expression, but to the nature of the experience. The discovery of antinomies has happened more than once in the history of philosophy. They are well known in the paradoxes of Zeno, the pupil of Parmenides.[3] Parmenides had taught that the existent is one, it is imperishable, indivisible, and perfect. All plurality,

[1] *Saṃy.*, iv, 54; this is the standpoint taken by the two *Prajñāpāramitā-hṛdaya-sūtras*, which declare that the skandhas, āyatanas, and dhātus (i.e. everything) are void.

[2] Ibid., iv, 295.

[3] Kant's antinomies were not quite the same. He found that antinomies arose when reason proceeded to draw conclusions from certain concepts that could not be verified in experience. But the antinomies arose from the same cause, the impossibility of making the terms of the concepts correspond with actual reality. For the latest treatment of Parmenides see F. M. Cornford in *Class. Quart.*, 1933, p. 97.

variety, coming into being, and destruction are empty words. This itself is a remarkable parallel to the doctrine of the Void, and the paradoxes of Zeno are an illustration of the same kind of dialectic as we find in Mahāyāna. If existence is many, said Zeno, it must be infinitely great and infinitely small. Motion is impossible, and so on.[1] The philosophical geniuses who followed Zeno were able to start afresh from a sounder standpoint, but the Indian philosophers never doubted that words were an adequate expression of things. For the Buddhists words were the verbal statement of the facts, or rather of the data, of sense experience. Instead of trying to restate their position they went forward, but actual experience had to be accounted for. Hence their theory of two kinds of truth, veiled or conventional truth (*samvṛti*), and truth in the highest sense (*paramārtha*). Truth in the highest sense is *tathatā*, "suchness," reality without any qualifications, the absolute. It cannot even be called existent, for existence implies relation to a possible non-existent. As it is beyond all relation it is inexpressible.

The work of Nāgārjuna[2] on the doctrine of the Void consists of a series of verses (*kārikā*), on which he himself wrote a commentary called *Akutobhayā*, "the fearless," explaining and expanding the argument. There are other commentaries, the most important being the *Prasannapadā* by Chandrakīrti.

Nāgārjuna begins by discussing the nature of causation as expressed in the theory of dependent origination (*pratītya-samutpāda*) of the Causal Formula. Dependent origination is said to be characterized by being (1) without cessation, (2) without origination, (3) without cutting off, (4) not eternal, (5) not one, (6) not differentiated, (7) without coming, (8) without going. Its interpretation as a series of causes and effects is entirely rejected. The argument consists in showing that contradictions arise in whatever way their causal relations are considered, and then both alternatives

[1] The impossibility of motion is discussed by Nāgārjuna in his second chapter. The problem of Achilles and the tortoise is one of Zeno's paradoxes, but this rests on his assuming that a line divided into an infinite number of parts is necessarily infinite in length.

[2] The name of the school of Nāgārjuna is *Mādhyamika* "follower of the *madhyamā pratipat*, the Middle Way or Path ", and there is little doubt that the term is taken from the first sermon of Buddha, where the Middle Path is preached. But the old meaning was transformed, and for Nāgārjuna it was the middle path between asserting the real existence of dharmas and denying them in the sense of negating a possible real.

are denied. The actual paradox of Zeno about the impossibility of motion occurs here.

" There are no things at all that have arisen, either of themselves or from another, or from both, or without a cause." Arising out of itself would imply that itself already existed. If a thing could be caused from what is other to itself, then anything could be produced from anything. Following the moral rules might lead to hell and the ten sins to heaven. That a thing could arise without a cause is still more absurd. The Mādhyamika has no objection to using arguments which would not be valid for himself. They are valid for his opponent, and all that he has to do is to show the contradictory results.

" There are four kinds of conditions : cause (*hetu*), object (*ālambana*), the preceding moment (*anantara*), and the predominating condition (*adhipati*).[1] In these conditions no self-existence of the entities is found. When there is no self-existence, there is no related existence." Here the existence of any causal relation is denied, much as was done by Hume. By association we read causal relations into the sequence. " Effect is with conditions ; effect is not with conditions ; conditions are not without effects, nor with them."

" Suppose it is said that there are conditions if a thing arises causally. So long as they have not arisen, why are they not called non-conditions ? " This, says La Vallée Poussin, is the cornerstone of Mādhyamika dialectic. It occurs elsewhere in the form, " if there is no father without a son, how does the existence of a son come about ? If there is no son there is no father, and hence both father and son are unreal." [2] He goes on : " neither of the non-existent nor of the existent is there a cause. If a cause of the non-existent, of what is it the cause ? If of the existent, why a cause ? "

The next point is the relation between things considered as consciousness (*citta*), or any special form which it takes (*caitta*), and that which is dependent on it, the object. If the consciousness exists in its own right, it is useless to consider an object. If the object already exists before the consciousness arises, then there is no question of relation

[1] This is the analysis of causal conditions as stated by the Sarvāstivādins, *Abhk.*, ii, 61 ff. It has been well discussed by O. Rosenberg, *Die Probleme d. buddh. Phil.*, ch. 15.

[2] *Bodhicaryāv.*, ix, 114.

to what is non-existent. There is no cessation (disappearance) of things which have not originated, and the preceding moment disappears in the effect, so that there is no cause.

The " predominating condition " is the condition as stated in the general formulation of cause, " when this exists, that exists." But as there is no real entity in entities the formula becomes meaningless. The result does not exist in any one of the conditions nor in all of them. Cloth cannot be perceived in the loom, nor in the threads, nor in the shuttle. If from such conditions something appears which was never in them, why does not a result appear from non-conditions ? " Therefore there is nothing that has a condition, no result without a condition ; as there are no results, how are there any conditions or non-conditions ? "

The history of the theories of the conception of cause in philosophical systems suggests that it is not surprising that contradictions should arise when the popular conception is analysed. The Buddhists had not even one conception. They had the Causal Formula, with a whole series of examples of causal sequence. No analysis was ever successful in interpreting them consistently. The only uniform expression ever reached was, " this being so, that happens," and this was so generalized that the scholastics had been able to find four different types of cause or conditional relation. It was not to Nāgārjuna's interest to find a better concept. The more defective the current concepts were, the easier it was for him to prove them all inconsistent. But that was only one half of the doctrine. Behind everything inconsistent and unreal or " void " there was an absolute reality. From the first there had been, though it was not conceived cosmically, but as a permanent attainable state, and from the first it was attainable not by reasoning processes, but by direct intuition. This method, the practice of concentration, was as essential in Mahāyāna as it had ever been.

As Dr. Schayer says, the normal means for attaining the mystic end is the methodically exercised practice of Yoga. In the long-prepared ecstasy the saint has beheld and grasped the all-unity, and although he awakes again to normal life, i.e. is again brought back to the distinction of subject and object, perceives colours, sounds, etc., feels feelings, and thinks thoughts, yet his consciousness of reality is fundamentally transformed by his post-ecstatic retrospection, just in this sense that now everything actual appears empty and unreal, dreamlike and illusory.[1]

Whatever the Void means—and it was only an old term adapted to a new concept—the fundamental fact for the Buddhist was this reality. How it was interpreted in relation to the Doctrine and the person of Buddha will be seen later. There are still other points in the teaching of Nāgārjuna which will make his position clearer.

He proceeds through all the characteristic doctrines of the Vaibhāshikas, treating them in the same way—on the impossibility of motion, on the sense faculties, the skandhas, action and actor, the truth of pain, the self, time, etc. In the chapter on Binding and Release *saṃsāra*[2] itself is said to be unreal. " If the saṃskāras transmigrate, they do not transmigrate as anything permanent nor as impermanent, and the argument for the existence of a being is just the same." Here the saṃskāras are the elements of which all compound things consist. But nothing is permanent except the three uncompounded things, and if the compounds are impermanent they perish as soon as they arise. This assumes the doctrine of momentariness (*kshaṇikavāda*), according to which each thing consists of a series of moments. Nor does the individual (*pudgala*) transmigrate. " If it is said that an individual transmigrates, he must be sought in fivefold way in the skandhas, in the āyatanas and the dhātus, but he (apart from these) does not exist. Who then transmigrates ? " The ātman is as unreal as the son of a barren woman. " From one form of grasping (*upādāna*) to another it would have no existence in *saṃsāra* ; as it is without existence and without grasping, how does it transmigrate ? " There is no transmigration of an ātman, adds the commentator, and as there is no transmigration of compounded things either, therefore there is no transmigration at all.

But all this is true of Nirvāṇa itself. It is a dream, a magician's deluding, says the commentator, quoting the passage in the *Ashṭasāhasrika* given above (p. 216). Yet, says an objector, though you deny transmigration and Nirvāṇa, yet there are binding and release. Nāgārjuna

[1] *Augewählte Kapitel aus der Prasannapadā*, p. xxiv.

[2] *Saṃsāra* may mean transmigration ; here it is rather the world of change in which transmigration takes place.

replies: "Compounded things, whose nature is arising and passing away, are neither bound nor released; nor is a being, as said above, either bound or released." But surely, says the objector, grasping is a bond, and as that is real there is binding. No, is the reply, for that which is already bound cannot come into the state of being bound, and that which is not bound is free from binding. It is the same argument which has already been used to prove the impossibility of motion. "The bound is not released, and the not bound is likewise not released. If the bound were released, binding and releasing would be simultaneous."

Those who say, "I shall attain Nirvāṇa when I am without grasping, and Nirvāṇa will be mine," hold a great false notion, the belief in a real self (*satkāyadṛṣṭi*). Here the doctrine of non-self is turned against the whole Hīnayāna scheme of salvation. The commentator quotes a long passage from a Mahāyāna sūtra, the *Dhyāyitamushṭi-sūtra*. In a conversation with Mañjuśrī the Lord describes the whole career of the disciple who enters the Order, keeps the moral laws, thinks that all compounds are transitory, feels revulsion, practises the path, and realizes tranquillity. He thinks, "I am released from all pains, there is nothing more for me to do, I am an arhat." Thus he forms the idea of a self, and at the time of death he is convinced of the rebirth (*utpatti*) of the self, so that doubt and uncertainty arise, and uncertainty about the enlightenment of an enlightened one. When he dies, he falls into the great hell, because although all things are unoriginated he imagines them as real.

The true Mahāyāna doctrine according to this sūtra is, "he who looks upon all compounds as not arisen has understood pain. He who looks upon all things as unoriginated has abandoned the cause of pain. He who looks upon all things as utterly extinguished has realized its cessation. He who looks upon all things as utterly void has practised the Way. He who thus looks upon the four noble Truths forms no idea or notion that 'these things are good, those things are bad, these things are to be abandoned, those things are to be realized, pain is to be understood, its origin is to be abandoned, its cessation is to be realized, the Way is to be practised.' And why? Because there is no thing which he imagines as real; fools and common people do so, and thus they feel passion, hatred, and delusion. He neither accepts or denies any *dharma* (thing), and thus his mind clings to nothing in the three worlds. He looks upon the whole three worlds as unborn."

It is with reference to this Scripture (Āgama), says the commentator, that Nāgārjuna states the question of Nirvāṇa from the point of view of absolute truth : " where there is no attribution of reality to Nirvāṇa and no withdrawal of *saṃsāra*, how can *saṃsāra* and Nirvāṇa be there distinguished in thought ? " They are thus identical, or at least proved to be identical. They are no more different than the waves of the ocean are different from the ocean.

Nāgārjuna discusses the question of Nirvāṇa in full in chapter 25. " If everything is void, there is no origination and no passing away ; of what is there Nirvāṇa either by abandonment or by cessation ? " The commentator first gives a fair statement of the Hīnayāna view. " Now with regard to this the Lord has described a twofold Nirvāṇa of individuals who have practised the religious life, followed the teaching of Buddha, acquired the greater and lesser doctrines, namely, Nirvāṇa with the remainder of a substratum of rebirth (*upadhi*) and Nirvāṇa without a remainder. The first is understood as due to complete abandonment of the depravities, ignorance, passion, etc. . . . It is like a village in which all the gangs of robbers have been destroyed.[1] But the Nirvāṇa in which even the mere skandhas no longer exist is Nirvāṇa without such a remainder.[2] It is like a village which, after the gangs of robbers have been destroyed, has itself been annihilated."

But, says Nāgārjuna, " if everything is non-void (real in the popular sense), there is neither arising nor passing away. Of what is there Nirvāṇa either by abandonment or cessation ? " The Hīnayānist replies, " if there is Nirvāṇa, there will indeed be no depravities or skandhas when Nirvāṇa is attained, hence their destruction will be Nirvāṇa." The reply as stated by the commentator is, " get rid of your false view (*grāha*). If things exist really, they cannot become non-existent. As Nāgārjuna says, ' The limit of Nirvāṇa is also the limit of *saṃsāra* ; not the finest distinction is found between them.' It must be understood that there is

[1] The simile of the village and robbers goes back to *Saṃy.*, iv, 175.

[2] The word *parinirvāṇa*, sometimes supposed to be the term for complete Nirvāṇa, is not used ; see p. 122.

no abandoning of anything through Nirvāṇa, nor the ceasing of anything. Hence Nirvāṇa is the destruction of all false imaginings, as has been said by the Lord:

> No real thing is of such a nature that it passes away;
> A thing that is not does not exist at all.
> He who imagines that things exist and exist not
> Will never make pain to cease.

The meaning of the verse is that in Nirvāṇa without a remainder there is non-existence through the utter disappearance of things, whether the depravities, karma, birth, or the skandhas. This all schools admit. Now things which are in Nirvāṇa do not exist at all. They are like the fear of a rope mistaken for a snake, which disappears when a light is brought in. As for existence in *saṃsāra,* fools and common people who believe in a self and selfhood are like people suffering from ophthalmia who see unreal hairs and flies floating before them."

The conclusion is drawn that Nirvāṇa is neither (1) existent, (2) nor non-existent, (3) nor existent and non-existent, (4) nor non-existent and not non-existent. The fourfold denial is another instance of direct connection with the older schools, for it is the same fourfold division as we find in the four undetermined questions about the existence of a Tathāgata after death. Here it is applied to the existence of Nirvāṇa. Existence is related to non-existence and to cause and effect. The reality of Nirvāṇa is beyond all conditions. The doctrine is one that is found differently expressed in other religions. The ultimately real is nowhere found in transient things. Nothing can be said of it but "no, no". But it can be apprehended in mystic intuition, and if this is knowledge, it is a knowledge entirely different from that of ordinary experience. Of this knowledge Nāgārjuna does not speak, but it is the counterpart of his attitude to the knowledge and experience of the senses, which he analyses and pulverizes. It is the attitude of the mystic who with the experience of the one reality knows that all else is empty and vain. This one reality, which is not to be called anything, not even real, is Nirvāṇa.

Buddhism, which began with the mysticism of yoga-practices, also ended with it. For the mystic, the ultimately real of his experience was *tathatā,* "suchness." As the goal of his attainment it was Nirvāṇa, and as the object of his thought it was Buddha as the *dharmakāya*, "the body of the doctrine," or (with the ontological meaning of *dharma*) "the body of the nature of things." Like other forms of mysticism that try to express the inexpressible, Mahāyāna developed a mystic symbolism. This will be seen in the other great Mahāyāna school, that of the Yogāchāras.

The Middle doctrine of Nāgārjuna appears later than the earliest form of the doctrine of the Void, as taught in the sūtras of the Perfection of Wisdom, but it cannot be assumed that all the sūtras of this class are earlier than Nāgārjuna. They probably continued to be composed and revised. As they were intended for the edification of the laity they glorify the career of the bodhisattva and preach the great merits of hearing the recitation of each sūtra.

The introductory verses of the *Daśabhūmika* end with the words, "let those desirous of enlightenment hear the *Daśabhūmika* uttered, which has been proclaimed as the pure middle course that avoids (the extremes of) annihilation and permanence." These verses may be later than the sūtra itself, but evidently we have here an instance of the popular teaching going on at the side of the philosophical. The *Suvarṇaprabhāsa-sūtra* is a still more striking instance of the popular aspect. It contains the same four introductory verses as the *Daśabhūmika*, but with its own name substituted. This makes the line unmetrical, and implies that here at least there is an addition. The popularity of this sūtra is shown by the frequency with which it was translated into Chinese, Tibetan, and other languages, and these translations, with their changes and additions, allow us to see the growth of doctrine as well. According to the editor, Mr. Idzumi, it was first translated into Chinese about A.D. 412–426. This translation, like the Sanskrit itself, contains no explicit reference to the three bodies of a Buddha. In later versions a special chapter on the subject is inserted, and the rise of the doctrine can be certainly placed between the second and fifth centuries A.D.

The *Suvarṇaprabhāsa*, even more than the *Lotus*, shows the popular side of Mahāyāna teaching. The first chapter is devoted to its merits and the benefits of hearing it. The second has the same title as chapter 15 of the *Lotus*, on

The length of life of the Tathāgata, and the teaching is the same :

> The Buddha does not attain Nirvāṇa,
> The Doctrine does not pass away ;
> But for the sake of ripening beings
> He makes a show to attain Nirvāṇa.

This teaching is given to Ruchiraketu, and then follows the story of his having a dream and going to Buddha, before whom he makes the bodhisattva's vow to attain enlightenment.

The rest consists of chapters all very instructive to the laity, but without any inner connection. The four Great Kings come and tell how the sūtra has given them heroism and strength. The goddess Sarasvatī gives a spell against evil planets and dreams, and other gods and goddesses appear. Then follows a discourse on the duties of kings and stories of the former deeds of bodhisattvas. Some of them are formal jātakas with identification of the characters at the end. Chapter 6 is called *The Void,* and it undertakes to give in summary what other sūtras have given at length. It consists simply of thirty mixed trishṭubh verses, which might have been inserted from anywhere. The body is described as an empty village, in which the senses run about like six thieves (the same simile as used by Nāgārjuna, p. 224). The elements are like four snakes, and the conclusion is that all things are void and have arisen through conditions from ignorance.

Philosophically there is little to be gleaned from these sūtras. Their religious conceptions of bodhisattva practice and worship were shared by the Yogāchāras, but philosophically the Yogāchāras, though retaining the fundamental concept of the void, made a great advance by starting from a psychological standpoint.

Note on the Later Schools

The later schools were once classed according to the four divisions given by Mādhava in his *Sarvadarśanasaṃgraha.* This is a work of the fourteenth century, and merely shows us how the Buddhist schools appeared to a Hindu at that time. Even so, what we learn from it is not the fundamental teaching, but the points of dispute which had been selected for refutation by the orthodox schools. The schools mentioned are two of the older group (Hīnayāna), the Vaibhāshikas (Sarvāstivādins) and the Sautrāntikas, and the two chief Mahāyāna schools, the Mādhyamikas and the Yogāchāras.

More details are given by Tāranātha in his history of Buddhism.[1] It contains much that is unhistorical and fantastic, and it is not necessary here to discuss it in detail. Its value for us is that it was written by one who had the Buddhist literature behind him, and we can now see what that literary development was.

This first began in the Abhidharma schools. Besides the Sarvāstivādin group the chief schools were the Sautrāntikas and the Sāṃmitīyas.[2] Of these we have no complete accounts, but the *Abhidharmakośa* discusses many of their views. The author Vasubandhu undertook to expound Sarvāstivāda doctrine, though he appears to have been inclined to the Sautrāntikas. The name Sautrāntika implies that they rejected the Abhidharma works as an authority, and accepted only the *sūtrāntas*. The Sāṃmitīyas are best known for holding, like the Vātsīputrīyas, the pudgala doctrine, the view that though the individual does not exist apart from his parts, yet he is something more than the mere sum of them. Another important Hīnayāna school is well known as the Mahāsanghika, whose buddhological doctrines, if not the school itself, became merged in Mahāyāna.

It is clear, both from the Mahāyāna sūtras and the systematic works, that the chief opponents of the early Mahāyāna controversialists were the Sarvāstivādins. These continued to flourish at the side of the Mahāyānists, for Vasubandhu's great work on Abhidharma belongs to the fifth century.

We have seen the scope of Nāgārjuna's work. It was a systematization of the doctrine that first appears in the Mahāyāna sūtras. But this was probably only the final outcome of what had already been taught in a systematic form in the monasteries.[3] Another author who contributed to it was Āryadeva, and it continued to flourish and be commented on for centuries.

[1] The contents have been well analysed by Professor P. L. Vaidya in his *Etudes sur Āryadeva*.

[2] On these two schools, see *ERE*.

[3] P. L. Vaidya, ibid., p. 20, puts Nāgārjuna A.D. 170–200, and Āryadeva A.D. 200–225.

There is a similar course of development in the next great school, the Yogāchāra. We find a popular presentation in sūtra form, and then a systematic treatment by several scholars. Again, it is a natural surmise that when the sūtra was set forth there was already a systematic treatment in the monasteries, and that what we have now in the works of Asanga and Vasubandhu represents the form that it had taken in one of the centres of learning. After this there were no more important metaphysical developments. There was a subtle change in the religious side in the movement known as Tantrism, which affected both Buddhist and Hindu schools. In both cases it appears as an alien growth, but in the mysticism of the Yogāchāras there was a natural soil for its development.

The later we go the clearer become the traces in Buddhist literature of contact with the orthodox Hindu schools. There is a passage in Chandrakīrti's commentary on Nāgārjuna which gives us an interesting glimpse of the state of philosophical parties in the seventh century A.D.[1] He refers to the different ways in which reality is asserted. (1) There are those who imagine the real existence of entities, and they are said to be the three Hindu schools of Karma-mīmāṃsā, Vaiśeshika, and Sānkhya, and the Vaibhāshikas. (2) Those who deny existence are the Nāstikas, the materialists or nihilists. (3) There are those who deny the existence of past and future, of moral character (*avijñapti*),[2] of unconscious mental elements, but assert it of the rest. These appear to be the Sautrāntikas. (4) There are those who deny the real existence of the falsely known (*parikalpita*), but assert it of that which exists (relatively) through conditions (*paratantra*), and of that which is thought in its true nature (*parinishpanna*). These are the Yogāchāras, who had already become an important school. There appears to be no recognition here of the holders of upanishadic doctrine, nor of the form which it finally took as the Vedānta.

[1] *Madhyamakavṛ*, 523.
[2] Thus reading with Stcherbatsky, not *vijñapti*; cf. p. 162.

CHAPTER XVIII

THE DOCTRINE OF CONSCIOUSNESS ONLY: THE THREE BODIES: TANTRISM

THE *Lankāvatāra-sūtra* is important not only as the chief canonical text for the doctrine of subjective idealism but also on account of its curious literary character as a sūtra. It is essentially the same doctrine as is later found in the Yogāchāra of Asanga and Vasubandhu.[1]

Professor Suzuki (*Studies*, 171) says that it was not written as a philosophical treatise to establish a definite system of thought, but to discourse on a certain kind of religious experience, and that what philosophy or speculation it offers is only incidental as an introduction necessitated by the rational nature of humanity. It may be true that this was the writer's motive, but it is also true, as Professor Suzuki's valuable and important studies show, that the philosophical system was there, and that the author was not slow in attacking rival systems. It is not systematic, but sūtras, as we have seen, were not systematic. They were popular expositions of the instruction given orally in the monasteries. The *Lankāvatāra* evidently belonged to a Mahāyāna school which existed alongside of the Prajñāpāramitā movement. It accepted the doctrine of the Void, the career of the bodhisattva, and the unreality of things perceived by the senses. But while the school of Nāgārjuna started from the standpoint of logic, and showed the impossibility of making any statement free from contradictions, the *Lankāvatāra* started from a psychological standpoint, and found a positive basis in actual experience.

Nothing definite can be said about the date of the *Lankāvatāra*. It was first translated into Chinese about A.D. 430, and again in A.D. 443, but it was then already a composite work, and it may have existed much earlier

[1] Suzuki refuses to call it Yogāchāra. It is, however, one formulation of the system that held the doctrine of Vijñānavāda, the existence of consciousness only.

in a simpler form.[1] Still it appears to be later than the Prajñāpāramitā group of sūtras. Much of it is in verse, and the polemical matter seems to be further removed from the period when Mahāyāna had to defend itself against the older Buddhist schools. It shows its hostility to the careers of disciples and pratyekabuddhas, but more prominent than these are the tīrthakaras, the " heretics ", who in this sūtra are the representatives of the orthodox schools such as Nyāya and Sānkhya, which are mentioned by name. The full title is *Saddharma-lankāvatāra*, " the entrance of the good doctrine into Lankā." Lankā usually means Ceylon, but here there is no traceable reference to the Pāli legend of Buddha's three visits to Ceylon. Lankā is here a city on the peak of Mount Malaya,[2] and it is the citadel of Rāvaṇa, the rākshasa with ten heads. The literary reference comes rather from the *Rāmāyaṇa*, but the monster of the epic appears here as a good Buddhist layman.

When the sūtra opens Buddha was just coming out of the palace of the nāgas beneath the ocean, where he had been preaching for a week. He looked at Lankā and smiled, for he remembered that previous Buddhas had taught the doctrine there. Rāvaṇa, being inspired by the power of Buddha, invited him to come and teach the doctrine of inner perception and the real existence of mind (*citta*). Buddha then went to Lankā in Rāvaṇa's chariot, and he and his attendant bodhisattvas were adorned by yaksha girls and boys with necklaces of pearls and gems. He created other mountain peaks, on which he himself with Rāvaṇa was seen. Suddenly they all vanished, and Rāvaṇa found himself alone. He had a sudden revulsion of feeling (*parāvṛtti*), and realized that what he perceived was only his own mind. Then through his former roots of goodness he was able to understand all treatises, and with his yoga power he could see things as they really are. He heard a voice from the sky saying, " it is to be known through the inner self," and Buddha explained to him that thus was the way of training. It is the way of the yogis, the sons of Buddha, i.e. the

[1] It contains (88), apparently an allusion to the parable in the *Lotus*, where a man attracts his boys with toy animals, but afterwards gives them real ones, and in refuting the idea of cause (84) it uses two of the arguments used by Nāgārjuna.

[2] Malaya is usually a mountain in Malabar, but a district of that name in Ceylon is mentioned in *Mhvs*.

bodhisattvas, who advance beyond the views and attainments of disciples, pratyekabuddhas, and heretics. This is the realization of the great yogis, who crush the doctrines of others, who destroy evil heresies, who are skilled in rejecting the heresy of a self and in producing a revulsion of mind by means of higher understanding.

In this way Rāvaṇa was taught the two fundamental truths of this school, the truth that everything external is due to a wrong interpretation of inner experience, and the truth that the apprehension of reality is reached by a sudden revulsion in which the truth bursts upon the yogi (by which is meant the bodhisattva) in his contemplation.

The whole scene then reappeared to Rāvaṇa in all its glory, and Buddha laughed. The whole assembly laughed, but Buddha laughed loudest. The reason was, as Buddha explained, that Rāvana wanted to ask a twofold question. He had already asked it of Buddhas in the past, and he will ask it of the Buddhas to come. Rāvaṇa was then allowed to put his question on the duality of things. It is said that things and non-things are to be abandoned. How can they be abandoned if they do not exist ? The answer is that duality is due only to the wrong imagination of the ignorant. Such people look upon the manifestations of mind as external things. They should be looked upon, like the horns of a hare, as belonging neither to reality nor non-reality, and in that consists their abandonment. " He who thus sees, sees rightly. They who see otherwise move in false imagination,[1] and grasp things as twofold, like a reflection of oneself in a mirror or in water, or one's shadow by the light of the moon or in a house, or like hearing an echo. Thus by grasping at their own false imagination they imagine things and non-things ; they go on imagining, and never attain tranquillity. The word tranquillity means " having one point " (*ekāgra*). It is the entrance into the Tathāgatagarbha, the realm of the noble knowledge of the inner self, whereby arises the highest concentration." [2]

That is the end of the chapter on the request of Rāvaṇa.[3]

[1] Suzuki says " discrimination ", but it should at least be called false discrimination. It consists in making a false distinction or positing of things as inner and outer.

[2] *Lank.*, 20.

[3] Nanjio's table shows that the first chapter is not in the earliest extant Chinese translation. It has evidently been added as a popular introduction

He appears no more, and the rest of the sūtra, except a collection of verses forming the last chapter, consists of an exposition of the doctrine that the world is nothing but mind (*cittamātra*), and that this is to be realized in a state of concentration. The teaching is given in answer to the questions of the bodhisattva Mahāmati, who appears only as a questioner, unlike the bodhisattvas in other sūtras, who through the power of Buddha often expound much of the doctrine themselves.

The general position is like that of the Mādhyamika school. All is void, all is *māyā*, there is no self either in the individual or in objects, nothing can be asserted or denied about individual things, and there are three yānas, but only for the sake of rousing the ignorant. But while the Mādhyamikas start from the standpoint of logic, and show the impossibility of making any statement free from contradictions, the *Lankāvatāra* has a psychological basis. It assumes the psychological analysis of earlier Buddhism, the skandhas, sense organs, and senses. As through each sense a particular kind of consciousness, i.e. state of awareness, arises, we get six consciousnesses, eye-, ear,- nose-, tongue-, touch-, and mind-consciousness. But besides these a seventh is distinguished, *manas*, mind itself. This, says Dr. Masuda, is self-consciousness. That is no doubt one aspect of it, but it seems to have claimed recognition for the same reason that Aristotle distinguished a common sense. Each of the six consciousnesses acts through only one sense, but there is a faculty, the *sensus communis*, which can distinguish and compare the data of each sense. Professor Suzuki says that mind-consciousness is the mind which remembers, judges, imagines, wills, etc., but *manas* is the deeply-seated consciousness in the soul which ignorantly clings to the ego-conception and reality of an external world.

This would be enough for a psychological theory, but this theory is only part of an ontology. There is an ultimate reality, real beyond anything that can be asserted of what comes within the range of experience. This is thought (*citta*) or mind, not mind as existing in the variety in which it is experienced, but without any differentiation, and called

to the doctrine that is to follow. This translation also omits the two last chapters, the ninth on spells, and the tenth consisting of a collection of verses. Chapter 8 on meat-eating has also no organic connection with the rest.

store-consciousness (*ālaya-vijñāna*). When the relation between this and the consciousness of ordinary experience has to be explained, it is done by means of similes. "Consciousness consisting of the skandhas, dhātus, and āyatanas, which are without a self or of anything of the nature of a self, arises from ignorance, karma, and craving, and it functions through being attached to grasping at things by means of the eye and all the organs, and makes the presentations of its store-mind appear as bodies and vessels, which are manifestations of its own mind (the store-consciousness). Unstable like a river, a seed, a lamp, wind, a cloud, it is subject to destruction from moment to moment." [1]

All things having been explained as mind or consciousness, the ultimate reality is then interpreted as the fundamental store-consciousness, and all the other terms which have been applied to this reality are also used here. It is suchness, the Tathāgata, Buddhahood, and mind, but mind stripped of everything transient and phenomenal. Hence it becomes superfluous to ask whether this mind or store-consciousness is universal or individual. It is conceived as the one reality beyond all differentiation, and any plurality would imply differentiation. But it is also spoken of in its state of evolution, in which it includes all differentiation. This is the Tathāgata-garbha, "the womb of the Tathāgata," in which all reality and difference is embraced.[2] Buddha, buddhahood, tathatā are one, but on the plane of relative reality there are differences. Hence it is possible to speak of many Buddhas, and the bodhisattva may exercise his "skill in means" by appearing to accept such differences in order to save beings.

There is a list of five categories (*dharma*) which elucidate the main features of the system. (1) *Nāma* name, (2) *nimitta* mark, (3) *vikalpa* false imagination or positing (discrimination), (4) *samyagjñāna* right knowledge, (5) *tathatā* suchness, reality. They are brought into relation with the three kinds of self-existence (*svabhāva*). Names and marks are

[1] *Lank.*, 68. *Vijñāna* "consciousness", *manas* "mind", and *citta* "thought", are often used interchangeably in the older literature. Here they have been differentiated, without always being exactly distinguished. *Citta* is sometimes the *ālayavijñāna*.

[2] The Tathāgatagarbha is described as "naturally bright and pure from the beginning, bearing the thirty-two marks within the body of every being, like a precious jewel wrapped in a dirty garment". *Lank.*, 77. Every being is essentially Buddha.

entirely unreal, they lead to attributing reality or self-existence to unrealities, an entirely wrong and wrongly imagined (*parikalpita*) construction of experience. This is *parikalpita svabhāva*. *Vikalpa* may be of the relatively true, as when a thing is thought of as related to certain conditions, when the self-existence is *paratantra*, dependent on another.[1] Right knowledge, knowledge free from names, marks, and conditions, is knowledge of *tathatā*, suchness, absolute reality. Such existence is *parinishpanna*, perfected. Another important term is *vāsanā*, literally " perfuming ". It is something which remains like a perfume after an action has been done. One form of it is memory, but it is wider than that. Habits result from it, and Suzuki translates it " habit-energy ", which he explains as " a kind of supersensuous energy mysteriously emanating from every thought, every feeling, or every deed one has done or does, which lives latently in the store-house called ālaya-vijñāna ".[2] It is the truth that " what we have been makes us what we are ", but it involves another aspect than that crystallized in the doctrine of karma. The escape from it, as all Buddhism asserts, is right knowledge, the attaining of Nirvāṇa, and that, as explained here, is " the getting rid of the mind-consciousness which wrongly imagines ", i.e. which makes a false construction of experience and imagines or posits an external world. It is also said to be " the realm of attaining to the inner self by means of noble knowledge, free from the false notions of permanency and annihilation, existence and non-existence ".[3]

Thus mind-consciousness as the cause of this false construction is to be got rid of. " Mind-consciousness arises through being attached to the distinguishing of external objects, and it nourishes the store-consciousness by its *vāsanās* (the results of its activity). Mind (*manas*) then follows with its attachment to the ideal of me and mine and its reflection thereon. It has no separate body or mark of its own, and it has the store-consciousness as its cause and support. Through its attachment to objects, which are really manifestations of its own thought (*citta*), the whole system of thought-constructions arises mutually conditioned. Like waves of

[1] When a rope is imagined to be a snake, the snake is entirely unreal. The rope itself is real, but only in a relative sense, *paratantra*. The rope has no existence in the highest sense.

[2] *Studies*, p. 178.

[3] *Lank.*, 99.

the sea stirred by the wind of objects, which are manifestations of its own thought (these constructions) arise and pass away. Thus when mind-consciousness is got rid of, the seven consciousnesses are got rid of." This riddance is brought about as in all mysticism by an inner experience, expressly characterized in the *Lankāvatāra* as a revulsion (*parāvṛtti*) which results in a sudden reinterpretation of the whole data of experience. We are familiar with it in its moral aspect as conversion.

The *Lankāvatāra*, like all monistic systems, finds its chief difficulty in explaining the relation of the many to the one. It resorts to similes, it explains that words are not the highest reality, and teaches that the truth is to be reached by direct realization. The Mādhyamikas had been able to deny the reality of all sense experience by showing the contradictions which resulted in any attempt to express it verbally. Their success depended on their assumption that the verbal expressions were the accurate and complete representation of the experience. Their tenet of an absolute reality did not really result from their dialectic. It was an unquestioned assumption which had lain there all along. It was so also in the *Lankāvatāra*, but there it was a positive conception, and it was asserted to be related in some way to the world of unreality. But it was a conception of an absolute unity, not a unity like the ego of Fichte, in which the difference of ego and non-ego was implicit. Hence every appearance of difference or differentiation had to be explained as being illusion, and reality as being beyond the reach of thought. Such idealism, like other Indian idealistic systems, does not look to find reality in the fullest and most harmonious statement of the facts of experience, but in emphasizing one fact (itself an abstraction), and in brushing away the rest as illusion.

There is another presentation of this system in Aśvaghosha's *Awakening of faith in the Mahāyāna*.[1] Stcherbatsky puts the recognition of *ālaya-vijñāna* and *tathatā* by Aśvaghosha in the first century A.D. This implies that he identifies the author of the *Awakening of faith* with the great Buddhist poet of the time of Kanishka. However,

[1] *Mahāyāna-śraddhotpāda.* It has been translated from the Chinese by D. T. Suzuki, who is preparing a revised version. The presumed Sanskrit original is not known.

there were several Aśvaghoshas, and it is certain that the doctrine of the work as there presented cannot be earlier than the Mādhyamika school. It may be later even than the *Lankāvatāra*, for Suzuki says that it seems to be an attempt at systematizing the philosophy of that sūtra. It is a work of the same school, and need not be separately considered.

The brothers Asanga and Vasubandhu are said to be the founders of the Yogāchāra school. They were the founders in the same sense as Nāgārjuna was the founder of the Mādhyamikas. In both cases there was a school in existence and popular expositions of the doctrine in sūtras. The genius of one or two men in each case resulted in a systematic exposition of the doctrines of an already existing school. The connection of Asanga and Vasubandhu does not seem to have been so close to the *Lankāvatāra* as was that of Nāgārjuna to the Prajñāpāramitā works, but it was essentially the system of that work which they expounded and elaborated. It is not necessary to hold that they were of exactly the same school, and naturally they applied their own methods of persuasion. When a doctrine was taught orally in separate monasteries, it would be inevitable that the originality of individual teachers would lead to new lines of thought. In this sense there may have been far more schools than we are aware of, but there were two definite Mahāyāna systems, the Mādhyamika and the Yogāchāra, and to one or the other of these all Mahāyāna schools belonged in essentials.

The home of Asanga and Vasubandhu was Peshawar in Gandhāra, and they are said to have lived in the second half of the fifth century A.D.[1] They wrote a number of works

[1] The life of Vasubandhu was written in the sixth century by Paramārtha. It has been translated by Takakusu in *T'oung-pao*, 1904. There were three brothers of Peshawar, all called Vasubandhu, who became Sarvāstivāda monks. We are concerned only with the first two. The eldest studied the doctrine of the Void, but could not grasp it. When in despair he was about to destroy himself, the arhat Piṇḍola came from the mythical island, Pūrvavideha, and taught him the Hīnayāna doctrine. But still unsatisfied, he went by his magic power to the Tushita heaven and learnt the doctrine of the Void from the future Buddha Maitreya. Thenceforth he was known as Asanga (he who is without attachment), but he was unable to convince people of the doctrine, so at his request Maitreya came down and in the course of four months recited the Yogācārabhūmi. He also taught Asanga a form of concentration through which he could understand all things, even the most abstruse Mahāyāna sūtras, and on these he wrote commentaries. Many more details are told about him, the most credible of which is that he converted his next younger brother Vasubandhu, who had already written

which are now the foundation of *vijñānavāda*, the doctrine of consciousness only. As is shown by the title of the school, *Yogāchāra*, "the practice of yoga," there was a strong mystical side. The list of their works as given by the Tibetan author Bu-ston (cf. *Muséon*, 1905, p. 144) includes five by a teacher called Maitreya, on which Asanga wrote commentaries. The view that there really was such a teacher can now be accepted as correct. It is not philosophically important, but it shows that there was a well established Vijñānavāda doctrine before Asanga.

The most important of the works of the brothers, owing to the fact that it was commented on by ten commentators, is Vasubandhu's *Triṃśakakārikā* or *Triṃśikā* (thirty verses). What we possess now is the Sanskrit text of the verses with a large work by Hiuen Tsiang, compiled from these commentaries, the *Vijñaptimātratāsiddhi*.[1] It is arranged much like the *Abhidharmakośa*, the exposition of Sarvāstivāda doctrine, which Vasubandhu wrote before his conversion. Much of it is occupied with the refutation of the views of other teachers.

The term *vijñaptimātra* is used like the term *vijñānamātra*, "consciousness only," but *vijñapti* means "information, indication", and it has been explained as "thought", as being that which is expressed by indication. Vasubandhu and his commentators are much more interested than the *Lankāvatāra* in explaining the nature of existence as it appears, the different kinds of causes, and their relation to the store-consciousness. Dr. Masuda, in his important study, says that in the Yogāchāra philosophy the store-consciousness (unlike the *Lankāvatāra*) is still throughout an individual consciousness.[2] This is so because the exposition

important Sarvāstivāda works. It had been usual to assume that this story of Maitreya was sheer invention intended to give authority to what was really Asanga's work. But Professor H. Ui has shown that the explanation is rather that Maitreya was a historical personage and the instructor of Asanga, and that in the legends he has been confused with Maitreya the bodhisattva. See H. Ui in *Indian Studies in Honor of C. R. Lanman*, 1929; G. Tucci, *Doctrines of Maitreya*[*nātha*] *and Asanga*, Calcutta, 1930.

[1] Translated from the Chinese as *La Siddhi de Hiuen Tsang*, by L. de la Vallée Poussin, Paris, 1928–9. Sthiramati's commentary in Sanskrit has also been published.

[2] *Der individualistische Idealismus der Yogācāra-Schule*, p. 43; cf. *Siddhi*, p. 447; one does not experience the bījas of another, and the eighth consciousness of one person does not develop into the bījas of another. But why the bījas should be thus grouped into individuals no form of Buddhism has ever explained.

starts from phenomena, and explains them as they appear in each individual. Yet, as he says (p. 40), their theory led to the conclusion that nothing but consciousness exists, and the substance of phenomena, or in their terminology "the true nature", is the absolute or suchness (*tathatā*). For Nāgārjuna also it was suchness, but he gave no positive explanation of the relation between phenomena and the absolute. Dr. Masuda holds that for Yogāchāra it consists in the two being "neither different nor non-different" (p. 43). Thus so far as the store-consciousness is non-different from the absolute it is entirely universal and undifferentiated, and the positive explanation involves a contradiction to be surmounted by the methods of the mystic.

But before the final conclusion is reached an elaborate system of epistemology and ontology is set out. We find the same general concepts as in the *Lankāvatāra*, the eight consciousnesses, the three forms of self-existence, and the *vāsanās*. The *vāsanās* (results of actions) are called seeds (*bīja*). These exist in the store-consciousness, and always in time bear fruit. What we have here is a theory which rests on the same data as the doctrine of karma. But while karma is only a theory of the moral consequences of willed action, the vāsanā theory is wider, and it is applied chiefly to explain the error of thought which posits an external world. Different views were held as to why the seeds should exist in the store-consciousness at all. One view was that they were natural and had always been there, another that they had all been produced by "perfuming". Dharmapāla's view was that there were some of both kinds.[1] This view of "natural" seeds shows that we have a theory which cannot be entirely identified with the karma theory. The question as to how the process began does not arise, for the question of an absolute beginning always remained an excluded question.

Like the Mādhyamikas the Yogāchāras spoke of the non-selfness of individuals as well as of things. The two beliefs, the belief in the real existence of self and of things were the two obstructions, the obstruction of the depravities, passion, etc. (*kleśāvaraṇa*), and the obstruction to attaining full knowledge (*jñeyāvaraṇa*). The store-consciousness, it has

[1] *Siddhi*, pp. 102 ff.; Masuda, loc. cit., p. 38. There is no reason to identify the Dharmapāla, who taught at Nālandā in the seventh century, with the Pāli commentator Dhammapāla. E. Hardy, *ZDMG.*, 1898, p. 105.

been said, covers all that we now refer to as the subconscious and the unconscious. It is probable that the psychological facts of the subconscious gave rise to the concept of the store-consciousness, but it is not, as in modern psychology, a mere extension of the group of facts that are included in the conscious. It is a metaphysical concept of a different order of being, an ultimate reality at the base of all phenomena. The store-consciousness is already differentiated by the *vāsanās*, which as seeds ripen and produce their fruit. When it evolves it develops touch, mental activity (*manaskāra*), feeling, perception, and will (*cetanā*).[1] These five correspond to the five factors of the individual, the skandhas, but the skandha theory has had to be modified according to the mind-alone theory. The first skandha, body (*rūpa*) implies the heresy of externality and is replaced here by its subjective element, touch. *Manaskāra* includes the *saṃskāras*, all the ideas or states of mental activity. Feeling (*vit, vedānā*) and perception (*saṃjñā*) remain the same, and the place of consciousness (*vijñāna*) is taken by *cetanā*. This is a difference of terminology, as the term *vijñāna*, used in other special senses in this system, is here avoided. *Cetanā* is mind in action, i.e. will, and includes consciousness. It is "the activity of mind" (*manaśceṣṭā*) according to the commentary.

This is the first transformation, the evolution of the seeds that have ripened in the store-consciousness. The second transformation is the evolution of *manas*, the seventh consciousness. "Depending upon the store-consciousness, and having that as its support, the consciousness called *manas*, which has the nature of cogitation, functions." This is the second transformation, in which the *manas* is accompanied by the heresy of a self. The third transformation is the perception of the sixfold object, body, sound, scent, taste, touch, and ideas (objects of thought). The idea of a self consisting of the skandhas thus becomes concrete. The seventh consciousness (*manas*) is associated with all the modes of sense and thought and the other non-material activities of the individual. These are the saṃskāras, all the possible non-material states of the individual, and they are given according to the Sarvāstivāda analysis which has been discussed above (p. 162).

[1] The following exposition is according to Vasubandhu's *Triṃśikā*.

The five sense-consciousnesses, sight, etc., arise in the store-consciousness, and they are always accompanied by mind-consciousness, except in the world of the unconscious gods (*asaṃjñisattvas*), in the two highest Attainments (p. 52), and in torpor and fainting.

The theory of knowledge is the same as that which we find in the *Lankāvatāra*. The transformation of consciousness itself results in false imagination (*vikalpa*). Everything thus imagined is in general *parikalpita*, falsely imagined, and has no self-existence. But things may be thought in a certain regular order as being due to causes or conditions. Such thought has a relative self-existence (*paratantra*), and it expresses the relative truth of things as perceived; but it becomes as false as the rest when the great revulsion takes place, when the non-self-existence of all things is realized, and everything is known to be only store-consciousness. This is perfected knowledge (*parinishpanna*).

It is not enough to be convinced of the truth that all is only consciousness. He who grasps an object and says, "this is *vijñaptimātra*," has not reached *vijñaptimātra*. If he had, there would be no object to grasp nor grasper.

> When consciousness does not apprehend an object, then it is established in *vijñaptimātratā*; for when there is nothing to grasp there is no grasping.
>
> (When) he is without mind, without apprehending, his knowledge is supramundane. There is revulsion from the object, through the abandonment of the two kinds of weakness.[1]
>
> That is the realm without āsravas, inconceivable, good, fixed, happy, with body released; this is what is called the dharma-body of the great Sage.[2]

This is the state attained by the bodhisattva when he reaches omniscience. The attaining of it is no mere theoretical study of the doctrine of the Void or of mind-only. It involves the practice of the career of the bodhisattva pursued for countless ages through higher and higher stages, with the perfect attainment of the six virtues and the acquiring of omniscience in every possible form (*sarvākārajñatā*), such as we have seen in the sūtras that describe the career. This state is buddhahood, "the dharma-body of the great Sage." The bodhisattva becomes not merely a Buddha, but Buddha, the ultimate undifferentiated reality, suchness.

[1] i.e. the two obstructions, belief in a real self and belief in the reality of things, p. 239.

[2] *Triṃśikā*, 28–30.

As Asanga (or rather Maitreya) says, " on the pure stage (free from the āsravas) there is neither oneness nor plurality of Buddhas; not oneness owing to their formerly having had bodies, not plurality because like space they have no bodies." [1] Here we have the usual explanation of the absolute unity posited by the system. There is thus also an infinity of Buddhas. They are beings who have completed the career and have taught the doctrine; they exist now in a state of bliss, but behind all illusion and relative truth they are the one universal reality.

From this threefold Mahāyāna conception has resulted the doctrine of the three bodies of a Buddha (*trikāya*). Many dogmatic views about the nature of a Buddha had already been established, and in some of them we can perceive principles which anticipated the later theory. But it was the application of an ontological theory to all forms of existence that led to their being organized in the Trikāya theory. All the elements of the doctrine are found, as Suzuki points out, in the *Lankāvatāra*, but it will conduce to clearness if the explicit theory of Asanga is first stated.[2]

The body of Buddhas is threefold. The essential body is the dharma-body (*dharma-kāya*), and it is distinguished by revulsion of the support, i.e. the revulsion which has turned from everything illusory to ultimate reality. It is the same for all Buddhas. It is said to be the " support " of the two others, for ultimately only it exists, and is hence called essential (*svābhāvika*). The second, the body of enjoyment (*sambhoga-kāya*), is " that through which Buddha affords enjoyment of the doctrine in assemblies ". As Buddhas are described in the sūtras as existing in all universes and preaching to great assemblies of bodhisattvas and gods, this body of enjoyment was a concept which made it possible to harmonize the doctrine of these sūtras with the apparently contradictory teaching about his Nirvāṇa. This body is said to be different in all Buddha-fields and assemblies. Buddhas reveal themselves to bodhisattvas in this body in the Akanishṭha heaven, the highest of the heavens of

[1] *Mahāyānālank.*, ix, 26.

[2] Ibid., ix, 59 ff.; cf. Bu-ston, p. 127. Asanga expressly speaks of three bodies, the dharma-body being the essential body and the true form of all. But a fourth was made by treating the essential body separately. La Vallée Poussin, "The three bodies of a Buddha," *JRAS.*, 1906, 943; Masson-Oursel, *JA.*, 1913, 581.

form. The transformation-body (*nirmāṇa-kāya*) is "that by which he works the good of all creatures", i.e. the person of the historical Buddha, who passed through all the stages of his existence, taught the doctrine, and attained Nirvāṇa. The doctrine that Buddha could appear with a mind-formed body is very old, and the Mahāsanghikas converted it into the doctrine that his earthly appearance was never anything else. Here it appears to harmonize the teaching of works like the *Lotus* and the *Suvarṇaprabhāsa*, that the Tathāgata has always existed, with the historical facts about Śākyamuni.

As the trikāya doctrine is based upon a body of dogmatic teaching about the nature of a Buddha, it is natural that earlier doctrines should be included in it. But these are not necessarily anticipations of it. When *dhammakāya* occurs occasionally in the Pāli, it is merely the body of doctrine.[1] The *Milinda-pañha* says that Buddha now exists in the body of the doctrine, that is, in the spoken word, and the statement is only the utterance of the rationalist, who took a negative view of the nature of Nirvāṇa but preferred not to put it in its boldest form.[2]

Such references in the Pāli to the "body of the doctrine" have been called hints or foreshadowings of the Mahāyāna theory of dharmakāya. It is true that Mahāyāna adopted the phrase, and in the *Ashṭasāhasrika* (94) even used it in the same sense, where it is said that the Buddhas are dharmakāyas, but that the monks are not to think of Buddha's physical body; they will look upon him as the perfected dharmakāya, namely, the Prajñāpāramitā-sūtra. The change of meaning was due to a deliberate substitution of another meaning of *dharma*, in the sense of real nature, or ultimate

[1] Dutt, *Aspects*, pp. 98 ff.; La Vallée Poussin, "The three bodies of a Buddha," *JRAS.*, 1906, 947; Bu-ston, *History of Buddhism*, tr. Obermiller, p. 131; Suzuki, *Studies*, p. 308.

[2] The *Milinda-pañha*, "Questions of Milinda," is a work now existing in Pāli (transl. Rhys Davids, 1890–4). It consists of dialogues between king Milinda and a Buddhist sage Nāgasena discussing many points of Buddhist doctrine. The Milinda of the legendary setting is a reminiscence of the Bactrian king Menander of the second century B.C. To what school it belonged is unknown, and it is unlikely that its original language was Pāli. The date may be the first or second century A.D. Its rationalistic tone once made it a convenient means of reading into the Pāli Canon the view that original Buddhism was "agnostic atheism". It has not been used here, as it is quite impossible to treat its doctrines as authoritative for Theravāda, or as anything more than the individual views of a member of an unknown Hīnayāna sect. Mrs. Rhys Davids thinks that the author (or authors) was not even a Buddhist. See *Milinda Questions*, p. 18.

truth, which in the first place is enlightenment. The commentary on the *Bodhicaryāvatāra* (ix, 38) defines enlightenment (*bodhi*) as " buddhahood, existence in the highest sense, free from self-existence whether single or multiple, neither originated nor ceased, neither annihilated nor eternal, liberated from all contingent existence, like space, and named dharmakāya ". Here dharmakāya is an entity, the most real of entities, and to become a true ontological conception it only needed the Yogāchāra theory, which identified Buddha with the suchness of absolute reality.

It was this theory which made it possible to combine the dharmakāya with the two other bodies into a theory of the triple body. In popular buddhology the Buddhas continue to exist in a state of bliss. They attain even as bodhisattvas a glorious body. This is the body of enjoyment, even before it was called so. For the transformation body the Yogāchāras already had before them the doctrine of a mind-formed body, and the Mahāsanghika doctrine that Buddha's whole earthly existence was nothing more than this. The trikāya theory was only a systematizing of the already existing doctrines. As Suzuki says, it was probably not until the Yogāchāra philosophy began to be crystallized into a system by Asanga and his predecessors that the conception of the triple body came to form a part of their programme.

The most instructive piece of evidence is the *Suvarṇaprabhāsa*. This belongs to the Prajñāpāramitā class of sūtras. Like these sūtras it contains in the Sanskrit version no doctrine of the triple body, but later forms of the sūtra as preserved in translations contain an additional chapter on the subject. This means that the doctrine in its developed form has been adopted and inserted. The Yogāchāra school is the most probable source, but even in this school its formulation must be later than the *Lankāvatāra*.

There were two further developments of Buddhist thought, but neither can be said to be developments of the doctrine. The first was the rise of a school of logic. Logic for the Buddhists and the Indian schools generally was always more than the rules of formal thought, and it never became separated from questions of epistemology. These had been raised by the Yogāchāras in their extremest form, and it is not surprising that Buddhist logic and a theory of knowledge should be elaborated in this school. The subject belongs rather to the general history of Indian logic, and the sources have not yet been fully investigated or even published. Stcherbatsky has done important work at it,[1] and Tucci is still discovering and editing logical works which must be examined before the history can be written.

The discussions in the *Kathāvatthu* show that the Pāli school had developed a logical method, and Stcherbatsky thinks that manuals of logic must have then existed. But nothing more than a method was then wanted, for epistemological questions had not then arisen.

There are two small treatises in Tibetan by Nāgārjuna, which contain references to the logical method of Nyāya. This, even if not the beginning of Buddhist logic, allows us to see what were the influences on its development.[2] It was the school of Asanga which gave the great impulse to its growth. Asanga, says Stcherbatsky, established a body of rules on the art of debate not materially different from the rules prescribed in the Nyāya school, and Vasubandhu is recorded to have composed three logical treatises. With Asanga's pupil Dignāga (early sixth century) and Dharmakīrti, the pupil of Īśvarasena, Dignāga's own pupil, Buddhist logic became a widely famous system. Several schools of commentators followed, and then, says Stcherbatsky, " the popular masses began to turn their face from that philosophic, critical, and pessimistic religion, and reverted to the worship of the great brahmin gods. Buddhism was beginning its migration to the north, where it found a new home in Tibet, Mongolia, and other countries."

Why Buddhism declined and almost disappeared in the land of its birth is still a matter of discussion, but there is one other development still to be mentioned, tantric Buddhism. This was certainly flourishing in the tenth century. It is not properly speaking a development of Buddhism, but an amalgamation with a form of religion called Tantrism, which affected certain branches both of Buddhism and Hinduism. Tantrism as a form of religion is of unknown origin, and may possibly have arisen among

[1] *Buddhist Logic* (with a translation of Dharmakīrti's *Nyāyabindu* and its commentary by Dharmottara), Leningrad, 1931–2.

[2] Stcherbatsky, loc. cit., i, 28.

some indigenous and non-Aryan people. It consists in giving a religious significance to the facts of sex. Such a development, at least in a certain stage of society, is not necessarily immoral. Its discussion, however, belongs to medical psychology. The unpleasantness of the subject has sometimes led writers to speak of it as mere debauchery, but a proper examination of the facts would probably show that it belongs to an exceptional but not abnormal social development. When introduced into a quite different state of society it must appear both abnormal and immoral. In any case a proper discussion of the subject could only be made by including and treating of the facts as they have existed in all the various forms of Hinduism and as they exist now. One peculiar feature of Buddhist Tantrism is that it adopted religious technical terms and applied them in new senses, so that what appear as quite ordinary expressions may bear a surprisingly different meaning, and a tantric sense may be lurking where least expected. It is usually found combined with two other factors, the use of magic formulas, and yoga-practice. All the three have this in common that they represent attempts to get beyond the hard world of facts and achieve the marvellous results imagined by the mystic.

The use of magic formulas and practices, as we have seen, is very old in Buddhism. It was discouraged, and it was forbidden to the monk, but it was never doubted that such practices might be effective. In Mahāyāna they were not only held to be effective, but were regularly taught in the sūtras. Yoga is also very old, and among yoga-practices were many which might be performed for worldly purposes. These practices, too, increased and were elaborated by Mahāyāna, and there is little doubt that they opened the way to Tantrism. It was among the Yogāchāras that Tantrism developed. The yogi practises his methods, and expects a wonderful result. But all his striving, if he is not of the mystic temperament, may leave him disappointed. Tantrism makes readier promises, and the subject can be studied in the works mentioned in the bibliography.

There is no reason to think that the decline of Buddhism was due to persecution. C. Bendall suggested that it was perhaps owing to Tantrism that Buddhism came to be discredited in India and disappeared. This explanation will scarcely hold, for Tantrism only affected certain schools, and the Tantrism of the Hindus still flourishes. In the absence of historical facts, the causes of the disappearance of Buddhism in India must remain hypothetical. The great difference of organization between Hinduism and Buddhism lay in the fact that the brahmin priests were not an ascetic body apart from the laity. They were a part of the social structure and an essential part in carrying out the rites and sacraments for the laity. In this function they were essential even for the Buddhist laity. While the Order continued there was a body in existence in open opposition to brahminism, and the disappearance of the Order meant the end of Buddhism. The Buddhist layman, who was all along a member of a Hindu caste, worshipped deities differing little from the Hindu gods. If the educated monk and his community disappeared, there was no essential principle to distinguish the Buddhist layman from the Hindu. Mr. Nagendranath Vasu has shown how in Orissa a form of Buddhism survived which became disguised as a form of Hinduism.[1] With the disappearance of the monks and the absence of any definite teaching the god Dharma became another of the numberless gods of India.

It is easy to see how the Buddhist Order may have disappeared. It depended for its existence on the generosity of the layman, and if his sense of duty to give alms became dulled, as it well might be with the corruption of the monasteries, the most distinctive feature of the Buddhist organization would be lost. There is plenty of evidence in the Buddhist books of corruption quite apart from the question of Tantrism. It is also likely enough that the Muhammadan invasion contributed to the destruction of the monasteries.[2]

The one place where Buddhism has remained is Nepal, Buddha's native land. When Hodgson during his residence in Nepal (1833–1843) was sending manuscripts to Burnouf, he also tried to obtain information about the doctrine from the Buddhists of the country. He set a questionnaire, arranged according to his own ideas of theology, often with leading questions, such as " how many avatāras of Buddha

[1] *The Modern Buddhism and its followers in Orissa.*

[2] The survival of Jainism is another interesting problem. It may be said that it survived because it preserved its monastic system. It was " the creed of a cultivated class, from which the masses are excluded ". Buddhism dissolved in popular bodhisattva worship.

have there been ? " (It was thus that he got the answer that the last seven Buddhas were avatāras.) " What is the motive of your good acts—the love of God—the fear of God —or the desire of prospering in the world ? " It was no wonder that the answers he obtained seemed to him "a sad jumble of cloudy metaphysics ", and that Burnouf was surprised that he could not discover in his manuscripts anything like the " Bauddha system " as described by Hodgson. Yet scholars continue to use his terms, some of which, like *dhyāni-buddha*, have never been found outside his writings.

Hodgson found four systems. The best known is that of Ādibuddha, which L. de la Vallée Poussin describes as " Buddhist in fact only in name and in so far as it employs Buddhist terminology ". Even the Hinduism on which it rests is of a degraded type. " It is well known," says the same scholar, " that Hodgson had recourse for his information to native scholars, whom he ceremoniously styles ' living oracles ', and who, in support of their statements supplied him with fragments of texts, which were not all authentic." When Hodgson's statements were challenged by Rémusat, he disclaimed any purpose " to meddle with the interminable sheer absurdities of the Bauddha philosophy or religion ". It may be possible some day to give an accurate description of the Nepalese religion, as has been partially done by La Vallée Poussin,[1] but it will scarcely add another chapter to the history of Buddhism.

[1] See his article " Ādibuddha ", in *ERE*.

CHAPTER XIX

BUDDHISM AND MODERN THOUGHT

THE spread of Buddhism into other countries does not properly form a part of the history of Buddhist thought, except in so far as the mingling of cultures may have produced new schools. Theoretically there was no development. All schools claimed to be holding the word of Buddha, and in one sense they were right. The Buddhism of Ceylon spread to Burma, Siam, and Cambodia.[1] There are sects and ecclesiastical differences, but the doctrine is still that of the Pāli Scriptures. The Tibetans and the Chinese, followed by the Koreans and Japanese, received Mahāyāna Buddhism. Now it is Japan which is chiefly active in devotion to the doctrine, and the schools of Japan still find the Buddha word in the sūtras of the Mahāyāna schools which they received from the Chinese.

The Buddhism of Tibet and the Far East is important in the first place through the fact that most of the Mahāyāna literature and a good number of Sarvāstivāda works were translated first into Chinese and later into Tibetan. From the Tibetan followed Mongolian translations. Since much of the literature in the original Sanskrit has disappeared, these translations come to be of the highest importance. The Tibetan translations, owing to the structure of the language, have been done in such a faithful manner that it is often possible to reconstruct the original Sanskrit. The translation of the Scriptures known as the *Kanjur* (*bkah-hgyur*) in 100 or 108 volumes was completed between the eleventh and thirteenth centuries. There is also a collection of commentaries and secular works known as the *Tanjur* (*bstan-hgyur*).[2] Tibetan Buddhism, except for some historical and grammatical works, has been little but

[1] Both in Burma and Cambodia there are traces of Mahāyāna, but at present Hīnayāna flourishes.

[2] An analysis of the *Kanjur* and a slighter one of the *Tanjur* was given by Csoma in *Asiatic Researches*, xx, 1836, ff. Revised edition by L. Feer, Lyons, 1881. There is a detailed analysis of the *Tanjur* in P. Cordier's *Catalogue du fonds tibétain de la Bibliothèque nationale*, Paris, 1909–1915.

a development of the less worthy elements introduced from India along with superstitions of its own.

In China, Mahāyāna entered on new phases of development. Legend places the introduction of Buddhism into China in A.D. 68, when the Emperor Min-ti invited two monks from north-west India to China, where they undertook to translate Buddhist works.[1] The work of establishing the doctrine was done through a series of Indian scholars and Chinese travellers. Among the travellers are three who stand out both on account of the records of their journeys as well as for the large number of works which they took back to China. Fa Hien travelled between A.D. 399 and 413. Hiuen Tsiang (Yuan Chwang), who spent some fifteen years in India (629–645), brought back hundreds of books. His work as translator and commentator gave a great impulse to the establishing of Yogāchāra doctrine, but he collected works of all schools, and it is chiefly due to him that we owe the preservation of the Vinaya of several schools. I-tsing travelled somewhat later (671–695), and followed Sarvāstivāda doctrine. He records the names of over fifty Chinese monks who travelled in India. The chief period of translation was between the fifth and the seventh centuries, but relations with India continued to the twelfth.[2]

In the sixth century Buddhism reached Japan by way of Korea. Schools had already arisen in China which became established in Japan. One school, however, the Nichiren sect, is recognized as due to the reforming activity of the Japanese Nichiren.[3]

It is only recently that studies have been made on a scale which will make it possible to give an adequate account of Chinese and Japanese Buddhism. Japanese scholars

[1] They are said to have taken with them and translated the *Sūtra of the forty-two Sections*. This is not a sūtra in the ordinary sense, but a fairly complete summary of the doctrine, made up chiefly of a collection of Buddha's utterances. There is no trace of Mahāyāna doctrines in it. It is given in *Sermons of a Buddhist Abbot*, by the Rt. Rev. Soyen Shaku, Chicago, 1906. The best account of the missions is in P. C. Bagchi, *Le Canon bouddhique en Chine*, Paris, 1926.

[2] See article by J. Takakusu on Yuan Chwang, etc., in *ERE*.

[3] There is a traditional list of twelve Japanese sects, which do not represent the actual conditions. See R. Fujishima, *Le bouddhisme japonais*. Some of the twelve were never sects, and Sir C. Eliot (*Enc. Brit.*, xii, 928) omits three and puts in their place three branches of the Tendai sect. There are, however, far more than twelve if branches are recognized. See p. 256.

have produced valuable works, and it is chiefly to them that we must look for further light.[1]

It was quite impossible for either Chinese or Japanese to recognize any chronological sequence in the mass of doctrinal works that they received. They could not even, like the Mahāyānists of India, set aside the Āgamas of the Tripiṭaka as superseded. Hence they invented quite artificial methods to explain the different portions of the literature as partial or complete revelations of the teaching. The Tendai school made five divisions: (1) the *Avataṃsaka-sūtra*, which was taught in the second week after the enlightenment, (2) the *Āgamas* (i.e. of the Sarvāstivādins), which for twelve years were taught at Benares, (3) certain Mahāyāna-sūtras, such as the *Lankāvatāra* and *Suvarṇa-prabhāsa*, which were taught for eight years, (4) the *Prajñāpāramitā-sūtras*, for twenty-two years, and lastly (5) the *Saddharmapuṇḍarīka* (the *Lotus*) and the *Mahā-nirvāṇa-sūtra*, taught for eight years.[2] The two last sūtras are the Scriptures at the Tendai (T'ien-t'ai) school, which reached Japan in the eighth century. As will have been seen (p. 185) the *Lotus* does not expound metaphysical questions. It is really a theology preaching an eternal Buddha and an infinity of bodhisattva saviours. Its philosophical principles are those of the Void and conventional and absolute truth. The Rev. Yamakami says, " the mountains soar high up in the air, the water flows in the river, stars adorn the sky, the flowers beautify the earth: all these have distinctive existences. These existences, however, are not real, but are only conventional. In other words, they are subject to the law of causation; they could not have their respective existences without causes and conditions. This law of causation is technically called ' the principle of conventionality ' in the Tendai school. And the ' law of causation ', according to this school, is nothing but an active principle of the Truth or Reality; hence individual existences in the universe are not independent manifestations apart from the Reality . . . We must not,

[1] O. Rosenberg's *Die Probleme der buddhistischen Philosophie* is not only a work of fundamental importance for the history of Buddhism, but gives a special treatment of Chinese and Japanese Buddhism drawn from Japanese sources. It contains an extensive bibliography. An extremely important work for Japanese Buddhism is *Habogirin*, an encyclopædic dictionary of Chinese and Japanese Buddhism, now being issued by S. Lévi and J. Takakusu.

[2] Fujishima, loc. cit., p. 71; cf. Rosenberg, p. 255.

therefore, forget that in every phenomenon or individual we may recognize the light of Truth. Or more buddhistically speaking, we should comprehend that the mountains, which soar high up in the air, the water which flows in the stream, the stars that adorn the sky, or the flowers which decorate the earth, are all manifestations of the supreme reality; therefore we may enjoy the enchanting views of the realm of Truth through their manifestation." [1]

This beautiful nebulosity may even be harmonized with the thoughts of a Tennyson or a Rousseau, but how does the philosophy behind it compare with the metaphysical systems of the West? East and West have each been occupied with their special problems. Has either anything to learn from the other? The doctrine of the Void with its inconceivable reality and its relative truth looks much like the deserted tabernacles of Schopenhauer and Herbert Spencer, but its actual value still awaits adequate exposition and estimation as philosophy.

From the religious point of view the differences are more fundamental. To the West the theology or buddhology of the Lotus is fantastic, and Mahāyāna, having deserted the historical standpoint of early Buddhism, had nothing but this to put in its place. In theology most of the great world religions have avoided pantheism. No Indian system of monism has been able to escape it.

But not even the Rev. Yamakami finds the Tendai school final. It is the *Avataṃsaka*, he finds, which marks the final development of Buddhist philosophy. This (and the Tendai) are the last and also the best products of Buddhist thought. There are also four other schools which seek to realize these doctrines by experiment and practice, the *Mantra* (*Shingon*), the *Dhyāna* (*Zen*), the *Sukhāvatīvyūha* (*Jodo*), and the Japanese *Nichiren* school.

The *Avataṃsaka* (*Kegon*) school takes its name from the Scripture of that school, the *Buddhāvataṃsaka-sūtra*, "discourse of the adornments of Buddha." [2] It is really a collection of sūtras, one of them being the *Daśabhūmika*, which has already been discussed (p. 204). Mr. Suzuki describes it as "the consummation of Buddhist thought, Buddhist sentiment, and Buddhist experience. To my mind, no

[1] *Systems*, p. 274.
[2] Analysis in Vasiliev, *Buddhism*, p. 173.

religious literature in the world can ever approach the grandeur of conception, the depths of feeling, and the gigantic scale of composition, as attained by this sūtra. It is the eternal fountain of life from which no religious mind will turn back athirst or only partially satisfied . . . Here not only deeply speculative minds find satisfaction, but humble spirits and heavily oppressed hearts, too, will have their burdens lightened. Abstract truths are so concretely, so symbolically, represented here that one will finally come to a realization of the truth that even in a particle of dust the whole universe is seen reflected—not this visible universe only, but a vast system of universes, conceivable by the highest minds only." [1]

Although this sūtra was, we are told, the first preached by Buddha, men of slow intellect, like Śāriputra and Maudgalyāyana, were unable to understand a word of it. Hence for their sakes he taught the Hīnayāna doctrine, to disciples the four Truths, and to Pratyekabuddhas the Chain of Causation. With this sūtra we still stand on purely Indian ground, for the philosophy is that of the Yogāchāra. What it means for a Japanese can be seen from the impressive words of Mr. Suzuki. There is no doubt that Buddhism of that kind is religion. One point may be noticed here in connection with the universal character of Mahāyāna. The goal for everyone is Buddhahood, but in order to attain the Truth as understood by Yogāchāra it is also necessary through long ages to fulfil the career of a bodhisattva and become a Buddha, and yet not in the highest sense a Buddha, but Buddha, Tathatā, absolute reality. Other schools, especially those popular with the laity, chose a less arduous way.

The mystical side of Yogāchāra was emphasized by the teaching of the Zen school,[2] which was brought to China from south India by Bodhidharma in the sixth century. Suzuki has shown [3] that the school held their teaching to be contained in the *Lankāvatāra-sūtra*, but their tendency was to reject any external doctrinal statement as authority. Their whole method and system was meditation (*dhyāna*). As Ma-tsu, a pupil of Bodhidharma, said, " O monks, when

[1] *Studies*, p. 95.
[2] Chinese *shan*, from Skt. *dhyāna*.
[3] *Essays in Zen Buddhism* and *Studies*, p. 44.

you each believe that you yourself are the Buddha, your mind is no other than the Buddha-mind. The object of Bodhidharma who came from Southern India to this Middle Kingdom was to personally transmit and propagate the supreme law of One Mind by which we are all to be awakened to the truth."[1] That is all the teaching, and there remains hardly anything in the system characteristic of Buddhism. Suzuki says that it "grew up as a native product of Chinese genius". It reached Japan as late as the twelfth century.

Of the *Shingon* or *Mantra* school little is known. The terms that are used are those of Tantra, but more information is wanted. One peculiar method of its propaganda, says Rosenberg, was that it interpreted the doctrines of other religions in a Buddhist sense, and the gods of Shintoism were explained as incarnations of various Buddhas and Bodhisattvas.

For both schools of Mahāyāna full enlightenment and salvation are attained only by ages of striving and sacrifice in the career of the bodhisattva. That ideal remained, but in the *Jodo* (Pure Land) school there is another tendency, although the final end remained the same. This was to aim at being reborn in Sukhāvatī, the Happy Land, the heaven of the Buddha Amitābha at the western point of space, and this was achieved, as has been seen, by devotion to Amitābha and Avalokiteśvara and sharing in their merits. It was not a substitute for the goal of enlightenment, for Avalokiteśvara's vow was that he would go on taking beings to Sukhāvatī to hear the doctrine preached by Amitābha until all should be set in the highest enlightenment.

The idea of sharing in the merits of a saintly being is not peculiar to Mahāyāna or even to Buddhism, and it contains an element of truth. No being is morally self-made. There is no calculating the extent to which the moral development of one individual may be due to the influence of others. But this is not the way in which Buddhism looked at it. Good karma produced a store of merit, which might be transferred to others. The idea is found even in the Pāli Jātakas, and it is much extended in the worship of the bodhisattvas, and can be seen in its fullest extent in the Scriptures of this school, the two *Sukhāvatīvyūha-sūtras* and the *Amitāyurdhyāna-sūtra*. There we are told: "Not on account

[1] Suzuki, *Studies*, p. 46.

of a mere root of goodness are beings born in the Buddha country of the Tathāgata Amitāyus. Whatever son or daughter of good family shall hear the name of the Lord Amitāyus, and having heard it shall reflect upon it, and for one, two, three, four, five, six, or seven nights shall reflect upon it with undisturbed minds, when they come to die the Tathāgata Amitāyus attended by the assembly of disciples and followed by a host of bodhisattvas will stand before them, and they will die with unconfused minds. After death they will be born even in the Buddha-country of the Tathāgata Amitāyus, in the world Sukhāvatī."[1]

This, says Rosenberg, is the latest stage of the dogmatic development of Buddhism in Japan. The teaching began in China in the seventh century and a century later in Japan. The sūtras represent the development of the most popular form of Buddhism among the laity in India, and so it remained in Japan.

The history of the schools of Japan represents the stages of doctrinal development, but all this had little significance for the laity. Modern popular Buddhism shows three general tendencies. There is the form which has combined with the shamanistic superstitions of the people, their belief in spirits and demons, and the use of spells and amulets, especially in the Shingon sect. Another group holds the belief in Amida (Amitābha) and rebirth in his Pure Land. The higher clergy of this sect consist of the aristocracy and the most cultured class of Japanese society. The third tendency is that of mystic contemplation. "In this sect Shamanism is rejected in principle, as well as the belief in any saving power. Everyone can and must by himself reach the knowledge of the truth through contemplation . . . In medieval Japan the warrior aristocracy joined this sect, as lovers of the beautiful and at the same time as men who admired the concentration and self-denial of the contemplative mystic."[2] It was thus, in form at least, a return to the earliest Buddhism.

Behind all this is the Buddhism which is cultivated by the students in the monasteries. There the dogmatic systems remain, and work is being done by Japanese scholars

[1] Smaller *Sukhāvatīvyūha*, § 10. All three sūtras are conveniently translated in *SBE*, vol. 49.

[2] Rosenberg, *Probleme*, 281.

which is of the highest importance for the historical study of Buddhism. Professor Takakusu, describing present activities, says that Buddhism in Japan is represented by thirteen sects and fifty-eight sub-sects. Each sect has its own college instituted solely for the benefit of scholars who make a special study of its particular doctrine. Of these colleges those ranking as universities are the Ryukoku Daigaku of the Nishi Hongwanji Temple (the Shin sect), the Otani Daigaku, of the Higashi Hongwanji Temple (the Shin sect), the Rissho Daigaku (the Nichiren sect), the Komazawa Daigaku (the Soto sect), and the Rengo Daigaku (the Tendai, Jodo, Shingon of the new school, and Yuzunembutsu sect). Besides these there is the Toyo Daigaku, one of the most well-known schools in Tokyo. Almost all the leading universities and colleges have introduced more or less provisions for Buddhistic research, and in each of the State universities one or more chairs of Buddhist literature have been founded, which are in charge of competent professors and assistant professors.[1]

Mahāyāna has never made any impression on the West either as religion or philosophy. Presented by the early investigators as a tissue of absurdities or niaiseries, it is still commonly looked upon as nihilism or subjectivism. Now it is beginning to be recognized as more than this, but a full exposition of its metaphysical theories still awaits the complete publication of its authoritative texts and commentaries.

It is, however, possible to recognize in Mahāyāna two theories which are philosophical systems, Weltanschauungen in the true sense. They have parallels with Western systems, and they deserve investigation. Nāgārjuna's doctrine of the Void may be said to strike on the same rock as the Vedānta of Śankara. They both explain experience in such a way that the experience to be explained has no longer any reality. Then it has to be denied explicitly, and yet the experience itself is the basis of the negative conclusion. Hence the doctrine of relative and absolute truth. But even there is the recognition, even if inadequate, of a universally admitted principle. Experience only becomes real when interpreted, and every philosophical system is a reinterpretation more or less adequate. Every interpretation and every

[1] *The Young East*, 1925, p. 1.

system becomes false in the light of a more complete co-ordination. The relative truth which was rejected by Nāgārjuna was that of the everyday conception of the world expressed in the traditional terms of language. Everyone knows that this is false. The sun does not rise, thunderbolts do not fall. Is it possible to restate this conception so as to reach an exact statement of the truth of experience ? It has not been done yet in a final sense, and Nāgārjuna did not stop to ask. He was so sure of absolute reality and of a means of attaining it by direct intuition that he swept away every interpretation as relative and hence false. To the mystic the exact nature of the structure of the world or the atom was of no more importance then than it is now. That is why the Mahāyānists accepted the Sarvāstivāda cosmology as we find it in the *Abhidharmakośa*. It was a scientific presentation of everyday experience. In the third chapter of that work we have the elements of a system of natural science, including psychology. One of its most characteristic features is its reduction of time as well as matter to a series of atomic elements, and hence the existence of the individual to a sequence of moments. It had no importance for metaphysics, for the individual, even if reduced to a flow of time atoms, still remained a flow.

The philosophy of the Yogāchāras was a positive step forward in attempting to reinterpret the data of experience. Unlike modern idealism it did not accept the distinction of self and not-self, but denied it. It was solipsism rather than idealism. Both this theory and the relativity theory of Nāgārjuna need further study, not so much as a part of Buddhism, but in connection with the related Hindu theories of natural science and metaphysics.

It is as a religion that Buddhism has come into contact with Western thought, and this has been through the Pāli tradition, the Buddhism of Ceylon, Burma, Siam, and Cambodia. It was unfortunate that it was once expounded by scholars who took a pleasure in describing it as agnostic atheism, and who even spoke of " the antinomy of an entity or soul ". Not even Kant put the soul into his list of antinomies.

Buddhism agrees with the other world-religions in recognizing an ultimate eternal reality, but it nowhere describes this reality in positive language. Mahāyāna

Buddhism indeed came to describe the Tathāgata in terms hardly to be distinguished from the monotheistic terminology of Hinduism, but this was only relative truth. In reality there was only the inexpressible absolute, and this differed from the earlier conception of Nirvāṇa by being described not only as an individual state, but as a cosmological ultimate. God is a cosmological ultimate, but evidently this bare concept cannot be made to cover what is meant by God in a theistic system.

Early Buddhism allows of no possibility for the concept of a saviour. Later Buddhism does, but there is a fundamental difference from the Christian doctrine. The doctrine of bodhisattvas with their merits corresponds rather with saint-worship. They do not save beings in the sense of bringing them to perfect enlightenment. They make their way easier, and bring them to the heaven where they may hear the preaching of the doctrine that is to lead the way to omniscience.

In the transference of merit a parallel to the doctrine of grace can be seen. Such transference is not peculiar to Mahāyāna. There is a Jātaka story (No. 190) of a sea-spirit (nāga) who saved a shipwrecked disciple, but who refused to save his companion until the disciple allowed him to share in the merit of his having kept the commandments. But not even in Mahāyāna did this develop into a general scheme of salvation, though it is likely enough that the worshippers of Avalokiteśvara and Amitābha may have not looked beyond the Happy Land promised to them. There is a stricter resemblance to the doctrine of grace when we find the bodhisattvas uttering enlightened truth through being inspired by Buddha's power, but here, too, the doctrine never became a general scheme.

The mystical element in religion was shared by Buddhism with other Indian religions, and was carried through consistently. Mere faith and works are never final. Mere devotion, as in Krishna-worship, cannot bring salvation. The doctrine of rebirth had made this conclusion seem obvious. He that does many good deeds shall receive many rewards, but salvation rests upon a knowledge of the truth.

Morals has not always been a part of religion, but all religions that have developed a theology have come to recognize that ultimate reality cannot be separated from the ultimate truth of morals. Fortunately for Indian ethics it early became possible to separate the question of ethics from the question of the morality of the gods, for the tales of the gods were as little edifying as those of Greek mythology. This was done through the doctrine of karma combined with the doctrine of repeated births. Karma became a law of moral cause and effect, which even the gods could not escape.

These doctrines became the basis of Buddhist ethics, but the real greatness of the ethical system was due to the actual detailed teaching of a moral genius. Such doctrines as the forgiveness of enemies or compassion for the weak are revelations to which human consciousness may gradually awaken when they are set before it. They do not become realized by deduction from abstract principles. The doctrine of karma was one which lent itself to a mechanical conception of the heaping up of good actions. Buddhism did not entirely escape, but the Founder made the greatest advance in Indian ethics by insisting on motive as the standard of moral judgment.

The insistence on morals throughout the disciples' career is all the more remarkable in that good action was never a means to the final end. Princess Sumanā once asked Buddha what would be the difference between two men, one of whom had been bounteous in a former life and one not. "The bounteous one will surpass the other in being long-lived, of good appearance, happy, famous, and powerful." What will happen if they enter the Order ? The bounteous one will surpass the other in five similar ways. What will be the difference if they both win arhatship ? "In that case I say, Sumanā, there is no difference at all between release and release." [1]

The doctrine of rebirth made the non-ātman theory a very different thing from what to a Western mind is implied by a denial of the soul. If there is no soul, then the only other alternative is

> To drop head foremost in the jaws
> Of vacant darkness and to cease.

It would not be to the point, even if it were true, to say that this, according to Buddhist principles, is the result of denying the ātman. It is a result that the Buddhists never drew.

[1] *Angut.*, iii, 32.

Ajita's doctrine of annihilation at death was denied throughout the whole history of Buddhism. The individual being had existed before, and he would exist again. He was only a bundle of changing skandhas, changing from moment to moment, and from life to life, and it was only Nirvāṇa which could bring about their final dissolution. His personal identity remained to such an extent that he could come to remember his former existences. This was no accommodation to popular belief, for this doctrine of remembrance was part of the formal teaching, and it remains so still. The question of the dissolution of personality only becomes urgent when it is asked what takes place with the cessation of rebirth. Naturally no one can give an answer to that except the one who has reached that state, and what the Scripture says about it has already been recorded.

The disputes and assertions and misunderstandings that have taken place on this very point have given it an unnecessary prominence. There is less need now for many words, for the literature is becoming accessible which makes obsolete much that was written before the texts were understood or even known.

Leading up to this ultimate and fundamental problem is the whole religious and philosophical system, which maintained the continuity of its religious doctrines from their earliest appearance in the mists of historical legend to their disappearance from India in an almost equal gloom. It absorbed much of the culture of its Hindu surroundings during its thousand years of growth, and at the same time transformed it. Now it has become a part of the culture of the East. It will long continue to furnish matter for historical and philosophical research as well as problems of future social and religious development.

APPENDIX I

THE SCRIPTURES

The changes that have taken place in the conception of Buddhism as a religion and a philosophy are largely due to the piecemeal way in which the original documents have been brought to light. When Burnouf in 1844 issued his *Introduction à l'histoire du Buddhisme indien,* he mentioned as his chief predecessors Abel Rémusat,[1] the Chinese scholar, and the Moravian missionary Isaac Jacob Schmidt [2] as having thrown more light on the origin of Indian Buddhism than all those who up to that time had undertaken the study of the subject. Yet Rémusat's investigations were limited to Chinese works, and Schmidt, a scholar whose great merits have never been fully recognized, drew all his information from Mongolian and Tibetan translations. Burnouf was the first to investigate some of the Sanskrit originals, and his task was made possible through the enterprise of B. H. Hodgson, who was British Resident in Nepal from 1833 to 1843. During this time Hodgson sent from Nepal a large number of copies of Sanskrit manuscripts to various libraries in Europe, and it was chiefly on the basis of those sent to the Société Asiatique of Paris and to himself that Burnouf wrote his *Introduction.* But these documents were mainly representative of Mahāyāna, and their relation to the earlier Pāli and Sanskrit works was quite unknown.

Burnouf was well aware of the importance of Pāli for the prosecution of his subject. In fact everything of a chronological nature that he had to say came from Pāli works. He was (with Lassen) the first to make the Pāli language known in Europe,[3] and his unpublished papers show that he had copied Pāli manuscripts and inscriptions, and had

[1] Jean Pierre Abel Rémusat (1788–1832), professor of Chinese at the Collège de France.

[2] I. J. Schmidt (1799–1847). The latest account of his work is by F. Babinger in *Festschrift für Friedrich Hirth,* Berlin, 1920.

[3] *Essai sur le pali,* par E. Burnouf et Chr. Lassen, Paris, 1826.

made extensive studies in grammatical, doctrinal, and historical works.[1] But the whole of the Pāli Canon was still in manuscript, and although George Turnour of the Ceylon Civil Service (1799–1843) had issued translations of portions, and in 1837 had published the text and translation of the first thirty-eight chapters of the *Mahāvaṃsa*, it was not till 1855 that any portion of the Canon was published in Europe. Since then, through the labours of V. Fausböll, H. Oldenberg, and especially T. W. Rhys Davids, the whole of the Canon of the Theravāda school is now printed.[2]

Other forms of a complete Canon, those of the Sarvāstivāda schools, once existed in Sanskrit. These as a whole have been lost, but translations exist in Tibetan and Chinese, and the Sanskrit originals of portions have survived and are gradually being published.

The remains of another important Canon, that of the Lokottaravādins, exist in the *Mahāvastu*. This is an Avadāna, a form of literature later than the suttas, based on the Vinaya of the Lokottaravādins, and it contains a large number of suttas and other portions of the Canon of that school. The great development known as Mahāyāna led to new schools and the production of a great number of new canonical works. These also exist in translation in Chinese and other languages, and those which survive in Sanskrit are being studied and made accessible.

There have been disputes between scholars as to the relative value of the Sanskrit and Pāli sources. Burnouf's documents belonged chiefly to late schools, and it was impossible in his time to distinguish those portions which really were comparatively early. Then the Pāli Canon was discovered. It was more complete than anything else that had been found. It claimed, like the Sanskrit works, but with more vraisemblance, to be the actual word of Buddha, and it was on the material of this Canon that expositions of Buddhism were written by Pāli scholars. The protests of the Sanskritists were largely unavailing; as a matter of fact

[1] *Papiers d'Eugène Burnouf conservés à la Bibliothèque Nationale*, Paris, 1899.

[2] There are now also editions printed in Ceylon and Burma, and especially in Siam. The last edition of the splendid text of the Canon, issued under the patronage of the King of Siam, was published at Bangkok in 1926–8 and the commentaries in 1920.

they were unable to point to a Sanskrit Canon at all comparable to the Pāli. But the grounds of their objection were well put by L. de la Vallée Poussin.

This scholar pointed out that the Pāli scholars relinquished the examination of Northern sources, and took no account of them. "They are passionately attached to the exegesis of the Southern [i.e. Pāli] Scriptures, which are in appearance more archaic and better documented. The results of these labours are of the highest importance, both for the history of religions in general, as well as for that of Buddhist and Indian ideas. Oldenberg's book is a perfect exposition: Pāli Buddhism cannot be better described, or the intellectual and moral factors more artistically demonstrated, and the idea which a Sinhalese doctor makes of his religion and destiny more precisely set out. Oldenberg's error was to entitle his book: *Buddha, his life, his doctrine, his community*. He should have added, 'according to Pāli sources and the principles of the Sinhalese Church.' Now by commenting on the Sinhalese traditions without exactly fixing their date and character there is a risk of falsifying the history of Buddhism in its general spirit and in its very signification. . . . Too easily persuaded that they know primitive Buddhism, European [Pāli] exegetes regard the different Canons of the Churches of the North as almost modern compositions, in which heretical, adventitious, and heterogeneous doctrines have become definite in the course of centuries." [1]

To estimate this accusation fairly it is necessary to recognize to what extent the Pāli exegetes were right. It is a fact that there are numerous works in Sanskrit which are "almost modern compositions". It is also true that in them there is much that is heretical, adventitious, and heterogeneous. This is not mere modern theory. It is admitted by the authors of these late works themselves. They taunted the older schools with clinging to the letter rather than the spirit. They even admitted that their opponents' teaching really was the Buddha-word, but maintained that Buddha taught it to the simple-minded merely as a preliminary, and meant it to be superseded by the higher doctrine, the new goal of life and the new philosophical conceptions which they called Mahāyāna. Stcherbatsky

[1] *Bouddhisme, études et matériaux*, pp. 2 ff., London, 1898.

declares that Buddhism "resulted, 500 years after the demise of the Master, in what may be called a quite new religion, reposing on a quite different philosophic foundation ".[1]

If this were all, it would appear that the Pāli scholars were right. But to show that the Pāli sources are older does not prove that they are primitive. These scholars assumed that all the works in Sanskrit showing a connection with Pāli must have been translated from Pāli. But these related Sanskrit works are distinct both from the Mahāyāna compositions and the Pāli, and belong to the Canon of the Sarvāstivāda and its branches. These schools had translated them, not from the Pāli of the Theravādins, but from their own Scriptures in the Prakrit dialect in which they were at first composed. It is now possible to see how they all developed from one nucleus of doctrine preserved by memory, but were gradually differentiated owing to the precarious method of their preservation in widely separated communities.[2]

The language of the Pāli Canon is described by the commentators as Māgadhī (the language of Magadha). There can be no doubt that this was the original language, but it is now usually held that Pāli as we know it must have developed in the west of India, and the probability is that the present Pāli Canon comes from a Buddhist community of monks in the region of Ujjenī (Ujjain), who adapted it to their own dialect. It still retains traces of an earlier dialect in the verse passages. The Sarvāstivāda schools went further, and turned the whole of their Canon into Sanskrit, though in this case also traces of a popular dialect, a form of Prakrit, appear in the metrical passages. The *Mahāvastu*, which also aims at being Sanskrit, preserves many more traces of its original Prakrit.

[1] *The conception of Buddhist Nirvāṇa*, p. 4, Leningrad, 1927. Nevertheless L. de La Vallee Poussin, at least as late as 1902, continued to hold that the Mahāyāna was as old as the Sinhalese doctrine. "Nous ne pensons pas que les traditions, les vinayas et les dogmes du Grand Véhicule, ni même ceux du Véhicule tantrique soient moins archaïques ou moins anciens." *Journ. As.*, ii, 1902, p. 238.

[2] This is now recognized by de la Vallée Poussin. "Nous parlons, au singulier, du Canon. Il n'est pas douteux qu'un corps considérable d'Écritures a servi de base aux deux canons que nous connaissons, canons des sectes sthaviriennes, le canon de langue pâlie et le canon sanscrit des Sarvâstivâdins : on peut désigner ce corps d'Écritures sous le nom de Canon bouddhique." *Le dogme et la philosophie du Bouddhisme*, p. 97.

The Tipiṭaka

Franke has stated " that the books of the Canon as *a whole* are not authentic ; that the Canon was not composed and compiled in one and the same period of time . . . that even the first two Piṭakas (to say nothing of the Abhidhamma) cannot possibly have been presented as finished before either the ' first ' or the ' second ' Council, even if these events took place at the intervals assigned to them."[1] This conclusion, in the sense that we do not possess a verbatim report of the discourses, is so obvious that it scarcely needed stating, but it is quite negative. We know that the Buddha-word—everything that Buddha was held to have given as a rule or taught as a doctrine—was preserved for centuries by memorizing. The statement in the Pāli Chronicles that the Scriptures were first written down in Ceylon in the reign of Vaṭṭagāmaṇi (29–17 B.C.) is of little significance. There may have then been such an official recension, but it is probable that much had been written down before. However that may be, the practice of learning it by heart was for long the only means of preserving it ; there was thus no means of preserving a definite order, or even of being certain that any discourse was really the word of the Master.[2]

The disciples felt these difficulties, for we find in the Scriptures a discourse attributed to Buddha giving four rules for determining the genuineness of any doubtful passage. We can accept the fact that the monks found these rules necessary and made use of them, without supposing that Buddha, forseeing the difficulties to come, actually formulated them. The rules are, (1) if a monk says that he has heard directly from the Lord anything as being the Dhamma, the Vinaya, or the teaching of the Master, it is to be compared with the Sutta or shown to exist in the Vinaya. If it does not correspond, it is not the word of the Lord, and is to be rejected. The same method is to be used (2) if a monk says he has received it from an assembly (*sangha*) of monks with a leader, or (3) from a number of learned elders who

[1] *JPTS.*, 1908, p. 2.

[2] One of the earliest means of classifying them was to divide them into small groups (usually ten) and to record the titles of the suttas of each group in a verse called an *Uddāna*.

have acquired the Āgamas, and who know by heart the Dhamma, the Vinaya, and the Māṭikā, or (4) from such a single learned elder.[1]

The division of the Scriptures into two classes, discipline and doctrine, was inevitable. But in these rules we find a third division, the Māṭikā, a term now applied to the lists of subjects discussed in the class of Abhidhamma, but also used as a synonym of Abhidhamma. This last class, though not recognized by some schools and evidently later than the others, now forms the third part of the Triple Basket, the Tipiṭaka (Skt. *Tripiṭaka*). The term *piṭaka* as a division of the Canon is not in the Scriptures, but must be as old as the third century B.C., for the term *peṭaki*, "reciter of the Piṭaka", occurs in inscriptions of that date.[2] The term *pañca-nekāyika*, "reciter of the five Nikāyas," also occurs, showing that the division of the Suttas into Nikāyas or Āgamas already existed. The arrangement of the whole Tipiṭaka is as follows :—

A. Vinaya-Piṭaka

The rules of discipline, contained in two chief sections followed by a minor work.

I. *Sutta-vibhanga.*[3] Consisting of the Pātimokkha rules, each rule being followed (1) by a verbal commentary explaining each word of the rule, (2) an account of the incident which led to the promulgation of the rule, sometimes forming extensive legends, (3) special cases and exceptions. The portion of the Pātimokkha which deals with the summoning of the Uposatha is given in the Mahāvagga under the rules for holding Uposatha.

[1] *Ang.* ii, 167 ; *Dīgha*, ii, 123. This sutta is itself an example of how accretions could occur. The four rules at some period existed, and some pious monk, doubtless convinced that they were Buddha's own rules, turned them into a sutta, which Buddha was supposed to have uttered a day or two before his death. Its unhistorical character is shown by the fact that it includes the Māṭikā, and refers to the Āgamas. Āgama is the Sarvāstivāda term for the collections usually called Nikāyas in Pāli.

[2] This and other terms are discussed by Rhys Davids in *Dial.* i, p. xii. In *Av. Śat.* No. 84 *tripiṭa* as the name of a knower of the three Piṭakas occurs.

[3] The arrangement of this portion can be seen from the analysis of the Pātimokkha above, p. 15 ff.

II. The Khandhakas

1. *Mahāvagga* (Great Series)

(1) Rules for admission to the Order.
(2) Uposatha meeting and recital of the Pātimokkha.
(3) Residence during Retreat in the rainy season (*vassa*).
(4) The ceremony concluding Retreat (*pavāraṇā*).
(5) Rules for the use of leather for shoes, dress, and furniture.
(6) Medicine and food.
(7) The kaṭhina ceremonies for the annual making and distributing of robes.
(8) Material of robes, sleeping regulations, and rules for sick monks.
(9) The modes of executing official acts of the Order.
(10) Proceedings in case of dissensions.

2. *Cullavagga* (Small Series)

(1, 2) Rules for dealing with offences that come before the Order.
(3) Reinstatement of monks.
(4) Rules dealing with questions that arise.
(5) Miscellaneous rules for bathing, dress, etc.
(6) Dwellings, furniture, lodgings.
(7) Schism.
(8) Treatment of travelling monks, those living in the forest, etc., and the duties of teachers and novices.
(9) Exclusion from the Pātimokkha.
(10) The ordination and instruction of nuns.
(11) History of the first Council at Rājagaha.
(12) History of the second Council at Vesālī.

III. *Parivāra.* A supplement containing summaries and classifications of the rules. It may be peculiar to the Theravādins, as the *Dīpavaṃsa* speaks of its rejection by the Mahāsanghikas, but other schools had a supplementary work.

The Sarvāstivāda Vinaya follows the same general arrangement. The first portion, the *Vinaya-vibhanga*, corresponds to the *Sutta-vibhanga* ; the second portion, the *Vinayavastu*, corresponds to the *Khandhakas*, and instead of the *Parivāra* it is followed by the *Vinayakshudraka*, " minor Vinaya work," and *Uttaragrantha*.[1] The last consists of a series of questions on Vinaya put to Buddha by Upāli.

The *Vinayavastu* of the Mūla-Sarvāstivādins shows evident correspondences in arrangement and subject matter to the *Khandhakas* of the Pāli :—

(1) *Pravrajyavastu* (admission to the Order).
(2) *Poshadhavastu* (Uposatha).
(3) *Varshavastu* (Retreat).
(4) *Pravāraṇavastu* (ceremony concluding Retreat).
(5) *Kaṭhinavastu* (material for robes).
(6) *Cīvaravastu* (rules for robes).
(7) *Carmavastu* (leather for shoes).
(8) *Bhaishajyavastu* (medicines).
(9) *Karmavastu* (official acts).
(10) *Pratikshayavastu* (possibly on dwellings and lodgings).
(11) *Kālākālasampadvastu* (on the right and wrong times).
(12) *Bhūmyantarasthacaraṇavastu* (rules for travelling monks).
(13) *Parikarmaṇavastu* (executing proceedings).
(14) *Karmabhedavastu* (probably corresponds to the Pāli section on different kinds of official acts, and the following section to different kinds of meetings).
(15) *Cakrabhedavastu*.
(16) *Adhikaraṇavastu* (rules dealing with cases that arise).
(17) *Śayanāsanavastu* (rules for beds).

B. Sutta-Piṭaka (Dhamma)

The doctrinal portion, the Dhamma (Dharma), exists in four or five collections called in Pāli Nikāyas, in the other schools Āgamas. The separate discourses are usually known as suttas (sūtras) or suttantas (sūtrāntas), but an earlier term used in the suttas themselves is *dhammapariyāya*, " section of doctrine." [2] The separation of this portion into four or

[1] This the order in *Mvyut.* 65. In the Tibetan the *Vinayavastu* comes first. It has seventeen divisions, which only partially correspond with the above. The two *Prātimokshas* and the *Bhikkhunī-vibhanga* are numbered separately.

[2] *Suttanta*, as has been shown by Mr. E. H. Johnston, is a collective term formed from *sutta*, but there is no real difference of meaning. The difference appears to be due to the usage of different classes of reciters of portions of the Scriptures. The term *sutta* (*sūtra*), lit. " thread ", refers in brahminical works to short aphoristic sentences intended to be committed to memory. With the Buddhists it is any part of this division of the Scriptures, which

five collections is as early at least as the third century B.C., as the term *pañcanekāyika,* "knowing the five Nikāyas," shows. This classification appears to have been a purely formal one due to convenience in committing to memory, the groupings being into (1) long suttas, (2) medium long, (3) grouped suttas, (4) suttas arranged on a numerical principle. It is not surprising that there should be other doctrinal works which did not fit into the fourfold scheme. The Theravādins formed them into a fifth Nikāya, but much of the material existed also in other schools, and among the Sarvāstivādins, a school with a long continuous growth in India, there was an enormous development, as will be seen in the discussion of the nine Angas. The Pāli order and arrangement is as follows :—

1. *Dīgha-Nikāya* (*Dīrghāgama*)

The collection of long discourses, thirty-four suttas arranged in three vaggas or series.

1–13. *Sīlakkhandha-vagga.*—Each of these has incorporated in it a list of moral rules known as the Sīlas. Most of the suttas describe the training of the monk in three stages, beginning with these moral rules, proceeding to the practice of concentration (*samādhi*), and ending with *paññā,* the full knowledge of the arahat. Several of them discuss the views of the brahmins on sacrifice and sacred knowledge, the doctrines of various religious schools, the value of caste and self-mortification, and expound leading doctrines.

14–23. *Mahā-vagga.*—Most of these suttas are not properly discourses but legends. The most important is the *Mahāparinibbāna-sutta,* an account of the last days and death of Buddha and the distribution of his relics. Two others are really portions or extensions of this, the *Mahāsudassana-sutta,* in which Buddha on his death-bed tells of his former existence as king Sudassana, and the *Janavasabha-sutta,* an extension of another discourse which Buddha delivered on his last

may be a discourse or poem, but which is always given as a separate utterance of Buddha or a disciple. Its earlier sense is seen in the *Pātimokkha,* where it is applied to each Vinaya rule, and in the title *Sutta-vibhanga.* The term *dhammapariyāya* was used by Asoka in the form *dhammapaliyāya* in the edict in which he recommends portions of Scripture to the monks and nuns for study. *Inscriptions of Asoka,* ed. Hultzsch, p. 173. Dr. Walleser holds that *sutta* is from Skt. *sūkta,* "well spoken, a hymn," and this certainly fits the discourses very well, but when the Canon was turned into Sanskrit nothing was known of this derivation, nor do the Jains recognize it.

journey. Other legends are the *Mahāpadāna-sutta*, an account of the last seven Buddhas with the life of Vipassin Buddha down to the beginning of his preaching ; *Mahā-Govinda-sutta*, a previous life of Buddha as Mahā-govinda, recorded by a heavenly musician, who went up to the heaven of Brahmā to hear it ; *Mahā-Samaya-sutta*, the " great Assembly " of gods who visit Buddha, and who are described by him in a long poem. The most important doctrinal discourses are the *Mahānidāna-sutta* on the Chain of Causation, the *Mahā-Satipaṭṭhāna-sutta*, on the four contemplations with commentary on the Four Truths, and *Pāyāsi-sutta* given by the elder Kumārakassapa, on the doctrine of a future life and reward of actions.

24–34. *Pāṭika-vagga.*—This is the most miscellaneous section, and it indicates that definite doctrinal beliefs about the nature of a Buddha had become much developed by the time the collection was made. Two suttas show Buddha explaining the origin and development of the universe (after its periodical destruction) and the differentiation of castes. There is the legend of the universal king (*cakkavattin*), a prophecy about the next Buddha (Metteya or Maitreya), a discourse on the thirty-two bodily marks of a universal king (which are also the marks of a Buddha), and a spell to serve as protection against evil spirits, which was given to Buddha by the Four Great Kings. It became the Buddha-word when Buddha repeated it to the monks. The *Sigālovāda-sutta*, the one discourse addressed to a layman, is really a poem with a prose commentary. The last two, *Sangīti* and *Dasuttara*, are long lists of classified doctrinal terms, and are ascribed to Sāriputta.

2. *Majjhima-Nikaya* (*Madhyamāgama*)

The division of discourses of medium length, 152 suttas in fifteen vaggas. There is the same description as in the *Dīgha* of the life of the monk in the three stages of morality, concentration, and enlightenment. This in several suttas is brought into connection with the story of Buddha's enlightenment and first preaching. There are several other legends of Buddha's life, his descent from heaven and his birth (No. 123), his debates with the Jains (Nos. 35, 56, 58, 79, 101, 104), his foster-mother as a nun (No. 146), the schism of Devadatta (Nos. 29, 58), and several discussions on caste (Nos. 84, 93, 96). Some are in the form of commentaries, and several show a tendency to the Abhidhamma style of exposition with classified lists of terms. Twenty-one of them are attributed to disciples.

3. *Saṃyutta-Nikāya* (*Saṃyuktāgama*)

The division of "connected" suttas in five vaggas divided into groups (saṃyuttas) and these again into smaller vaggas of separate suttas. Many short poems and scraps of verse are collected in the first, called :—

(1) *Sagātha-vagga*, "series with verses." They are grouped in saṃyuttas according to the characters appearing in them, the gods, the king of the Kosalas, Māra, etc.
(2) *Nidāna-vagga*, this, like the following, does not indicate the subject of the whole, but only of the first ten saṃyuttas on the Nidānas, the twelve links of the Chain of Causation.
(3) *Khandha-vagga*, beginning with suttas on the five khandhas.
(4) *Saḷāyatana-vagga*, beginning with suttas on the six senses.
(5) *Mahā-vagga*, "the great series," beginning with suttas on the Eightfold Path.

4. *Anguttara-Nikāya* (*Ekottarikāgama*)

Anguttara means "(one) member beyond", and *ekottarika* "having one (member) beyond". The division is purely numerical, beginning with suttas discussing lists of one thing, lists of two, three, etc., up to eleven. The first gives a list of the one sight, the one sound, the one scent, etc., which occupies the thought of a man or woman. The last is a list of the eleven good and eleven bad qualities of a herdsman, and the corresponding qualities of a monk. It is in eleven *nipātas* (groups), each divided into vaggas, which usually contain ten suttas.

5. *Khuddaka-Nikāya*

The division of minor works. The contents of this Nikāya have varied at different times. The following fifteen are at present recognized in Ceylon :—

(1) *Khuddaka-pāṭha.* "The reading of small passages," nine short formulæ and suttas mostly occurring in other parts of the Scriptures.

(2) *Dhammapada.* "Words of the Doctrine," a collection of 423 stanzas arranged in twenty-six vaggas.

(3) *Udāna.* An udāna is a solemn utterance spoken under the influence of emotion. This is a collection of eighty udānas spoken by Buddha, mostly in verse, and accompanied by the legends of the circumstances that led to their being uttered.

(4) *Itivuttaka.* A collection of 112 short suttas in four nipātas with verses. The verses are usually introduced by *iti vuccati,* "thus it is said."

(5) *Suttanipāta.* "Collection of suttas," in five vaggas. They are in verse with occasional prose introductions and contain some important legendary matter.

(6) *Vimāna-vatthu.* "Stories of celestial mansions," eighty-five poems in seven vaggas, in which beings who have been reborn in one of the heavens explain the acts of merit that led to their reward.

(7) *Peta-vatthu.* "Stories of petas," in which the petas are ghosts condemned to a special unhappy existence. There are fifty-one poems on the same model as the *Vimāna-vatthu.*

(8) *Thera-gāthā.* "Verses of the elders," stanzas attributed to 264 elders.

(9) *Therī-gāthā.* A similar collection of stanzas attributed to about a hundred nuns.

(10) *Jātaka.* Tales of Buddha's previous births. There are verses in each tale, and only those supposed to be uttered by the destined Buddha are the canonical part. The tales themselves form the commentary on the verses, and are said to be a translation from the Sinhalese, which is itself a translation from an earlier Pāli form. The number 547 does not give the exact number of tales, owing to the practice of embedding one tale within another, and several tales occur more than once with different verses.

(11) *Niddesa.* "Exposition," divided into *Mahā-* and *Culla-Niddesa.* The former is a verbal commentary on the fourth vagga (*Aṭṭhaka*) of the *Suttanipāta,*

and the latter on the fifth vagga (*Pārāyaṇa*) and on the *Khaggavisāṇa-sutta* in the first vagga. They contain much Abhidhamma material.

(12) *Paṭisambhidā-magga.* "The way of analysis," an analysis of various concepts, knowledge, heresy, the practice of breathing while meditating, etc. In method and material it is really an Abhidhamma work.

(13) *Apadāna.* Accounts in verse of the lives and previous lives of monks and nuns.

(14) *Buddhavaṃsa.* "History of the Buddhas," in which, in response to a question by Sāriputta, Buddha gives an account in verse of his first forming in the presence of Dīpankara Buddha the resolve to become a Buddha, with the life of Dīpankara and the succeeding twenty-four Buddhas, including an account of himself.

(15) *Cariyā-piṭaka.* "The basket of conduct," i.e. the conduct of the future Buddha in order to attain the ten Perfections (*pāramī*), forming thirty-five tales from the *Jātaka* versified. Only seven of the ten Perfections are illustrated.

There has never been any general agreement even among the Theravādins about the number of works in this Piṭaka. The whole fifteen are mentioned in Buddhaghosa's commentary on the Vinaya, but in the Chinese translation of this commentary No. 1 is omitted, showing that the original text of Buddhaghosa did not admit it.[1]

He also records two earlier traditions, one that the reciters of the *Dīgha* omitted the first and the last three, calling the rest the "Minor book" (*khuddaka-gantha*) which they placed in the Abhidhamma-piṭaka; the other that the reciters of the *Majjhima* included all but the first, and placed them in the Sutta-pitaka. The Siam edition omits 6–10 as well as the last three.

The four Āgamas of the Sarvāstivādins have been compared with the corresponding Nikāyas by Professor Anesaki,[2] and

[1] No. 1, consisting of a series of short texts mostly from the suttas, was intended for novices. When they were once collected into a separate book it would be almost inevitable that it should be treated as Scripture.

[2] *Some problems of the textual history of the Buddhist Scriptures*; and *The four Buddhist Āgamas in Chinese.* Trans. As. Soc. Japan, xxxv, parts 2, 3, 1908; *Le sagātha-vagga du Saṃyutta-nikaya et ses versions chinoises. Muséon*, 1905, pp. 23 ff.

in more detail by Professor C. Akanuma.[1] The result is to show a close correspondence in the case of the *Dīgha*. The Chinese has thirty suttas, two of which are not found in the Pāli. Several of those in the Pāli Dīgha are in other books of the Chinese. The order of the suttas is different, but the same vaggas were known, for the ten in the Chinese which come last correspond to the Sīla-vagga. In the Majjhima there are 222 suttas as against 152 in the Pāli, and nineteen of them are not in the Chinese. The material also varies more than in the Dīgha, for many suttas of the Chinese Majjhima occur in the Pāli Saṃyutta and Anguttara, and *vice versa*. The differences are greatest in these two last. We may conclude that there was once a common stock of suttas learnt by heart. Probably differences in what was remembered had already begun between the two schools. The beginnings of the classification must have originated while the schools were in close connection, but it evidently went on and was completed in each independently.

C. Abhidhamma-Piṭaka

Unlike the two other Piṭakas the Abhidhamma of the Theravādins is quite distinct from that of the Sarvāstivādins. That of the Theravādins consists of seven independent works. The tradition is that they were thought out by Buddha in the fourth week after his enlightenment :—

(1) *Dhammasangaṇi*. "Enumeration of dhammas," i.e. mental elements or processes.

(2) *Vibhanga*. "Distinction or determination." Further analysis of the matter of the foregoing.

(3) *Dhātukathā*. "Discussion of elements." On the mental elements and their relations to other categories.

(4) *Puggalapaññatti*. "Description of individuals," especially according to their stages along the Noble Path.

(5) *Kathāvatthu*. "Subjects of discussion," discussions and refutations of doctrines held by other schools.

(6) *Yamaka*. "Book of pairs," called by Geiger an applied logic. The subject matter is psychological, and the analysis is arranged in pairs of questions.

[1] *The comparative catalogue of Chinese Āgamas and Pāli Nikāyas.* (In Japanese.) Nagoya, Japan, 1929.

(7) *Paṭṭhāna.* "Book of relations," an analysis of the relations (causality, etc.) of things in twenty-four groups.

The Abhidhamma of the Sarvāstivādins also consists of seven works,[1] one main work followed by six supplements, and unlike the Theravādin Abhidhamma they are not attributed directly to Buddha, but to seven disciples, four of whom are elders recognized by the Theravādins.

(1) *Jñāna-prasthāna,* by Kātyāyanīputra. "The course of knowledge." It is a long work, and discusses most of the philosophical concepts (bonds, karma, material elements, organs, concentration, views) involved in attaining knowledge.

(2) *Sangīti-paryāya,* by Mahā-Kaushṭhila or Śāriputra. "Section for recitation." It consists of lists of doctrinal terms arranged numerically like the *Sangīti-sutta* in the *Dīgha,* on which Takakusu thinks it is modelled.

(3) *Prakaraṇa-pāda,* by Vasumitra. "Work (on Abhidhamma)." A discussion on dhammas (doctrinal concepts). Vasumitra is the name of a well-known Sarvāstivādin author.

(4) *Vijñāna-kāya,* by Devaśarman. "Group (of subjects) on consciousness." Chinese tradition puts the author a century after Buddha's death.

(5) *Dhātu-kāya,* by Pūrṇa or Vasumitra. "Group (discussing) mental elements."

(6) *Dharma-skandha,* by Śāriputra or Maudgalyāyana. "Aggregate of dharmas," discussing the chief philosophical concepts as in No. 1.

(7) *Prajñapti-śāstra,* by Maudgalyāyana. "Book of instruction." The instruction is on cosmological and secular matters, the qualities of a Bodhisattva and a Buddha, etc.

Although there is some similarity in these titles to the Abhidhamma works of the Theravādins, the works are quite independent. When we consider that the other two Piṭakas

[1] They now exist only in Chinese translations, and have been summarized and analysed by Professor Takakusu (*JPTS.* 1904–5, pp. 67 ff.). The Sanskrit names of six of the works omitting Vijñāna-kāya are given in *Mvyut.* 65. *Bu-ston* says that the Vaibhāshikas of Kashmir regard them as belonging to the word of Buddha (trans. by E. Obermiller, p. 49).

have a common basis, it is possible to draw the important conclusion that the existing Abhidhamma works are much later than the contents of the first two Piṭakas, and arose when the two schools were definitely separated. Their sectarian character is also indicated by a description of the Abhidhamma Piṭaka quite different from these, which is given in the account of the first Council in the Dharmagupta Vinaya.[1] This account lets us know what the author of it imagined the primitive Abhidhamma to be, and he must have relied on his knowledge of the Dharmagupta Canon of his time. But although this school was a branch of the Sarvāstivādins, there is no recognition of the Abhidhamma as understood either by the Theravādins or Sarvāstivādins.

The word *abhidhamma* is found in the suttas. It means " further dhamma " or " special dhamma ". In *Majjh.*, i, 214, two monks are said to hold an abhidhamma discussion (*abhidhammakathā*). The same procedure is referred to in *Ang.*, iv, 397, where a monk who duly knows the four Truths is asked a question about *abhidhamma* and *abhivinaya*, but leaves it alone and cannot expound it. Evidently an elaboration and analysis of the doctrinal principles is intended, just as *abhivinaya* would mean a casuistic discussion of the rules of discipline. There is no separate Abhivinaya, for the elaboration of the rules of discipline exists in the Vinaya itself. The codification of such principles requiring exposition would give rise to the *māṭikā* (*mātṛkā*), the " lists ", which form the basis of the Abhidhamma books, and now form a kind of table of contents. The elaboration of these principles, their definition and their proof by adducing sutta passages would form Abhidhamma proper. This is in fact what we actually find in the two existing Abhidhamma collections. They are two sets of text-books compiled by two schools of teachers who independently undertook to expound the same subject matter.

The Nine or Twelve Angas

What we may conclude from the Angas throws an important light on the growth of the Sarvāstivāda Canon. In several places in the Pāli suttas [2] there is a list of nine divisions of

[1] Quoted below, p. 278. [2] *Majjh.* i, 130.

the Dhamma: *sutta*, *geyya*, *veyyākaraṇa*, *gāthā*, *udāna*, *itivuttaka*, *jātaka*, *abbhutadhamma*, *vedalla*. It does not appear to have been originally an actual classification of the works in the Scriptures, but a description of the respective types of sutta. Three of them, however, *udāna*, *itivuttaka*, and *jātaka* are the names of actual works. But the probability is that the terms were at first used generally like the rest to describe the character of the composition. There are still many udānas and jātakas in various parts of the Scriptures not included in the works of those names.

These nine are also included in an extended list of twelve angas, which have been quite arbitrarily called a *Mahāyāna* list. It is given in the *Mahāvyutpatti*, 62, and to the above list it adds *nidāna* and *avadāna* after *udāna*, and at the end *upadeśa*.[1] Also instead of *vedalla* it has *vaipulya*, which is placed after *jātaka*. As the *Mahāvyutpatti* contains much Sarvāstivāda material, it cannot be concluded that the list of twelve angas belongs to Mahāyāna. Several Mahāyāna works have lists of less than twelve. The *Lotus*, ii, 44 (p. 45), has a list of nine. So has the *Dharmasangraha* (62), and the *Kāraṇḍa-vyūha* has a list of ten and one of eleven. They all omit *avadāna*, which is a characteristic type of work of the Sarvāstivādins.

Buddhaghosa defines the angas more than once,[2] but it is evident that in the case of several of the items all he knows about them is a number of suttas which happen to bear the name of the anga. *Sutta* is said to include the Vinaya, certain suttas in verse, and " other utterance of the Tathāgata named sutta ". *Geyya* is sutta which contains gāthās, especially the first vagga of the Saṃyutta-nikaya. *Veyyākaraṇa* is the whole Abhidhamma-piṭaka and other utterances not among the other eight angas.[3] *Gāthā*, " verses," are the *Dhammapada*, *Thera-* and *Therī-gāthā* and those verses in the *Suttanipāta* not called suttas. *Udāna*, *itivuttaka*, and *jātaka* are the works so named. *Abbhutadhamma* consists of the suttas that describe " wonderful events ". *Vedalla* is described by giving a list of six suttas, two of which have the title *vedalla*. They

[1] It also reads *itivṛttaka* (thus-happened) for *itivuttaka*, doubtless a wrong sanskritization.

[2] *Dīgha. com.*, p. 23.

[3] For the Sarvāstivādins *vyākaraṇa* is a prophecy by Buddha about the future destiny of a person.

are said to be in the form of question and answer and to give joy and satisfaction.[1]

The importance of the list of twelve angas lies in the fact that it shows the growth of other types of Scripture which could not be placed in the Piṭakas. That these types began not with Mahāyāna can be seen from the fact that they exist as Sarvāstivāda works. We cannot assume that the Sarvāstivādins borrowed a Mahāyāna form, for it is chiefly the Sarvāstivāda avadānas that were incorporated in the Mahāyāna Canon. We also find definite evidence for the Sarvāstivāda origin of avadāna and other additional terms in the Vinaya of the Dharmaguptas, a branch of the Sarvāstivādins. The passage is important enough to be quoted. It occurs in the account of the first Council, where Ānanda after reciting the Āgamas is said to have recited the Abhidharma Piṭaka.

> So also he (Ānanda) replied concerning the Jātaka Sūtra, the " good " Nidāna Sūtra, the Vaipulya Sūtras, the Adbhuta (dharma) Sūtras, the Avadāna Sūtras, the Upadeśa Sūtras, the Ku-i Sūtra (Vyākaraṇa), the Dharmapada Sūtra, the *Po-lo-yen* Sūtra, the " concourse of dangers " Sūtra, the verses of the Holy One (Muni-gāthā), all these, composing the miscellaneous collection of Sūtras, he spoke of; so also of others, in which difficulties and no difficulties in meaning were discussed, all these in their turns he spoke of, and so was collected the Abhidharma Piṭaka.[2]

It is not clear whether the " miscellaneous collection of sūtras " is a part of the Abhidhamma, or whether a fifth Āgama is implied, but the point is not here important. We find in it Nidāna, Avadāna, and Upadeśa, the three forms supposed to belong to Mahāyāna.

The Sarvāstivāda Avadānas

It was natural in a literature preserved so long by memory,

[1] The meaning is uncertain. In form *vedalla* (**vaidalya*) would be an abstract formed from *vidala*, like *vaipulya* from *vipula*. Skt. *dala* means a fragment, and it may be suggested that *vidala*, " split open, expanded," would mean fragmentary, and *vedalla* a sutta of fragments. This would suit the fact that those suttas are of a miscellaneous character and as it were made up of fragments. The term *vaipulya* is quite distinct, and appears to be a deliberate replacing of the earlier term. Although it is best known as a Mahāyāna term it was used, as will be seen, by the Dharmaguptas. It means abundance or fullness, and though the exact reason for its use cannot be proved, it was probably a term descriptive of the very extensive later suttas which were excluded from the four Āgamas.

[2] This is Beal's version, *Abstract of four lectures*, p. 79, with the omission of some of his comments. The *Po-lo-yen* is probably the *Pārāyaṇa* of the *Suttanipāta*, and the " Concourse of dangers " (rather, " dangers of intercourse ") the *Khaggavisāṇasutta*.

and one in which original composition continually went on, that there should be spurious and apocryphal works claiming a place in the Canon. It would not be easy to insert an additional sutta in the four Nikāyas after they had been classified and numbered, but there was always a number of unclassified works, and even when the Theravādins placed them in an additional Nikāya no agreement was ever reached as to what it contained. The literary activity of the Sarvāstivādins was even greater, for they continued to exist in India with a great system of education and centres of literary activity. The three forms of composition, *nidāna*, *avadāna*, and *upadeśa* became definite types of literature.[1] Of these, *avadāna* is the most important. Whatever the derivation of the word may be, there is no doubt that it means " heroic feat, glorious achievement ", but this describes only the contents, and does not tell how as a class of composition Avadāna is to be distinguished from the rest. Yet the actual Avadānas have a very distinct character. They are either single works or a number of these works made into a collection. One of the best known is the *Divyāvadāna*, the divine Avadāna, and consists of thirty-eight tales. A number of them are evidently tales which illustrate the occasion leading to the formulation of a Vinaya rule, and S. Lévi has proved that most of the work is compiled from the tales in the Vinaya of the Mūla-Sarvāstivādins. Three other important Avadānas were evidently compiled in the same way, the *Avadāna-śataka*, the *Karma-śataka*, and the *Damamūka*.[2] It was easy for such works to be admitted as Scripture, for the tales of which they were composed mostly originated in canonical works, and any composition which contained sayings of Buddha might be reckoned as the Buddha-word.

The Avadāna differs from Jātaka first in being a later form of literature. Jātakas occur in the earlier parts of the Canon, and are tales about previous existences of Buddha.

[1] The names also occur in Pāli. But *nidāna* " cause, occasion ", has remained the name of an introductory composition explaining the occasion or motive of a work. The Pāli word *apadāna* makes it probable that the form *avadāna* is a Prakrit form representing *apa-*, but the derivation is uncertain. As a type of literature the Pāli Apandāna has nothing to do with the Sarvāstivādin Avadāna. There is the *Mahāpadāna-sutta* in the *Dīgha*, and the *Apadāna*, a work in verse in the *Khuddaka-nikāya*, neither of them having any connection as a literary form with Avadāna. *Upadeśa* is " instruction ", and it remained with that general meaning in the Pāli.

[2] For these, see Bibliography, p. 294.

It was by the Theravādins that this type was cultivated. They made a special collection, and were able to include secular tales and fables of any kind provided that one of the characters in the tale was the future Buddha. In the same way the Sarvāstivādins made collections of Avadānas. Their special feature is that an incident is told of a character in Buddha's time, and it is then explained by Buddha as the result of some heroic act (*avadāna*) done in a previous existence. It is thus possible for Jātaka and Avadāna to overlap. The Avadānas have an important doctrinal significance, as they contain evidence for the rise of new dogmas during the centuries when the Canon as represented by the Vinaya and Āgamas was closed. This is seen also in the Avadāna of another school, the *Mahāvastu*.[1]

The Mahāvastu and Lives of Buddha

What has been said of the structure of the Avadāna applies also to the work of another school, the *Mahāvastu*. This is a work on a much larger scale than the others, but constructed in the same way. It has not always been recognized as an Avadāna, though it calls itself one. Even its introductory statement has been misunderstood, which is, " the beginning of the Great Story (*Mahāvastu*) of the Vinaya-piṭaka according to the text of the Mahāsanghikas, the Lokottaravādins of Madhyadeśa." [2] This seems plain enough, and it is at least clear that this is what the work actually is. It is not the Vinaya but the " Great Story " of the career of Gautama Buddha, as conceived by an adherent of the Lokottaravāda school. In order to tell this he goes through the Vinaya and incorporates all the legends he can find. To what extent they were in his Vinaya we cannot say, but some of the poems, eulogies, and ballads come from other parts of the Canon.[3] In carrying out his

[1] The Pāli *Udāna* shows evidence of having developed in the same way. There are Udānas, " fervent utterances " of Buddha, scattered throughout the Scriptures. The work of this name is a collection of such utterances with the legends explaining when they were uttered. A considerable number are from the Vinaya.

[2] Āryamahāsaṃghikānāṃ lokottaravādināṃ madhyadeśikānāṃ pāṭhena vinayapiṭakasya mahāvastuye ādi. Vol. i, 2.

[3] He also has quotations from the *Vimānavatthu* and the *Buddhavamsa*, showing that these works, though the latest in the Pāli Canon, came from India. The wildest views have been expressed about the date of the work. It is evident that the portions contributed by the compiler must be much later than the canonical passages which he quotes. For our purpose it is

plan, his respect for the Scripture has prevented him from welding the matter into a consistent unity, but the scheme of the whole can be seen. It is the career of the Bodhisattva conceived not as the life of one man, but as one instance of the career of the Bodhisattvas, who dedicate themselves to ages of training and acquiring the requisite qualities for one who is to be a saviour of the world. It begins with a statement of the stages of the bodhisattva's career, and describes all the legendary events of Gautama's life down to his enlightenment and first public preaching to king Bimbisāra. The thread of the story often seems to be missing, because the connecting link between two portions of narrative may not be there, and also because two or more parallel accounts of the same events may be given, so that there is often an apparent regression. The narrative is often broken by jātakas introduced to explain the cause of the events recorded. Apart from its importance as an instance of the later canonical literature, the *Mahāvastu* is also of great value in preserving much of the older canonical material which it quotes from the Scriptures of the Lokottaravādins, and it throws light especially on the development of dogmatic views about a Bodhisattva and Buddha.

There are two other works of Avadāna type, closely related to the *Mahāvastu* in that they give a biography of Buddha. The first, which exists only in Chinese, has been translated by S. Beal under the title, *The Romantic Legend of Sâkya Buddha* (London, 1875), and he declared it to be a version of the *Abhinishkramaṇa-sūtra.* The Chinese title, however, is *Fo-pan-hing-tsi-ching*, which Nanjio (No. 680) restores as *Buddha-pūrva-caryā-sangraha-sūtra,* " Sūtra of the collection of the previous life of Buddha." It forms a better arranged account than the *Mahāvastu,* and it is easy to see that it is constructed from Vinaya material. Much of it corresponds closely with the Pāli Vinaya, but a note at the end states that it belonged to the Dharmaguptas, and it was doubtless based on their Canon. The note also mentions the names of five lives of Buddha as current in different schools. Beal's note seems to imply that they are different names of the same work. One of them is *Ta-sse,* which he correctly

only necessary to note that the canonical matter forming the bulk of the work belongs to a Hīnayāna school parallel to the Theravāda and Sarvāstivāda, and that it contributed to the buddhology of Mahāyāna.

interprets as *Mahāvastu,* and which is doubtless our *Mahāvastu,* as it belonged to the Mahāsanghikas. It is clear that not one book in the different schools is meant, but that each school possessed its own life of Buddha.[1]

Another title of one of these lives, given by Beal as that of the book of the Sarvāstivādins, is *Ta-chong-yen,* " Great magnificence," which Vasiliev identified with the *Lalita-vistara.* But the latter title means " extended account of the sports (of the Bodhisattva) ", and it is a Mahāyāna work. It is, however, easy to see that the *Lalita-vistara* is based largely on Sarvāstivāda material, and this material may even have been the work called " Great Magnificence ". The *Lalita-vistara,* besides containing much avadāna matter, still retains direct evidence of having once been a Sarvāstivāda avadāna, for it has two beginnings. After the usual introduction of a Mahāyāna sūtra, saying that the Lord once dwelt at Śrāvastī, it begins over again : " At that time the Lord was dwelling near the great city of Śrāvastī, honoured, reverenced, respected, worshipped." If the words " at that time " were omitted, we should have the same abrupt beginning as we find in the avadānas, followed by the same stereotyped list of epithets, *satkṛto, gurukṛto,* etc. This looks like a survival of the original beginning of an avadāna. The work is of much greater literary ability than the *Mahāvastu.* The narrative is well ordered, and much of it, both in prose and verse, corresponds closely to the Pāli, but is most probably from the Sarvāstivāda Canon. Besides this there are long verbose passages of purely Mahāyāna origin, as well as poems very different from the canonical verses which it quotes. They are often in elaborate metres and in very corrupt Sanskrit due to their having been adapted and Sanskritized as far as possible from a Prakrit dialect.

Another work may be mentioned here, though it is not canonical, as being the chief Pāli authority for Buddha's life. It is the introduction to the *Jātaka,* the *Nidāna-kathā,* " discussion of the causes or occasions (of Buddha's deeds recorded in the *Jātaka*)." It was composed in Ceylon, and the author has compiled the first part by quoting largely from the *Buddhavaṃsa.* The rest, from the decision to be born to the first preaching, is based on the Canon and the

[1] See Nanjio's note, *Cat.* No. 680.

old Sinhalese commentaries, to which the author directly refers. The reputation of the Pāli Canon has given a quite spurious authority to the *Nidāna-kathā*. It was treated as equally canonical, but whatever the age of that Canon, the *Nidāna-kathā* cannot be earlier than the fifth century A.D. The author probably knew the *Lalita-vistara* or one of the rival works, for he protests against the story that Buddha, when he was tempted by Māra's daughters in the guise of old women, condemned them to remain in that state.

Mahāyāna canonical literature

The origin of the Mahāyāna Scriptures is even more obscure than that of the original collections. In form they are a continuation of the same type of literature—discourses purporting to have been delivered at various places by Buddha usually during his earthly career. But they are expressly termed Mahāyāna sūtras, and they often attack the doctrine of the older collections. About their real origin naturally nothing is expressed in the works themselves. Everything that can be said about their date, authorship, and provenance is mere supposition.

Some of their characteristic doctrines can already be traced in the Avadānas of the Sarvāstivādins and Mahāsanghikas. Such doctrines must have been taught in the monasteries, and we find the teaching about bodhisattvas, the Perfections, and the two kinds of truth infecting even Ceylon Buddhism. The doctrine that bodhisattvas utter true teaching owing to their being inspired by the direct power of Buddha (*buddhānubhāvena*) is frequent in the Mahāyāna sūtras, and it is possible that their composers may have been influenced by some such theory, which would make it unnecessary to class all the sūtras as conscious fabrications.

Mahāyāna doctrine was expounded by Nāgārjuna in the second century A.D., and we can certainly hold that some of the sūtras were in existence a century, perhaps two centuries, earlier.[1] But we cannot point to any one of them and feel sure that it belongs to the first century B.C. The

[1] Mr. Kimura thinks that Buddha himself taught Mahāyāna. "It was a fact that Buddha preached his 'Introspectional doctrines' in an esoteric, mystical garb for the advanced disciples." *The terms Hīnayāna and Mahāyāna*, p. 56.

question of division into schools is also obscure. The two earlier Mahāyāna schools, that of Nāgārjuna and that of Vasubandhu, both called themselves Mahāyāna, and both taught the doctrine of the void and the career of the bodhisattva. We do not know how far their peculiar doctrines brought them into distinct opposition as sects. Many of the Mahāyāna sūtras are not sectarian at all. Some of them emphasize special doctrines of buddhology, or present imaginative mythology, which may have been accepted by any Mahāyāna sect. The most we can say about the sūtras is that they fall into groups. So far as they have sectarian features their relationship is rather that they arose in certain literary centres. The most distinctive in doctrine and probably the oldest is the Prajñāpāramitā group. Another group is that which emphasizes the worship of Amitābha. The *Lankāvatāra* is distinct from both, not only in its Yogāchāra doctrine, but also in its distinct literary character, which suggests South India.

The Mahāyāna literature as a whole now exists in Chinese and Tibetan translations. Not much is to be learned as to its origin from the present arrangement. In both countries Buddhist works continued to be introduced for centuries and translated. This was chiefly between the seventh and fourteenth centuries, and the works are arranged in systematic groups, which doubtless to some extent preserve the Indian arrangement.

The three Pitakas remained in name in the Mahāyāna schools. They retained the old Vinaya, which was that of one or other of the Sarvāstivāda schools from which they developed.[1] The Chinese who visited India took everything they could find, and they translated the Vinaya of several schools. The Tibetan Vinaya has essentially the same rules as the Pāli, but the commentarial part, though often containing the same legends, is much more extensive. A good idea of its contents can be obtained from Rockhill's *Life of the Buddha*, which consists chiefly of legends drawn from it.

[1] Dr. N. Dutt makes the astounding statement that "the Mahāyānists lacked a well-codified Vinaya corresponding to that of the Hīnayānists" (*Aspects*, p. 290), as if the schools that adopted Mahāyāna had not always been in possession of a well-codified Vinaya. The ancient Vinaya belonged as much to them as to the Hīnayānists. They added a compendium of rules for bodhisattvas, but even the bodhisattva, if he was a monk, still had the Vinaya rules to keep, and even though he began as a layman, he was always a monk in the higher stages of his career.

The Abhidharma was also preserved by the Mahāyānists, i.e. the seven Abhidharma books of the Sarvāstivādins. They were translated into Chinese with the two commentaries, and now exist only in that form. The teaching was systematized in Vasubandhu's *Abhidharmakośa* and its commentaries, and this was translated both into Chinese and Tibetan, but as this work is not a part of the Scriptures the Tibetan Canon contains no proper Abhidharma. But the Mahāyānists, wanting to have an Abhidharma of their own, made a quite artificial division by taking a group of their sūtras and commentaries and calling it Abhidharma. In the Tibetan they are the *Prajñāpāramitā* sūtras, and in the Chinese the *Vajracchedikā* with commentaries and a number of works by Maitreya, Vasubandhu, and others. Burnouf, although he knew the *Abhidharmakośa*, accepted the *Prajñāpāramitā* as amply representing the Abhidharma, and he added three or four similar sūtras. That is the reason why Abhidharma used to be translated " Metaphysics ".

The Tibetan Scriptures, known as the *Kanjur* (*bkah-hgyur*), " translation of precepts," are in seven divisions. The first is the Vinaya as described above (p. 267). The other six consist of sūtras and tantras, works giving instructions for the performance of spells and expounding tantric doctrine. The fifth division has the special name of sūtra, but all are in sūtra-form, except for a number of avadānas and poems. It is impossible to describe the whole in detail, and it will be sufficient to point out the most important sūtras, especially those which have been discussed above.[1] After the Vinaya in seven divisions follow :—

(2) *Prajñāpāramitā.*—There are five large recensions in 100,000, 25,000, 18,000, 10,000, and 8,000 verses respectively. They are in prose, and their length is reckoned according to the corresponding number of verses of thirty-two syllables. The shorter ones are said to be abridgments, but they are really independent treatments of the same subject matter. That in 8,000 verses, *Ashṭasāhasrika*, has been discussed above (p. 215). Then follow eighteen small works down to the *Ekāksharī*, which is the Perfection of wisdom in the one

[1] Csoma gave an analysis in *As. Res.*, vol. 20, 1836–9. In 1845 the Imperial Academy of St. Petersburg published the index of another recension with a preface by I. J. Schmidt. It contains 1,083 items of very varying length in 100 volumes.

letter A. The best known of these is the *Vajracchedikā* (p. 214).

(3) *Buddhāvataṃsaka* (Adornment of Buddha). This is a collection of sūtras in which Buddha appears on the top of Mount Meru and in various heavens. It is a glorification of Buddha and the career of the bodhisattvas. Some idea of it can be gained from the references to the *Daśabhūmika* above (p. 204) and from the words of Professor Suzuki (p. 252). It contains distinct Yogāchāra doctrine.

(4) *Ratnakūṭa* (Jewel-peak). This consists of forty-four sūtras, and several have been published. The *Rāshṭrapāla-paripṛcchā*, describes the qualities of a bodhisattva, and contains a striking prophecy of the decay of Buddhism both in doctrine and morals.[1] The *Prajñāpāramitā* in 700 verses appears in this section.

(5) *Sūtra.* This is the largest section, and includes all the sūtras, about 300, not elsewhere classified. The first is the *Bhadrakalpika-sūtra,* giving a list of all the Buddhas who have appeared and will appear in this "good cycle" (*bhadrakalpa*). Usually there are five including Maitreya, but according to this doctrine there are to be 1,000.[2] Then follows the well-known *Lalita-vistara* (p. 282), and among them are also the *Lankāvatāra* (p. 230), the *Lotus* (p. 179), the *Sukhāvatī-vyūha* (p. 193), the *Kāraṇḍa-vyūha* (p. 190), and the *Mahāmegha-sūtra,* a spell for obtaining rain. The list closes with a number of Sarvāstivāda works, several collections of avadānas, and single avadānas contained in the *Avadāna-śataka.* Last come thirteen sūtras translated, Feer says, from the Pāli, but the titles are Sanskrit, and the source is more like Sarvāstivāda. Two are not identifiable in the Pāli. It is significant that four of them are spells : the *Mahāsamaya-sūtra* (*Dīgha,* ii, 253), the *Aṭānāṭiya-sūtra* (*Dīgha,* iii, 194), and the two for removing eclipses, *Sūrya-* and *Candra-sūtra* (*Saṃy.*, i, 50). They all occur in the collection of spells used in Ceylon known as the *Paritta* or *Pirit-pota.*

(6) *Nirvāṇa.* This consists of two sūtras on the death of Buddha. The basis is the same as the *Mahāparinibbāna-sutta* of the Pāli. The sūtra lent itself to expansion, as it

[1] Ed. by L. Finot, who has translated the passage.

[2] It was translated from the Mongolian by I. J. Schmidt in 1834. F. Weller has analysed the names in *Tausend Buddhanamen des Bhadrakalpa.* Leipzig, 1928. The doctrine of the thousand Buddhas is given in Bu-ston's *History of Buddhism,* p. 90 (transl. Obermiller).

was easy to insert discourses which were held to have been given at the time. Similar expansions took place in the Pāli, but the additions were kept separate (p. 269).

(7) *Tantra.* This in the St. Petersburg edition is divided into two, 464 items of tantra proper and 262 dhāraṇīs. Dhāraṇīs, however, occur in both portions.

Many of these works are ritual magic with instructions for making the magic circles and performing the spells for curing diseases, rain-making, overcoming an enemy, taming animals, increasing understanding, winning long life, etc. The tantras introduce female divinities and demons, beings who supply energy to the Buddhas and bodhisattvas by union with them. The *Kālacakra*, says Csoma, is the first original work of a tantric system that originated in the north, and was introduced into India in the tenth century. It refers to the Muhammadans and mentions Mecca. The *Suvarṇaprabhāsa* is also placed in this section. This is rather an indication of its late date than of any special connection with tantra, but spells are prominent in it. It was a popular work, as is shown by the different recensions. The Tibetan version, like some of the other works, was translated from the Chinese. It is followed by five spells known as the *Pañcarakshā*, " the five protections " (for deliverance from diseases, pain, etc.). Manuscripts of these are very common and indicate their great popularity.

The Chinese have preserved their Canon in the form of the Tripiṭaka. The translations have been analysed by Bunyiu Nanjio in his *Catalogue of the Chinese translation of the Buddhist Tripiṭaka.*[1] The division of the sūtras is similar to that of the Tibetan, but there is no tantra class. It is more complete in preserving the Hīnayāna sūtras, which are kept quite distinct, as are also the Abhidharma and Vinayas of the older schools. Many works not strictly canonical, such as commentaries, have been included.

Another Tibetan collection of non-canonical works is the *Tanjur* (*bstan-hgyur*), " translation of commentaries." It consists of one volume of hymns (stotras), 87 volumes of commentaries on the tantras, and 136 on the sūtras. The last division also includes grammatical and medical works and original works by Tibetan authors.

[1] To this *Le Canon bouddhique en Chine* of Dr. P. C. Bagchi, Paris, 1926, makes valuable additions.

APPENDIX II

THE EIGHTEEN SCHOOLS

There are at least six accounts of the origin of the eighteen schools.[1] The best known is that of the Pāli Chronicles. The number eighteen is traditional, but in fact more than this number are recorded. The Chronicles get out of the difficulty by placing eighteen of them before the third Council. In the other accounts some of the names are dropped, evidently names of schools which no longer existed, and in their place are put others which had become prominent later. All represent the first secession as due to the Mahāsanghikas. Then according to the Chronicles the divisions were as follows :—

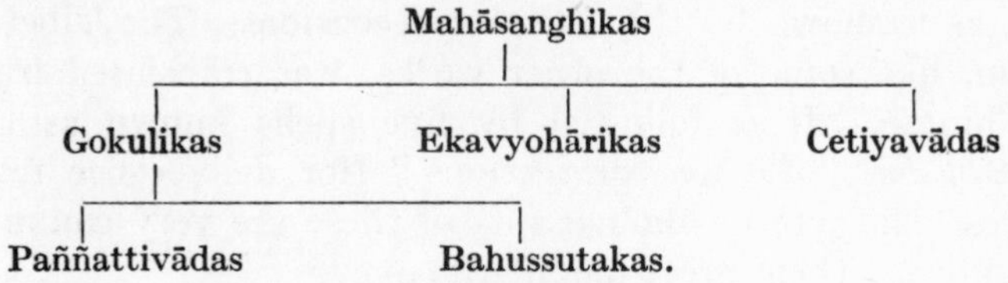

In Vasumitra this becomes :—

1. Mahāsanghikas.
2. Ekavyavaharikas.
3. Lokottaravādas.
4. Kaukkuṭikas or Kukkulikas.
5. Bahuśrutīyas.
6. Prajñaptivādas.
7. Caityaśailas.
8. Aparaśailas.
9. Uttaraśailas.

This is essentially the same list with additions. The Lokottaravādas are the real Mahāsanghikas, and the two last schools here added may be the Aparaseliyas and

[1] *Dpvs.* v, *Mhvs.* v ; Vasumitra in Masuda, *Origin and doctrines of the Early Indian Buddhist Schools,* and in Vasiliev, *Buddhismus,* p. 244 ; Bhavya in Rockhill, *Life of the Buddha,* p. 181 ; Tāranātha gives accounts according to five schools, p. 270.

Pubbaseliyas mentioned as late schools by the *Kathāvatthu* commentator. Bhavya and the rest have Pūrvaśailas for Uttaraśailas. The Gokulikas have become Kaukkuṭikas, Kukkulikas, and even Kaurukullakas. The *Kathāvatthu* commentator says that they declared all compound things to be utter *kukkulā*, cinderheaps, perhaps a doctrine developed out of their name. Nothing more is known of them. Gokula may be a quite independent name of local significance. There is further change in the Sarvāstivāda list [1] :—

1. Mahāsanghikas.
2. Pūrvaśailas.
3. Aparaśailas.
4. Haimavatas.
5. Lokottaravādas.
6. Prajñaptivādas.

Here four have disappeared, and the Haimavatas have been added. This can be explained if we suppose that the recorders did not depend merely upon traditional lists, but were influenced by the actual state of the sects as they knew them. What they recorded as Mahāsanghika sects would necessarily be those which claimed to belong to that group. From this point of view the Aparaśailas and Pūrvaśailas would be rightly included. They held Mahāsanghika doctrines, but being south Indian sects they are much later than the others. Their lateness is recognized by the *Kathāvatthu* commentator, though he shows their close connection with the Mahāsanghikas in doctrine. The most significant name is Prajñaptivāda, the doctrine that knowledge is not real but convention. It is probable that we have here a reference to the Mahāyāna epistemological theories.[2] These theories were certainly in existence when the above lists were compiled. It has been noticed that there is no direct connection between the Mahāyāna epistemology and the bodhisattva doctrine. The latter came from the Sarvāstivādins, and the Mahāyānists appear to have received their two characteristic doctrines from these two independent sources.

[1] This is the list of *Mvyut.*, discussed above (p. 38) ; it is given also by Tāranātha, p. 271, who attributes it to Vinītadeva.

[2] It is of course a complete anachronism to place its origin as early as the second century after Buddha's death.

The Haimavatas are classed by Vasumitra as Theravādins. The *Kathāvatthu* commentator merely mentions them (Hemavatas) as a late school. They were certainly not the old Theravāda, but they may in Vasumitra's time have claimed to be Theravādas or Sthaviras.

The next great secession from Theravāda is represented thus by the chronicles :—

Mahiṃsāsakas
- Sabbatthivādas
  - Kassapikas
    - Saṃkantikas
      - Suttavādas.
- Dhammaguttikas

Here too we have a group of closely related schools, of which the actual historical origin could hardly have been known. Then, treated as an independent secession,

Vajjiputtakas
- Dhammuttarikas
  - Bhadrayānikas
    - Chandāgārikas
      - Sammitīyas.

These two groups of eleven schools with the six of the Mahāsanghikas and the Theravāda itself form the eighteen schools recognized by the Chronicles. In these two last groups the best known schools occur, for they are those which continued in India until quite late times. Vasumitra makes both groups to be secessions from Sarvāstivāda. This school, he says, separated from the Theravāda at the beginning of the third century after Buddha's death. Then also in the third century the Vātsīputrīyas from the Sarvāstivādas. From the Vātsīputrīyas :

1. Dharmottarīyas
2. Bhadrāyaṇīyas
3. Sammatīyas
4. Channagirikas.

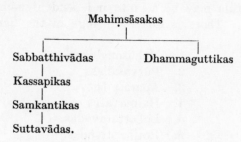

These, except for variations in the names, agree with those in the Chronicles.

Immediately afterwards also from the Sarvāstivādas the Mahiṃśāsakas separated, and from them :

1. Dharmaguptikas
2. Kāśyapīyas
3. Sautrāntikas or Saṃkrāntivādas.

These two groups with some other variations are treated in the Sarvāstivāda list as constituting the Sammatīya and Sarvāstivāda groups (p. 38).

Where the forms of the names differ from those in the Chronicles the probability is that the Sanskrit forms are right. The Vajjiputtakas of Vesālī were never a secession.[1] It was their practices, according to one tradition, which caused the first secession, but the first sect or school was the Mahāsanghika.[1] The later Vajjiputtakas, who seceded after the Sarvāstivāda group, are called Vātsīputrīyas in the Sanskrit. As these continued to exist in the north, where the accounts were compiled, the latter form is more likely to be correct. They were people of the Vatsa country, and it is not known whether Vatsīputra was the name of a leader or a general name for the people of the district. Dharmottarīya and Bhadrāyaṇīya also look like names formed from the personal names Dharmottara or Dhammuttara and Bhadrāyaṇa, and so with Dharmaguptika and Kāśyapīya. Bhadrayāna looks like a corruption. It is not really an addition to knowledge to translate Bhadrayānika " Lucky Vehicle " and Dhammaguttika " Normguard ". Still other names occur which do not furnish real information, even if we were sure of their etymology. There are half a dozen forms of Chandāgārika or Channagirika. The Chinese chose a form which means " Six-Towners ". The name probably comes from some place-name where the school was established, as was certainly the case with several names like Pūrvaśaila, " east rock ". Andhakas and Uttarāpathakas are collective terms used for southern and northern schools respectively.

The different accounts have much in common, for they were speaking to some extent of schools which existed round

[1] Mrs. Rhys Davids in the genealogical tree (*Points of Controversy*) makes the Vajjiputtakas the first secession with the Mahāsanghikas leading nowhere.

about them. When they give their views on the origin of the secessions they appear to be theorizing. One view makes the Sarvāstivāda originate from the Mahiṃśāsaka, and another view reverses this. It is a point on which the rival schools were not likely to agree, and the history of the schools did not begin to be written until long after exact knowledge of the original disputes was lost. How little was actually known about the circumstances of the secessions can be seen from the two entirely different accounts of the secession of the Mahāsanghikas. According to one account it was purely a matter of discipline, and according to another a series of doctrinal questions. Yet neither of these matters appear characteristic in the later history of that school. Przyluski rejects both explanations. He says that the Great Assembly (Mahāsangha) was the meeting of all believers, religious and lay people; that originally it was held on feast days, when the more learned preached the doctrine, and all publicly confessed their faults; that when the congregation of the religious was constituted, it became the custom in different groups to convoke only the Assembly in the strict sense, to the exclusion of the laics; that this practice had the advantage of safeguarding the prestige of the religious by permitting them to confess their faults behind closed doors; that it appears to have been inaugurated in the communities of the West; and that the Mahāsanghika sect, localized in the East, for long preserved the ancient custom, to which it probably owed its name.[1]

The Mahāvaṃsa tells us that besides the seventeen schools which arose in the second century after Buddha's death there were six later ones that arose in India and two in Ceylon:

> The Hemavatas, Rājagiriyas, and also the Siddhatthakas, the Pubbaseliya monks and also the Aparaseliyas,
> The Vajiriyas—these six also separated in Jambudīpa. The Dhammarucis and the Sāgaliyas separated in Ceylon.

These are sects which the Chroniclers and commentators evidently knew, but they tell us nothing of their origin. This makes it unlikely that the later accounts, which classify some of them with the older groups, knew anything of their real history. The Ceylon sects have been discussed above (p. 40).

[1] *Le Bouddhisme*, p. 29; no evidence is given for all this.

BIBLIOGRAPHY[1]

THE CANON

Pali Works

The Pāli *Sutta-piṭaka* and *Abhidhamma-piṭaka* have been published by the Pali Text Society between 1882 and 1927. The *Vinaya-piṭaka* was edited by H. Oldenberg in 1879–83, and is now being re-issued by the Pali Text Society. The text and translation of the *Pātimokkha* was published by J. F. Dickson, *JRAS.*, 1876, and the text by J. Minaev, St. Petersburg, 1869. The second part of the Vinaya, the *Khandhakas*, and the *Pātimokkha* were translated by Oldenberg and Rhys Davids in *Vinaya Texts*, Oxford, 1881–5. (SBE. 13, 17, 20.) The following parts of the *Sutta-piṭaka* have been translated:

Dīgha-nikāya. Dialogues of the Buddha, tr. by T. W. Rhys Davids and Mrs. Rhys Davids. 1899–1921. (SBB. 2–4.)

Majjhima-nikāya. Further Dialogues of the Buddha, tr. by Lord Chalmers. 1926–7. (SBB. 5, 6.)

Saṃyutta-nikāya. The Book of the Kindred Sayings, tr. by Mrs. Rhys Davids and F. L. Woodward. 1918–30. (PTS. Transl. Series, 7, 10, etc.)

Anguttara-nikāya. The Book of the Gradual Sayings, tr. by F. L. Woodward, 1932 ff. (PTS. Transl. Series, 22, 24.)

Khuddakapāṭha. Tr. by Childers, *JRAS.*, 1870, 309 ff., and also by Mrs. Rhys Davids in the next.

Dhammapada: Verses on Dhamma, and Khuddaka-pāṭha: the text of the Minor Sayings. Re-edited and tr. by Mrs. Rhys Davids. 1931. (SBB. 7.)

The Dhammapada, tr. from Pâli by F. Max Müller. Oxford, 1898. (SBE. 10.)

Buddhist Legends, tr. from the Dhammapada commentary by E. W. Burlingame. Cambridge, Mass., 1921.

The Udāna, tr. from the Pāli by D. M. Strong. 1902.

The Itivuttaka, tr. with an introduction and notes by J. H. More. New York, 1908.

The Sutta-nipāta, tr. by V. Fausböll. Oxford, 1898. (SBE. 10.)

Thera- and Therī-gāthā. Psalms of the Brethren, tr. by Mrs. Rhys Davids. 1913, and *Psalms of the Sisters*, by the same. 1909. (PTS. Transl. Series, 4, 1.)

The Jātaka together with its commentary, edited by V. Fausböll. 1877–97. (Tr. under the editorship of E. B. Cowell. Cambridge, 1895–1913. The introduction, *Nidāna-kathā*, tr. by Rh. Davids in *Buddhist birth stories*, 1880, new ed. by Mrs. Rhys Davids, 1925.)

Three of the Abhidhamma works have been translated:

[1] Place of publication if not stated is London. Full bibliographies in *Subject Index of the British Museum*, 1881 ff., and from 1928 in *Bibliographie bouddhique*, forming vols. 3, 5, 6, etc., of *Buddhica*, Paris, 1929 ff.

A Buddhist manual of psychological ethics, being a translation of the first book in the Abhidhamma Piṭaka entitled Dhamma-sangaṇi. With introductory essay and notes by C. A. F. Rhys Davids. 1900. The commentary, *Atthasālinī*, tr. as *The Expositor*, by P. M. Tin and Mrs. Rhys Davids. 1920–1. (PTS. Transl. Series, 8, 9.)

Puggala-paññatti, designation of human types, tr. by B. C. Law. 1924. (PTS. Transl. Series, 12.)

Points of Controversy, being a translation of the Kathā-vatthu, by S. Z. Aung and Mrs. Rhys Davids. 1915. (PTS. Transl. Series, 5.)

Sarvāstivāda Works

Prātimoksha-sūtra. Ed. by L. Finot, *JA.* i, 1913, 465 ff., with a translation from the Chinese by E. Huber. (Rockhill's *Life of the Buddha*, 1884, gives much material from the Tibetan Vinaya, the Dulva.)

Analysis of the Dulva (Vinaya) by A. Csoma Körösi, in *Asiatic Researches*, xx, Calcutta, 1836.

Some problems of the textual history of the Buddhist Scriptures, and the four Buddhist Āgamas in Chinese, by M. Anesaki, in *Trans. As. Soc. Japan*, xxxv, parts 2, 3, 1908.

The comparative catalogue of Chinese Āgamas and Pāli Nikāyas. By C. Akanuma. Nagoya, 1929.

Le Sagātha-vagga du Saṃyutta-nikāya et ses versions chinoises, par M. Anesaki, in *Muséon*, 1905, p. 23 ff.

Manuscript remains of Buddhist literature found in Eastern Turkestan. Edited by A. F. R. Hoernle. Vol. i. Oxford, 1916.

Bruchstücke des Sanskritkanons der Buddhisten aus Idykutṣari, in *Sitzb. der k. pr. Akad.*, 1904, p. 807 ff.

Avadānaçataka, edited by J. S. Speyer. St. Petersburg, 1906–9. (There is a translation from the Tibetan by L. Feer, Paris, 1891.)

Karmaçataka. Summarized in French from the Tibetan by L. Feer. *JA.*, 1901.

Divyāvadāna, edited by E. B. Cowell and R. A. Neil. Cambridge, 1886. (Portions are translated in Burnouf's *Introduction.*)

Damamūka. Hdzaṅs-blun oder der Weise und der Thor. Aus dem Tibetischen übers. und mit dem Originaltexte hrsg. von I. J. Schmidt. St. Petersburg, 1843.

Aśokāvadāna. Tr. in *La légende de l'empereur Açoka dans les textes indiens et chinois*, par J. Przyluski. Paris, 1923.

The Romantic Legend of Sâkya Buddha, tr. from the Chinese by S. Beal, 1875. See p. 281.

J. Takakusu. On the Abhidharma literature of the Sarvāstivādins. *JPTS.*, 1905. (Contains summaries of the seven Abhidharma works.)

Documents d'Abhidharma, trad. et annotés par L. de la Vallée Poussin. *BEFEO.*, xxx, 1931.

Mahāsanghika

Le Mahâvastu, publié par É. Senart. Paris, 1882–97. (Contains a summary of the contents in French. Portions of it are tr. by B. C. Law in *A study of the Mahāvastu.* Calcutta and Simla, 1930.)

Mahāyāna

Analysis of the Sher-chin [Prajñāpāramitā], Phal-chhen [Avataṃsaka], Dkon-séks [Ratnakūṭa], Do-dé [Sūtra], Nyáng-dás [Nirvāṇa], and Gyut [Tantra], being the 2nd—7th divisions of the Tibetan work, entitled the Kah-gyur, by A. Csoma Körösi, in *Asiatic Researches*, xx, Calcutta, 1839.

Analyse du Kandjour. L. Feer. Lyon, 1881. (Based on the above and on the Analysis of the Dulva.)

A catalogue of the Chinese translation of the Buddhist Tripiṭaka, by B. Nanjio. Oxford, 1883.

A comparative analytical catalogue of the Kanjur, by B. Sakurabe and Professor Teramoto. Kyoto, 1930–2.

Śatasāhasrika-prajñāpāramitā. Edited by P. Ghoṣa. Pt 1 ff. Calcutta, 1902 ff.

Ashṭasāhasrika-prajñāpāramitā. Edited by R. L. Mitra. Calcutta, 1888. (Tr. in part by M. Walleser as *Die Vollkommenheit der Erkenntnis*. Göttingen, 1914.)

Vajracchedikā. Edited by F. Max Müller. Oxford, 1881.

Sukhāvatī-vyūha (in two recensions). Edited by F. Max Müller and B. Nanjio. Oxford, 1883.

Buddhist Mahâyâna Texts. Oxford, 1894, 1927. (SBE. 49.) (Contains translations of *Buddha-carita* of Aśvaghosha, larger and smaller *Sukhāvatīvyūha*, *Vajracchedikā*, larger and smaller *Prajñāpāramitā-hṛdaya-sūtra*, and *Amitāyurdhyāna-sūtra*.

Saddharmapuṇḍarīka, edited by H. Kern and B. Nanjio. St. Petersburg, 1908–12. (Tr. by H. Kern. Oxford, 1884. S.B.E. 21.)

Kāśyapaparivarta, a Mahāyānasūtra of the Ratnakūṭa class, edited in the original Sanskrit, in Tibetan and in Chinese by Baron A. von Staël-Holstein. Shanghai, 1926.

Lalitavistara. Edited by R. L. Mitra. Calcutta, 1877, and by S. Lefmann, Halle a. S., 1902–8. (P. Foucaux edited the Tibetan version with French tr. as *Rgya tch'er rol pa*. Paris, 1847–8, and a version from the Sanskrit in 1884.)

Kāraṇḍavyūha. Edited by Satyabrata Samasrami, and pub. by Jibananda Vidyasagara. Calcutta, 1873.

Lankāvatāra-sūtra, edited by B. Nanjio. Kyoto, 1923. (Tr. by D. T. Suzuki, 1932.)

Udānavarga, tr. from the Tibetan by W. W. Rockhill. 1883.

Guhyasamāja-tantra. See Tantra below.

Aparimitāyurjñāna-sūtra, mit der tib. und chines. Version hrsg. und übers. von M. Walleser. Heidelberg. 1916.

Megha-sūtra, edited and tr. by C. Bendall. *JRAS*., 1880, p. 286 ff.

Suvarṇaprabhāsa-sūtra, edited by H. Idzumi. Kyoto, 1931. (Analysed and partly tr. from the Mongolian by I. J. Schmidt in *Mém. de l'Acad. Imp. des Sciences*. 6e série, sciences polit. Tom. 1, p. 225 ff. St. Petersburg, 1832.)

Bhadrakalpikā-sūtra. (Tr. by I. J. Schmidt in the above *Mémoires*, vol. 2, pp. 41–86. Analysed by F. Weller in *Tausend Buddhanamen des Bhadrakalpa, nach einer fünfsprachigen Polyglotte*. Leipzig, 1928.)

Tantra

Guhyasamāja-tantra or Tathāgataguhyaka, edited by B. Bhattacharyya. Gaekwad's Or. Ser., 53. Baroda, 1931. (Professor Winternitz in an important article in *IHQ*. 1933, p. 1 ff., points out that the Tathāgataguhyaka quoted by Śāntideva in his *Śikshāsamuccaya* is a different work. In the work here edited we find " the same unsavoury mixture of mysticism, occult pseudo-science, magic, and erotics, as in most of the other Buddhist Tantras ". The editor, although he admits that the work definitely asks its followers to disregard all social laws, thinks that Yoga and the Tantras are regarded as the greatest contributions of Sanskrit to world culture. In his *Introduction to Buddhist esoterism* (1932) he declares that "the Tantric culture is the greatest of all cultures, because it aims at the spiritual perfection and psychic development of man, and as such no one can deny that the Tantric culture is the greatest contribution made by India towards the world's civilization". His views are not shared by all Indians.[1])

Besides canonical works the following are important:

Matériaux pour servir à l'histoire de la déesse buddhique Tārā, par G. de Blonay. Paris, 1895.

Ādikarmapradīpa. (In *Bouddhisme, études et matériaux*, par L. de la Vallée Poussin, 1898. This contains valuable studies on tantric rites, maithuna or sexual union, spells, and the relations of Tantra with Śaivism.)

Subhāṣita-saṃgraha. Edited by C. Bendall. Louvain, 1905. (The editor holds that this work explains the decay, decrepitude, and dotage of Buddhism as shown in the Tantra-literature. A more convincing account was given by Mm. Haraprasad Sastri. See the important account of his life and work given by Dr. N. N. Law in *IHQ*. ix, 1933, p. 307.)

Les chants mystiques de Kāṇha et de Saraha ; les Dohā-koṣa et les Caryā, éd. et trad. par M. Shahidullah. Paris, 1928. (The author explains the "argot tantrique", by which technical religious terms were applied in obscene senses. The best general treatment is by L. de la Vallée Poussin in *ERE*, art. "Tantrism".)

The Post-Caitanya Sahajiā cult of Bengal. By M. M. Bose. Calcutta, 1930. (A study of a modern tantric sect. The author has also published the Bengali texts of the sect in *Sahajiyā sāhitya*. Calcutta, 1932.)

NON-CANONICAL WORKS

Buddhaghosa. *Visuddhimagga*. Edited by Mrs. Rhys Davids. 1920–1. Tr. by P. M. Tin as *The Way of Purity*. (PTS. Transl. Series, 11, 17, 21.)

Anuruddha. *Abhidhammatthasangaha*. JPTS. 1884. Tr. by S. Z. Aung and edited by Mrs. Rhys Davids as *Compendium of Philosophy*. (PTS. Transl. Series, 2.)

The Yogāvacara's Manual of Indian mysticism as practised by Buddhists. Edited by T. W. Rhys Davids. 1896. Tr. by F. L. Woodward as *Manual of a Mystic*. 1916. (PTS. Transl. Series, 6.)

M. Dharmaratna. *Satvotpatti-vinischaya and Nirvāṇa-vibhāga*. Tr. from the Sinhalese by H. M. Gunasekera as *An enquiry into the origin of beings and Discussions about Nirvāṇa*. Colombo, 1902.

Dharma-saṃgraha, prepared for publication by K. Kasawara and edited by F. Max Müller and H. Wenzel. Oxford, 1885.

Mahāvyutpatti. Edited by I. P. Minaev and N. D. Mironov. St. Petersburg, 1911.

[1] Mr. Bhattacharyya's views do not seem to be perfectly balanced. In his introduction to *Sādhanamālā*, vol. 2, p. xxxiii, he says, "it is indeed a pity that the Hindus, and also the Jainas to a certain extent, could not throw off the worthless and immoral practices enjoined in the Tantras even when Buddhism was stamped out of India."

Vasubandhu. *L'Abhidharmakośa*, trad. par L. de la Vallée Poussin. Paris, 1923–5.

T. I. Stcherbatsky. *The central conception of Buddhism and the meaning of the word "Dharma"*. 1923. (Translates portions of the preceding.)

Nāgārjuna. *Madhyamakavṛtti, Mūlamadhyamakārikās avec la Prasannapadā, commentaire de Candrakīrti*, publ. par L. de la Vallée Poussin. St. Petersburg, 1913.

—— *Die mittlere Lehre*, nach der tibetischen Version übertr. von M. Walleser. Heidelberg, 1911.

—— *Die mittlere Lehre*, nach der chinesischen Version übertr. von M. Walleser. Heidelberg, 1912.

T. I. Stcherbatsky. *The conception of Buddhist Nirvāṇa* (with tr. of Ch. 1 and 25 of Chandrakīrti's *Prasannapadā*). Leningrad, 1927.

Ausgewählte Kapitel aus der Prasannapadā (Ch. 5, 12–16). S. Schayer. Krakow, 1931.

Feuer und Brennstoff, by S. Schayer. (Tr. of Ch. 10 of the *Prasannapadā*.) Lwów, 1926.

Aśvaghosha. *Discourse on the awakening of faith in the Mahāyāna* (*Mahāyānaśraddhotpāda*), tr. from the Chinese version by D. T. Suzuki. Chicago, 1900.

Deux traités de Vasubandhu, Viṃśatikā et Triṃśikā, publ. par S. Lévi. Paris, 1925.

Matériaux pour l'étude du système Vijñaptimātra (with tr. of Vasubandhu's Vimśatikā and Triṃśikā) par S. Lévi. Paris, 1932.

Bodhisattvabhūmi, being fifteenth section of Yogācārabhūmi. Edited by U. Wogihara. 1. Tokyo, 1930. (Summary in English with notes by C. Bendall and L. de la Vallée Poussin in *Muséon*. 1905, etc.)

Śāntideva. *Bodhicaryāvatāra*, edited by I. P. Minaev. St. Petersburg, 1889. (French tr. by L. de la Vallée Poussin. Paris, 1907. Partial tr. by L. D. Barnett as *The Path of Light*. 1909.)

—— *Śikshāsamuccaya*. Edited by C. Bendall. St. Petersburg, 1897–1902. (Tr. by C. Bendall and W. H. D. Rouse. 1921.)

Uttaratantra. The sublime science of the Great Vehicle to salvation, being a manual of Buddhist monism. The work of Ārya Maitreya with a commentary by Āryāsanga. Tr. from the Tibetan by E. Obermiller. (Publ. in *Acta Orient.* ix, 1931, 81 ff. Dr. Obermiller discusses the five treatises of Maitreya, which were once attributed entirely to Asanga. He describes the fifth, the *Uttaratantra*, as "the exposition of the most developed monistic and pantheistic teachings of the later Buddhists and of the special theory of the Essence of Buddhahood [*tathāgata-garbha*], the fundamental element of the Absolute, as existing in all living beings".)

Chronicles and Travels

The Dīpavaṃsa, edited and tr. by H. Oldenberg. 1879.

The Mahāvaṃsa, edited by W. Geiger. 1908. (This consists of chapters 1–37. The continuation known as the *Cūlavaṃsa* was edited 1925–7. The former was translated by W. Geiger and M. H. Bode, 1912, and the latter by C. M. Rickmers. PTS. Transl. Series. 3, 18, 20.)

Mahābodhivaṃsa, edited by S. A. Strong, 1891. (PTS.)

Sāsanavaṃsa, edited by M. H. Bode, 1897. (PTS.)

Si-yu-ki, Buddhist records of the Western World, tr. from the Chinese of Hiuen Tsiang by S. Beal. 1884. (Contains also the travels of Fa Hien and Sung Yun.)

The life of Hiuen-tsiang by the Shamans Hwai li and Yen-tsing, with a preface containing an account of the works of I-tsing by S. Beal. 1885, new ed., 1911.

A record of the Buddhist religion as practised in India and the Malay Archipelago (A.D. 671–695) by I-tsing, tr. by J. Takakusu. Oxford, 1896.

Tāranāthae de doctrinae buddhicae in India propagatione narratio. Contextum tibeticum edidit A. Schiefner. Petropoli, 1863. (Trans. by Schiefner as *Târanâtha's Geschichte des Buddhismus in Indien*, 1869.)

History of Buddhism (*Chos-ḥbyung*), by Bu-ston, transl. from Tibetan by E. Obermiller. Heidelberg, 1931–2.

Eine tibetische Lebensbeschreibung Çâkjamuni's, im Auszuge mitgetheilt von A. Schiefner. *Mémoires présentés à l'Académie Impériale des Sciences par divers savants.* Vol. 6. 1851.

Modern Works

E. Burnouf. *Introduction à l'histoire du Buddhisme indien.* Paris, 1844.

R. S. Hardy. *Eastern monachism.* 1850.

—— *A manual of Budhism in its modern development.* 1853, 2nd ed., 1880.

V. P. Vasiliev. *Buddhism.* Vol. i. St. Petersburg, 1857. (German version 1860. French 1865.)

H. Oldenberg. *Buddha, sein Leben, seine Lehre, seine Gemeinde.* Berlin, 1881. (Trans. into English, 1882. 9th ed. of the German, 1921.)

—— *Die Lehre der Upanishaden und die Anfänge des Buddhismus.* Göttingen, 1915.

—— *Die Weltanschauung der Brāhmaṇa-texte.* Göttingen, 1919.

T. W. Rhys Davids. *Lectures on the origin and growth of religion as illustrated by some points in the history of Indian Buddhism.* (Hibbert Lectures.) 1881.

—— *Buddhism, its history and literature.* American Lectures. New York, 1896.

—— *Buddhist India.* 1903.

J. H. C. Kern. *Geschiedenis van het Buddhisme in Indië.* Haarlem. 1882–4. (German tr., Leipzig, 1884. French tr., Paris, 1901–3.)

—— *Manual of Indian Buddhism.* Strassburg, 1896.

R. S. Copleston. *Buddhism, primitive and present, in Magadha and Ceylon.* 1892. 2nd ed., 1908.

S. Kuroda. *Outlines of the Mahāyāna.* Tokyo, 1893.

I. P. Minaev. *Recherches sur le Bouddhisme,* trad. du russe. Paris, 1894.

L. Waddell. *The Buddhism of Tibet or Lamaism.* 1895.

J. A. Eklund. *Nirvāṇa, en religionshistorisk undersökning.* (With résumé in German.) Upsala, 1899.

D. T. Suzuki. *Outlines of Mahāyāna Buddhism.* 1907.

—— *Essays in Zen Buddhism.* 1927.

—— *Studies in the Lankāvatāra Sūtra.* 1930.

M. Walleser. *Die buddhistische Philosophie in ihrer geschichtlichen Entwicklung.* 1–3. Heidelberg, 1904–12.

G. Schulemann. *Die Geschichte der Dalailamas.* Heidelberg, 1911.

Yamakami Sogen. *Systems of Buddhistic Thought.* Calcutta, 1912.

C. A. F. Rhys Davids. *Buddhism.* 1912.

—— *Buddhist psychology.* 1914. 2nd ed. 1924.

—— The unknown co-founders of Buddhism. *JRAS.*, 1927, p. 193 ff.

C. A. F. Rhys Davids. *Gotama the Man.* 1928.
—— *Sakya or Buddhist origins.* 1931.
—— *Manual of Buddhism.* 1932.
M. E. Lulius van Goor. *De Buddhistische non geschetst naar gegevens der Pāli-literatuur.* Leiden, 1915
J. Jaini. *Outlines of Jainism.* Cambridge, 1916.
W. Geiger. *Pāli Literatur und Sprache.* Strassburg, 1916.
—— and M. Geiger. *Pāli Dhamma vornehmlich in der kan. Lit.* München, 1920.
B. M. Barua. Prolegomena to a history of Buddhist philosophy. Calcutta, 1918.
—— *A history of pre-Buddhistic Indian philosophy.* Calcutta, 1921.
W. Winternitz. *Geschichte der Indischen Litteratur.* Vol. 2. *Die buddhistische Litteratur und die heiligen Texte der Jainas.* Leipzig, 1920.
Sir C. Eliot. *Hinduism and Buddhism.* 1921.
S. Schayer. *Vorarbeiten zur Gesch. der Mahāyānistischen Erlösungslehren.* München, 1921.
W. M. McGovern. *An introduction to Mahāyāna Buddhism.* 1922.
—— *A manual of Buddhist philosophy.* Vol. 1, 1923.
Cambridge History of India. Vol. i, edited by E. J. Rapson. Cambridge, 1922.
S. N. Dasgupta. *A history of Indian philosophy.* Cambridge, vol. 1, 1922 ; vol. 2, 1932.
B. C. Law. *The life and work of Buddhaghosa.* Calcutta, 1923.
—— *Chronology of the Pali Canon.* Calcutta, 1932. (Part of a forthcoming history of Pali literature.)
—— *Buddhistic Studies.* Edited by Dr. B. C. Law. Calcutta, 1932.
—— *Geography of early Buddhism.* 1932.
—— Pali Chronicles, and Non-canonical Pali literature. *Annals of the Bhandarkar Or. Research Inst.* Vol. 13. Poona, 1932.
—— Nirvāṇa and Buddhist laymen. Ibid., vol. 14, 1933.
A. B. Keith. *Buddhist philosophy in India and Ceylon.* Oxford, 1923.
P. Oltramare. *La théosophie bouddhique.* Paris, 1923.
S. Dutt. *Early Buddhist Monachism* 600 B.C.–100 B.C. 1924.
N. Dutt. *Early history of the spread of Buddhism and the Buddhist schools.* 1925.
—— *Aspects of Mahāyāna Buddhism.* 1930.
S. Z. Aung and M. Walleser. *Dogmatik des modernen südlichen Buddhismus.* Heidelberg, 1924.
O. Rosenberg. *Die Probleme der buddh. Philosophie.* Heidelberg, 1924.
L. de la Vallée Poussin. *Nirvāṇa.* Paris, 1925.
—— *La morale bouddhique.* Paris, 1927.
—— *Le dogme et la philosophie du Bouddhisme.* Paris, 1930. (With bibliography.)
C. Formichi. *Il pensiero religioso nell'India prima del Buddha.* Bologna, 1925. (French tr. by F. Hayward revised by the author. Paris, 1930.)
J. Masuda. *Der individualistische Idealismus der Yogācāra-Schule.* Heidelberg, 1926.
J. Scheftelowitz. Neues Material über die manichäische Urseele und die Entstehung des Zarvanismus. *Z. f. Indol.*, 1926, p. 317 ff.
A. Guérinot. *La religion djaïna.* Paris, 1926.
S. Tachibana. *The ethics of Buddhism.* Oxford, 1926.

R. Kimura. *A historical study of the terms Hīnayāna and Mahāyāna and the origin of Mahāyāna Buddhism.* Calcutta, 1927.
S. K. Belvalkar and R. D. Ranade. *History of Indian philosophy.* Vol. 2. Poona, 1927.
E. J. Thomas. *The life of Buddha as legend and history.* 1927. 2nd ed. 1930.
J. W. Hauer. *Das Lankāvatāra-Sūtra und das Sāṃkhya.* Stuttgart, 1927.
—— *Die Dhāraṇī im nördl. Buddhismus.* Stuttgart, 1927.
E. Abegg. *Der Messiasglaube in Indien und Iran.* Berlin, 1928.
E. Wolff. *Zur Lehre vom Bewusstsein (Vijñānavāda) bei den späteren Buddhisten, unter besonderer Berücksichtigung des Lankāvatāra-sūtra.* Heidelberg, 1930.
G. Tucci. *On some aspects of the doctrines of Maitreya[nātha] and Asanga.* Calcutta, 1930.
R. Grousset. *Les civilisations de l'Orient. L'Inde.* Paris, 1930.
A. David-Neel. *With mystics and magicians in Tibet.* 1931.
J. Przyluski. *Le Bouddhisme.* Paris, 1932.

Chinese and Japanese Buddhism [1]

R. Fujishima. *Le bouddhisme japonais.* Paris, 1889.
J. J. M. De Groot. *Le code du Mahāyāna en Chine.* Amsterdam, 1893.
H. Haas. *Die Sekten des japanischen Buddhismus.* Heidelberg, 1905.
—— *Amida Buddha unsere Zuflucht. Urkunden zum Verständnis des japanischen Sukhāvatī-Buddhismus.* Leipzig, 1910.
H. F. Hackmann. *Buddhism as a religion, its historical development and its present conditions.* 1910.
R. F. Johnston. *Buddhist China.* 1914.
M. Anesaki. *Nichiren, the Buddhist prophet.* Cambridge, Mass., 1916.
—— *History of Japanese religion.* 1930.
O. Rosenberg. *Die Weltanschauung des modernen Buddhismus im fernen Osten.* Heidelberg, 1924.
A. K. Reischauer. *Studies in Japanese Buddhism.* New York, 1925.
M. W. De Visser. *Ancient Buddhism in Japan.* Paris, 1930.
E. Steinilber-Oberlin and K. Matsuo. *Les sectes bouddhiques japonaises.* Paris, 1930.
Hôbôgirin : Dictionnaire encyclopédique du Bouddhisme d'après les sources chinoises et japonaises, publ. sous la direction de S. Lévi et J. Takakusu, rédacteur en chef, P. Demiéville. Tokyo, 1929 ff.

Neo-Buddhism

P. Dahlke. *Buddhist essays.* 1908.
—— *Buddhism and science.* 1913.
—— *Buddhism and its place in the mental life of mankind.* 1927.
E. Holmes. *The creed of Buddha.* 1908.
G. Grimm. *Die Wissenschaft des Buddhismus.* Leipzig, 1923.
—— *The doctrine of the Buddha, the religion of reason.* Leipzig, 1926.
D. Goddard. *The Buddha's Golden Path : a manual of practical Buddhism based on the teachings and practices of the Zen sect, but interpreted and adapted to meet modern conditions.* 2nd ed., 1931.

[1] Important bibliography in O. Rosenberg, *Die Probleme der buddh. Philosophie.*

ADDENDA

Anuruddha. *Abhidhammatthasangaha. an Outline of Buddhist Philosophy.* Pali text, transl. and explanatory notes. Part I, by Nārada Thera. Colombo. 1947.

The Dhammapada. Transl. and text with notes and index. By Narada Thera. Colombo, 1946.

Buddhadatta Thera. *The early Buddhist councils and the various Buddhist sects.* (*Univ. of Ceylon Review*, 1948).

Early Buddhist Scriptures, transl. by E. J. Thomas, London, 1935.

The Road to Nirvāna (translations from the Pāli Scriptures), by E. J Thomas. London, 1949.

The Quest of Enlightenment (translations from the Scriptures of the Indian Sanskrit schools). By E. J. Thomas. London, 1949.

E. Waldschmidt. *Beiträge zur Textgeschichte des Mahāparinirvāṇasūtra* (Nachrichten von der Ges. d. Wiss. zu Göttingen. Philol-hist. Kl. Fachgruppe III. N.F.II, 3.) Göttingen, 1939.

Die Uberliefering vom Lebensende des Buddha. Eine vergleichende Analyse des Mahāparinirvāṇasūtra und seiner Textentsprechungen. (Abh. der Akad. d. Wiss. in Göttingen. Philol-Hist. Kl. 3. Folge, 29,30.) Göttingen, 1944-8.

Ásvaghoshá. *Buddhacaritá*, ed. by E. B. Cowell. Oxford, 1893. (English transl. in SBE. 49. E. H. Johnston has transl. ch. X-XVII from the Tibetan in *Acta Orientalia*, vol. 15, 1937).

Vijnaptimatratasiddhi (*la Siddhi de Hiuan Tsang*). French transl. by L. de La Vallee Poussin. Paris, 1928-9.

T. I. Stcherbatsky. *Buddhist Logic* (with a transl. of Dharmakirtis *Nyāyabindu* and its commentary by D. Larmottara). Leningrad, 1931-2.

B. C. Law. *South India as a centre of Pāli Buddhism.* (Krishnaswami Ayangar Com. vol.), 1936.

Some Jaina Canonical Sutras, Bombay, 1949.

J. Evola. *La dottrina del risveglio : Śaggio sull' ascesi buddhista.* Bari, 1943.

J. G. Jennings. *The Vedāntic Buddhism of the Buddha.* London, 1947.

INDEX